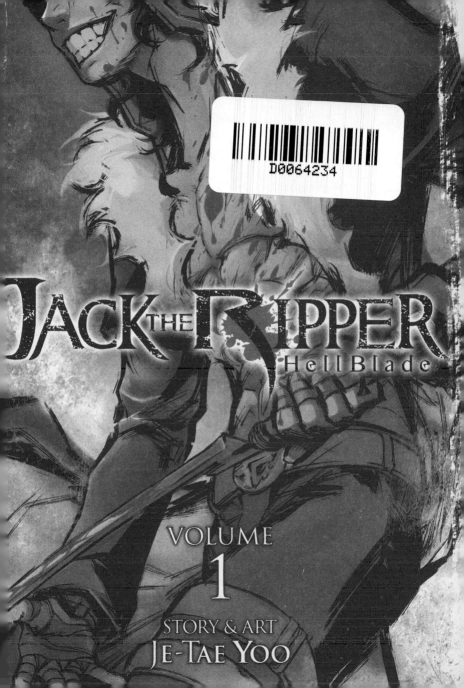

JACK THE RIPPER
Hell Blade

VOLUME
1

STORY & ART
JE-TAE YOO

JACK THE RIPPER
Hell Blade
VOLUME 1

STORY & ART BY
Je-tae Yoo

STAFF CREDITS

translation	**Lauren Na**
adaptation	**Janet Houck**
lettering & design	**Nicky Lim**
assistant editor	**Shanti Whitesides**
editor	**Adam Arnold**
publisher	**Jason DeAngelis**
	Seven Seas Entertainment

JACK THE RIPPER: HELL BLADE VOL. 1
©2009 by YOO Je-tae, Daewon C.I. Inc.
All rights reserved. First published in Korea as HELL BLADE VOL. 1
in 2009 by Daewon C.I. Inc.
English translation rights arranged by Daewon C.I. Inc. through Topaz Agency

ISBN: 978-1-935934-76-9

Printed in the USA

First printing: July 2012

10 9 8 7 6 5 4 3 2 1

FOLLOW US ONLINE: **www.gomanga.com**

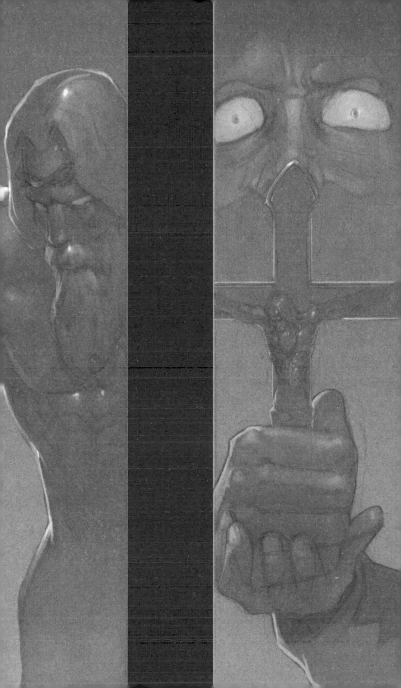

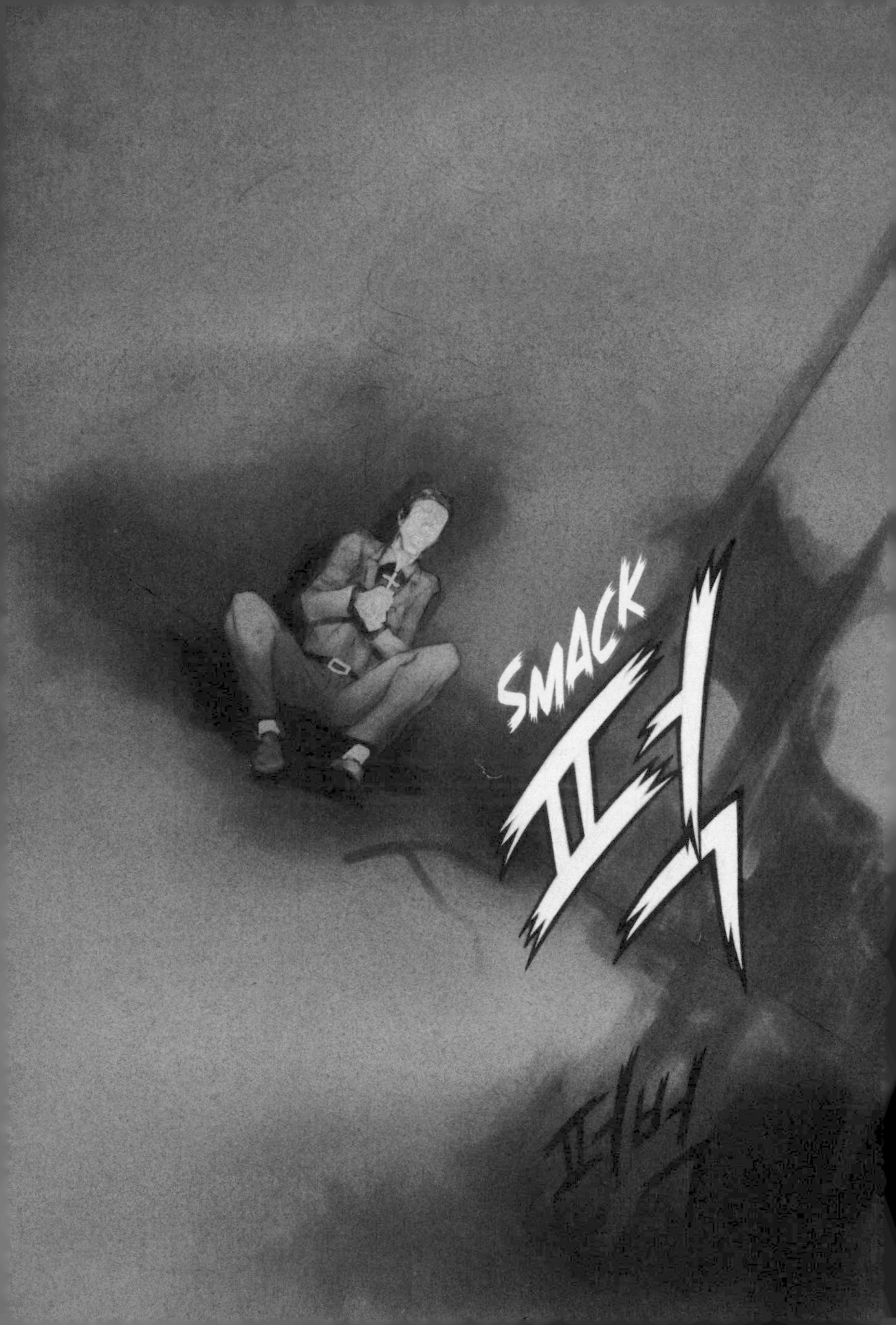
SMACK

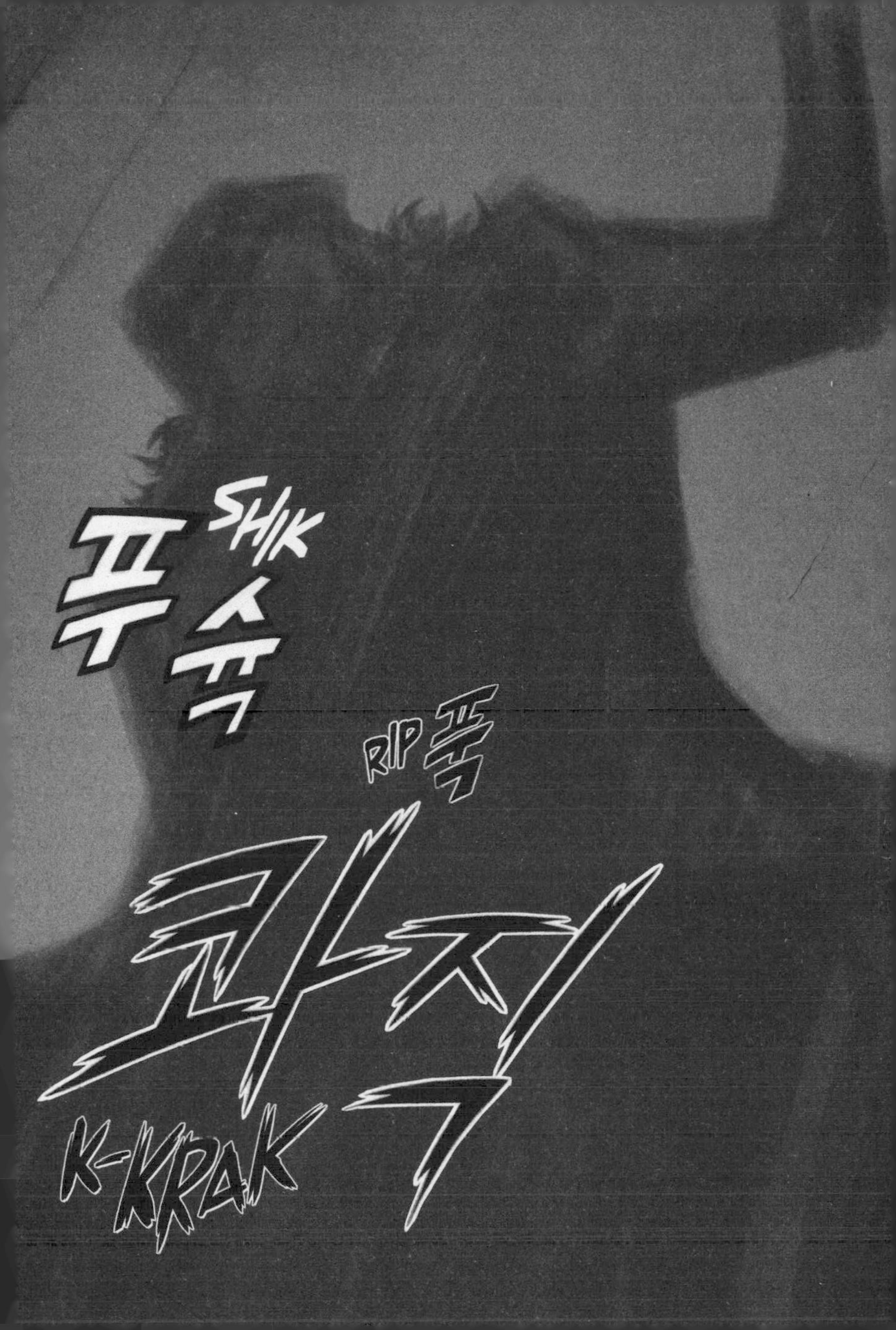
푸슉
SHIK
RIP 푹
콰직
K-KRAK

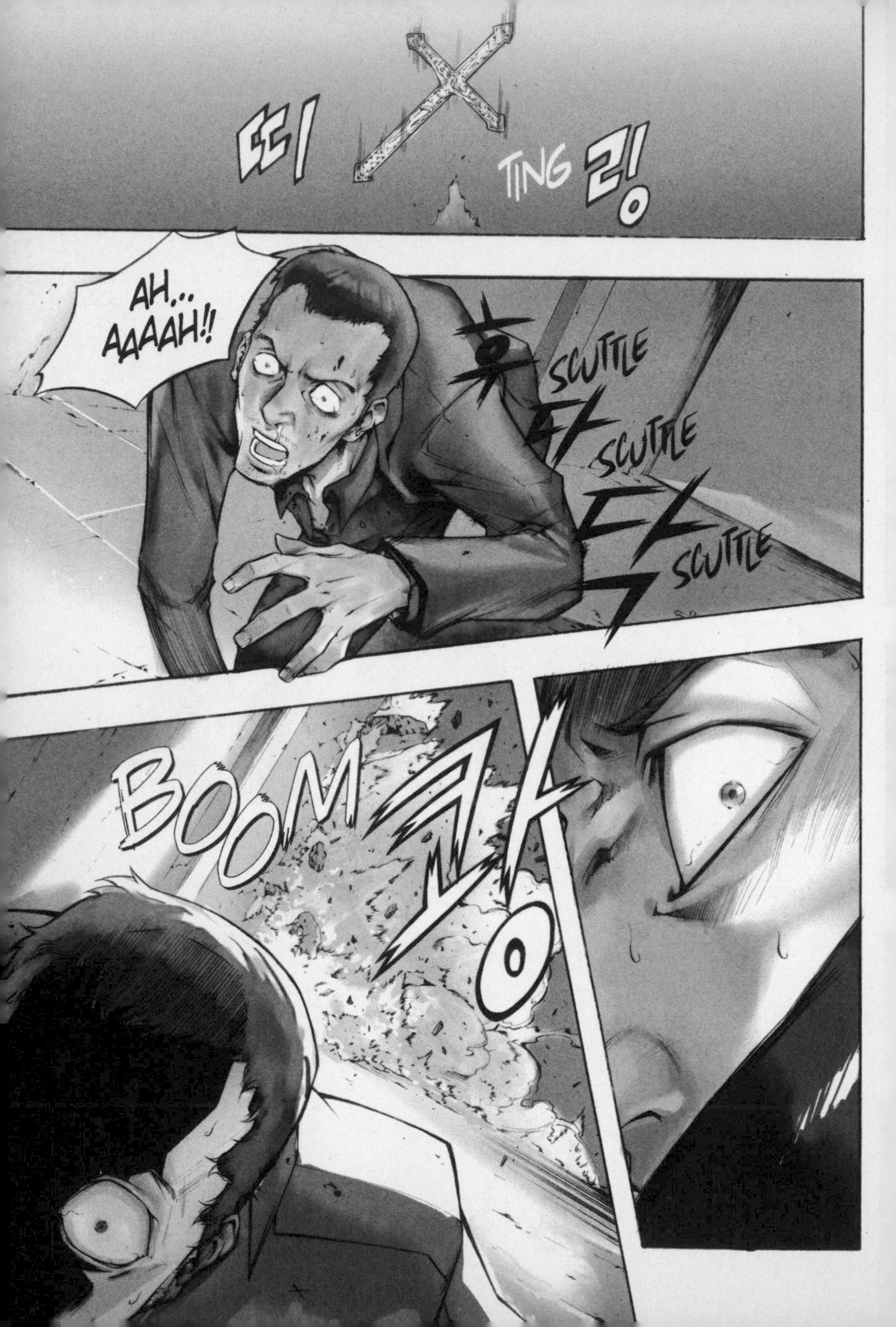
띠
TING
링!
AH... AAAAH!!
후다닥
SCUTTLE
SCUTTLE
SCUTTLE
BOOM
쾅!

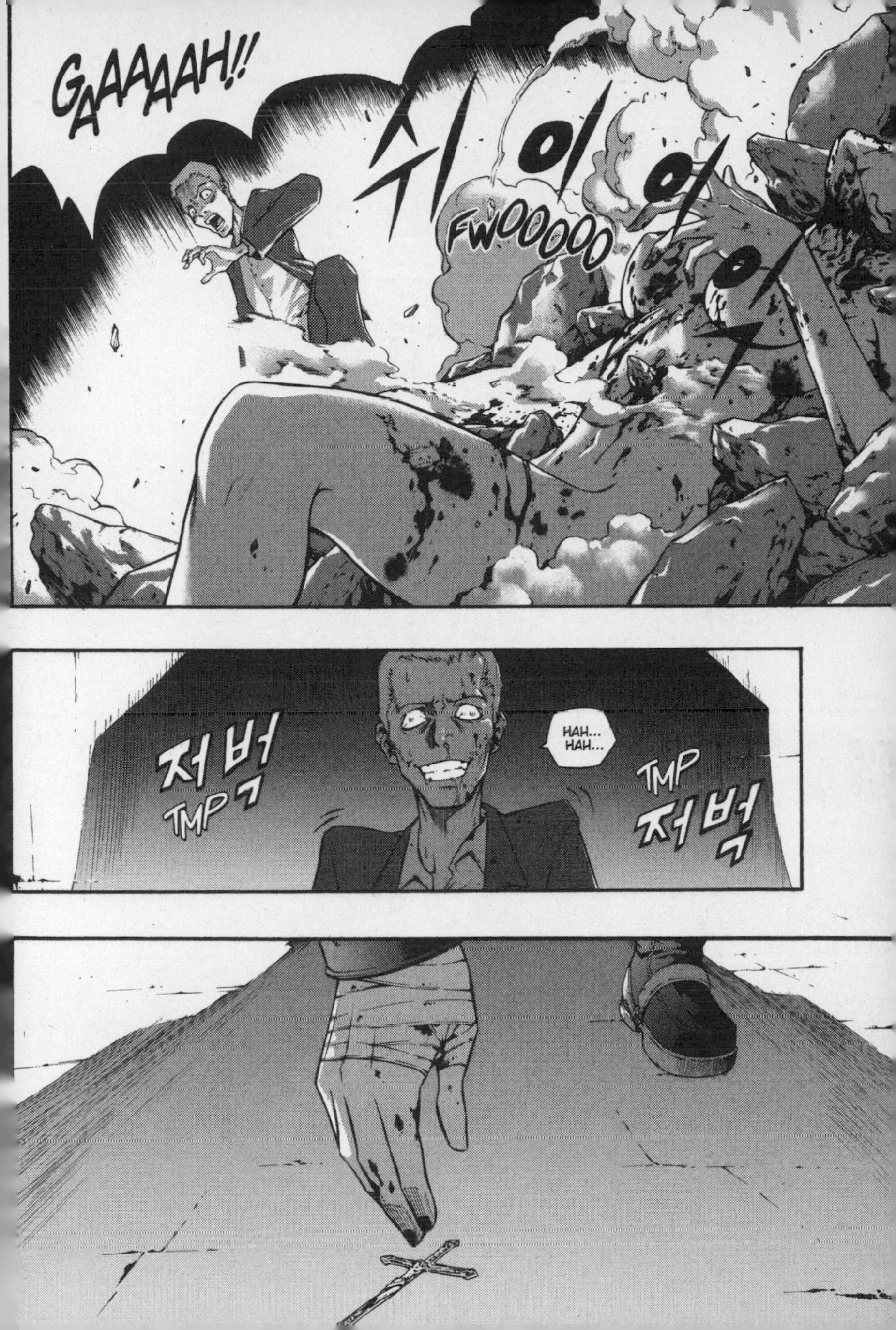
GAAAAAH!!
쉬이이익
FWOOOOO
저벅
TMP
HAH...
HAH...
TMP
저벅

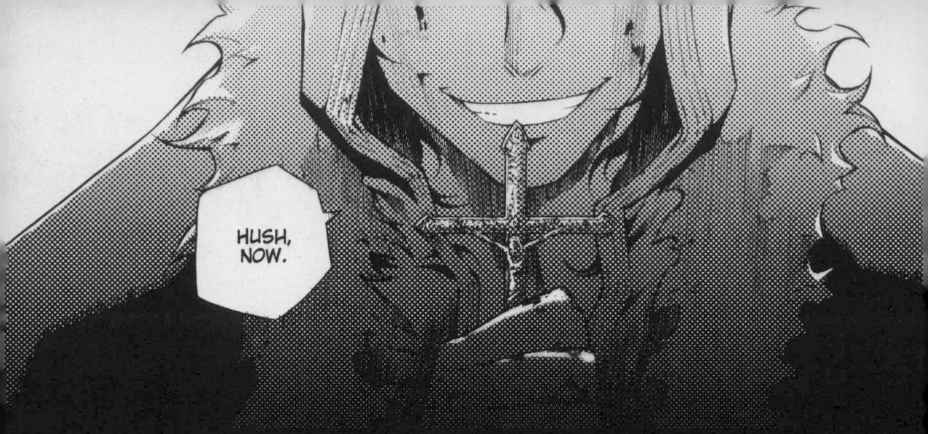
HUSH, NOW.

EPISODE 1

WALKING IN THE MIDNIGHT (1)

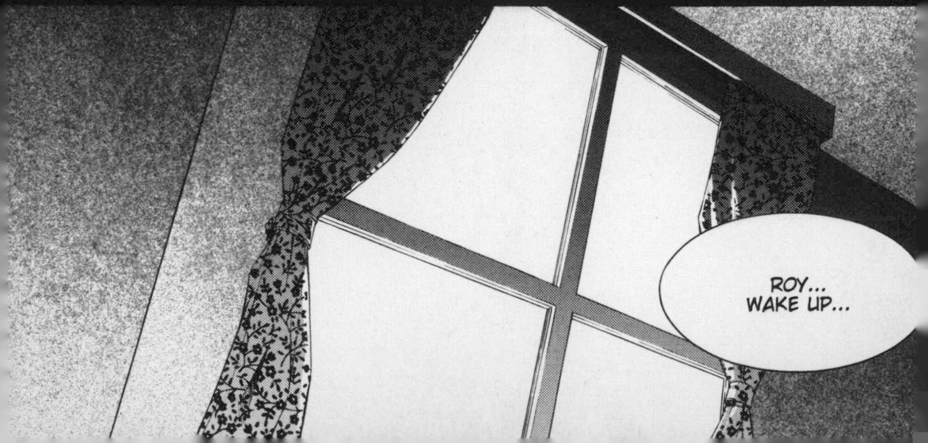
ROY... WAKE UP...

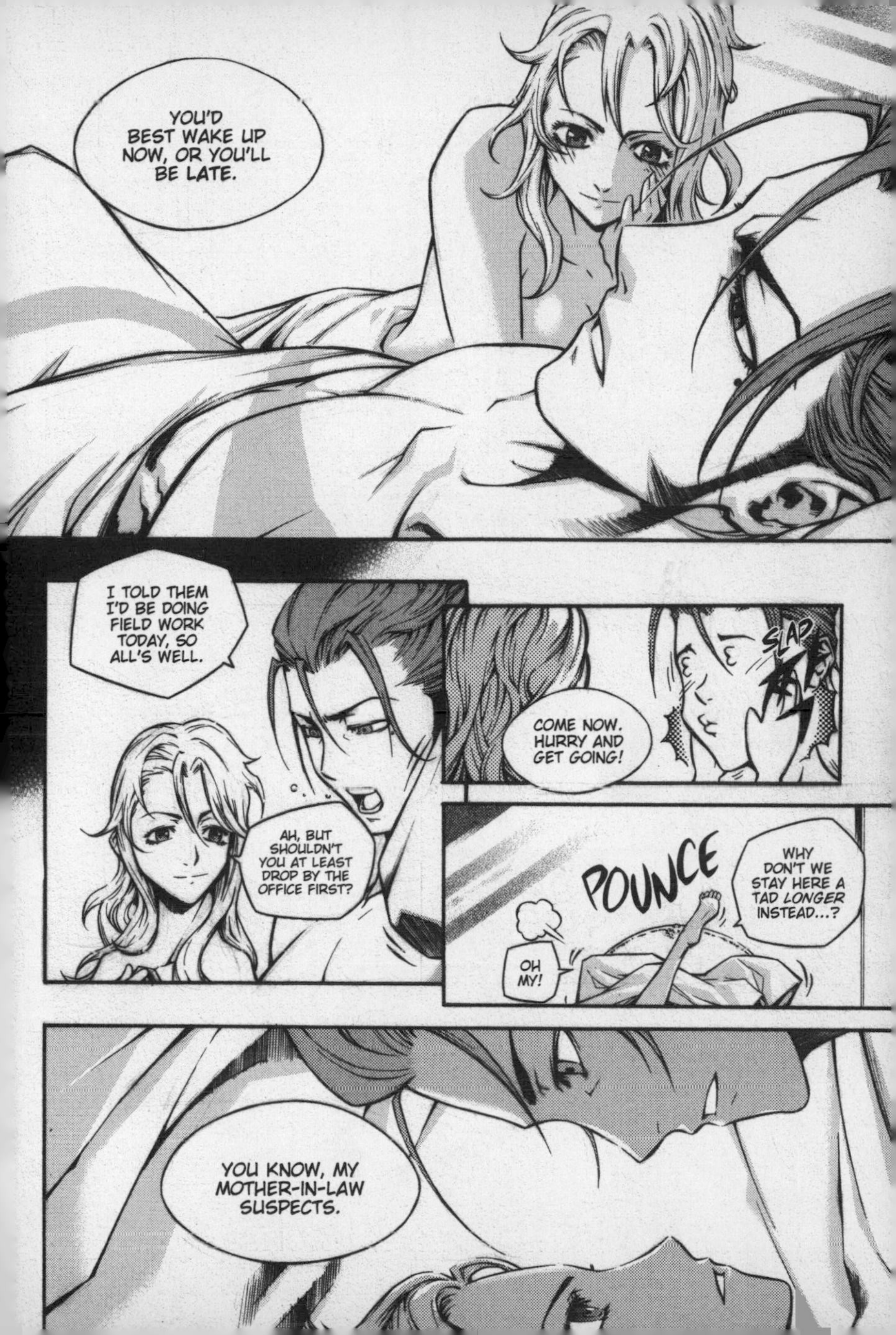
YOU'D BEST WAKE UP NOW, OR YOU'LL BE LATE.
I TOLD THEM I'D BE DOING FIELD WORK TODAY, SO ALL'S WELL.
AH, BUT SHOULDN'T YOU AT LEAST DROP BY THE OFFICE FIRST?
SLAP
COME NOW. HURRY AND GET GOING!
POUNCE
WHY DON'T WE STAY HERE A TAD *LONGER* INSTEAD...?
OH MY!
YOU KNOW, MY MOTHER-IN-LAW SUSPECTS.

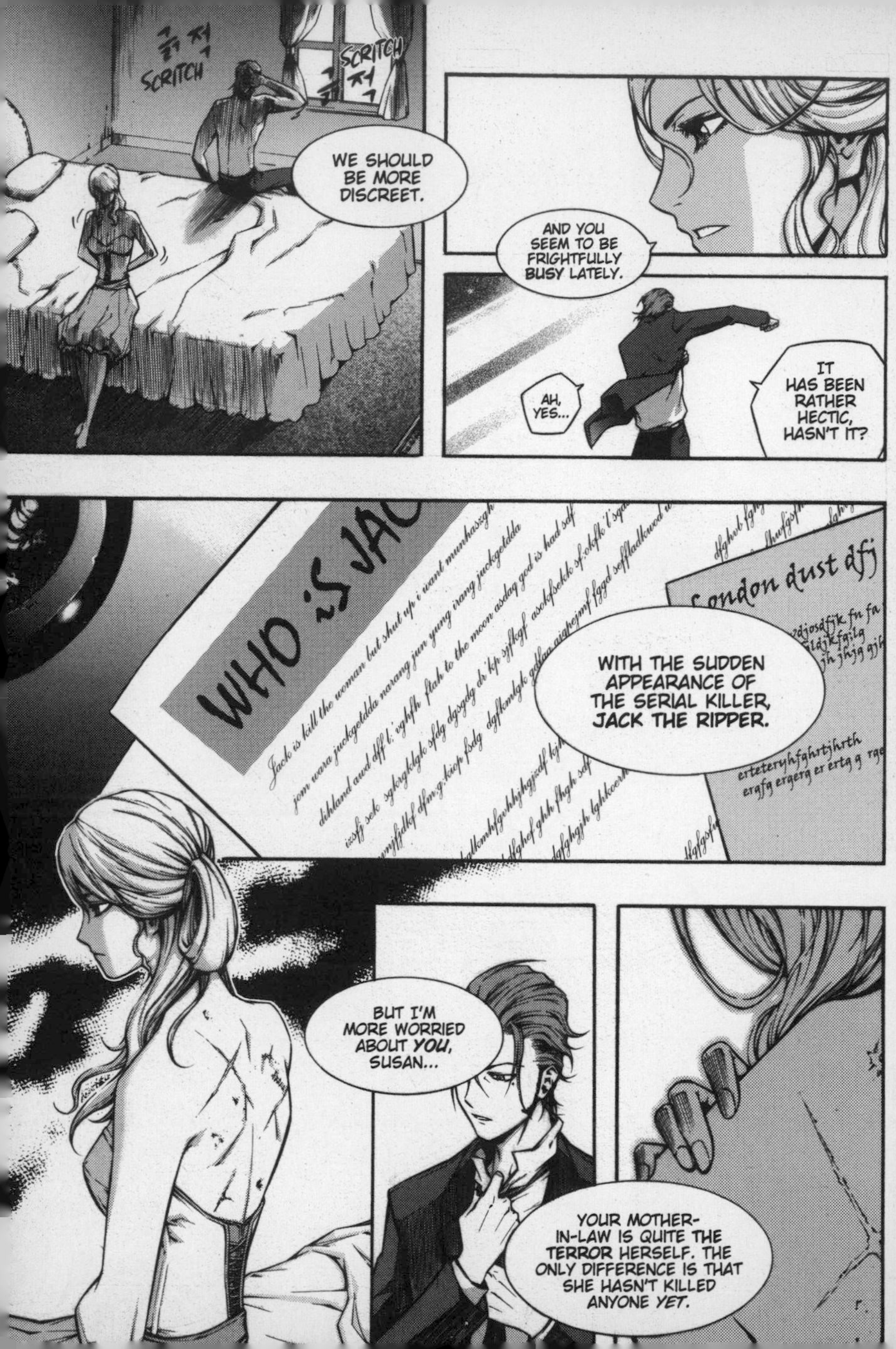
SCRITCH
SCRITCH
WE SHOULD BE MORE DISCREET.
AND YOU SEEM TO BE FRIGHTFULLY BUSY LATELY.
AH, YES...
IT HAS BEEN RATHER HECTIC, HASN'T IT?
WHO is JAC
London dust dfj
WITH THE SUDDEN APPEARANCE OF THE SERIAL KILLER, JACK THE RIPPER.
BUT I'M MORE WORRIED ABOUT *YOU*, SUSAN...
YOUR MOTHER-IN-LAW IS QUITE THE TERROR HERSELF. THE ONLY DIFFERENCE IS THAT SHE HASN'T KILLED ANYONE *YET*.

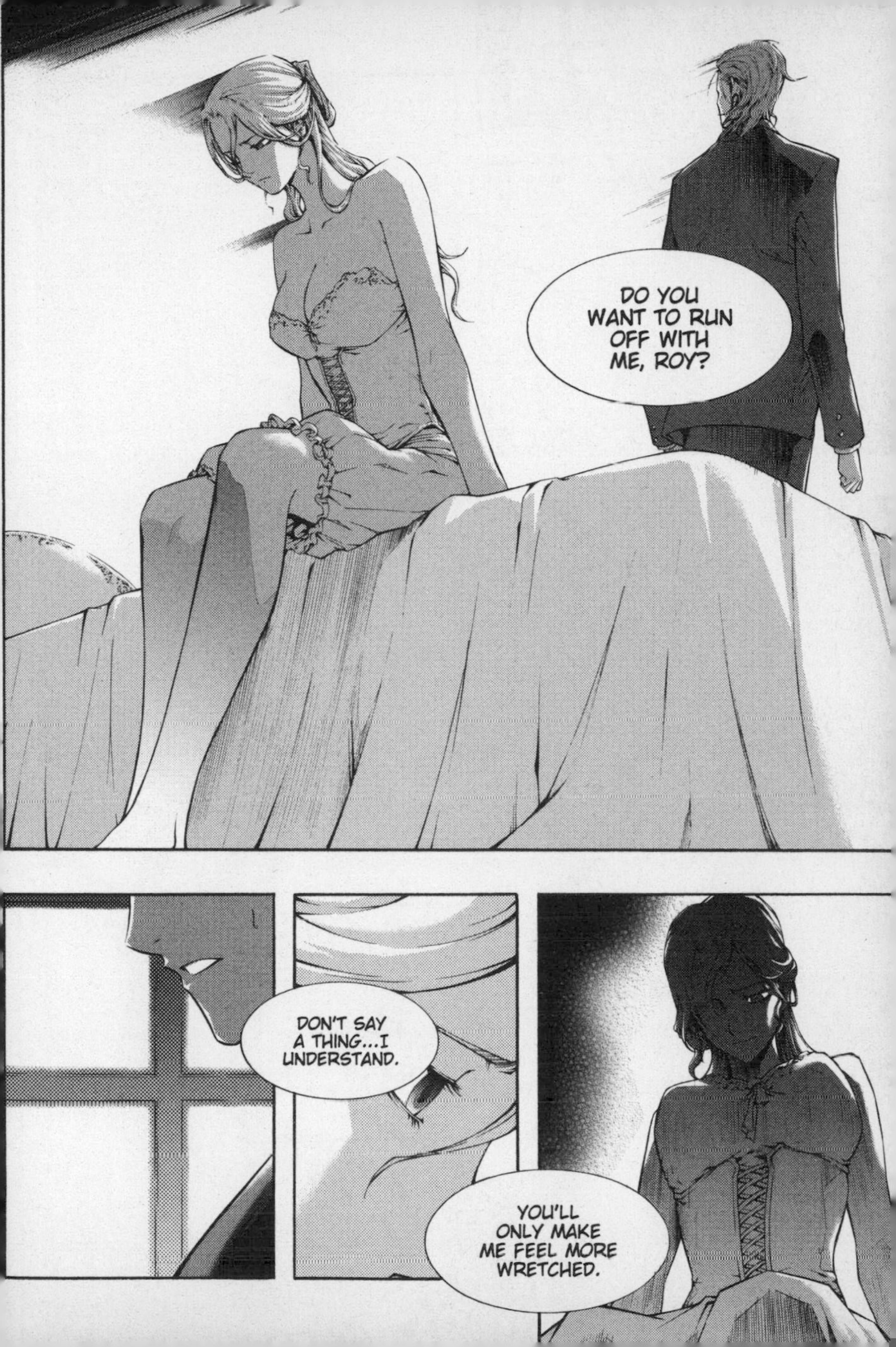
DO YOU WANT TO RUN OFF WITH ME, ROY?
DON'T SAY A THING...I UNDERSTAND.
YOU'LL ONLY MAKE ME FEEL MORE WRETCHED.

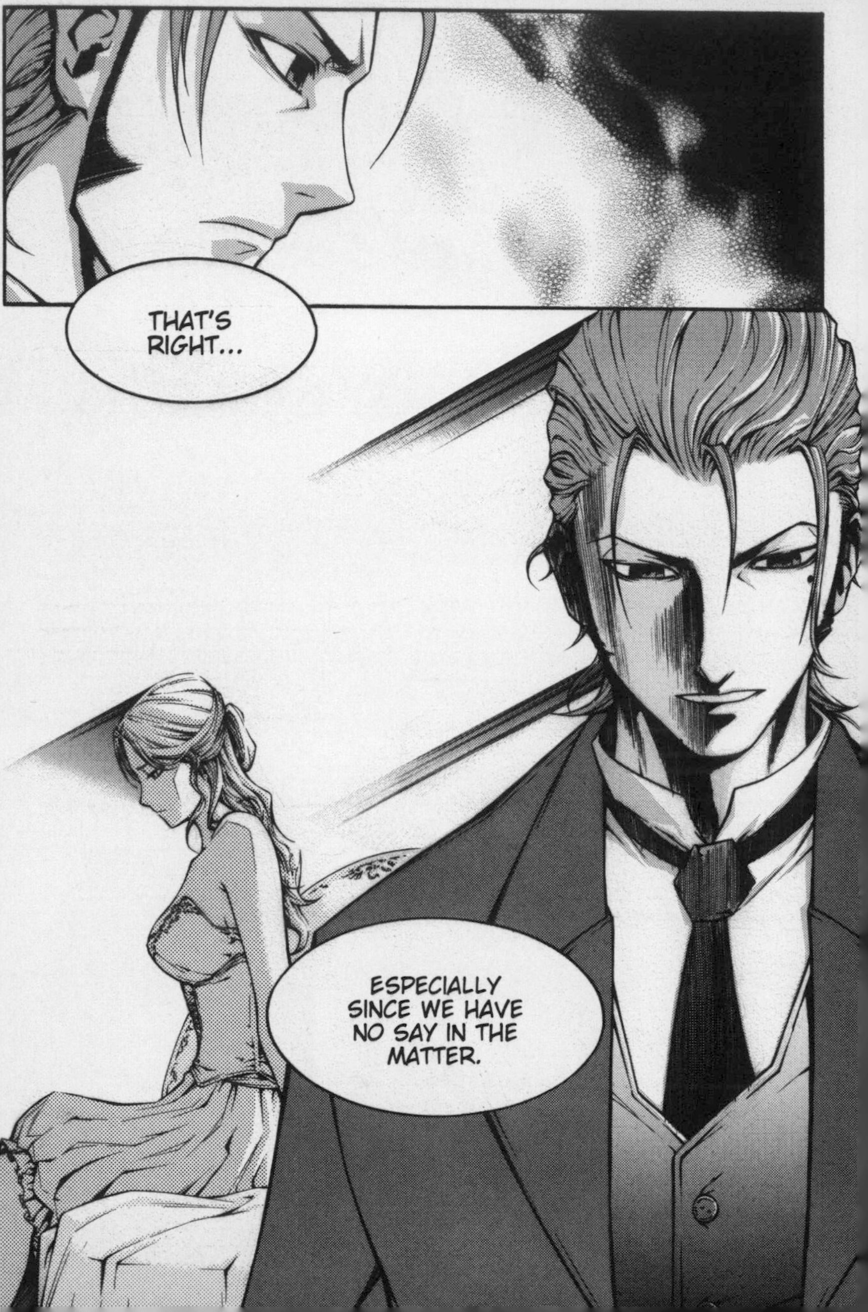
THAT'S RIGHT...
ESPECIALLY SINCE WE HAVE NO SAY IN THE MATTER.

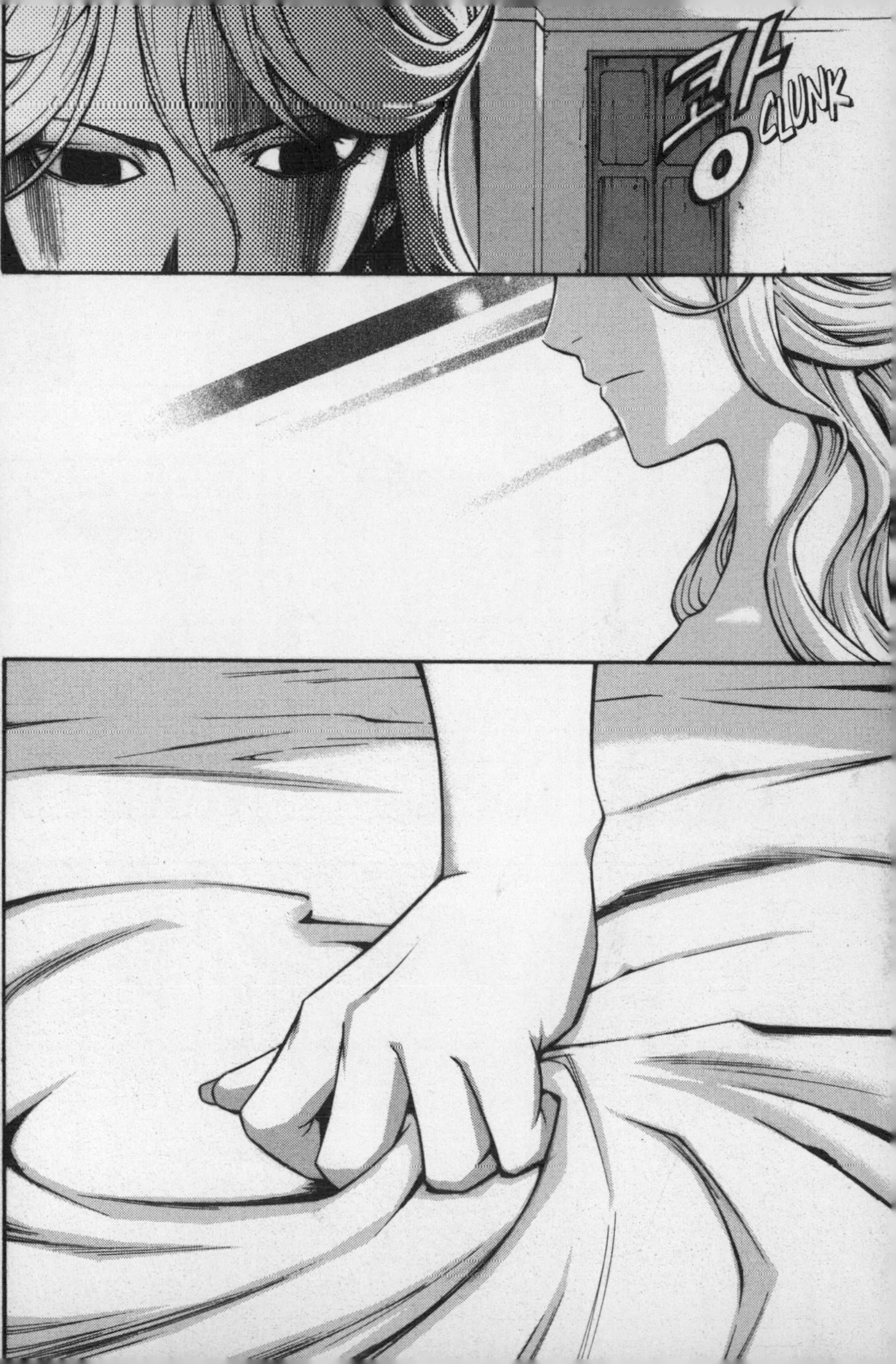
콰앙 CLUNK

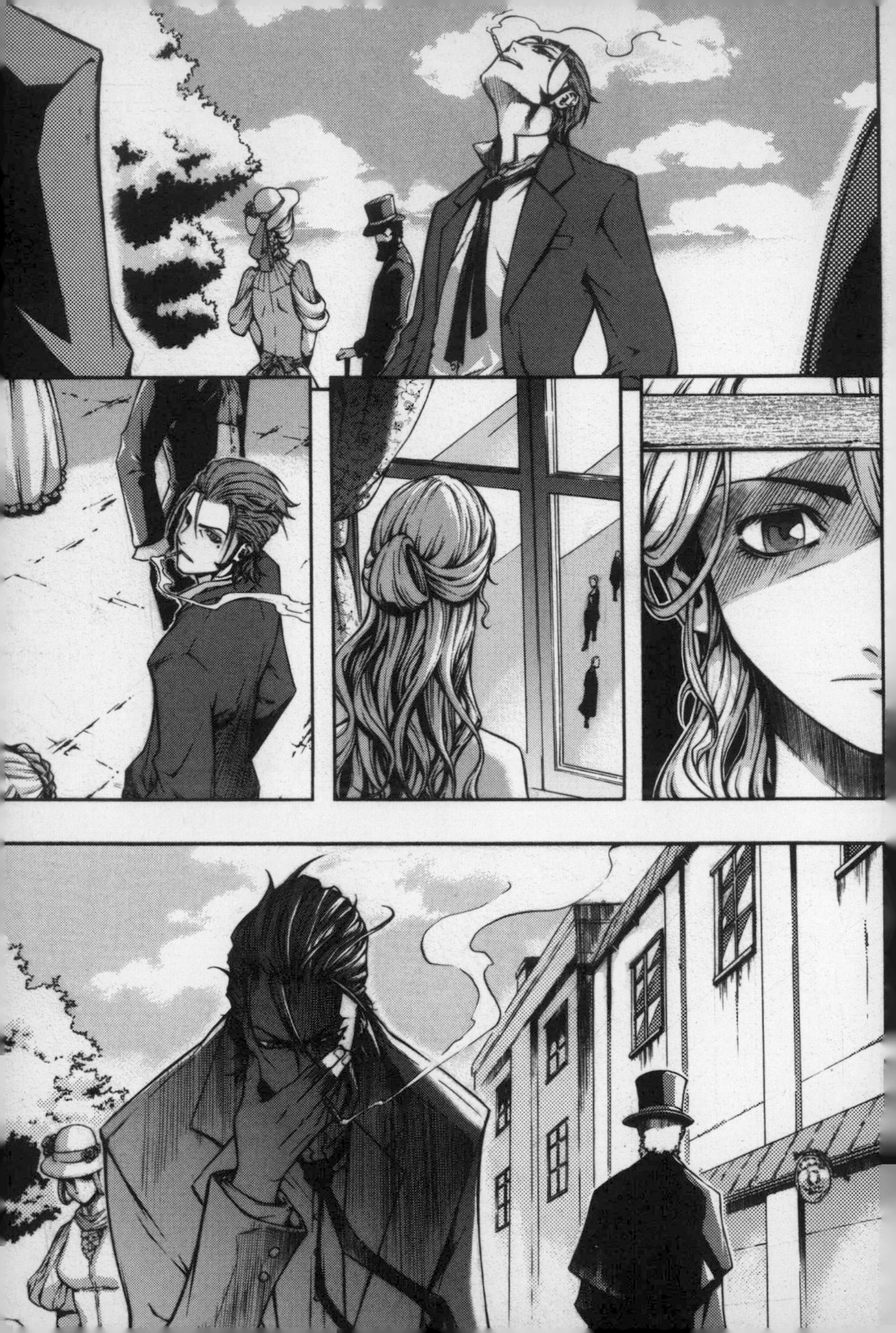

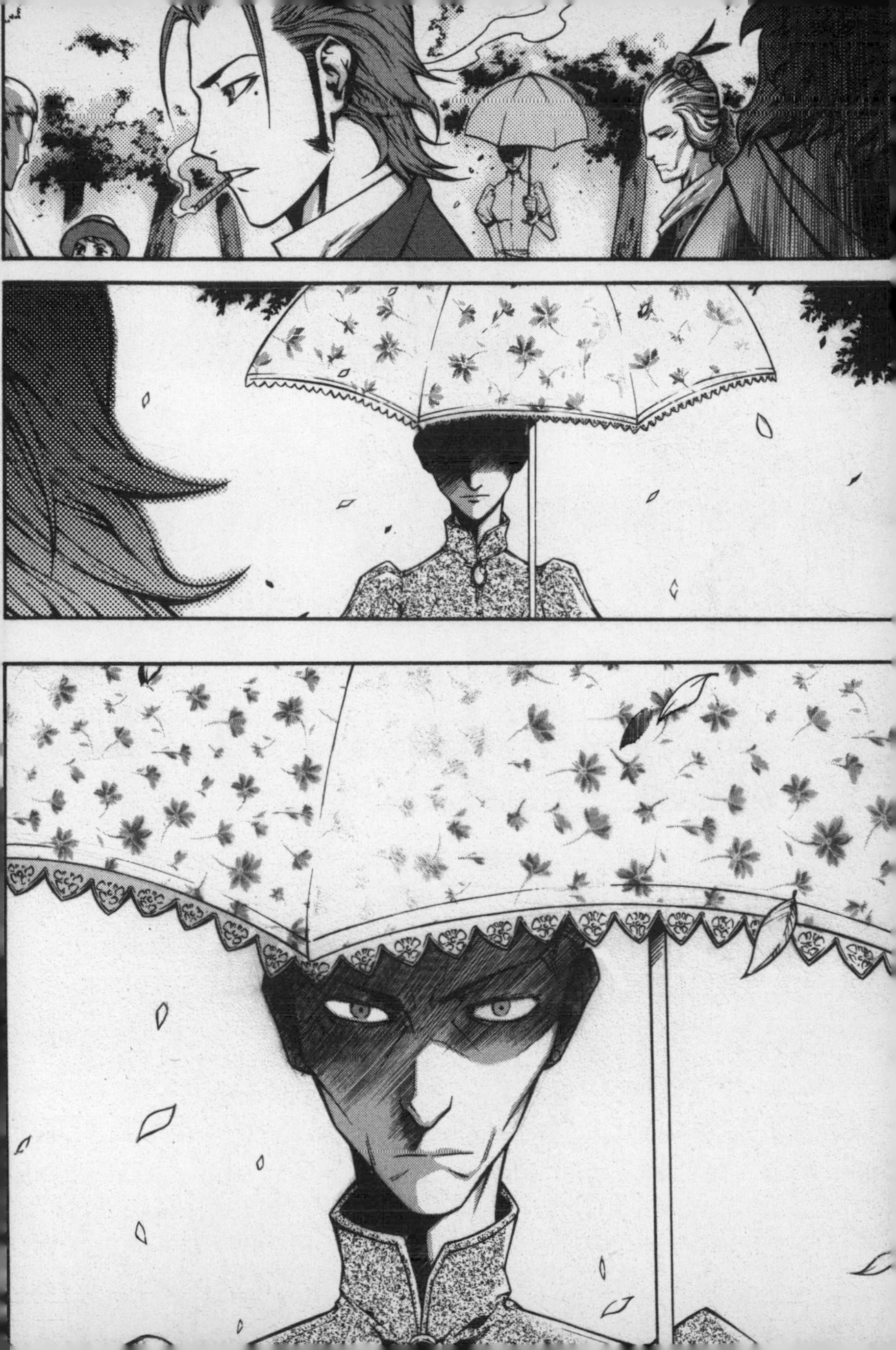

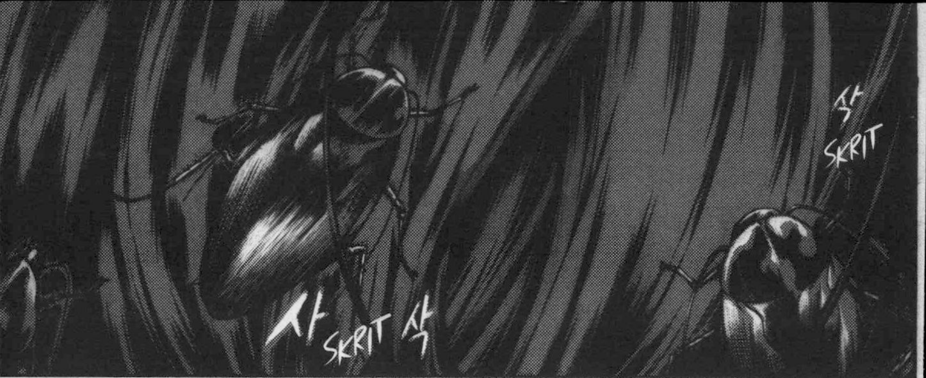
사 SKRIT 삭
삭
SKRIT
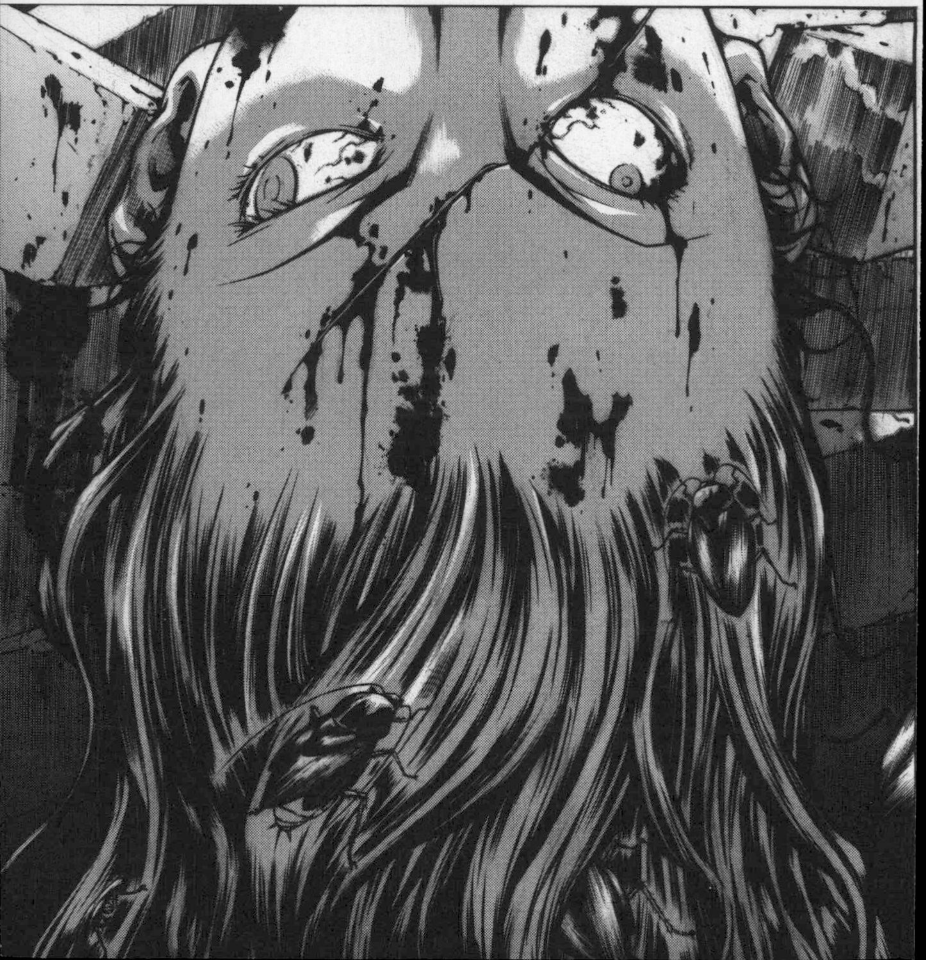

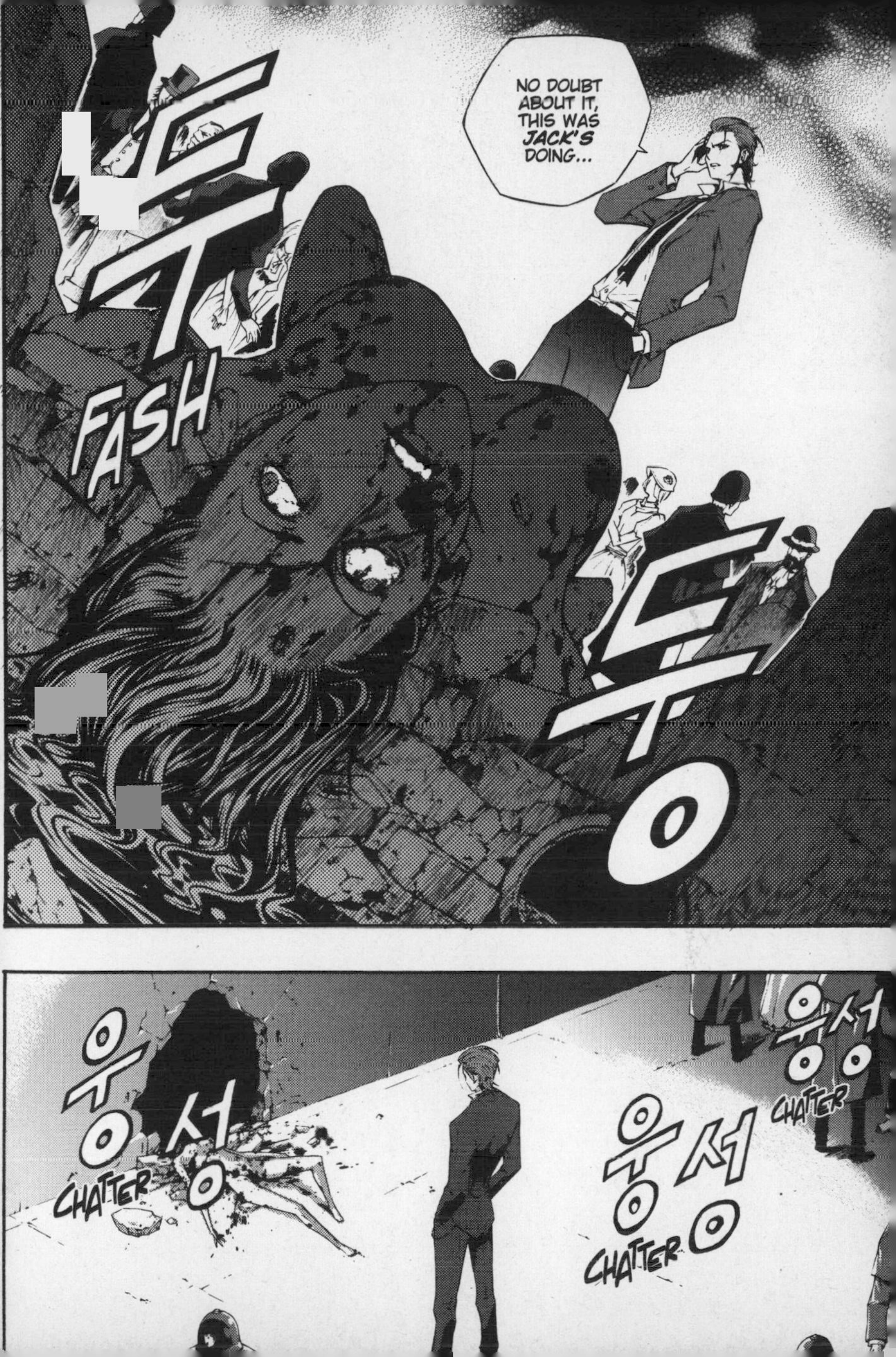
FASH
NO DOUBT ABOUT IT, THIS WAS JACK'S DOING...
웅성
CHATTER
웅성
CHATTER
웅성
CHATTER

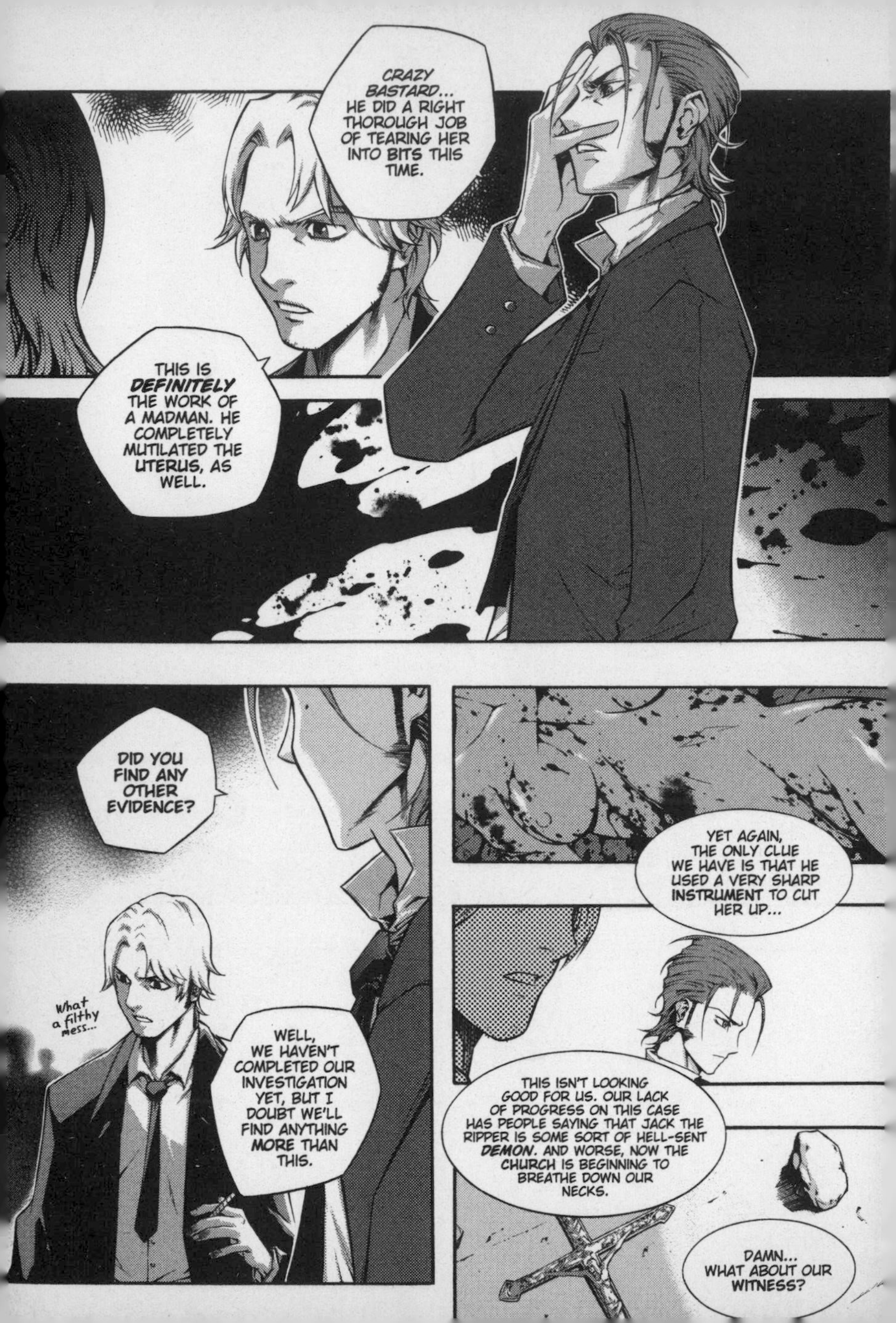
CRAZY BASTARD... HE DID A RIGHT THOROUGH JOB OF TEARING HER INTO BITS THIS TIME.
THIS IS DEFINITELY THE WORK OF A MADMAN. HE COMPLETELY MUTILATED THE UTERUS, AS WELL.
DID YOU FIND ANY OTHER EVIDENCE?
What a filthy mess...
WELL, WE HAVEN'T COMPLETED OUR INVESTIGATION YET, BUT I DOUBT WE'LL FIND ANYTHING MORE THAN THIS.
YET AGAIN, THE ONLY CLUE WE HAVE IS THAT HE USED A VERY SHARP INSTRUMENT TO CUT HER UP...
THIS ISN'T LOOKING GOOD FOR US. OUR LACK OF PROGRESS ON THIS CASE HAS PEOPLE SAYING THAT JACK THE RIPPER IS SOME SORT OF HELL-SENT DEMON. AND WORSE, NOW THE CHURCH IS BEGINNING TO BREATHE DOWN OUR NECKS.
DAMN... WHAT ABOUT OUR WITNESS?

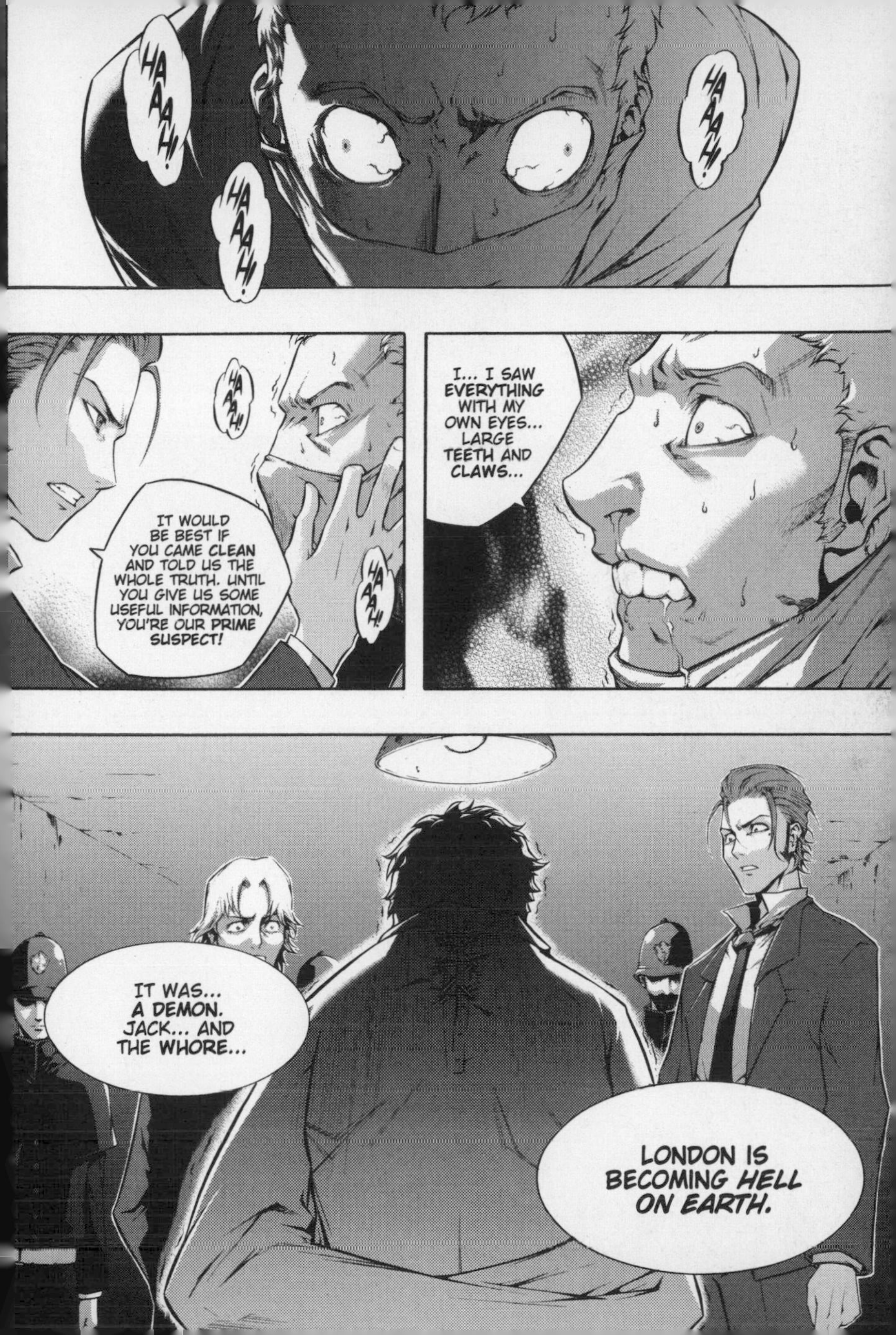
HAAAH!
HAAAH!
HAAAH!
HAAAH!
IT WOULD BE BEST IF YOU CAME CLEAN AND TOLD US THE WHOLE TRUTH. UNTIL YOU GIVE US SOME USEFUL INFORMATION, YOU'RE OUR PRIME SUSPECT!
HAAAH!
I... I SAW EVERYTHING WITH MY OWN EYES... LARGE TEETH AND CLAWS...
IT WAS... A DEMON. JACK... AND THE WHORE...
LONDON IS BECOMING *HELL ON EARTH.*

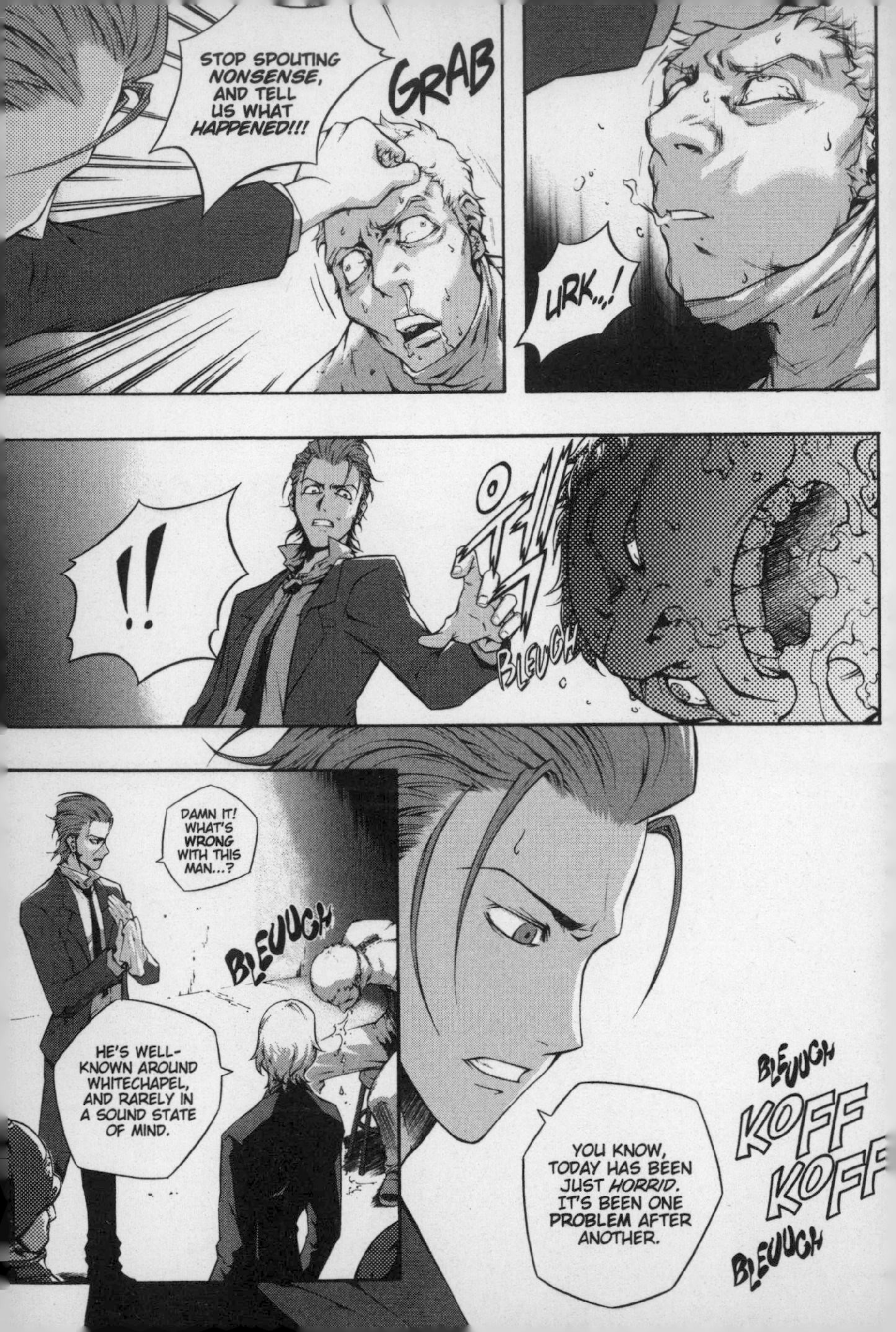
STOP SPOUTING NONSENSE, AND TELL US WHAT HAPPENED!!!
GRAB
URK...!
!!
BLEUGH
DAMN IT! WHAT'S WRONG WITH THIS MAN...?
BLEUUGH
HE'S WELL-KNOWN AROUND WHITECHAPEL, AND RARELY IN A SOUND STATE OF MIND.
YOU KNOW, TODAY HAS BEEN JUST HORRID. IT'S BEEN ONE PROBLEM AFTER ANOTHER.
BLEUUGH
KOFF KOFF
BLEUUGH

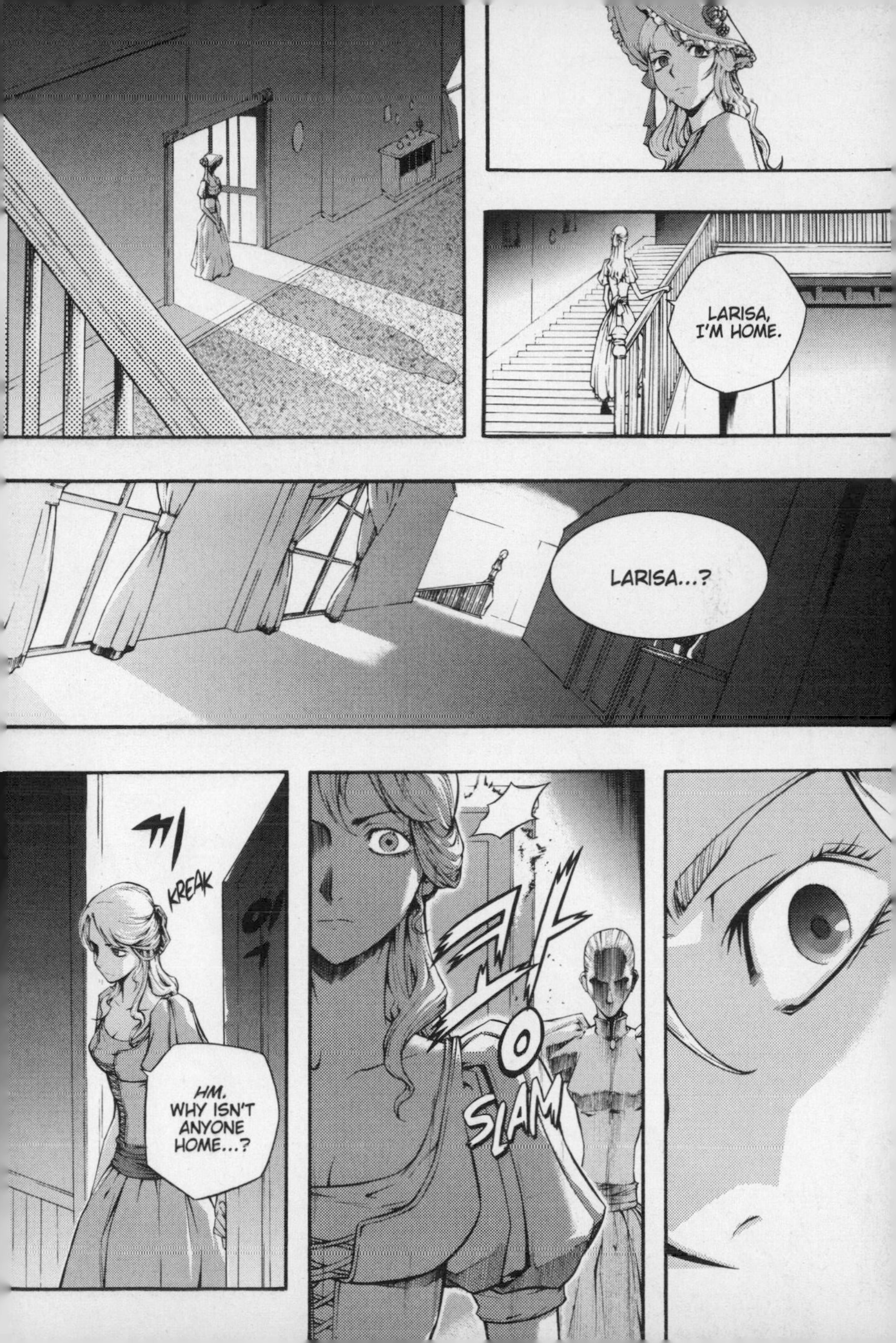
LARISA, I'M HOME.
LARISA...?
KREAK
HM. WHY ISN'T ANYONE HOME...?
SLAM

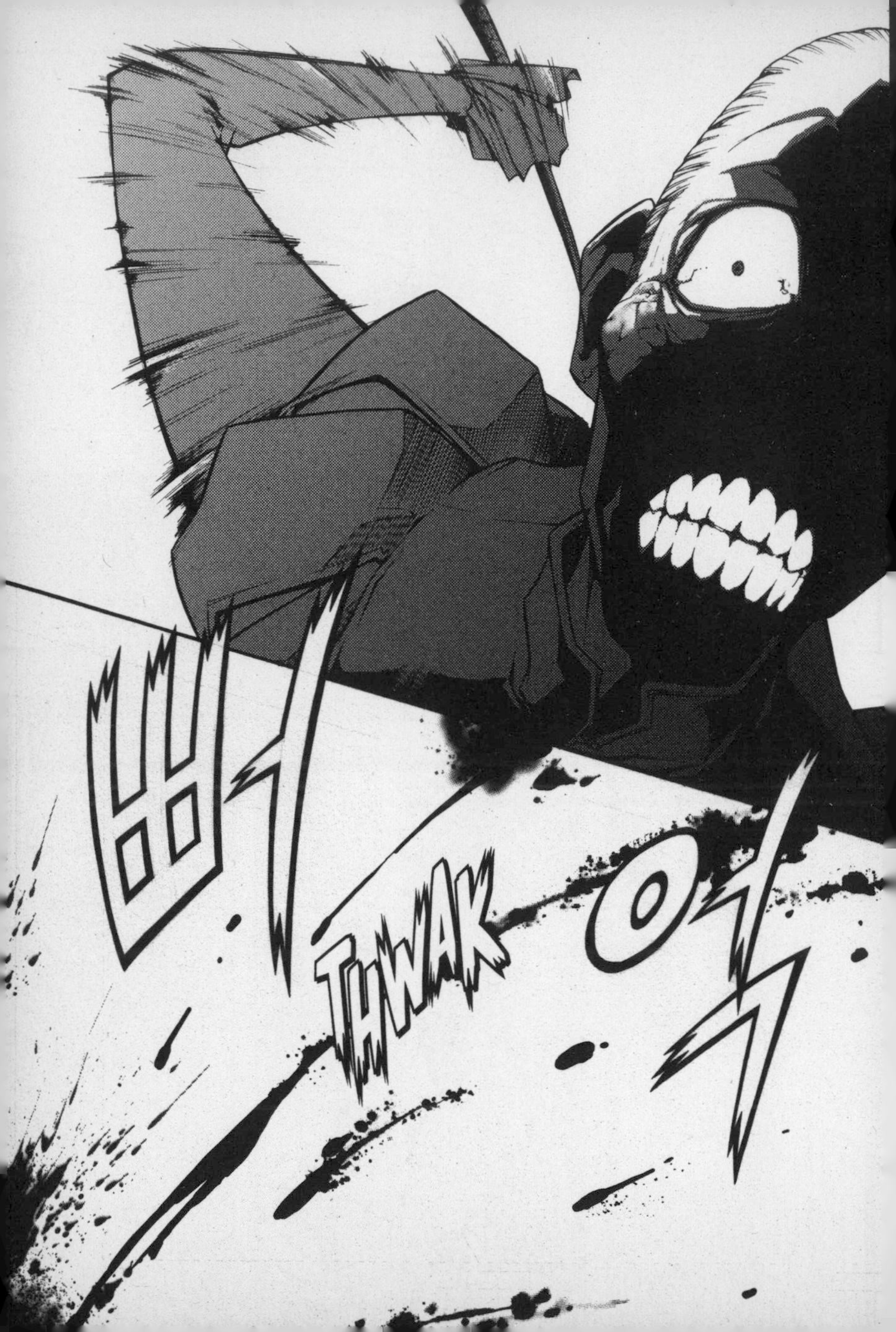

THWAK

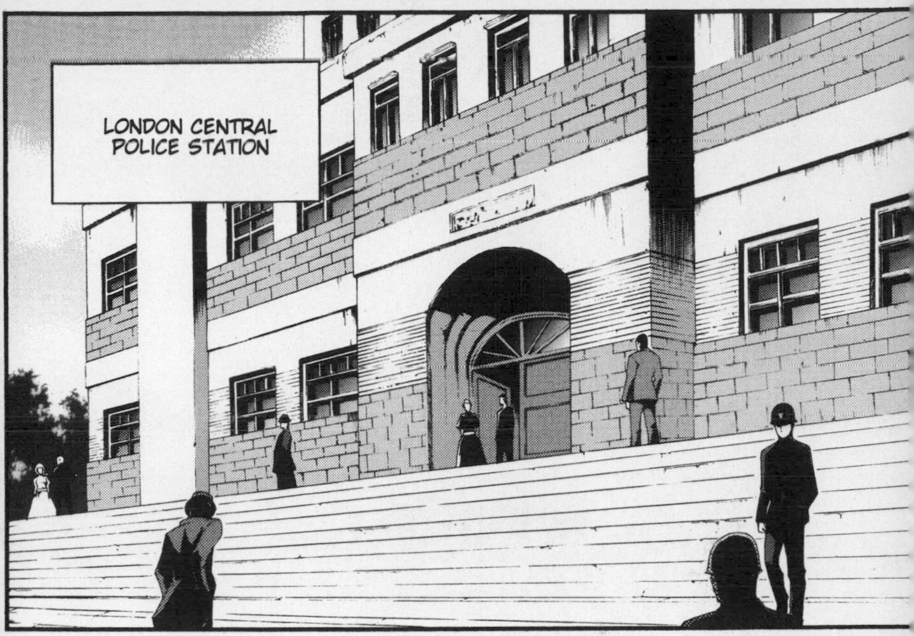
LONDON CENTRAL POLICE STATION
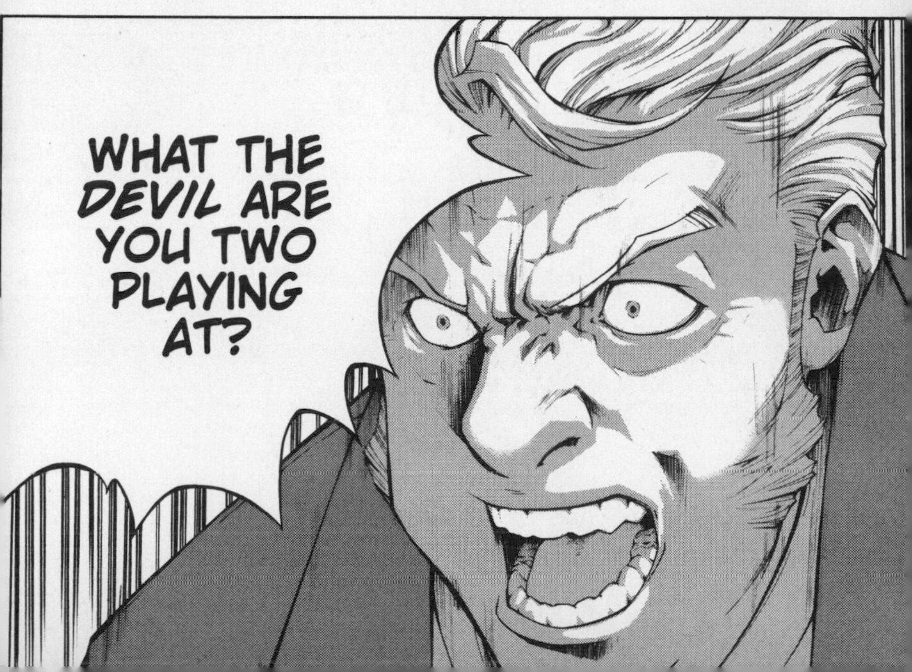
WHAT THE *DEVIL* ARE YOU TWO PLAYING AT?

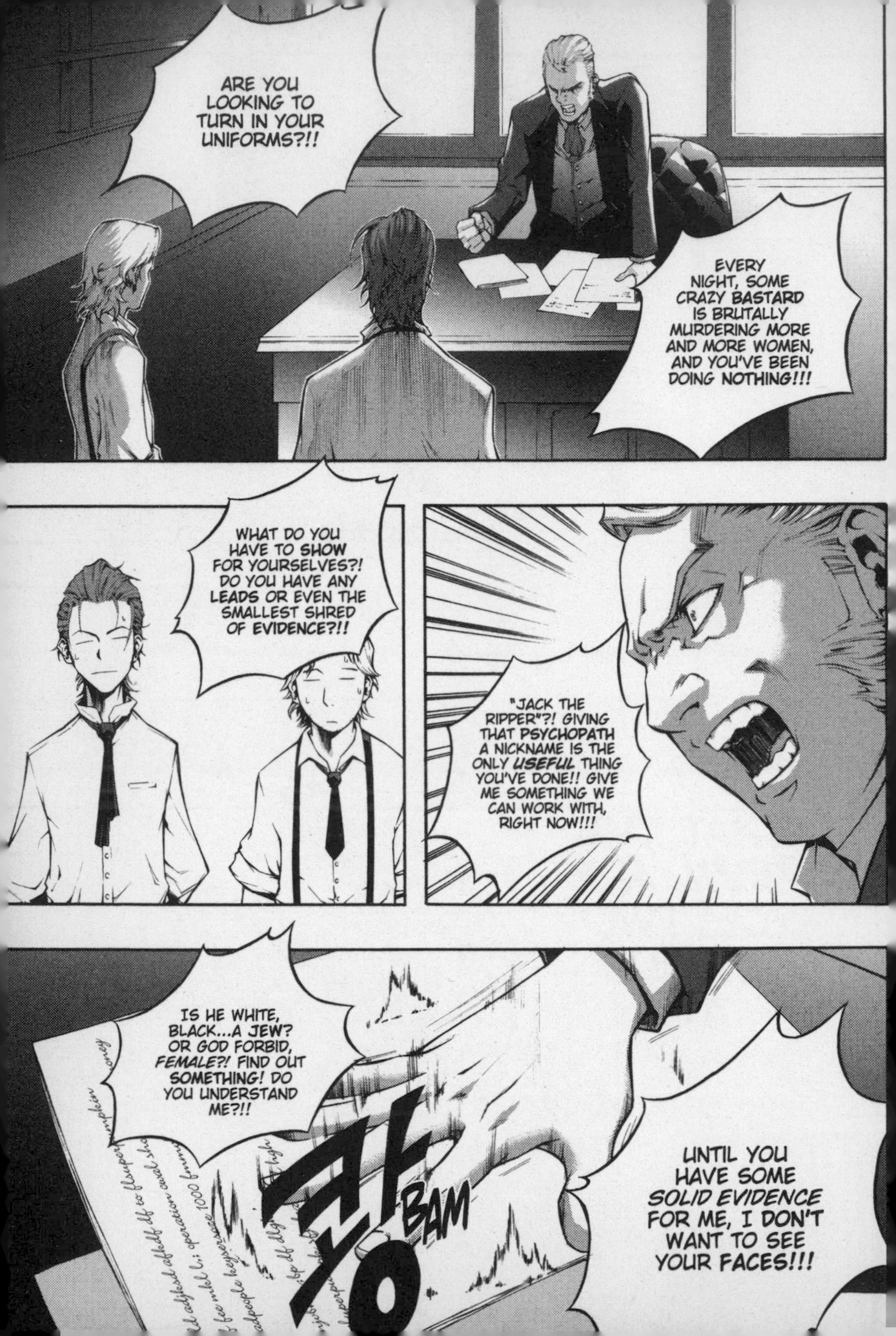
ARE YOU LOOKING TO TURN IN YOUR UNIFORMS?!!
EVERY NIGHT, SOME CRAZY BASTARD IS BRUTALLY MURDERING MORE AND MORE WOMEN, AND YOU'VE BEEN DOING NOTHING!!!
WHAT DO YOU HAVE TO SHOW FOR YOURSELVES?! DO YOU HAVE ANY LEADS OR EVEN THE SMALLEST SHRED OF EVIDENCE?!!
"JACK THE RIPPER"?! GIVING THAT PSYCHOPATH A NICKNAME IS THE ONLY USEFUL THING YOU'VE DONE!! GIVE ME SOMETHING WE CAN WORK WITH, RIGHT NOW!!!
IS HE WHITE, BLACK...A JEW? OR GOD FORBID, FEMALE?! FIND OUT SOMETHING! DO YOU UNDERSTAND ME?!!
BAM
UNTIL YOU HAVE SOME SOLID EVIDENCE FOR ME, I DON'T WANT TO SEE YOUR FACES!!!

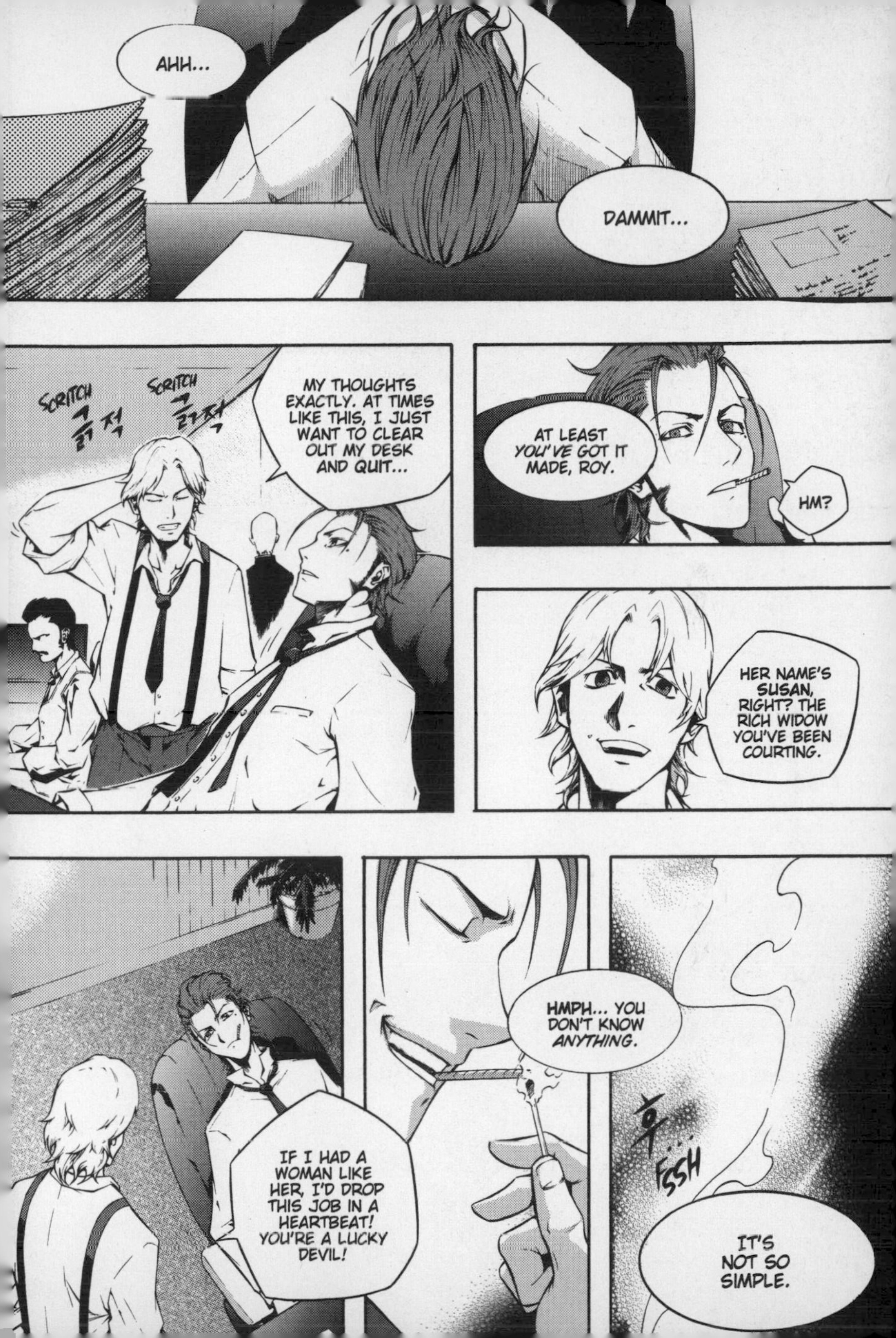
AHH...
DAMMIT...
SCRITCH
긁적
SCRITCH
긁적
MY THOUGHTS EXACTLY. AT TIMES LIKE THIS, I JUST WANT TO CLEAR OUT MY DESK AND QUIT...
AT LEAST *YOU'VE* GOT IT MADE, ROY.
HM?
HER NAME'S SUSAN, RIGHT? THE RICH WIDOW YOU'VE BEEN COURTING.
IF I HAD A WOMAN LIKE HER, I'D DROP THIS JOB IN A HEARTBEAT! YOU'RE A LUCKY DEVIL!
HMPH... YOU DON'T KNOW *ANYTHING*.
후...
FSSH
IT'S NOT SO SIMPLE.

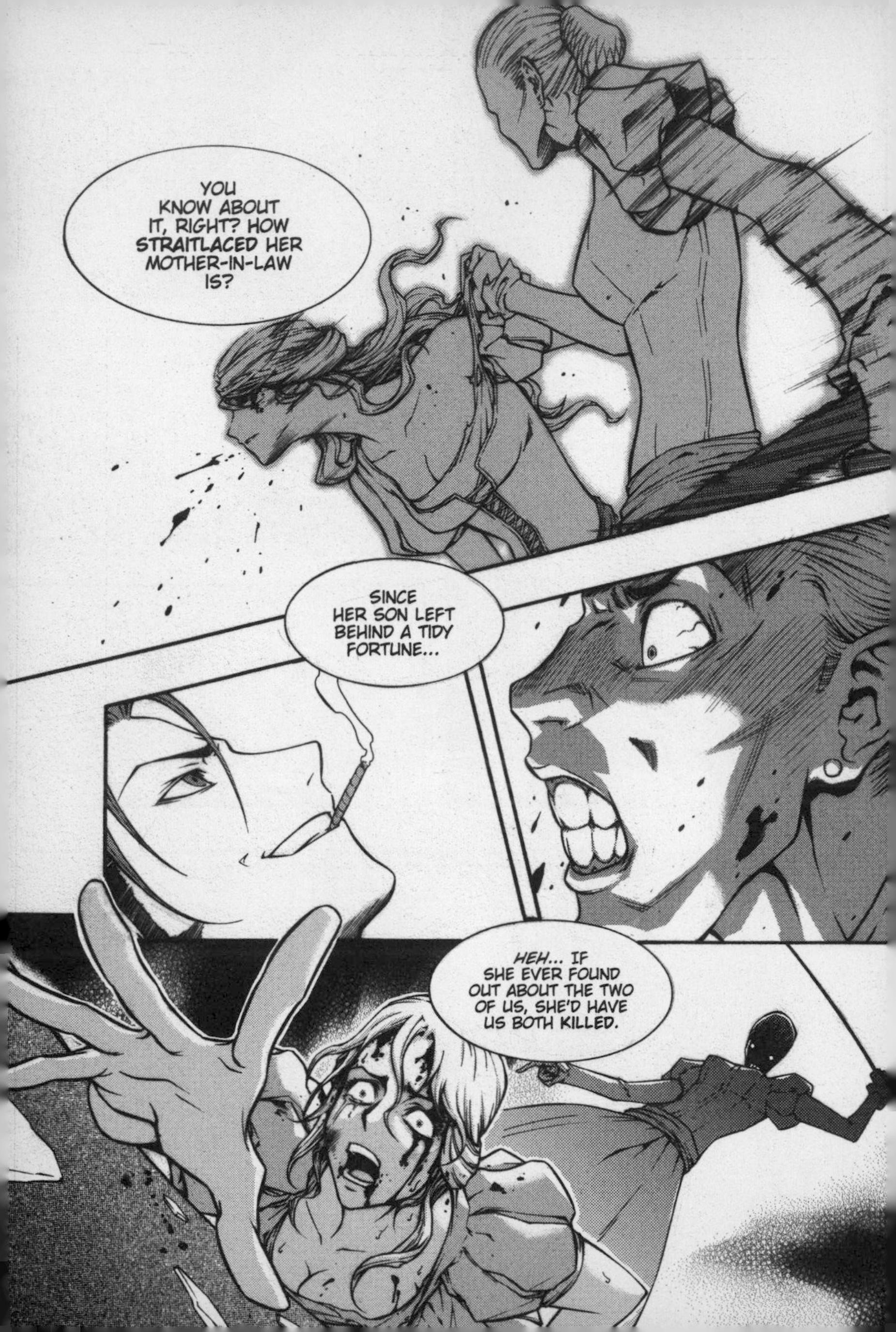
YOU KNOW ABOUT IT, RIGHT? HOW STRAITLACED HER MOTHER-IN-LAW IS?
SINCE HER SON LEFT BEHIND A TIDY FORTUNE...
HEH... IF SHE EVER FOUND OUT ABOUT THE TWO OF US, SHE'D HAVE US BOTH KILLED.

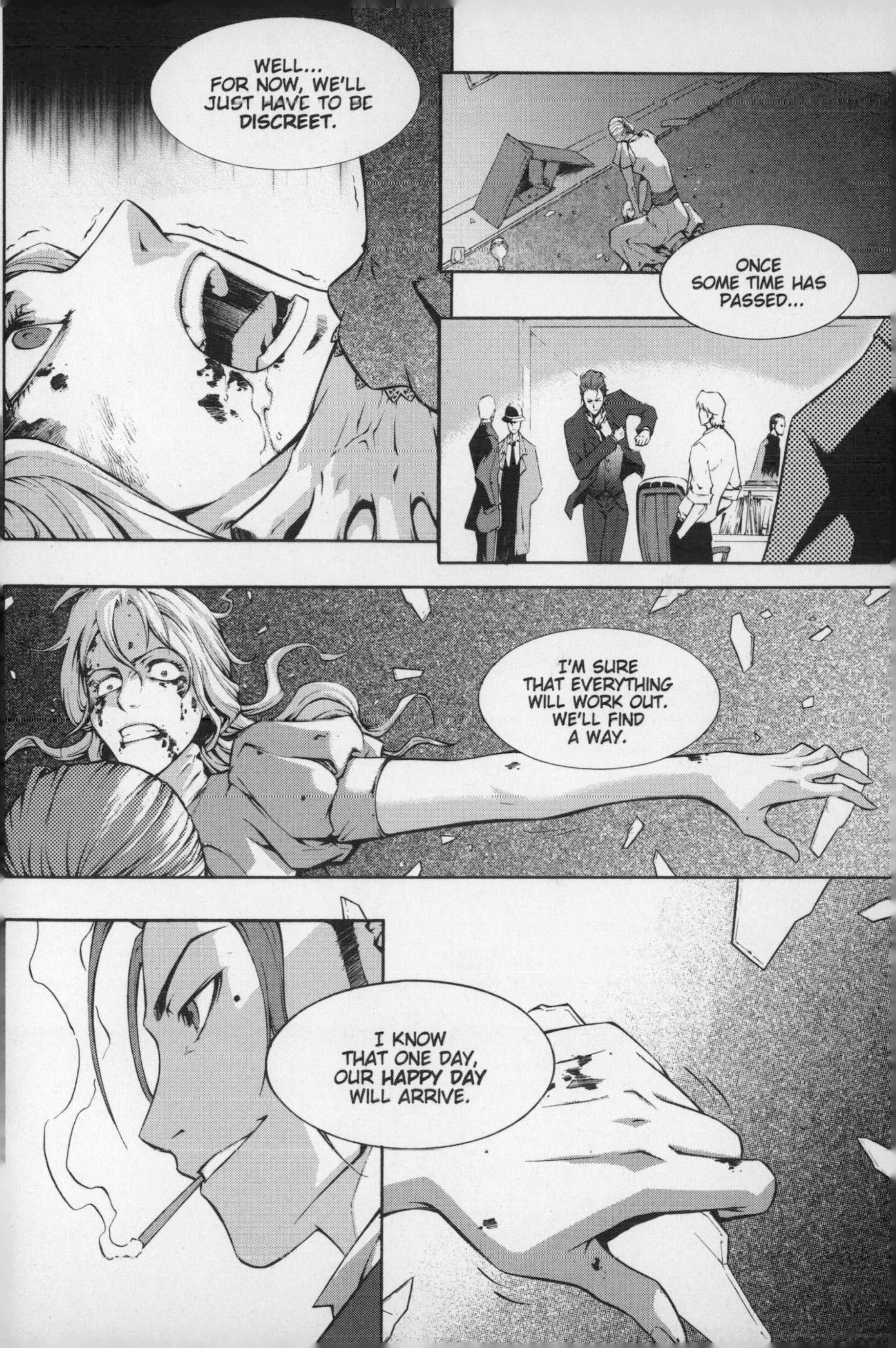
WELL... FOR NOW, WE'LL JUST HAVE TO BE DISCREET.
ONCE SOME TIME HAS PASSED...
I'M SURE THAT EVERYTHING WILL WORK OUT. WE'LL FIND A WAY.
I KNOW THAT ONE DAY, OUR HAPPY DAY WILL ARRIVE.

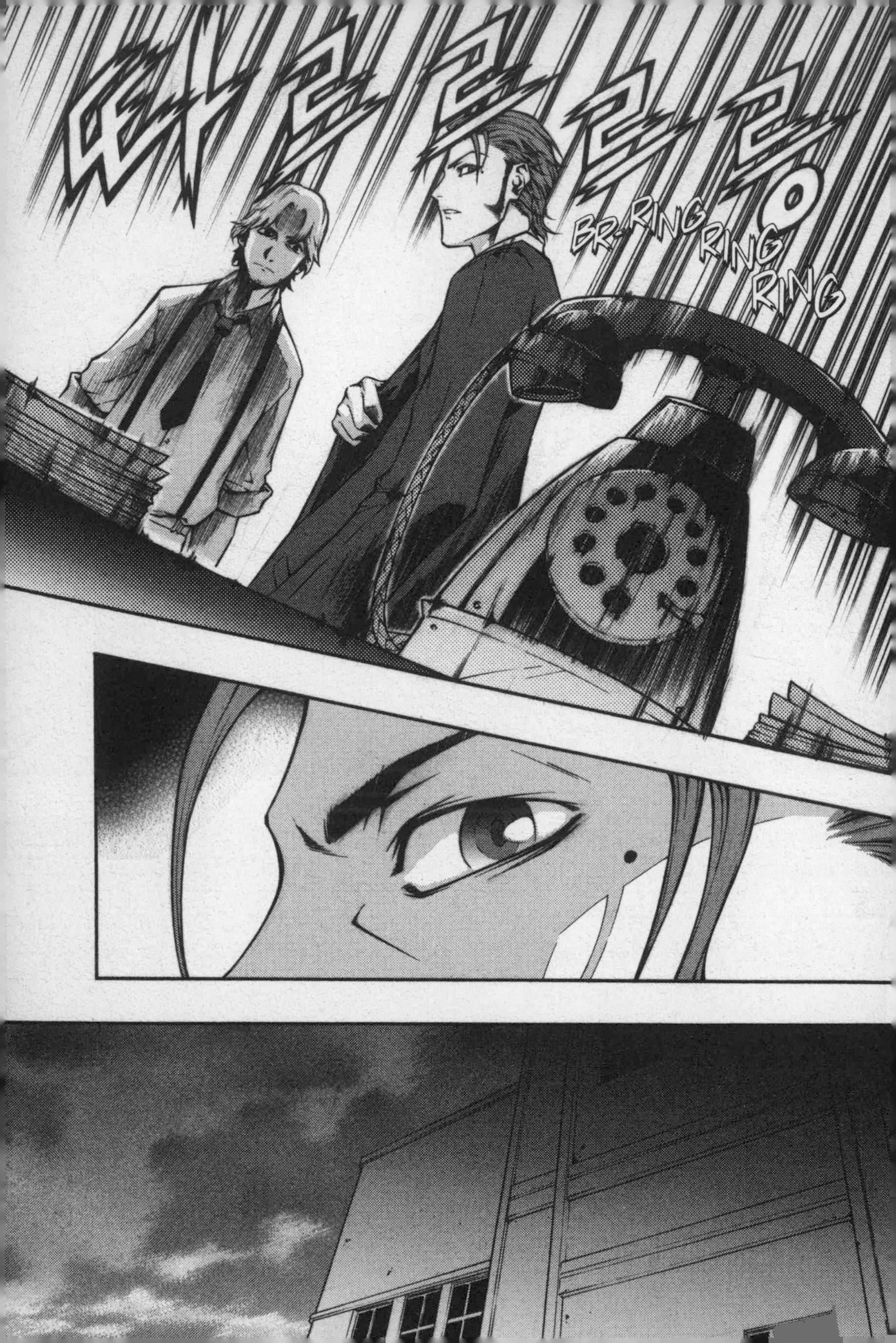
BR-RING RING RING

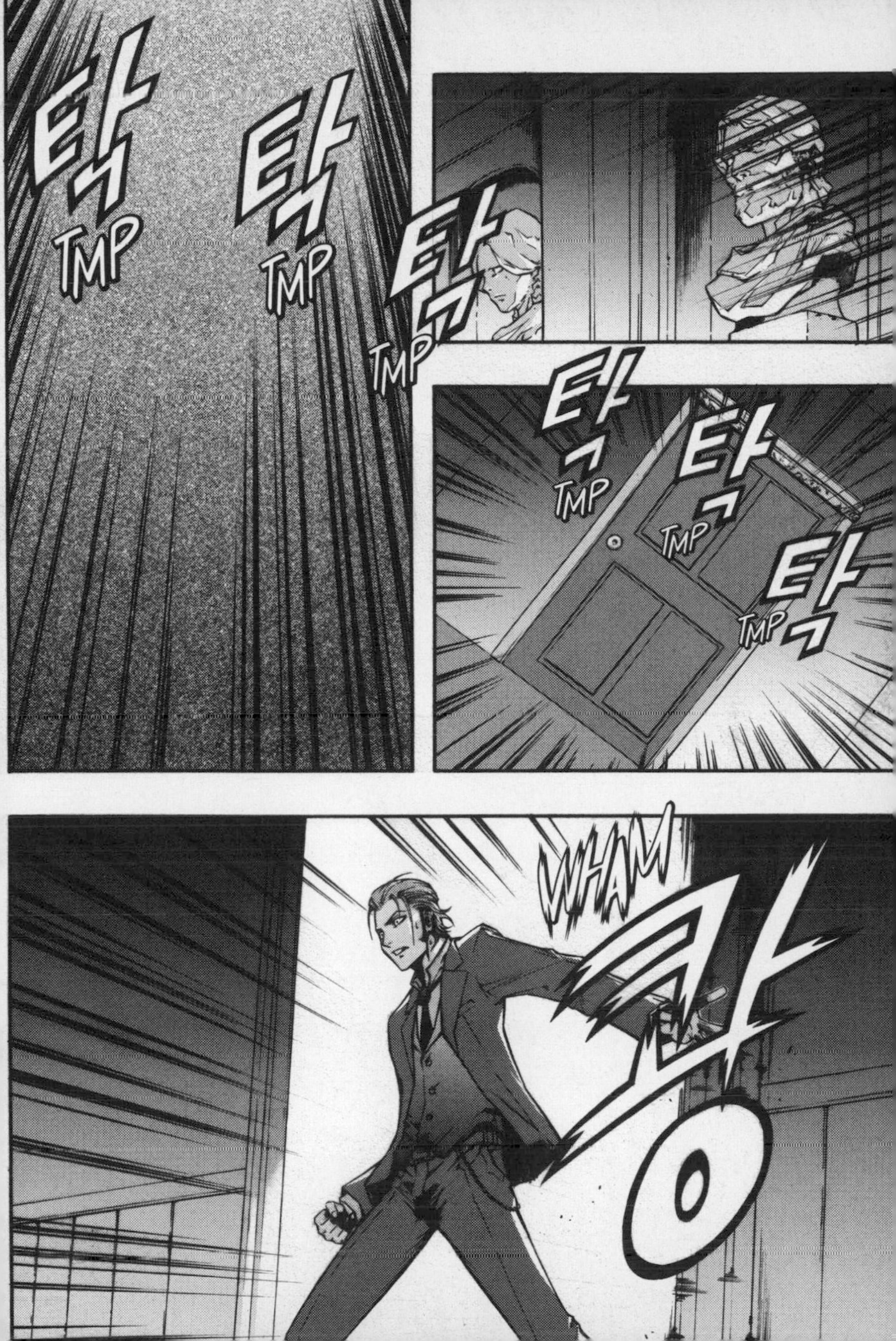

탁
TMP
탁
TMP
탁
TMP
탁
TMP
탁
TMP
탁
TMP
WHAM
캉

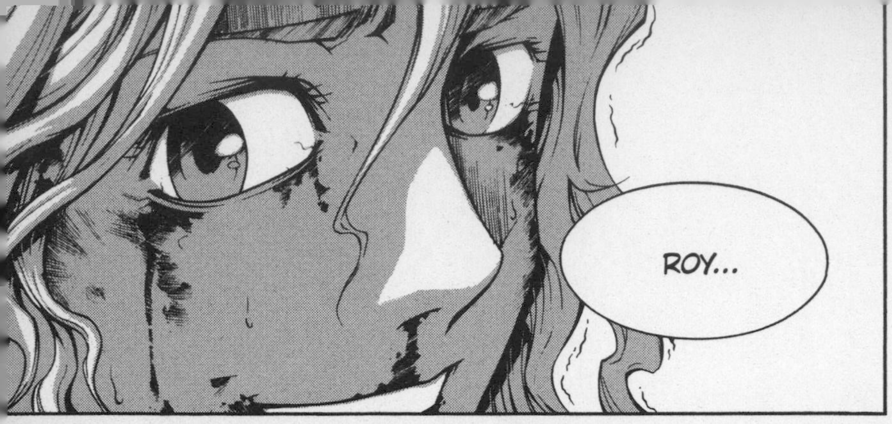
ROY...
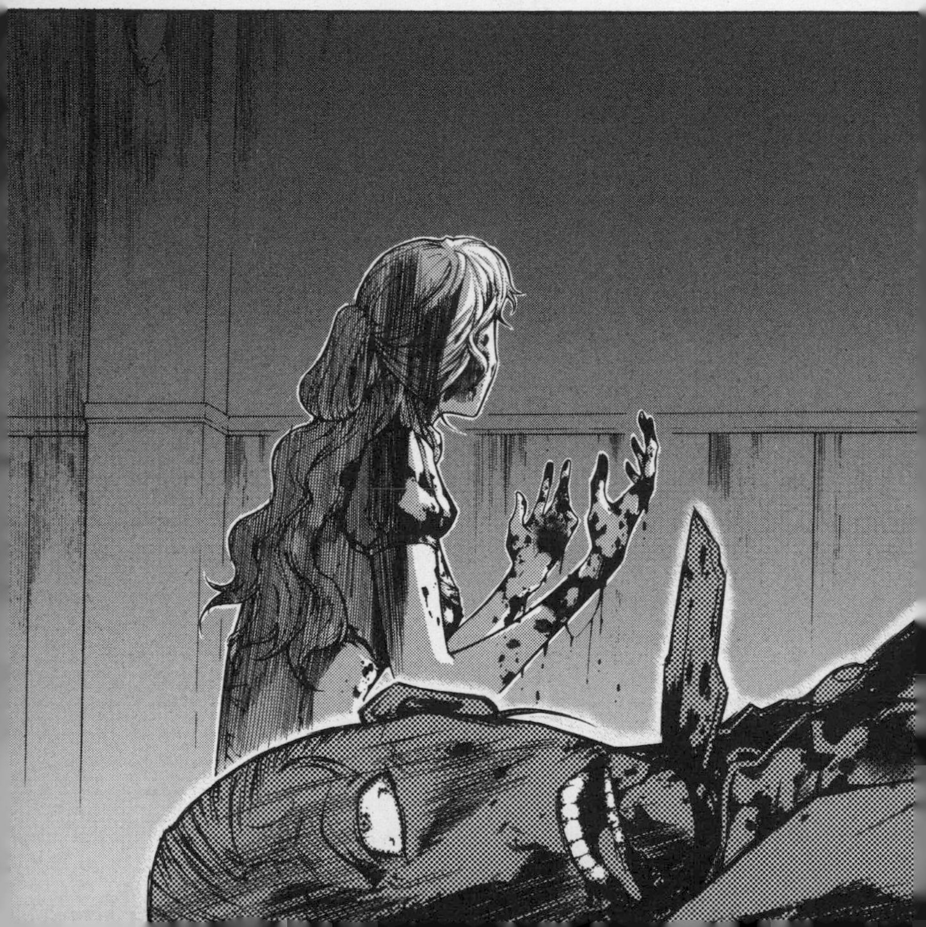

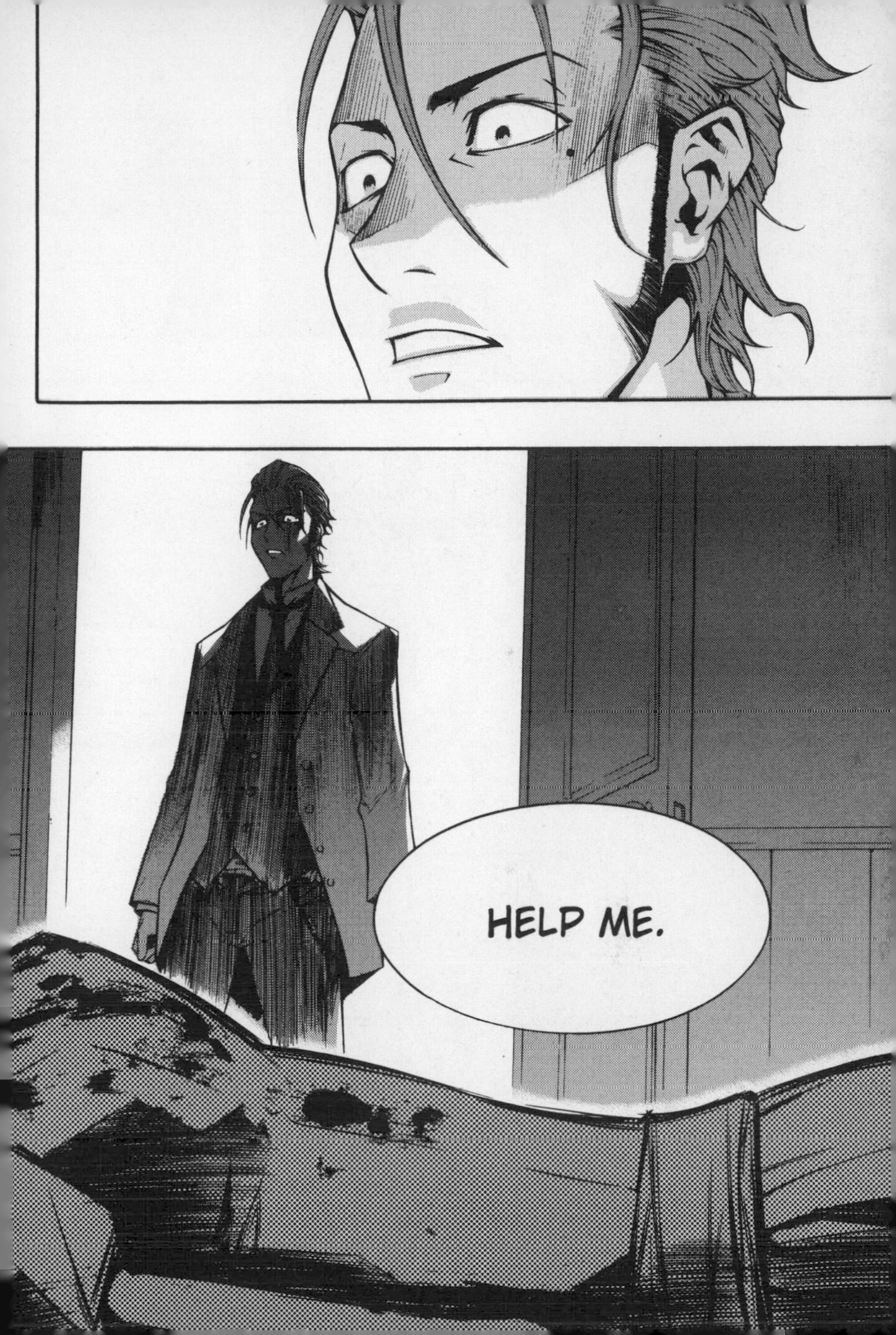
HELP ME.

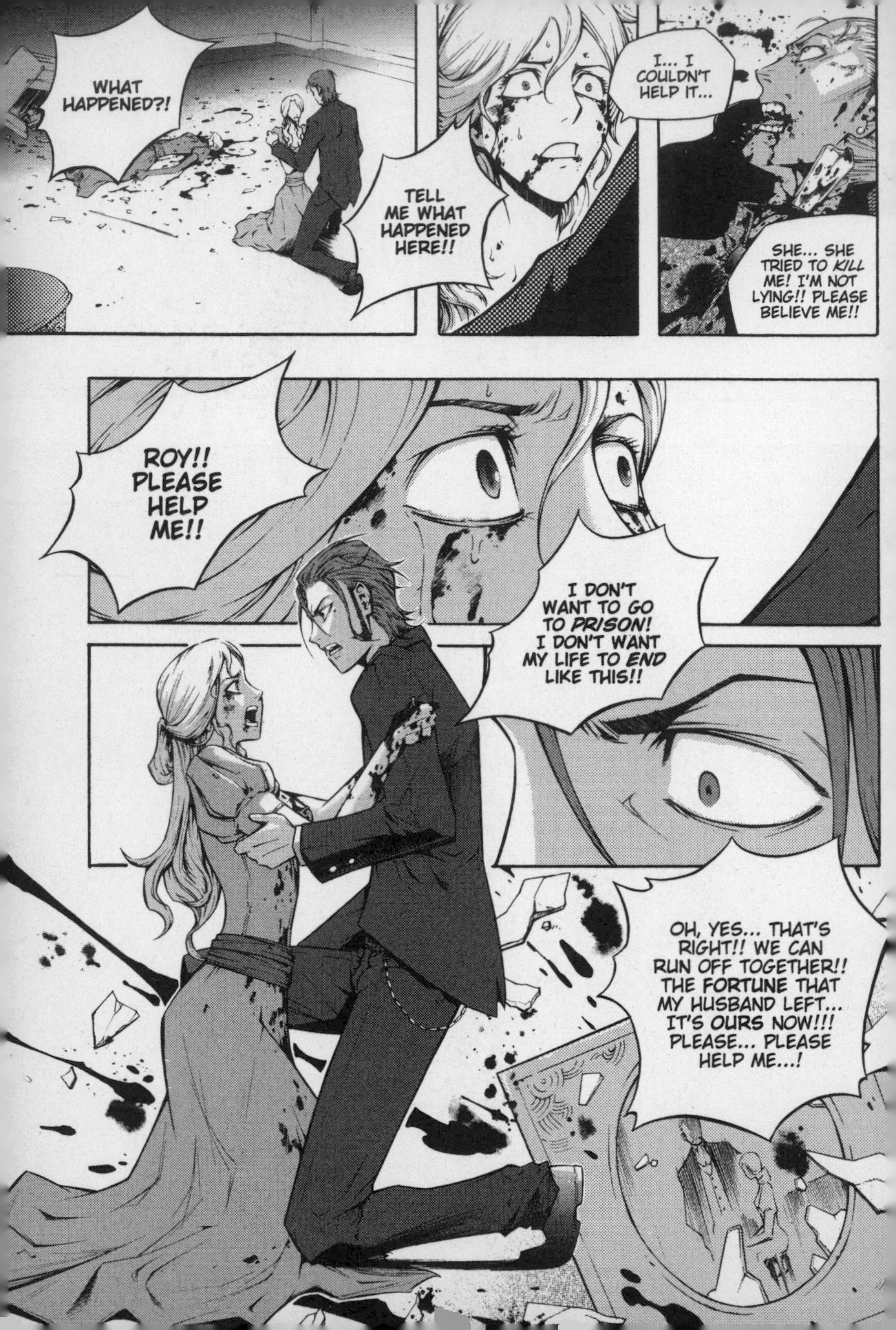
WHAT HAPPENED?!
TELL ME WHAT HAPPENED HERE!!
I... I COULDN'T HELP IT...
SHE... SHE TRIED TO KILL ME! I'M NOT LYING!! PLEASE BELIEVE ME!!
ROY!! PLEASE HELP ME!!
I DON'T WANT TO GO TO PRISON! I DON'T WANT MY LIFE TO END LIKE THIS!!
OH, YES... THAT'S RIGHT!! WE CAN RUN OFF TOGETHER!! THE FORTUNE THAT MY HUSBAND LEFT... IT'S OURS NOW!!! PLEASE... PLEASE HELP ME...!

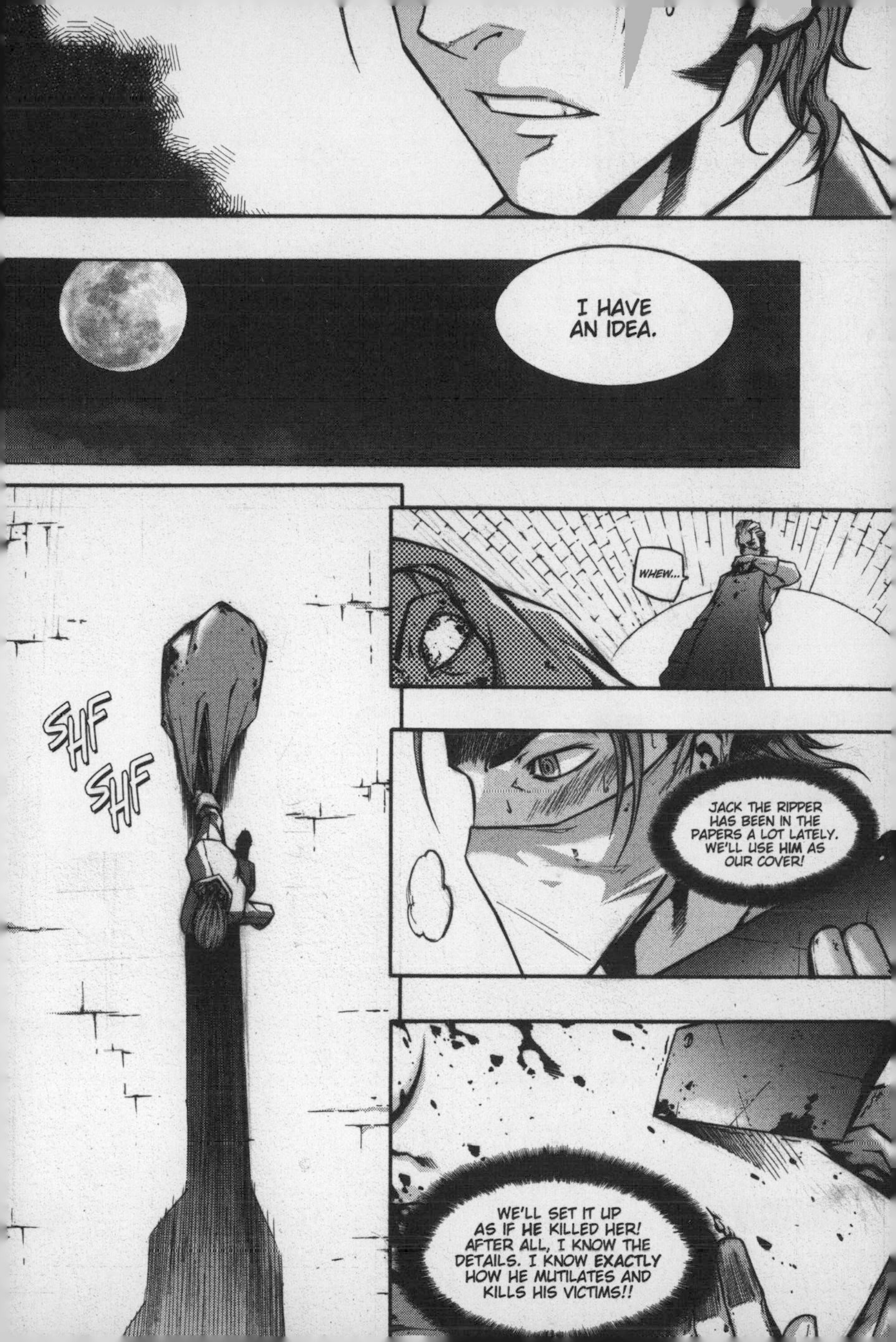
I HAVE AN IDEA.
SHF SHF
WHEW...
JACK THE RIPPER HAS BEEN IN THE PAPERS A LOT LATELY. WE'LL USE HIM AS OUR COVER!
WE'LL SET IT UP AS IF HE KILLED HER! AFTER ALL, I KNOW THE DETAILS. I KNOW EXACTLY HOW HE MUTILATES AND KILLS HIS VICTIMS!!

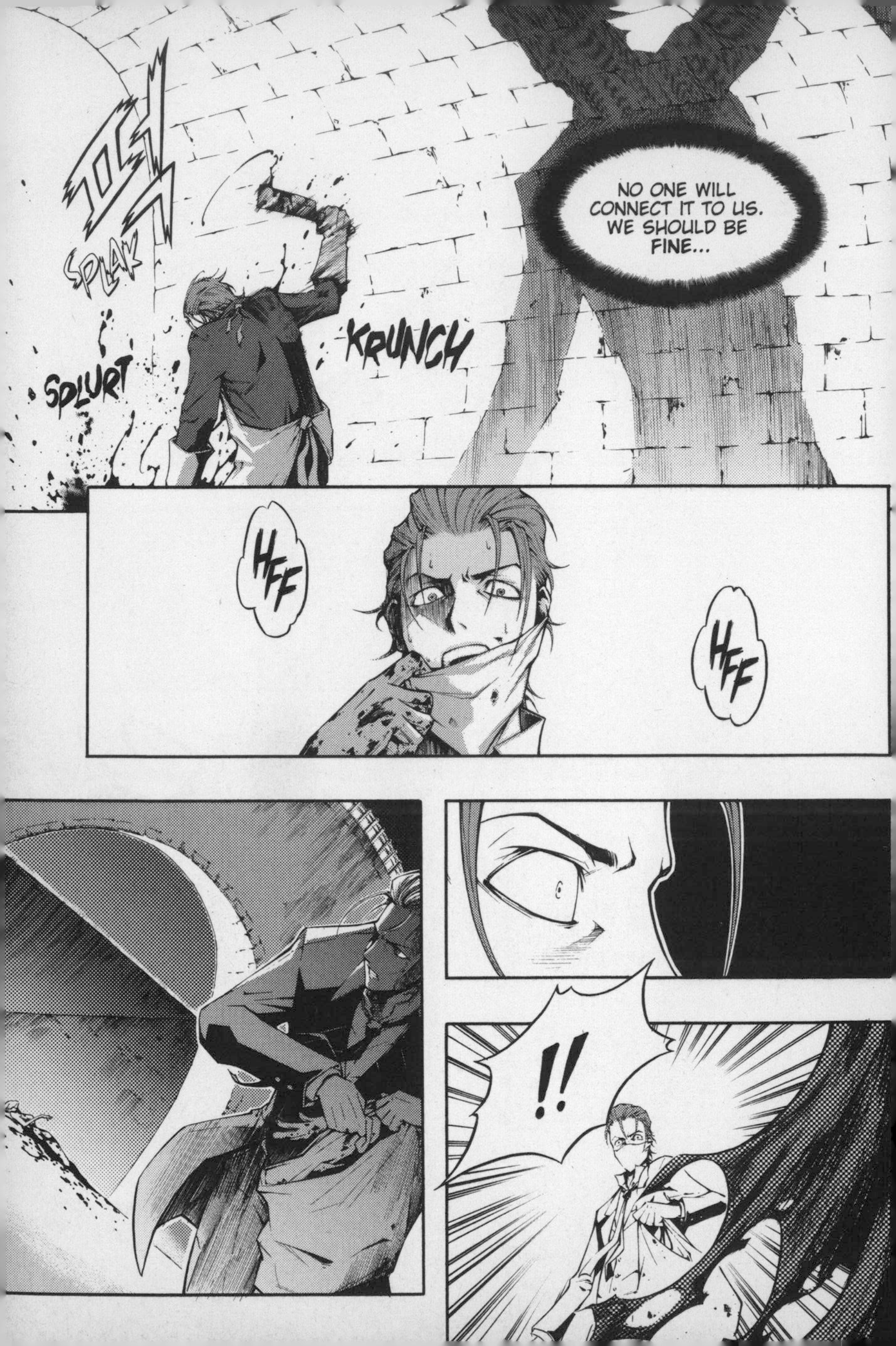
SPLAK
SPLURT
KRUNCH
NO ONE WILL CONNECT IT TO US. WE SHOULD BE FINE...
HFF
HFF
!!

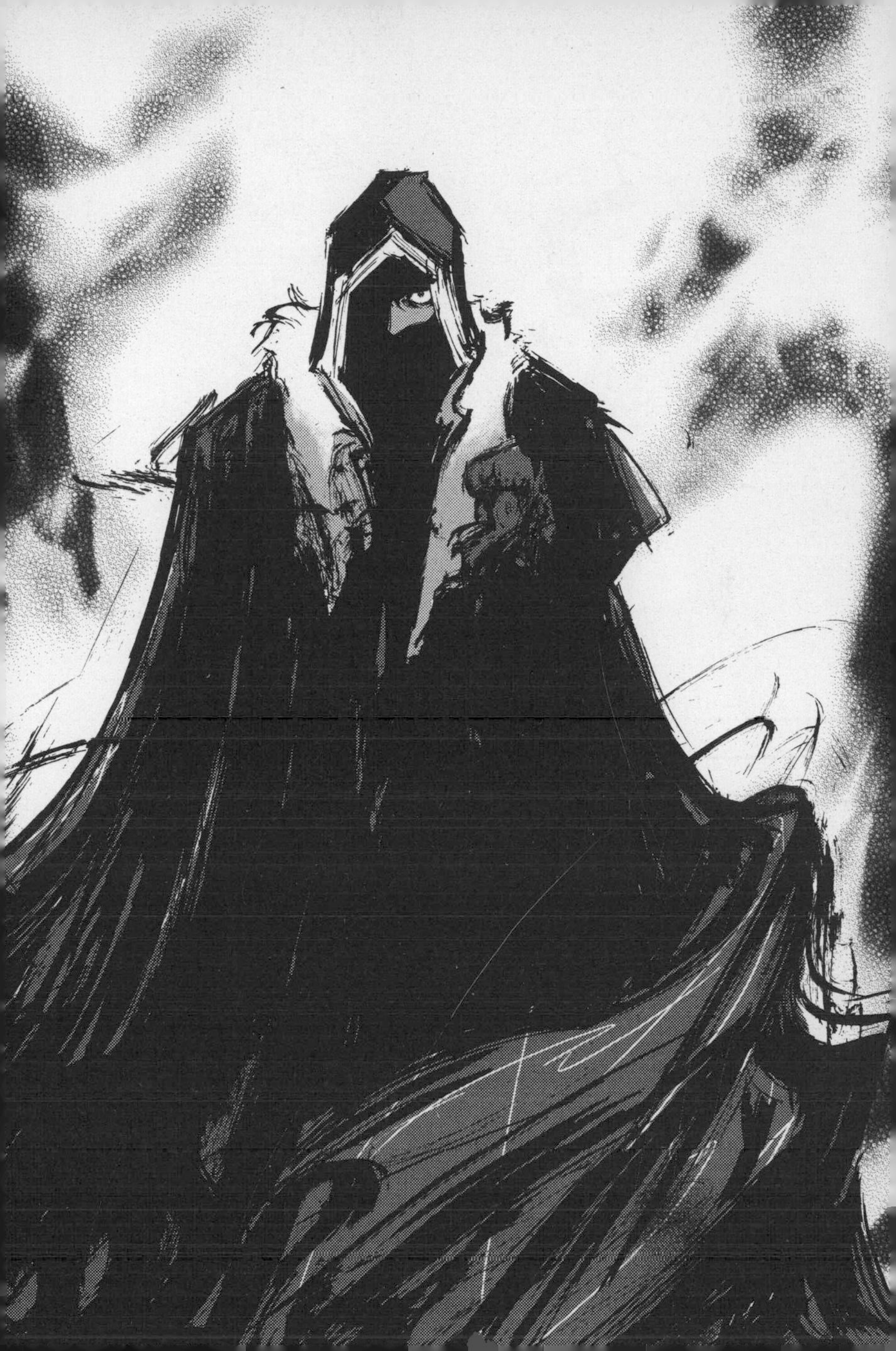

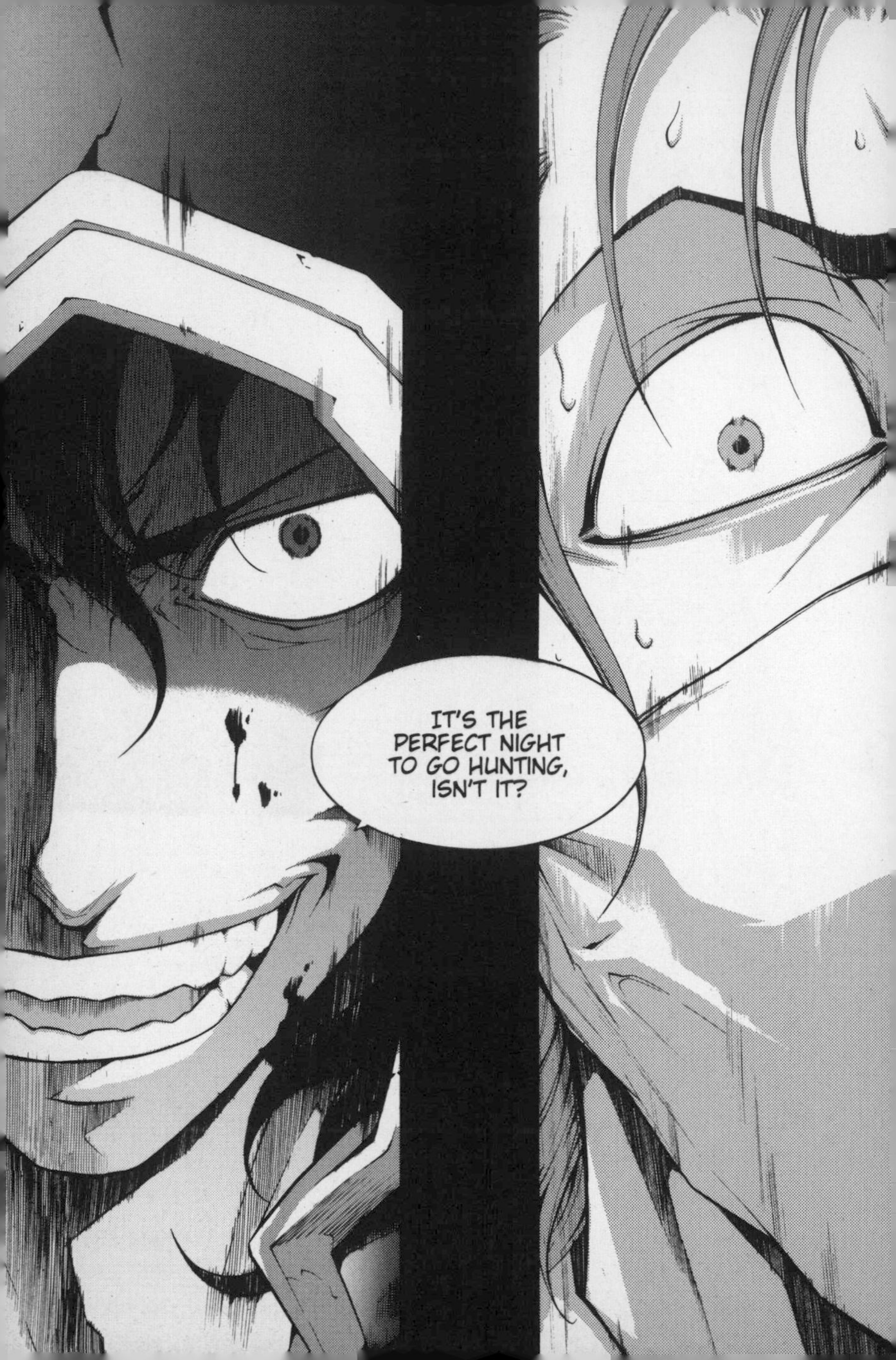
IT'S THE PERFECT NIGHT TO GO HUNTING, ISN'T IT?

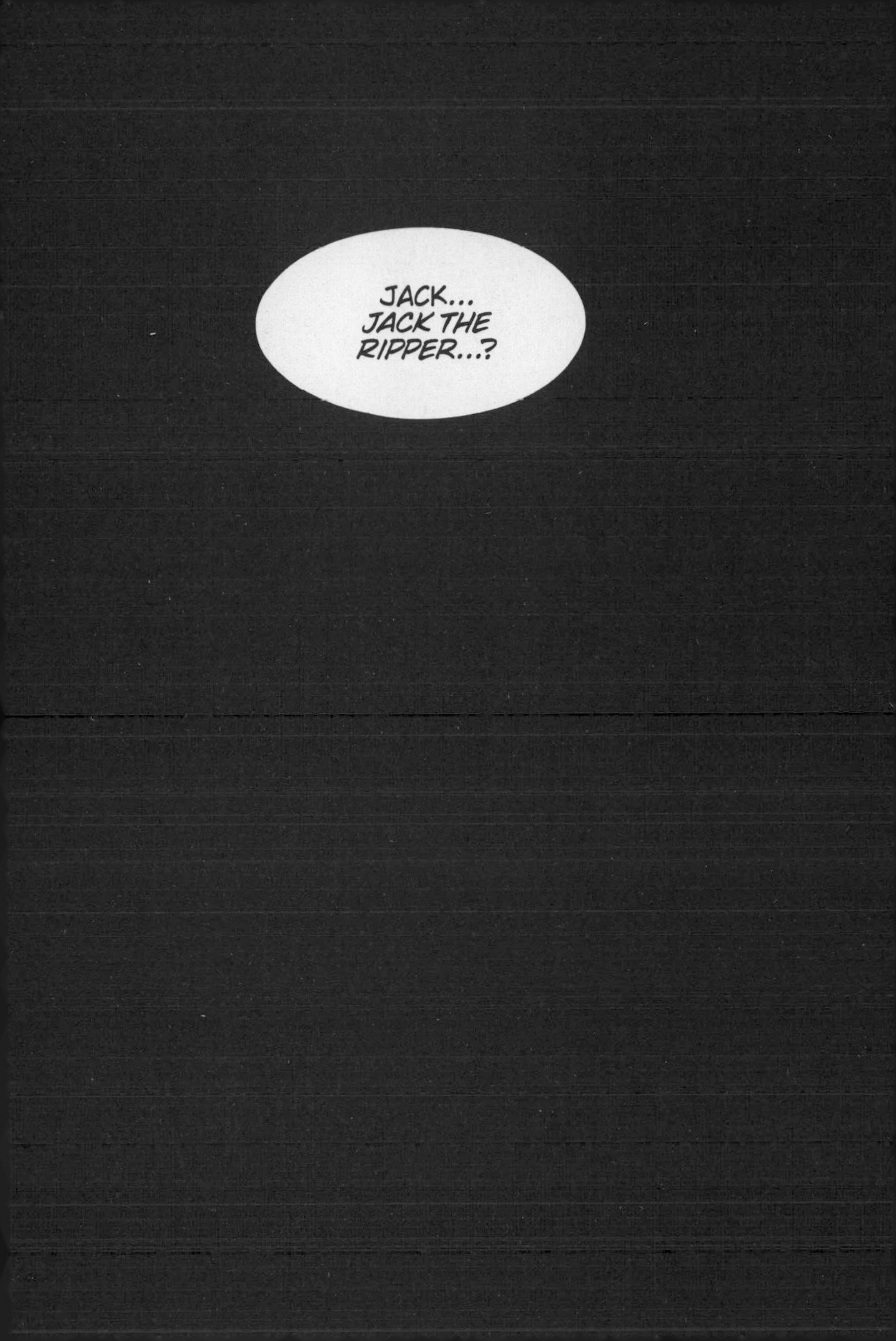
JACK... JACK THE RIPPER...?

JACK THE RIPPER
Hell Blade

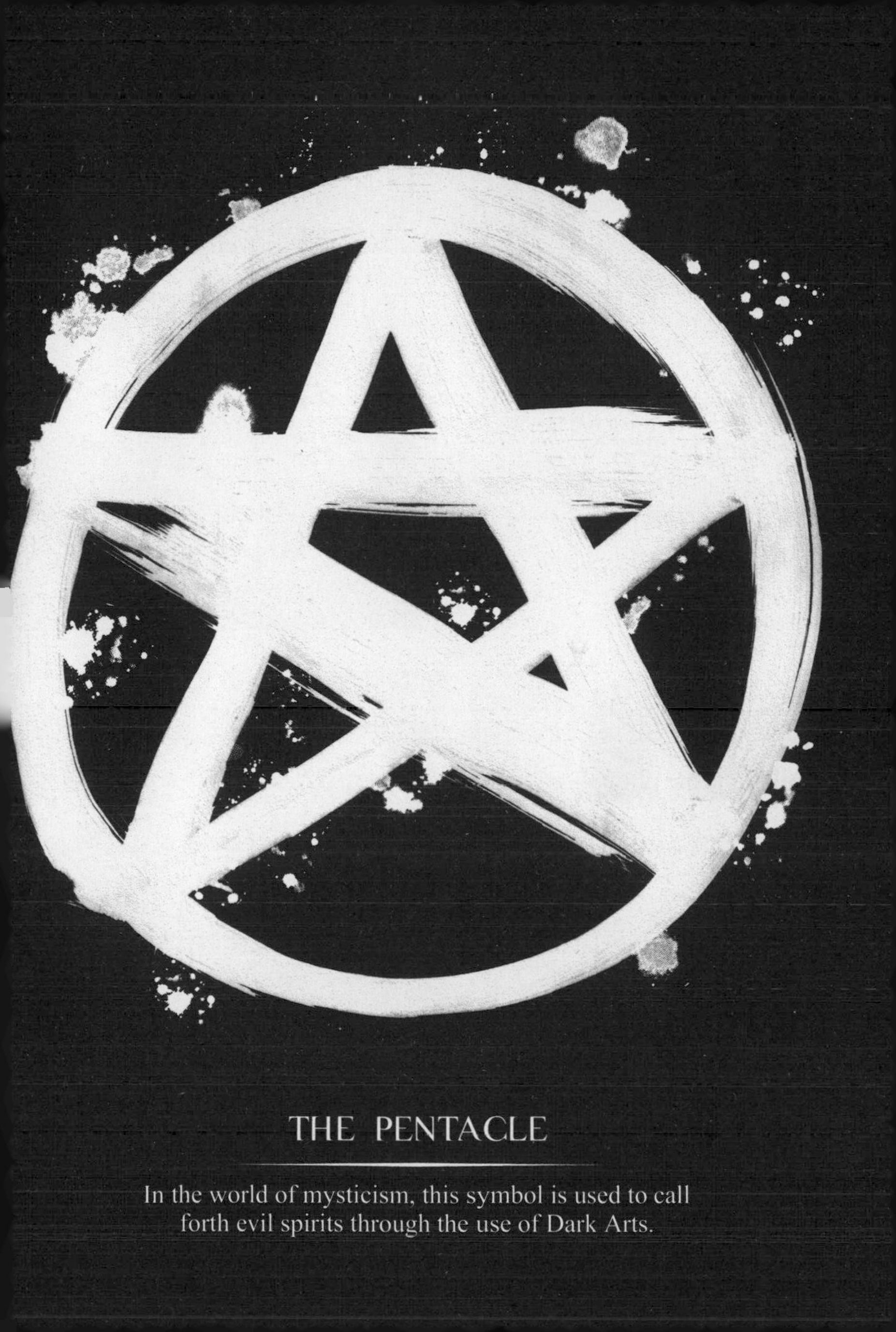

THE PENTACLE

In the world of mysticism, this symbol is used to call forth evil spirits through the use of Dark Arts.

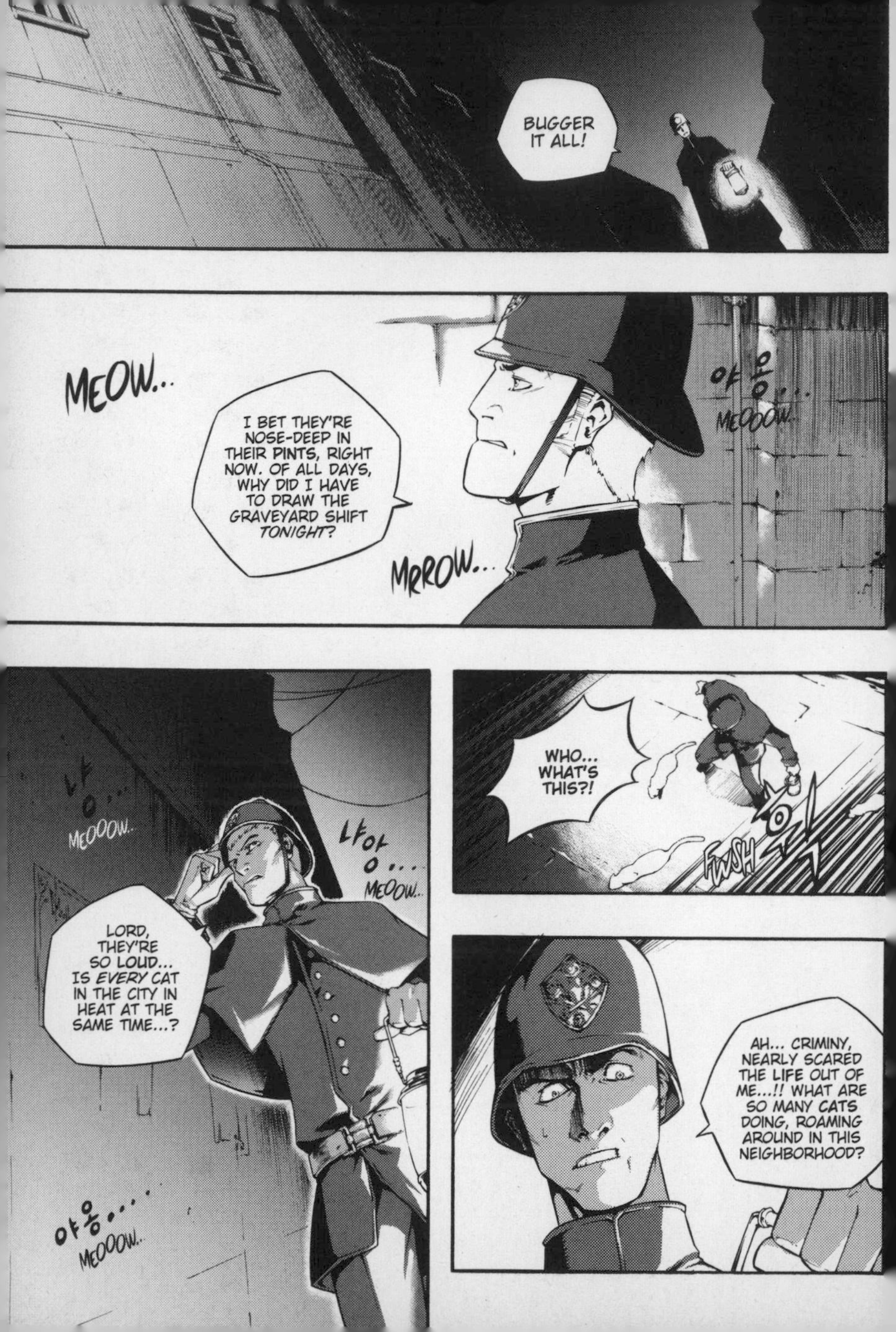
BUGGER IT ALL!
MEOW...
I BET THEY'RE NOSE-DEEP IN THEIR PINTS, RIGHT NOW. OF ALL DAYS, WHY DID I HAVE TO DRAW THE GRAVEYARD SHIFT *TONIGHT*?
야옹...
MEOOOW.
MRROW...
냐옹...
MEOOOW..
냐아옹...
MEOOW..
LORD, THEY'RE SO LOUD... IS *EVERY* CAT IN THE CITY IN HEAT AT THE SAME TIME...?
야옹...
MEOOOW..
WHO... WHAT'S THIS?!
FWSH
AH... CRIMINY, NEARLY SCARED THE LIFE OUT OF ME...!! WHAT ARE SO MANY CATS DOING, ROAMING AROUND IN THIS NEIGHBORHOOD?

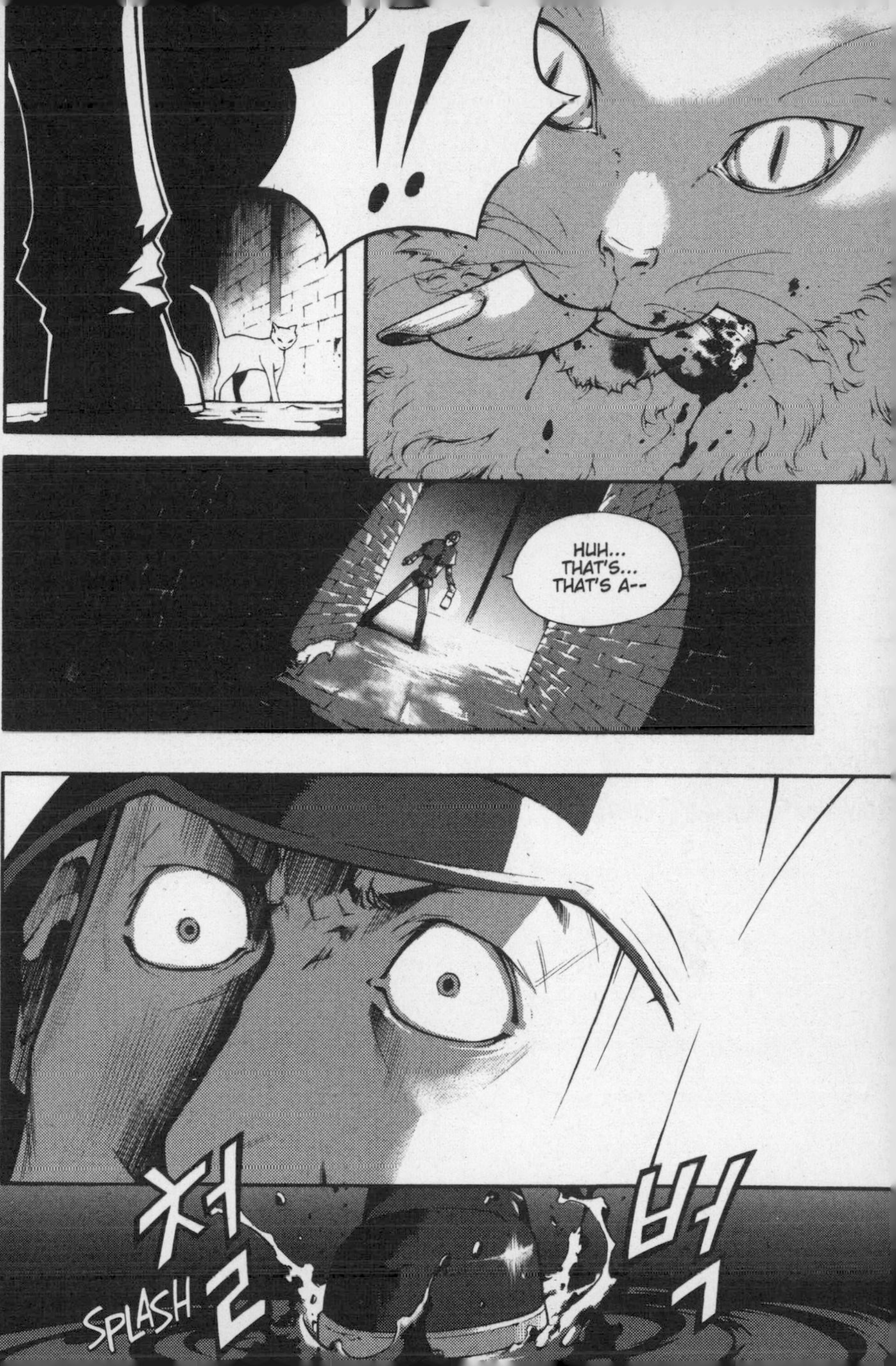
!!
HUH... THAT'S... THAT'S A--
SPLASH

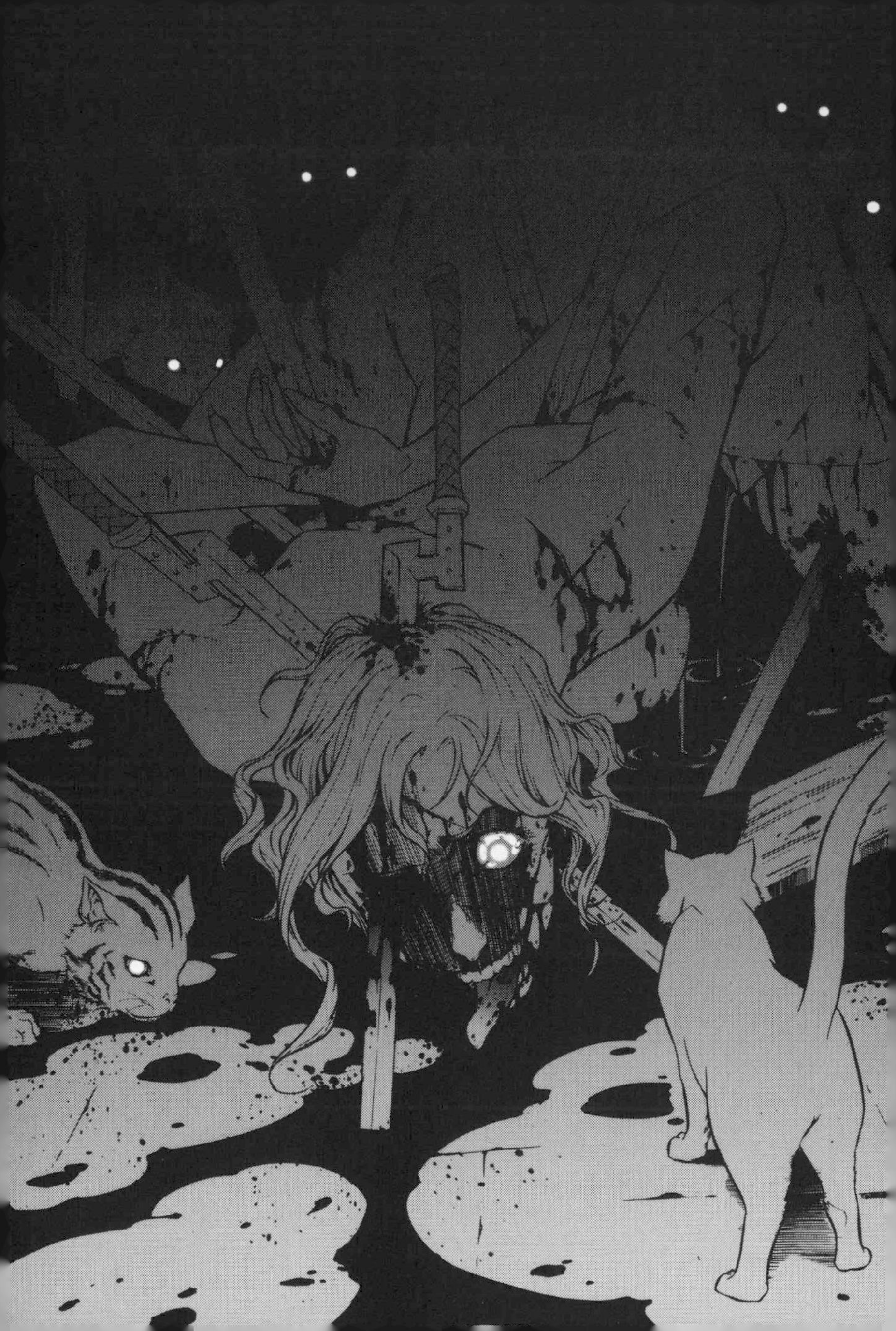

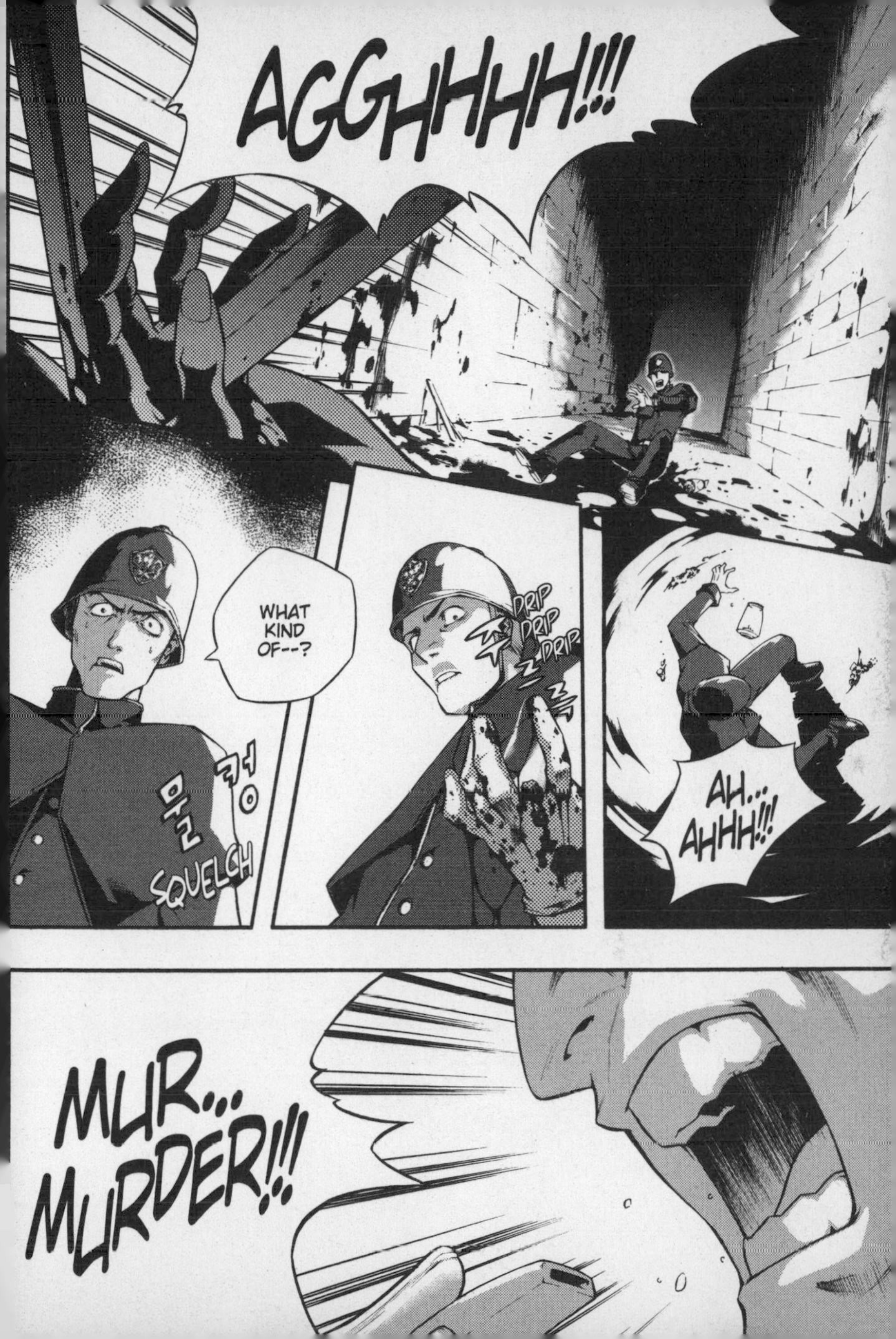
AGGHHHH!!!
WHAT KIND OF--?
SQUELCH
DRIP DRIP DRIP
AH... AHHH!!!
MUR... MURDER!!!

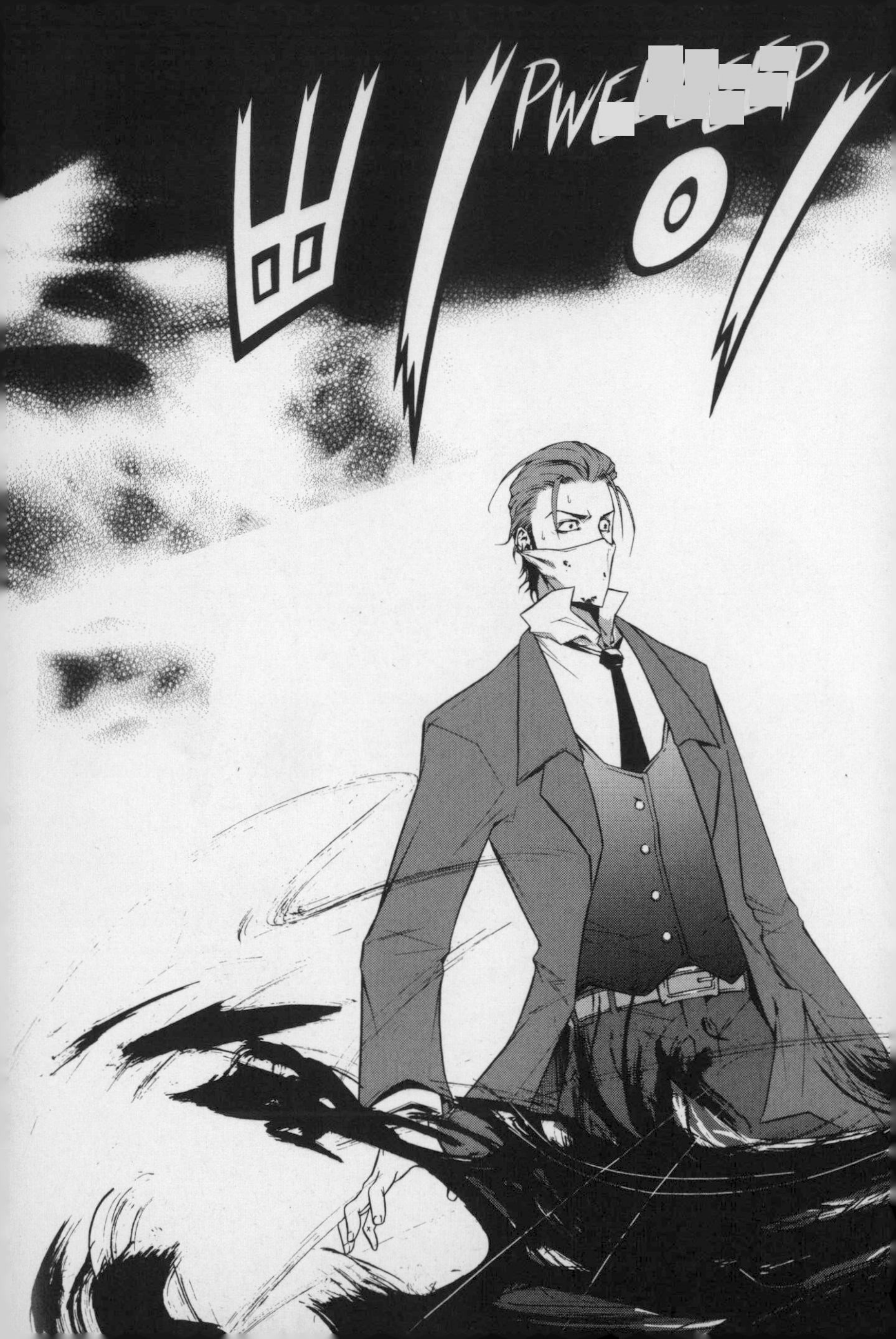
삐이
PWE

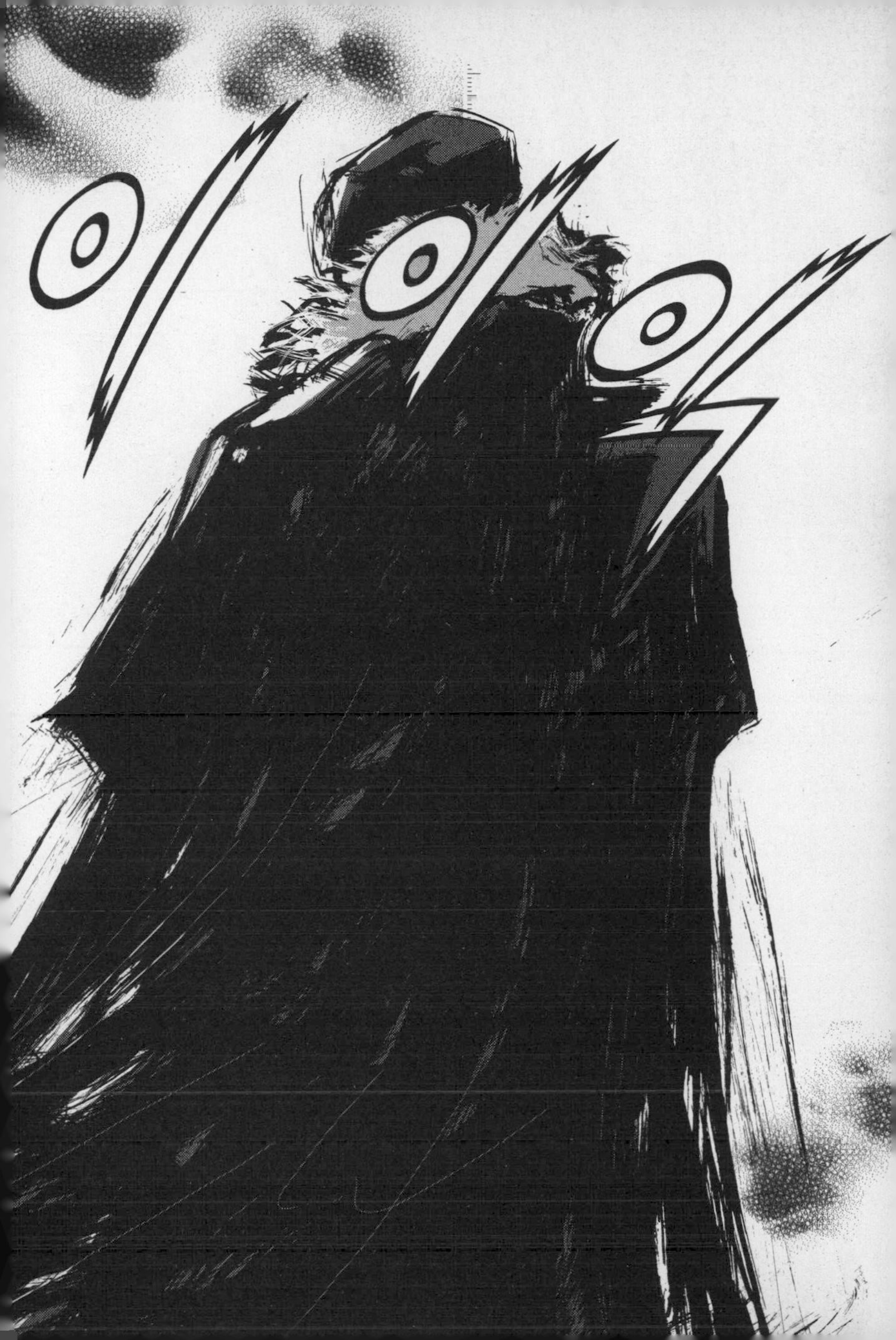

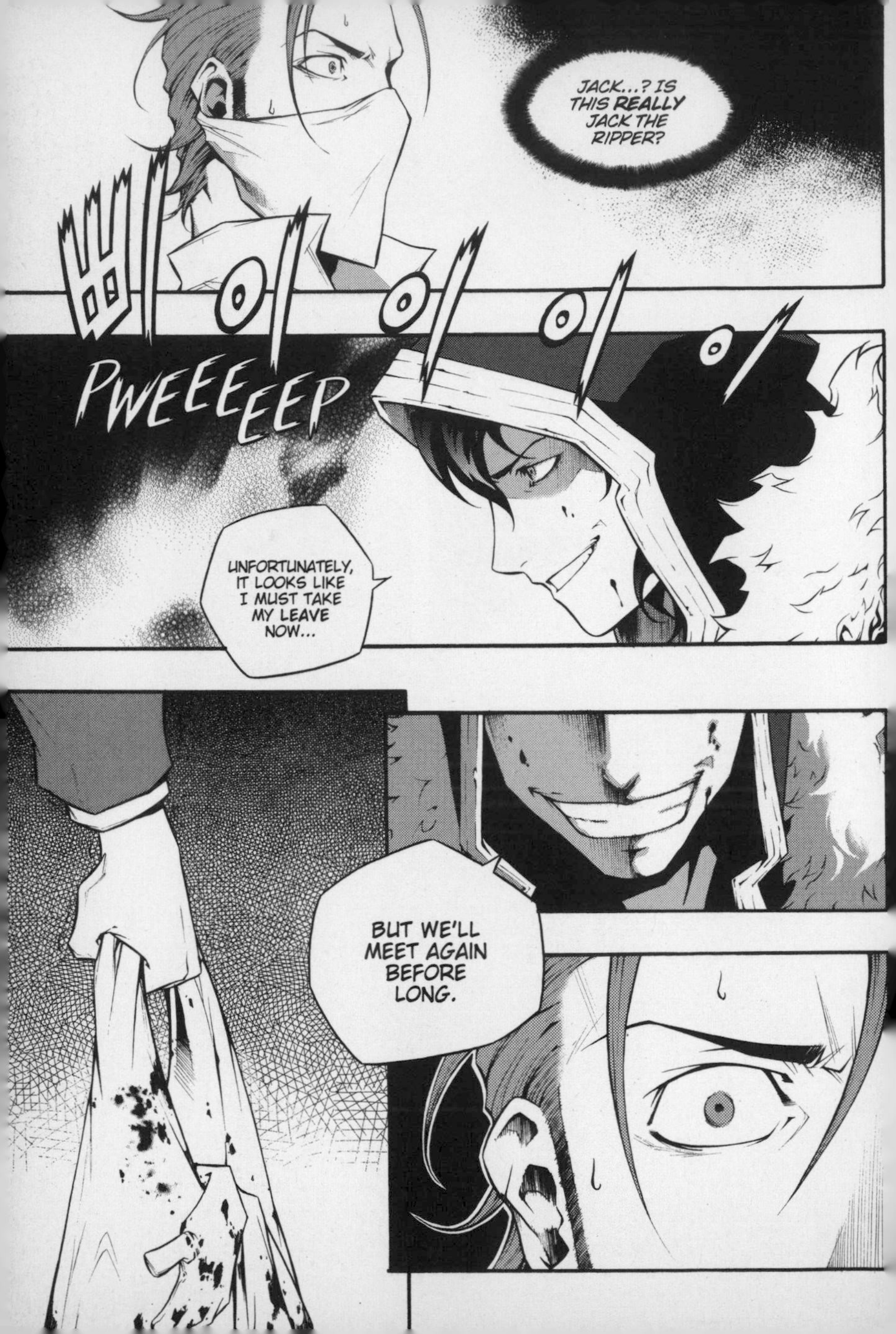
JACK...? IS THIS REALLY JACK THE RIPPER?
PWEEEEEEP
UNFORTUNATELY, IT LOOKS LIKE I MUST TAKE MY LEAVE NOW...
BUT WE'LL MEET AGAIN BEFORE LONG.

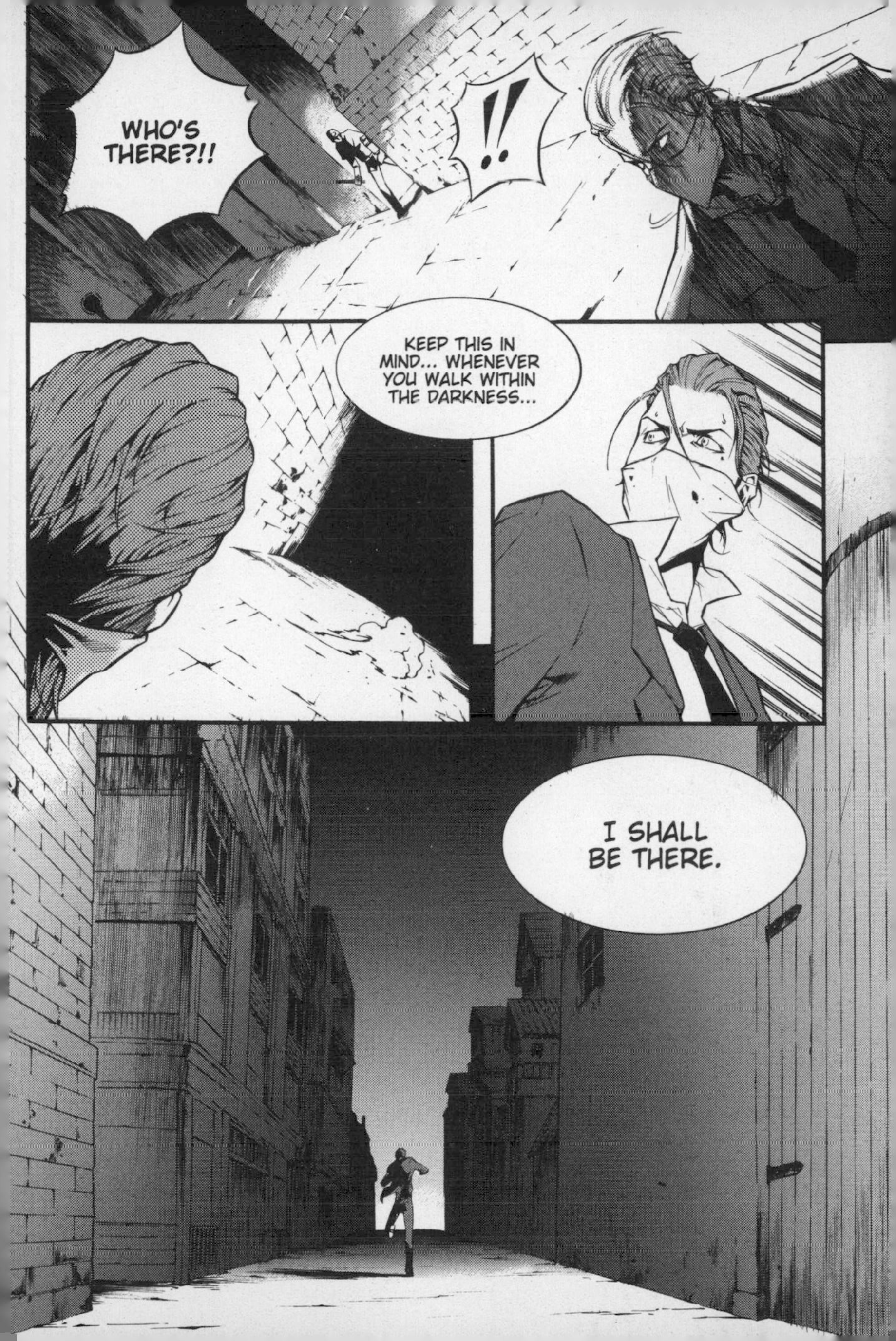
WHO'S THERE?!!
!!
KEEP THIS IN MIND... WHENEVER YOU WALK WITHIN THE DARKNESS...
I SHALL BE THERE.

EPISODE 2

WALKING IN THE MIDNIGHT (2)

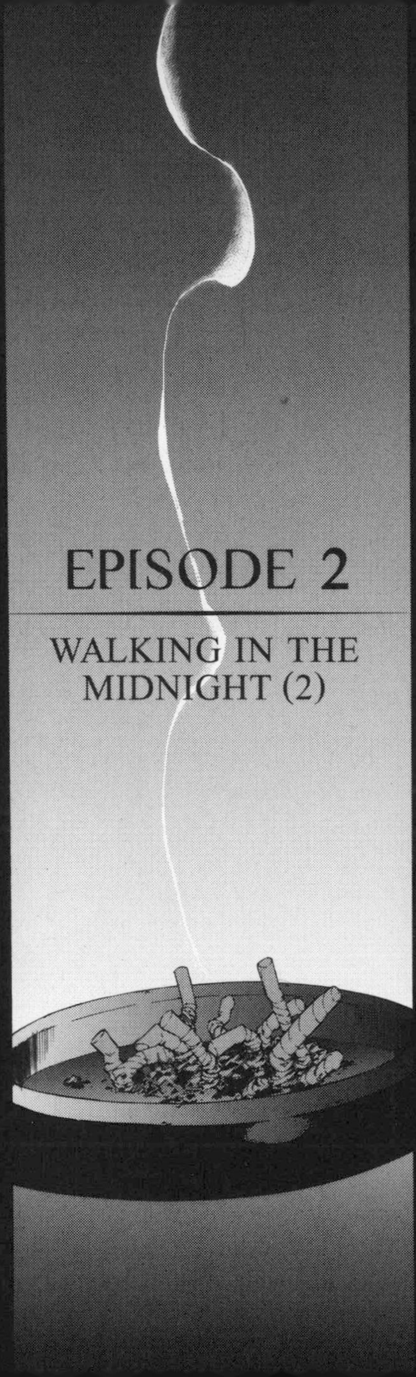

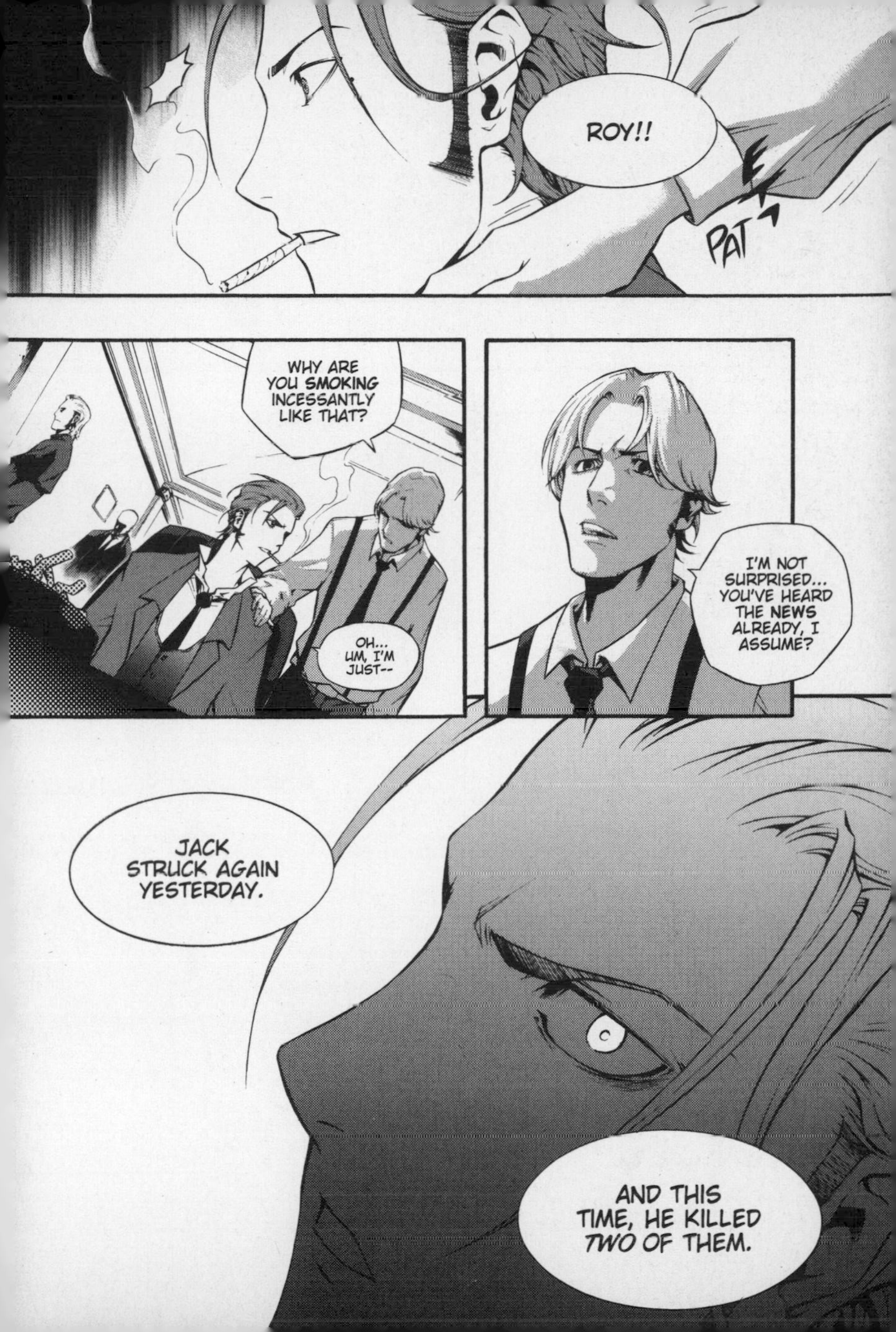
ROY!!
PAT
WHY ARE YOU SMOKING INCESSANTLY LIKE THAT?
OH... UM, I'M JUST--
I'M NOT SURPRISED... YOU'VE HEARD THE NEWS ALREADY, I ASSUME?
JACK STRUCK AGAIN YESTERDAY.
AND THIS TIME, HE KILLED *TWO* OF THEM.

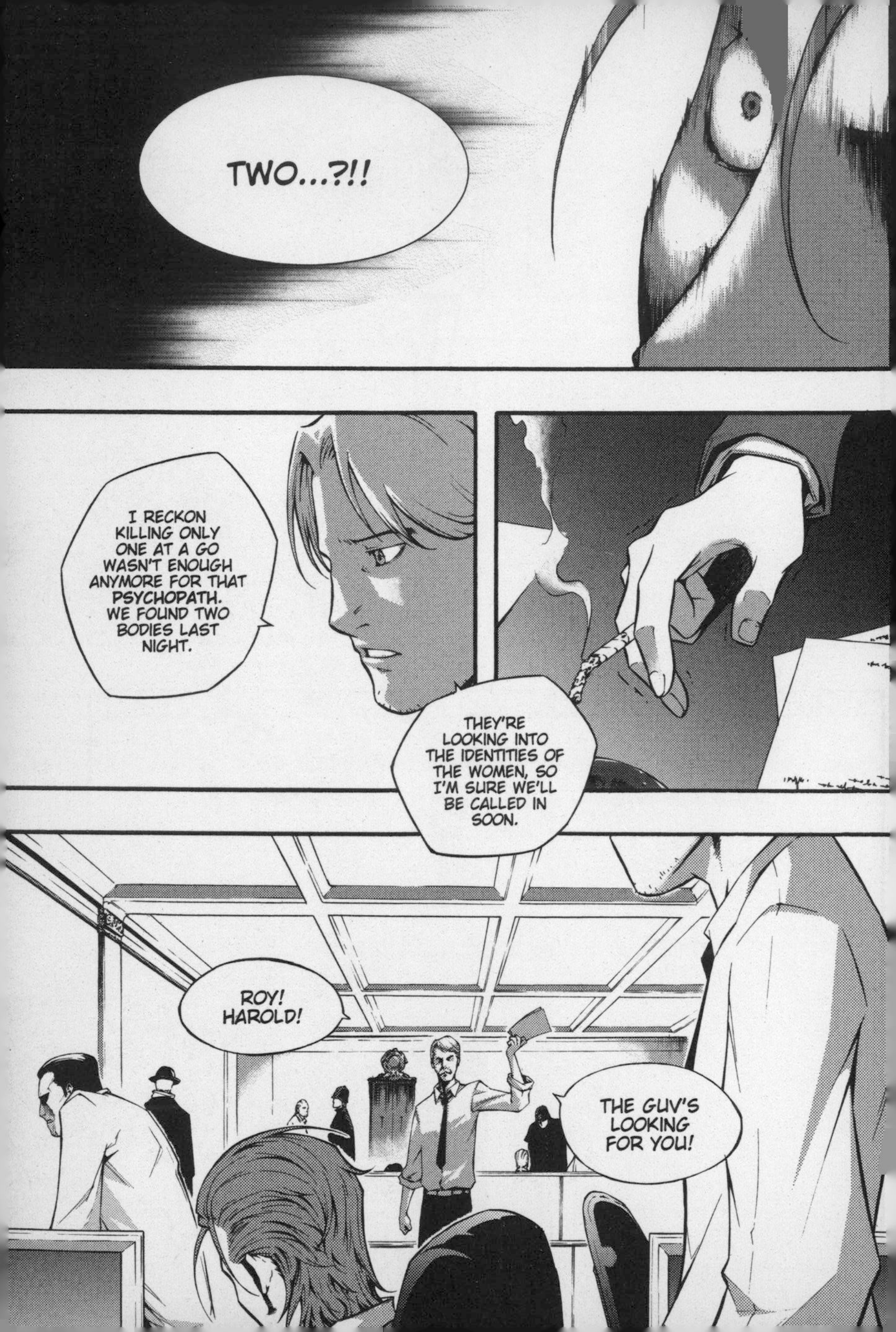
TWO...?!!
I RECKON KILLING ONLY ONE AT A GO WASN'T ENOUGH ANYMORE FOR THAT PSYCHOPATH. WE FOUND TWO BODIES LAST NIGHT.
THEY'RE LOOKING INTO THE IDENTITIES OF THE WOMEN, SO I'M SURE WE'LL BE CALLED IN SOON.
ROY! HAROLD!
THE GUV'S LOOKING FOR YOU!

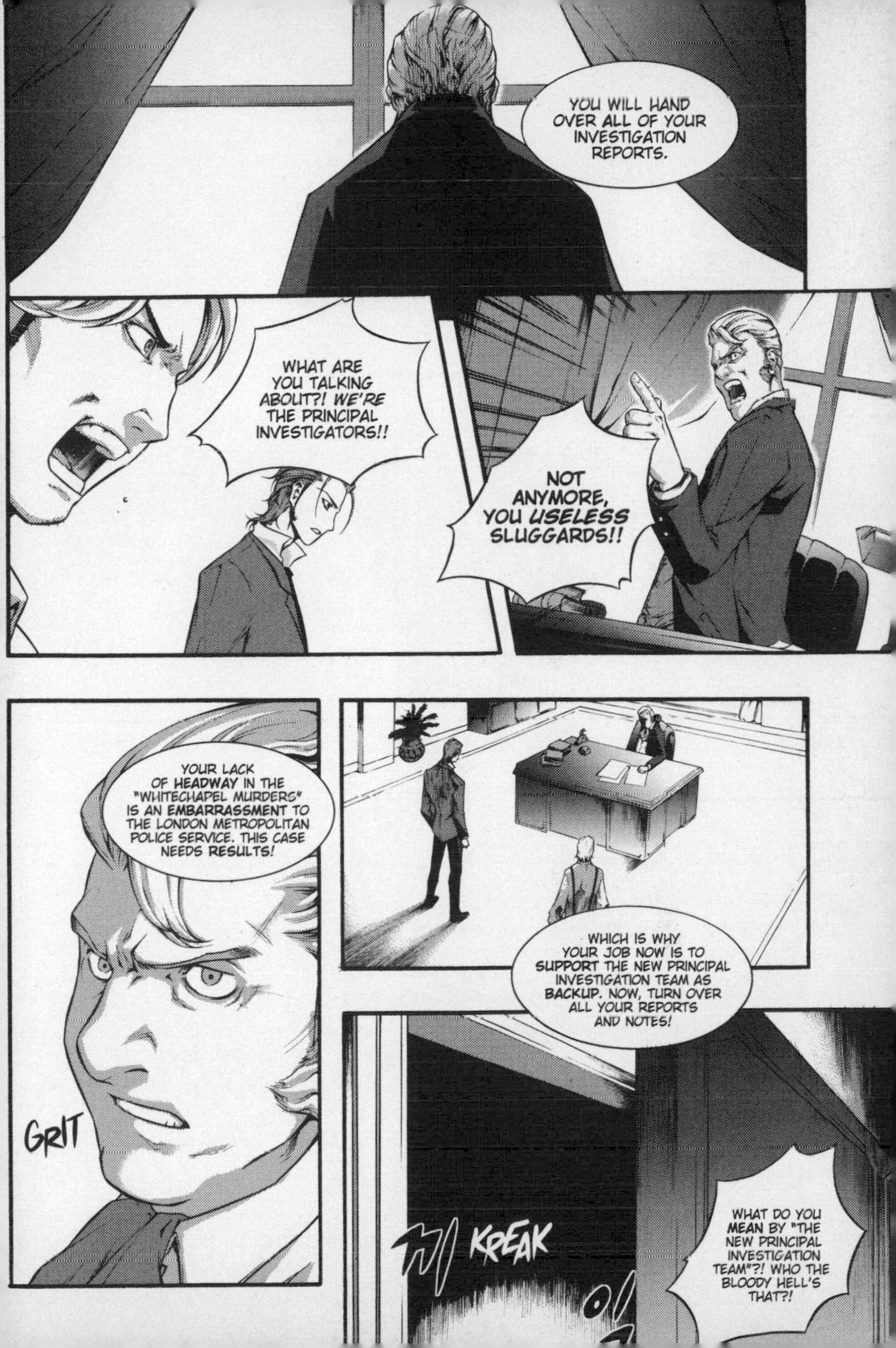
YOU WILL HAND OVER ALL OF YOUR INVESTIGATION REPORTS.
WHAT ARE YOU TALKING ABOUT?! WE'RE THE PRINCIPAL INVESTIGATORS!!
NOT ANYMORE, YOU USELESS SLUGGARDS!!
YOUR LACK OF HEADWAY IN THE "WHITECHAPEL MURDERS" IS AN EMBARRASSMENT TO THE LONDON METROPOLITAN POLICE SERVICE. THIS CASE NEEDS RESULTS!
GRIT
WHICH IS WHY YOUR JOB NOW IS TO SUPPORT THE NEW PRINCIPAL INVESTIGATION TEAM AS BACKUP. NOW, TURN OVER ALL YOUR REPORTS AND NOTES!
KREAK
WHAT DO YOU MEAN BY "THE NEW PRINCIPAL INVESTIGATION TEAM"?! WHO THE BLOODY HELL'S THAT?!

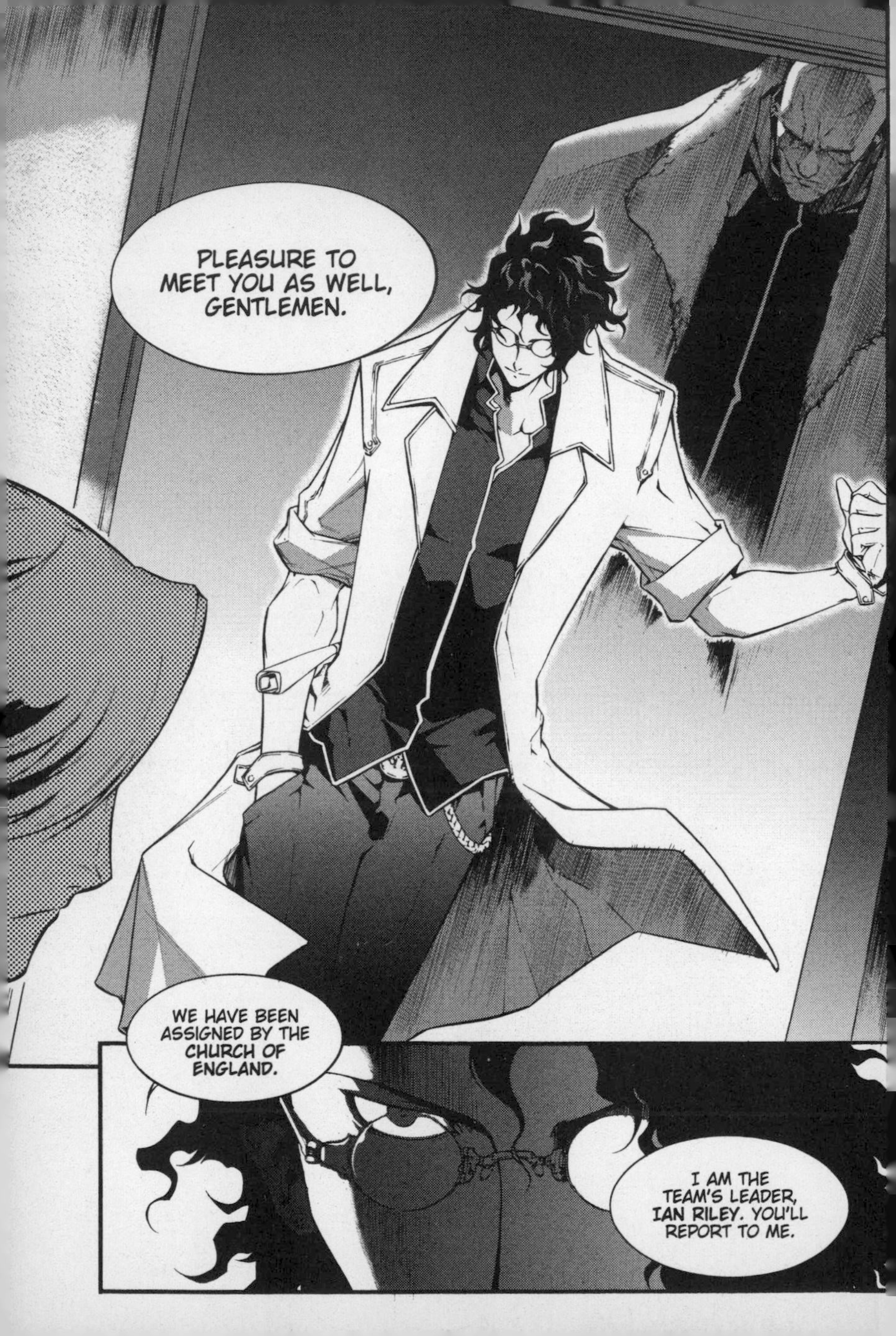
PLEASURE TO MEET YOU AS WELL, GENTLEMEN.
WE HAVE BEEN ASSIGNED BY THE CHURCH OF ENGLAND.
I AM THE TEAM'S LEADER, IAN RILEY. YOU'LL REPORT TO ME.

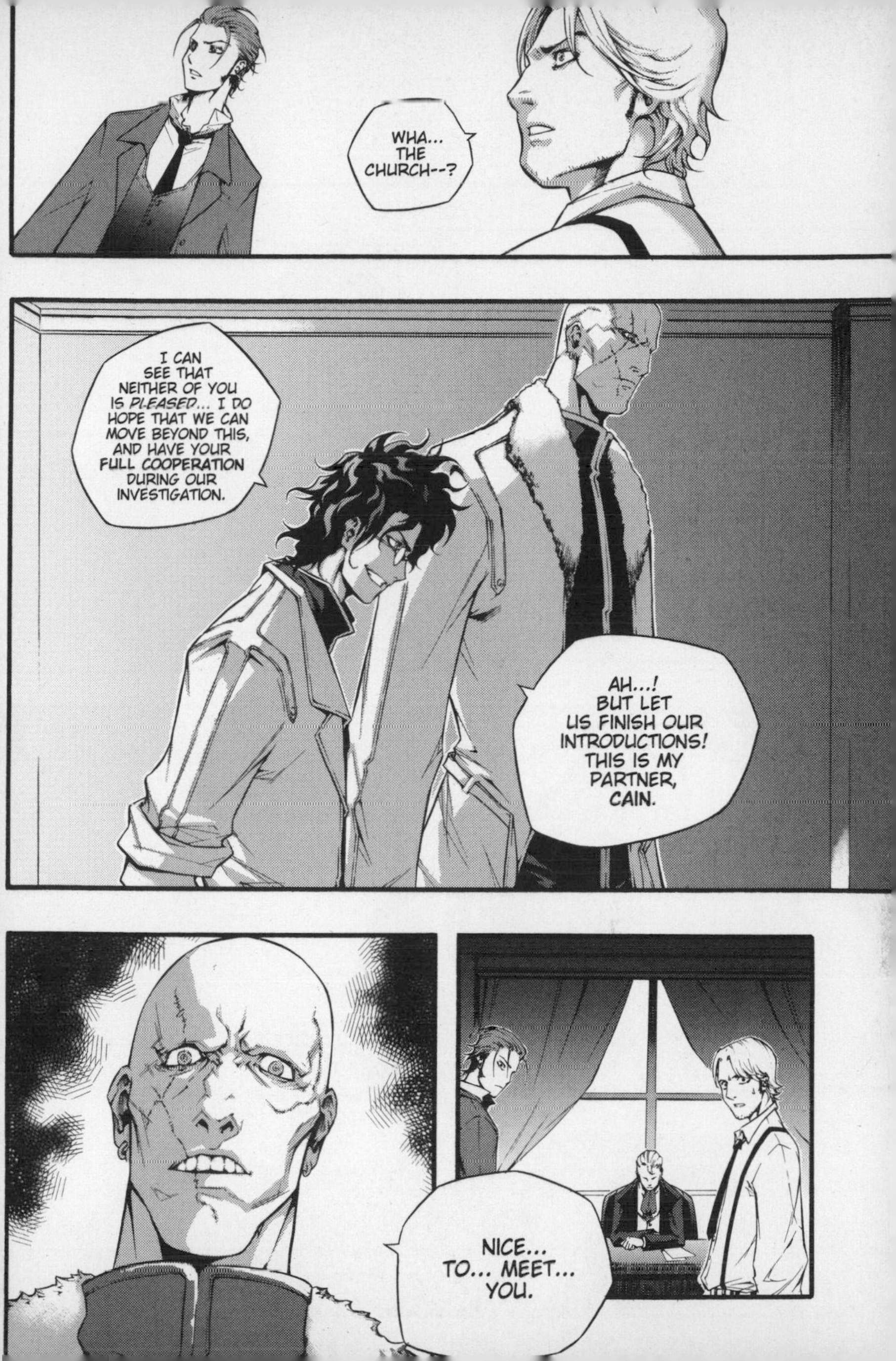
WHA... THE CHURCH--?
I CAN SEE THAT NEITHER OF YOU IS *PLEASED*... I DO HOPE THAT WE CAN MOVE BEYOND THIS, AND HAVE YOUR **FULL COOPERATION** DURING OUR INVESTIGATION.
AH...! BUT LET US FINISH OUR INTRODUCTIONS! THIS IS MY PARTNER, CAIN.
NICE... TO... MEET... YOU.

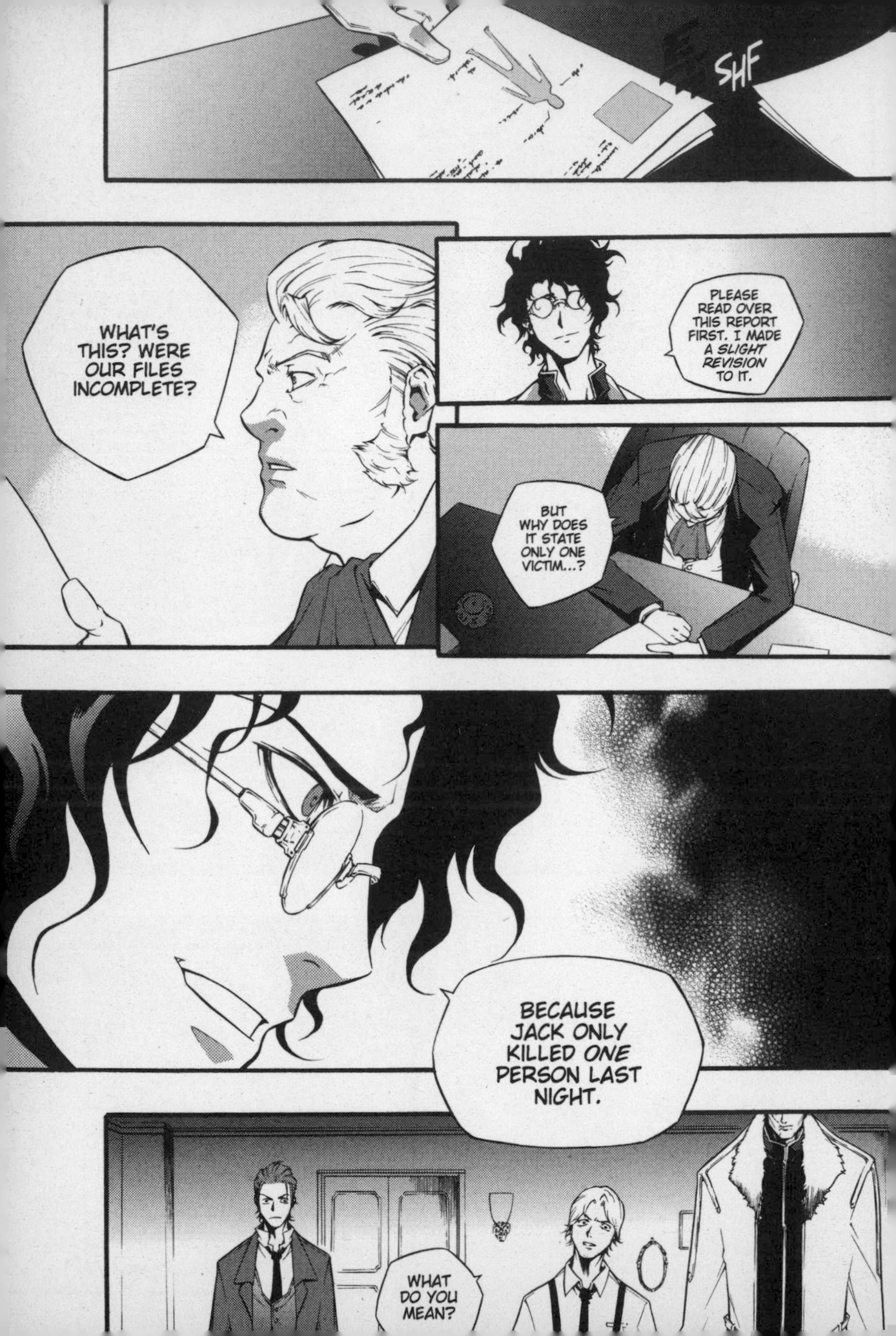
SHF
WHAT'S THIS? WERE OUR FILES INCOMPLETE?
PLEASE READ OVER THIS REPORT FIRST. I MADE A SLIGHT REVISION TO IT.
BUT WHY DOES IT STATE ONLY ONE VICTIM...?
BECAUSE JACK ONLY KILLED ONE PERSON LAST NIGHT.
WHAT DO YOU MEAN?

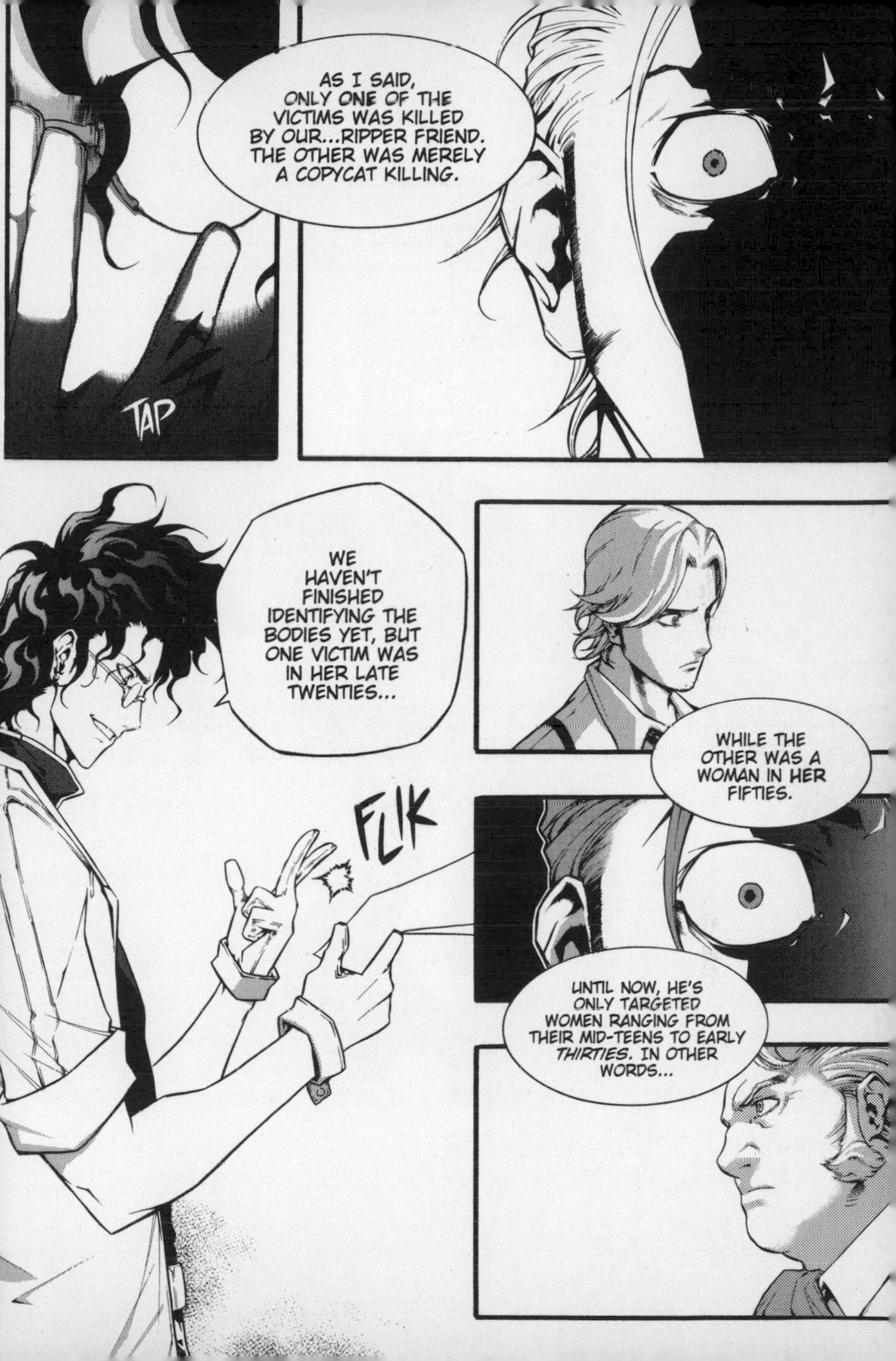
AS I SAID, ONLY ONE OF THE VICTIMS WAS KILLED BY OUR...RIPPER FRIEND. THE OTHER WAS MERELY A COPYCAT KILLING.
TAP
WE HAVEN'T FINISHED IDENTIFYING THE BODIES YET, BUT ONE VICTIM WAS IN HER LATE TWENTIES...
FLIK
WHILE THE OTHER WAS A WOMAN IN HER FIFTIES.
UNTIL NOW, HE'S ONLY TARGETED WOMEN RANGING FROM THEIR MID-TEENS TO EARLY *THIRTIES*. IN OTHER WORDS...

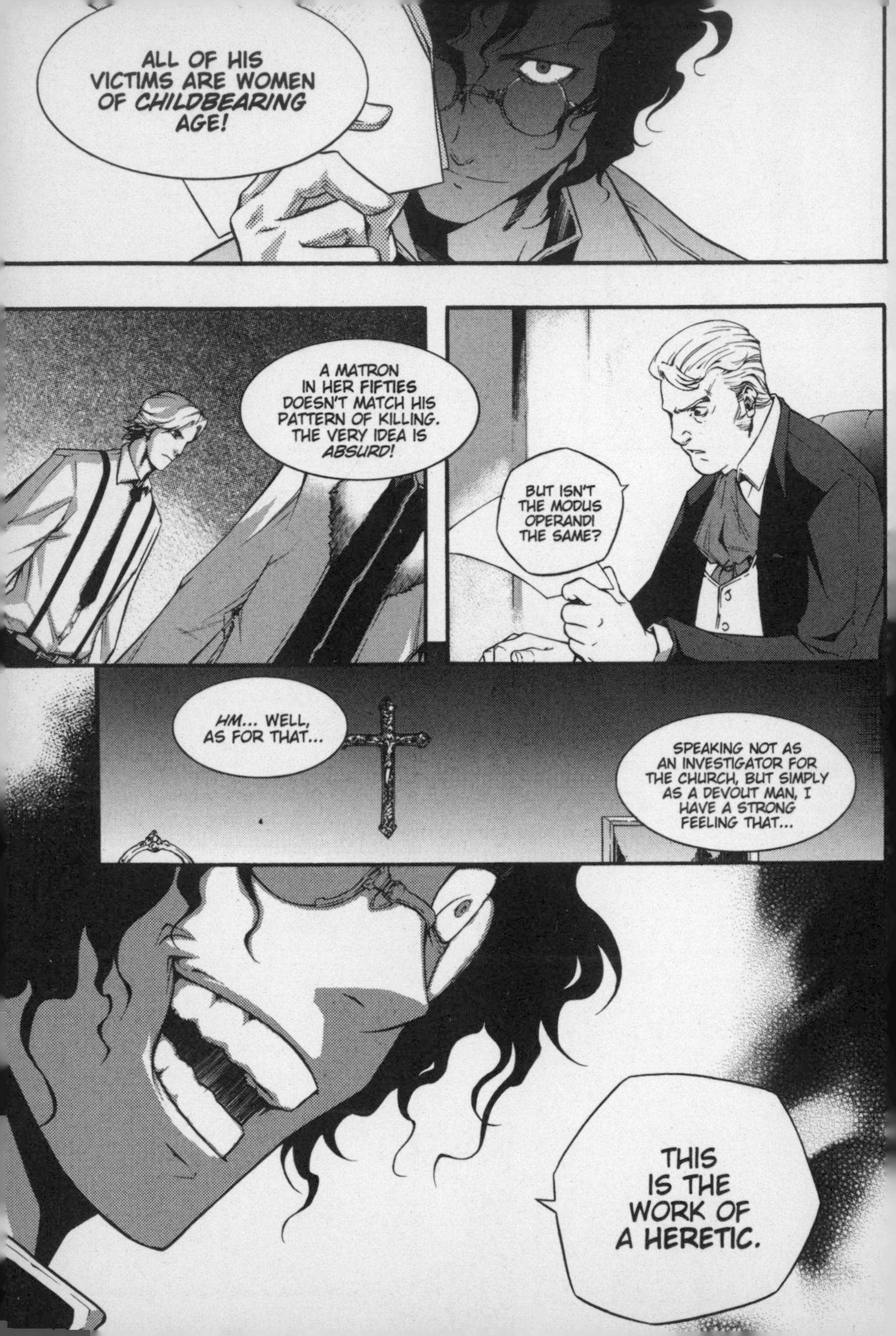
ALL OF HIS VICTIMS ARE WOMEN OF *CHILDBEARING* AGE!
A MATRON IN HER FIFTIES DOESN'T MATCH HIS PATTERN OF KILLING. THE VERY IDEA IS *ABSURD!*
BUT ISN'T THE MODUS OPERANDI THE SAME?
HM... WELL, AS FOR THAT...
SPEAKING NOT AS AN INVESTIGATOR FOR THE CHURCH, BUT SIMPLY AS A DEVOUT MAN, I HAVE A STRONG FEELING THAT...
THIS IS THE WORK OF A HERETIC.

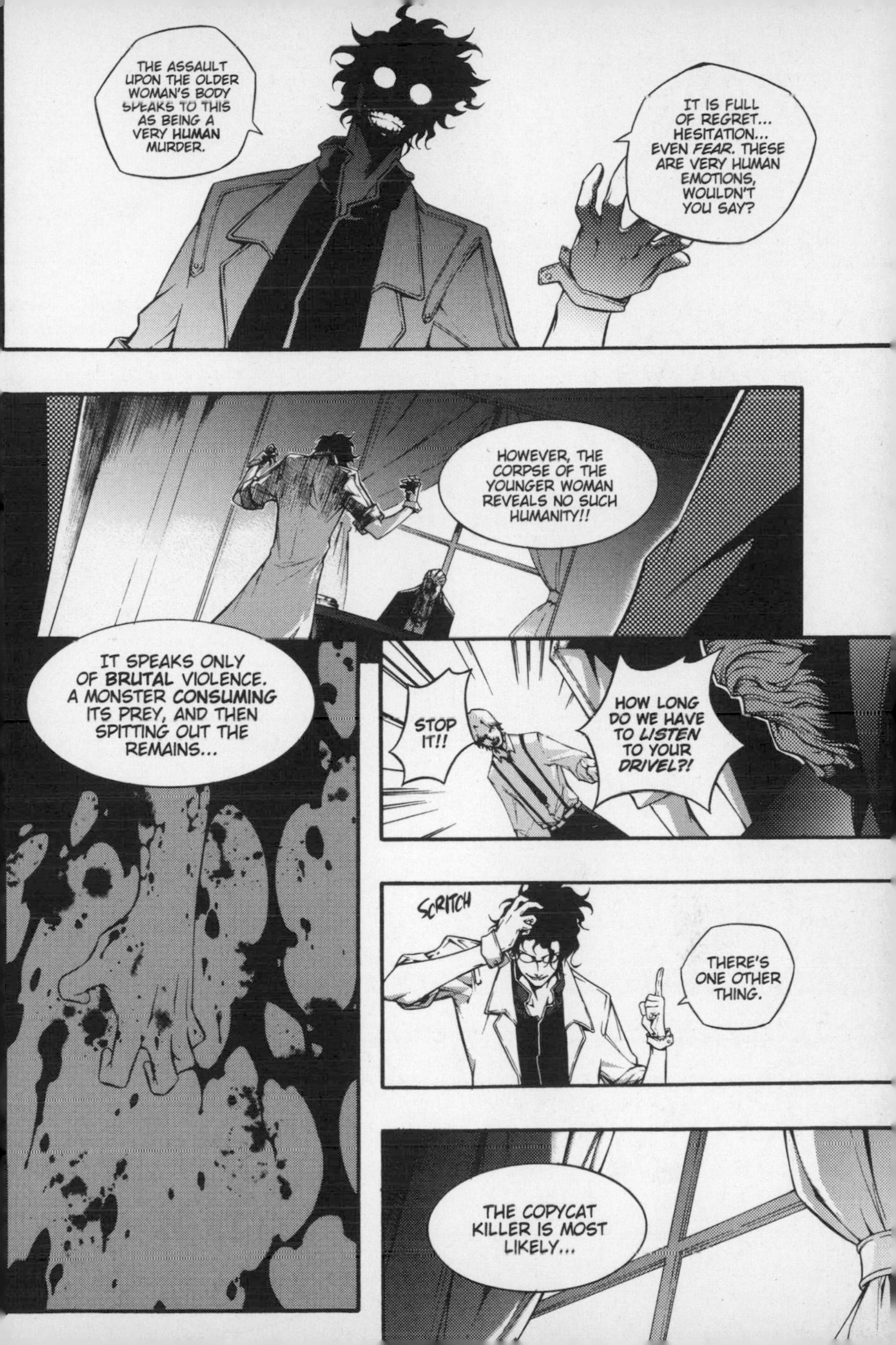
THE ASSAULT UPON THE OLDER WOMAN'S BODY SPEAKS TO THIS AS BEING A VERY HUMAN MURDER.
IT IS FULL OF REGRET... HESITATION... EVEN FEAR. THESE ARE VERY HUMAN EMOTIONS, WOULDN'T YOU SAY?
HOWEVER, THE CORPSE OF THE YOUNGER WOMAN REVEALS NO SUCH HUMANITY!!
IT SPEAKS ONLY OF BRUTAL VIOLENCE. A MONSTER CONSUMING ITS PREY, AND THEN SPITTING OUT THE REMAINS...
STOP IT!!
HOW LONG DO WE HAVE TO LISTEN TO YOUR DRIVEL?!
SCRITCH
THERE'S ONE OTHER THING.
THE COPYCAT KILLER IS MOST LIKELY...

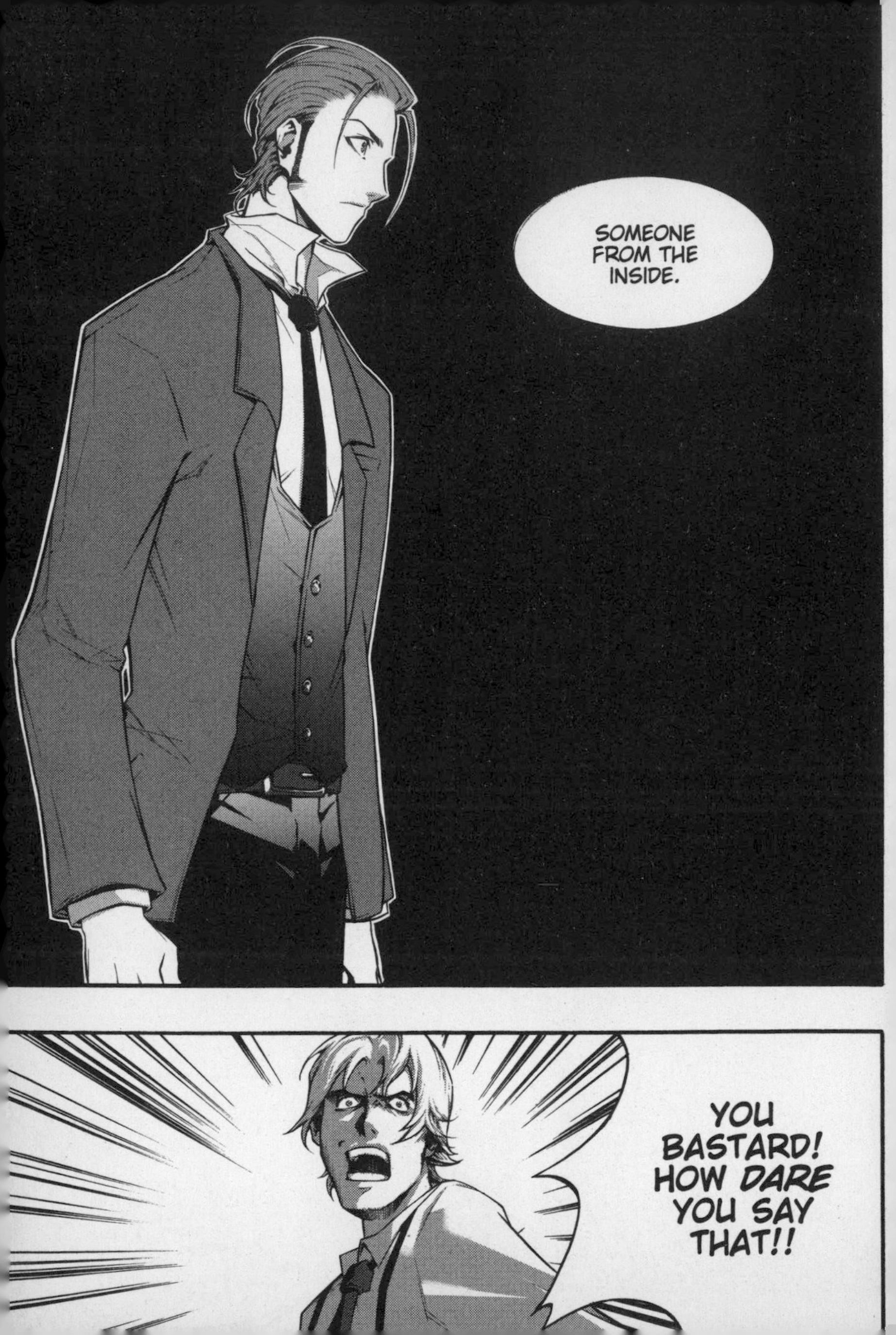
SOMEONE FROM THE INSIDE.
YOU BASTARD! HOW *DARE* YOU SAY THAT!!

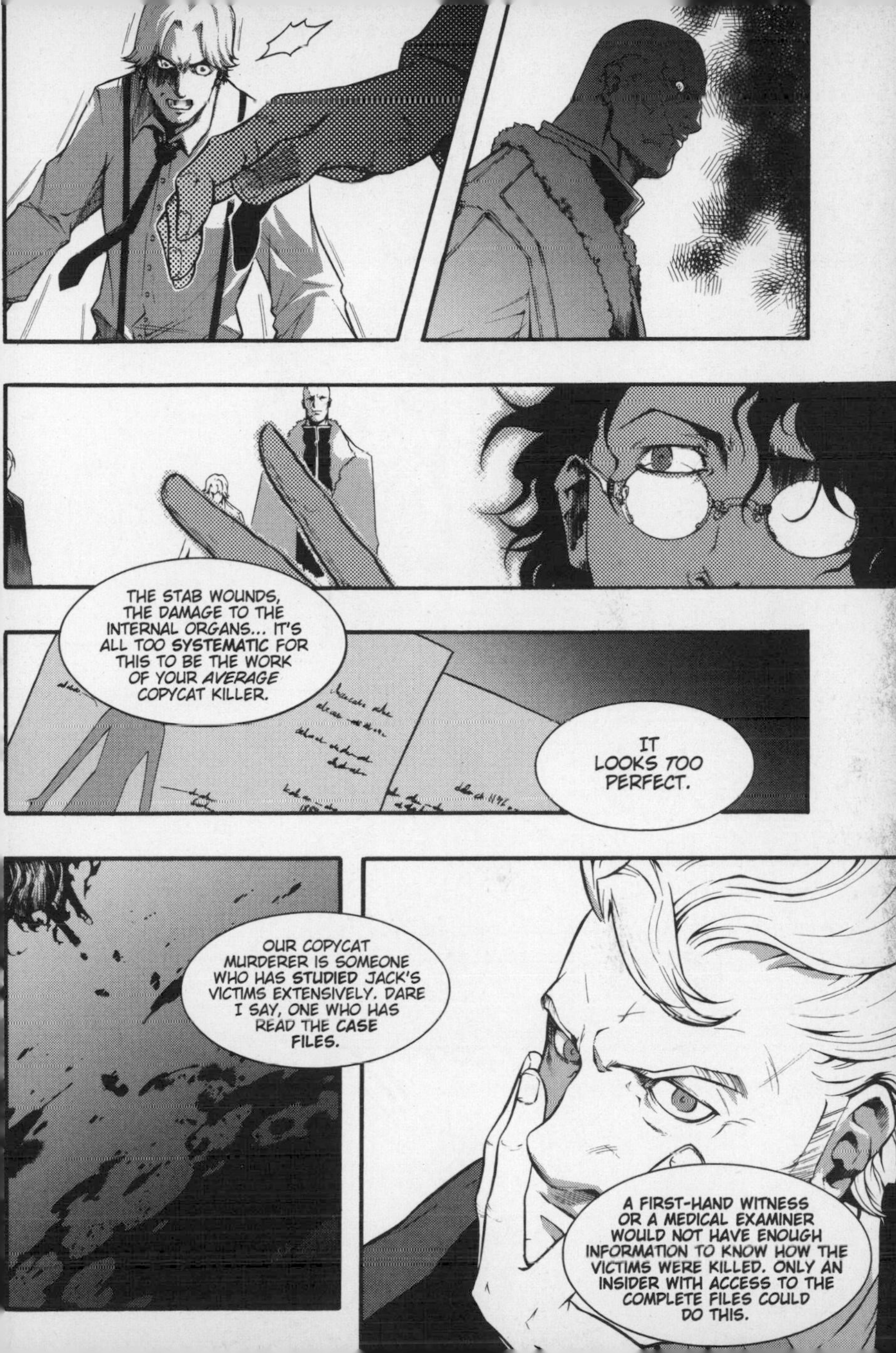
THE STAB WOUNDS, THE DAMAGE TO THE INTERNAL ORGANS... IT'S ALL TOO SYSTEMATIC FOR THIS TO BE THE WORK OF YOUR AVERAGE COPYCAT KILLER.
IT LOOKS TOO PERFECT.
OUR COPYCAT MURDERER IS SOMEONE WHO HAS STUDIED JACK'S VICTIMS EXTENSIVELY. DARE I SAY, ONE WHO HAS READ THE CASE FILES.
A FIRST-HAND WITNESS OR A MEDICAL EXAMINER WOULD NOT HAVE ENOUGH INFORMATION TO KNOW HOW THE VICTIMS WERE KILLED. ONLY AN INSIDER WITH ACCESS TO THE COMPLETE FILES COULD DO THIS.

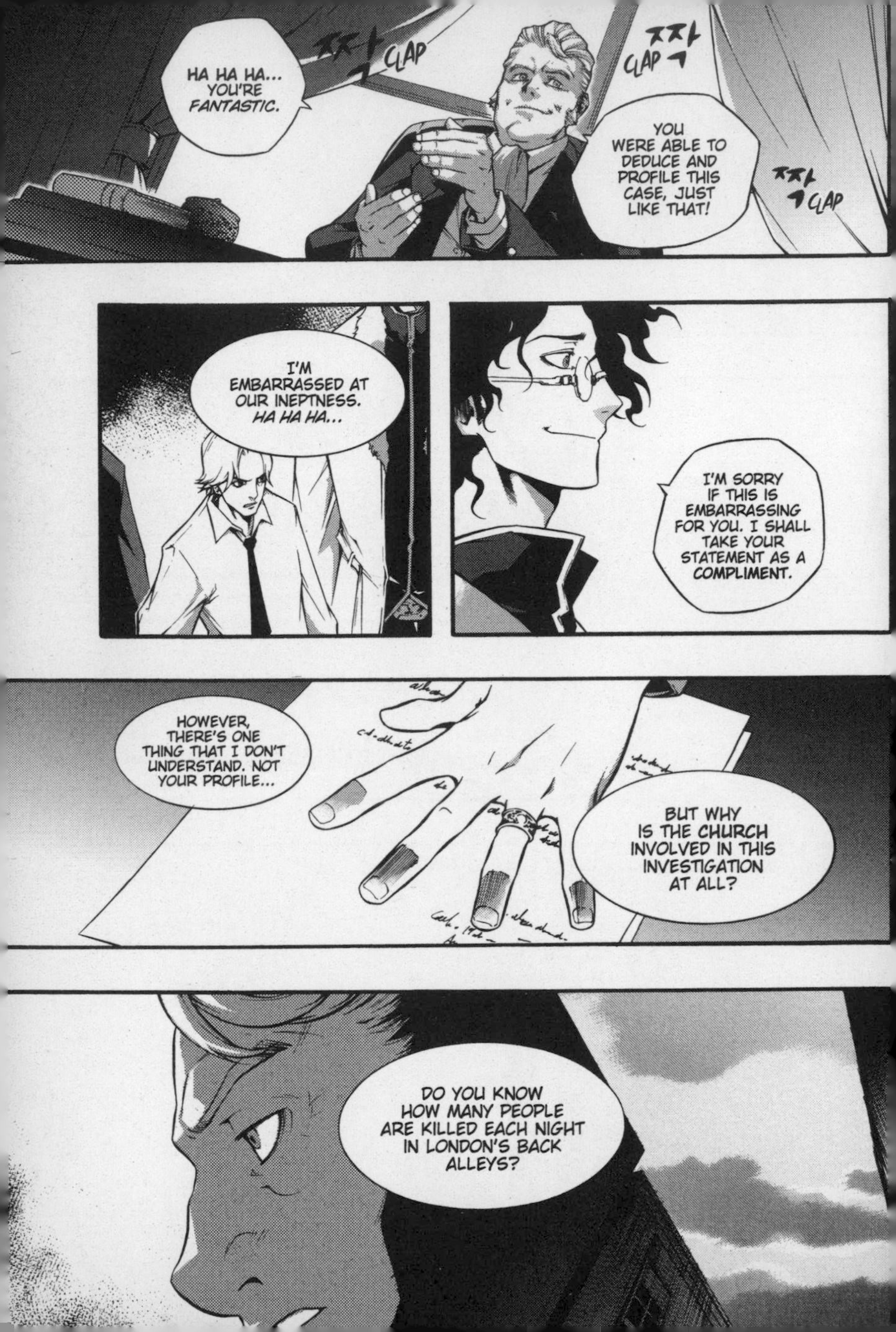
짝
CLAP
HA HA HA... YOU'RE FANTASTIC.
짝
CLAP
YOU WERE ABLE TO DEDUCE AND PROFILE THIS CASE, JUST LIKE THAT!
짝
CLAP
I'M EMBARRASSED AT OUR INEPTNESS. HA HA HA...
I'M SORRY IF THIS IS EMBARRASSING FOR YOU. I SHALL TAKE YOUR STATEMENT AS A COMPLIMENT.
HOWEVER, THERE'S ONE THING THAT I DON'T UNDERSTAND. NOT YOUR PROFILE...
BUT WHY IS THE CHURCH INVOLVED IN THIS INVESTIGATION AT ALL?
DO YOU KNOW HOW MANY PEOPLE ARE KILLED EACH NIGHT IN LONDON'S BACK ALLEYS?

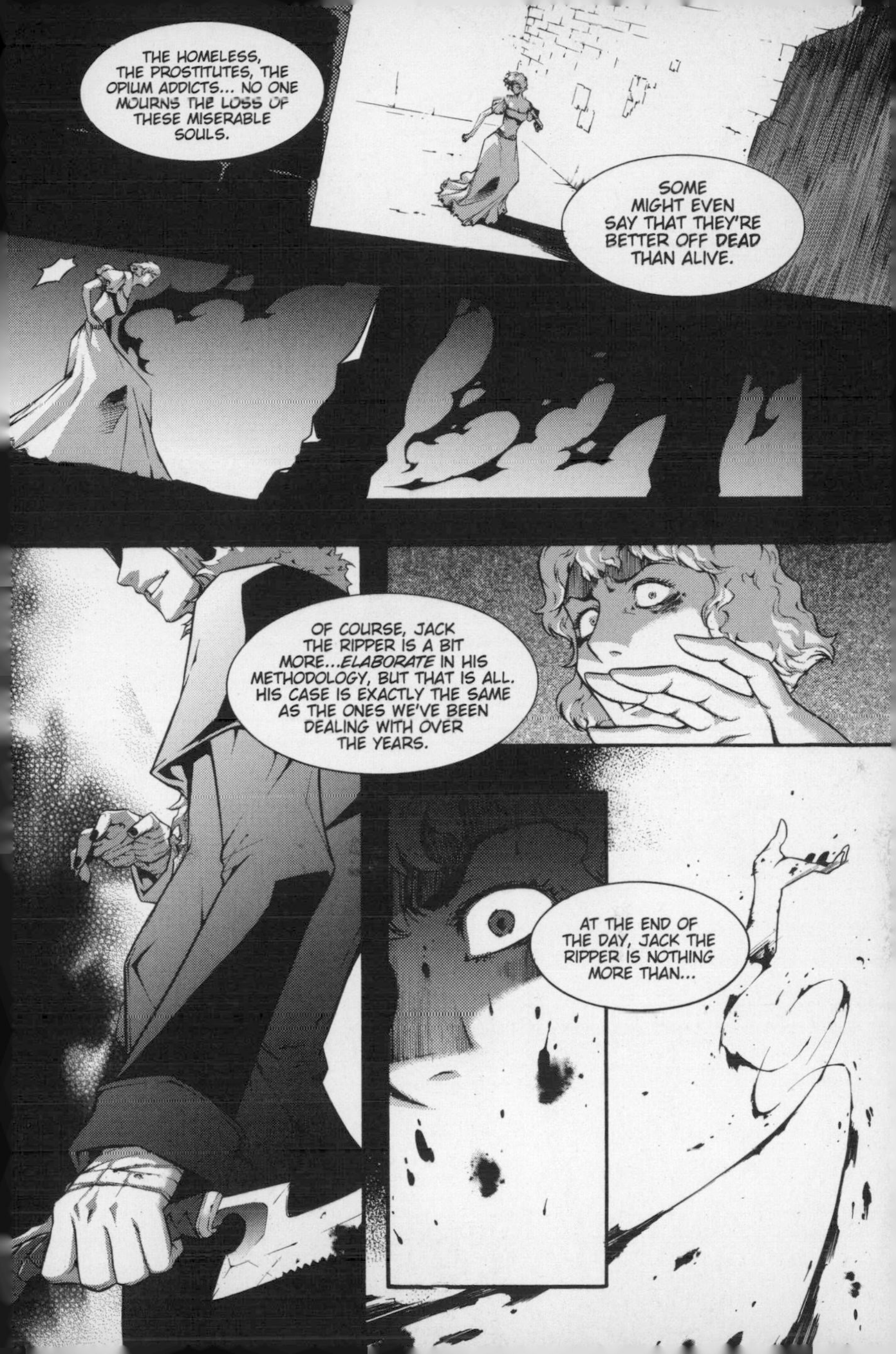
THE HOMELESS, THE PROSTITUTES, THE OPIUM ADDICTS... NO ONE MOURNS THE LOSS OF THESE MISERABLE SOULS.
SOME MIGHT EVEN SAY THAT THEY'RE BETTER OFF DEAD THAN ALIVE.
OF COURSE, JACK THE RIPPER IS A BIT MORE...*ELABORATE* IN HIS METHODOLOGY, BUT THAT IS ALL. HIS CASE IS EXACTLY THE SAME AS THE ONES WE'VE BEEN DEALING WITH OVER THE YEARS.
AT THE END OF THE DAY, JACK THE RIPPER IS NOTHING MORE THAN...

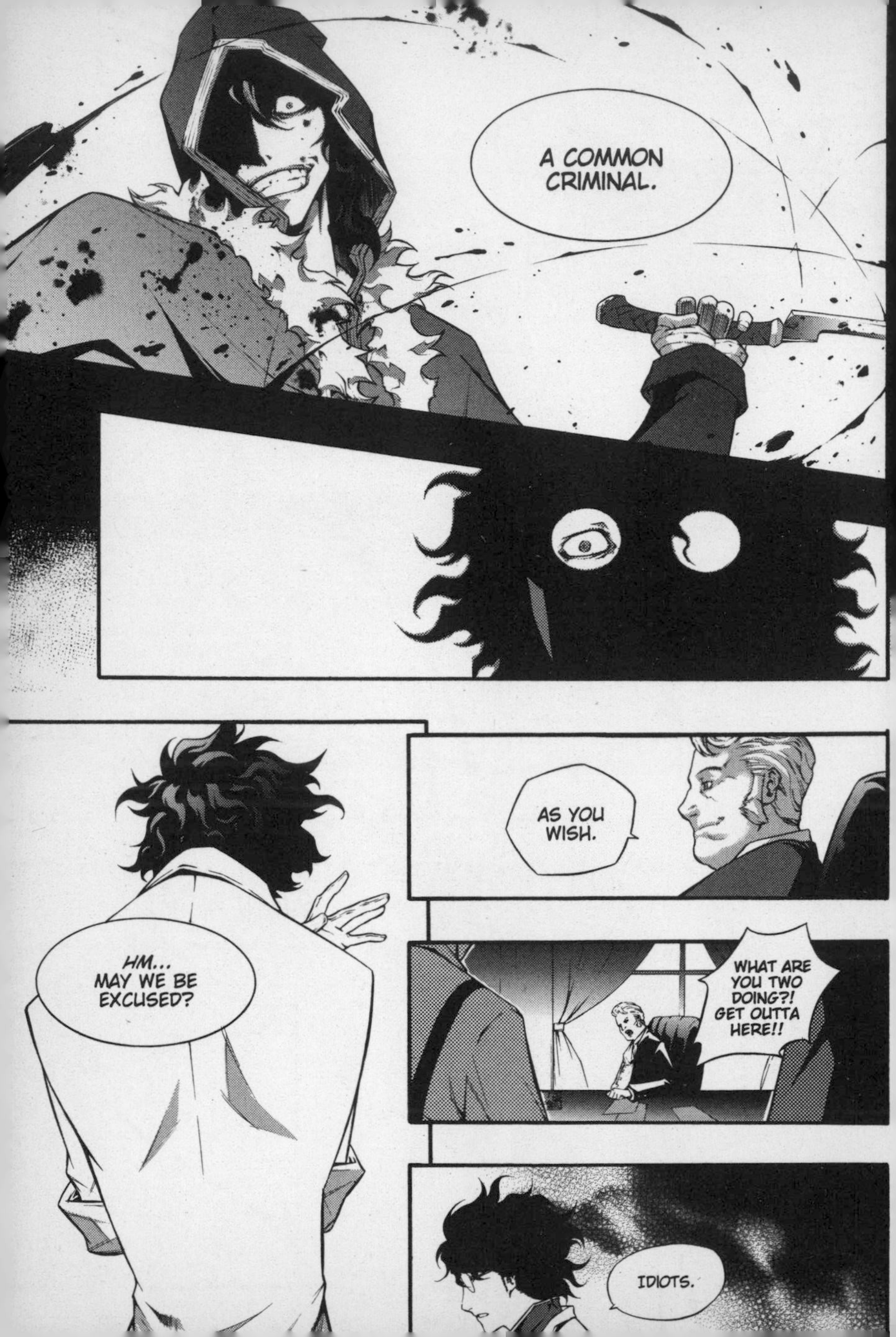
A COMMON CRIMINAL.
HM... MAY WE BE EXCUSED?
AS YOU WISH.
WHAT ARE YOU TWO DOING?! GET OUTTA HERE!!
IDIOTS.

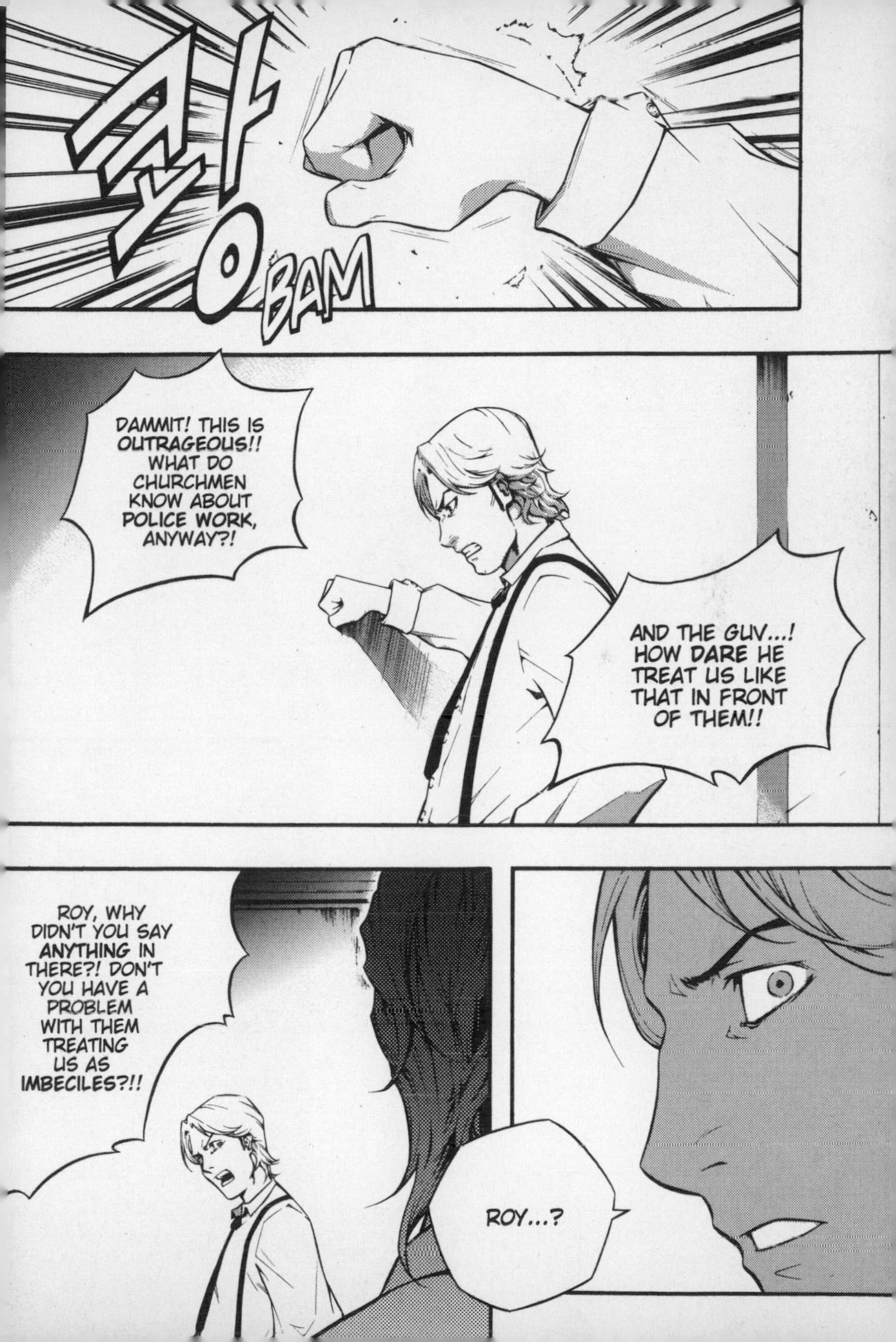
BAM
DAMMIT! THIS IS OUTRAGEOUS!! WHAT DO CHURCHMEN KNOW ABOUT POLICE WORK, ANYWAY?!
AND THE GUV...! HOW DARE HE TREAT US LIKE THAT IN FRONT OF THEM!!
ROY, WHY DIDN'T YOU SAY ANYTHING IN THERE?! DON'T YOU HAVE A PROBLEM WITH THEM TREATING US AS IMBECILES?!!
ROY...?

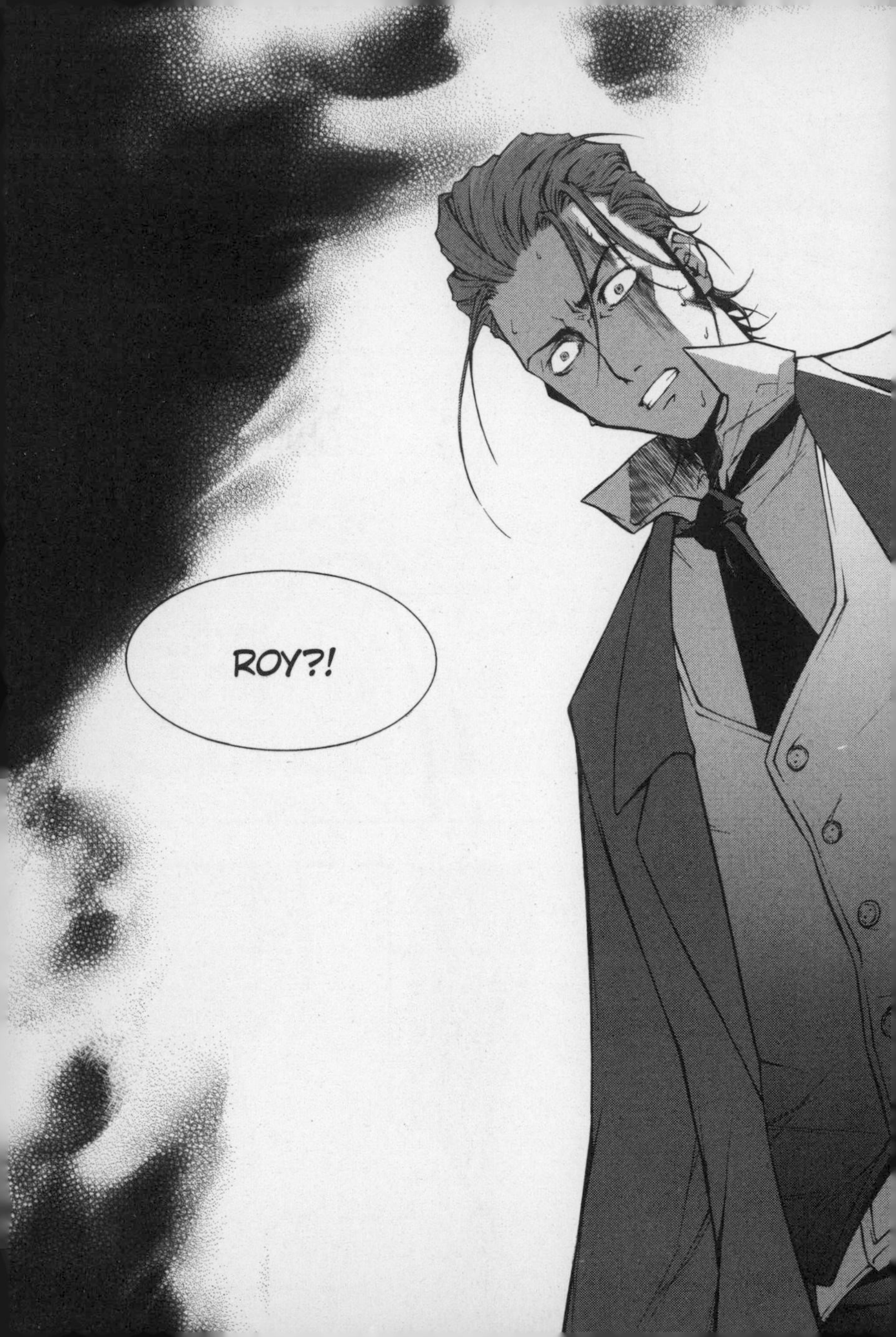
ROY?!

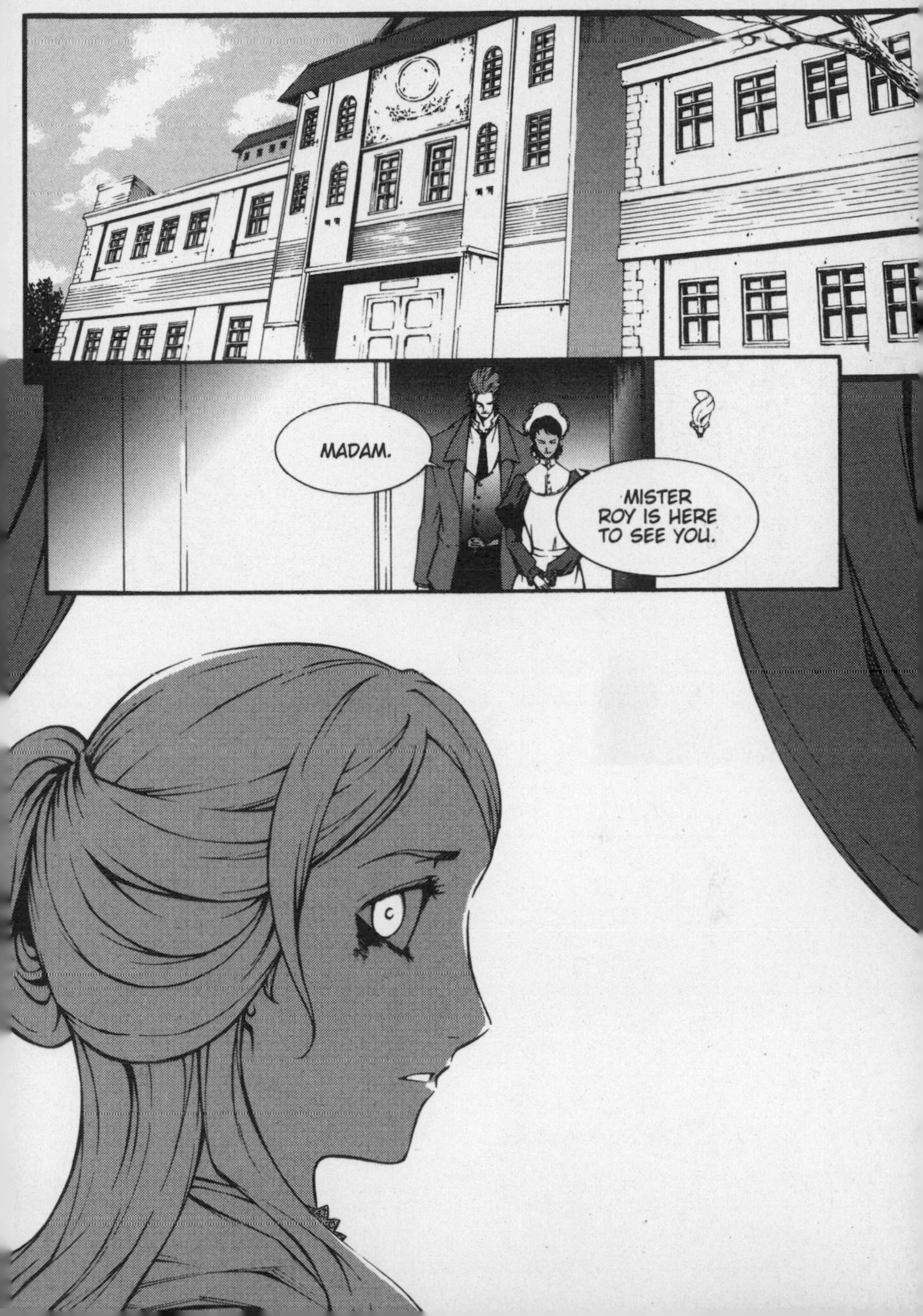
MADAM.
MISTER ROY IS HERE TO SEE YOU.

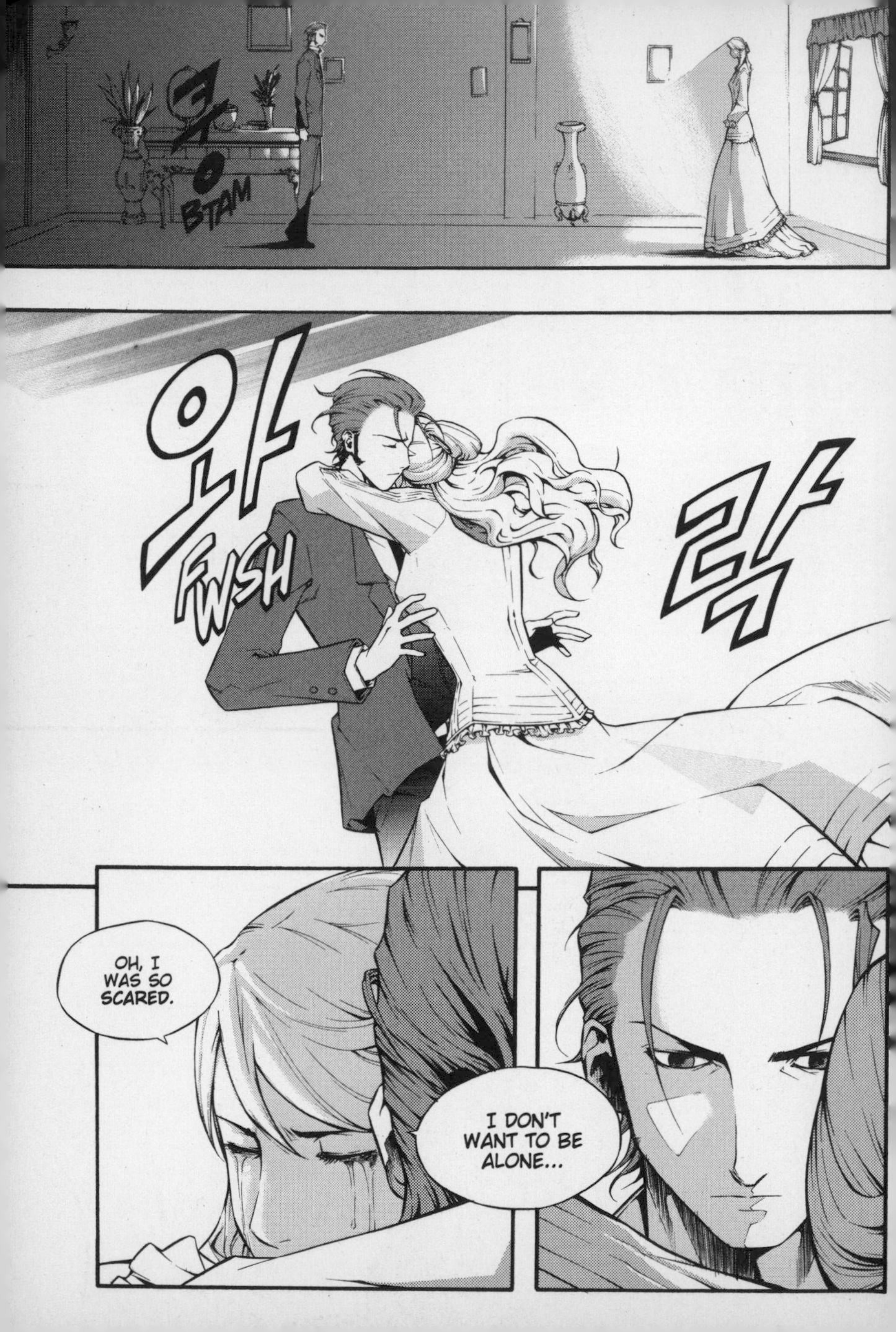
BTAM
와
FWSH
락
OH, I WAS SO SCARED.
I DON'T WANT TO BE ALONE...

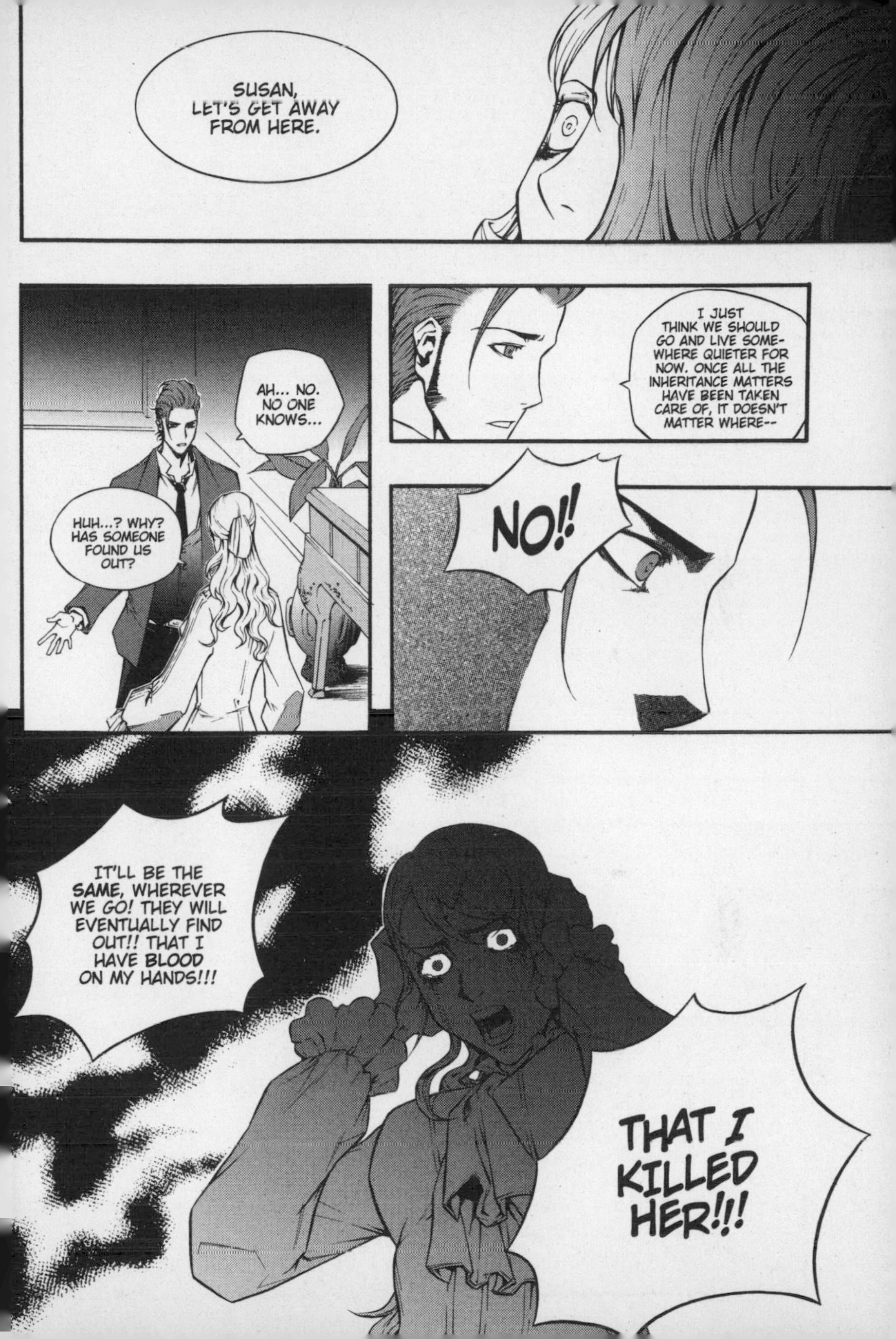
SUSAN, LET'S GET AWAY FROM HERE.
AH... NO. NO ONE KNOWS...
HUH...? WHY? HAS SOMEONE FOUND US OUT?
I JUST THINK WE SHOULD GO AND LIVE SOMEWHERE QUIETER FOR NOW. ONCE ALL THE INHERITANCE MATTERS HAVE BEEN TAKEN CARE OF, IT DOESN'T MATTER WHERE--
NO!!
IT'LL BE THE SAME, WHEREVER WE GO! THEY WILL EVENTUALLY FIND OUT!! THAT I HAVE BLOOD ON MY HANDS!!!
THAT I KILLED HER!!!

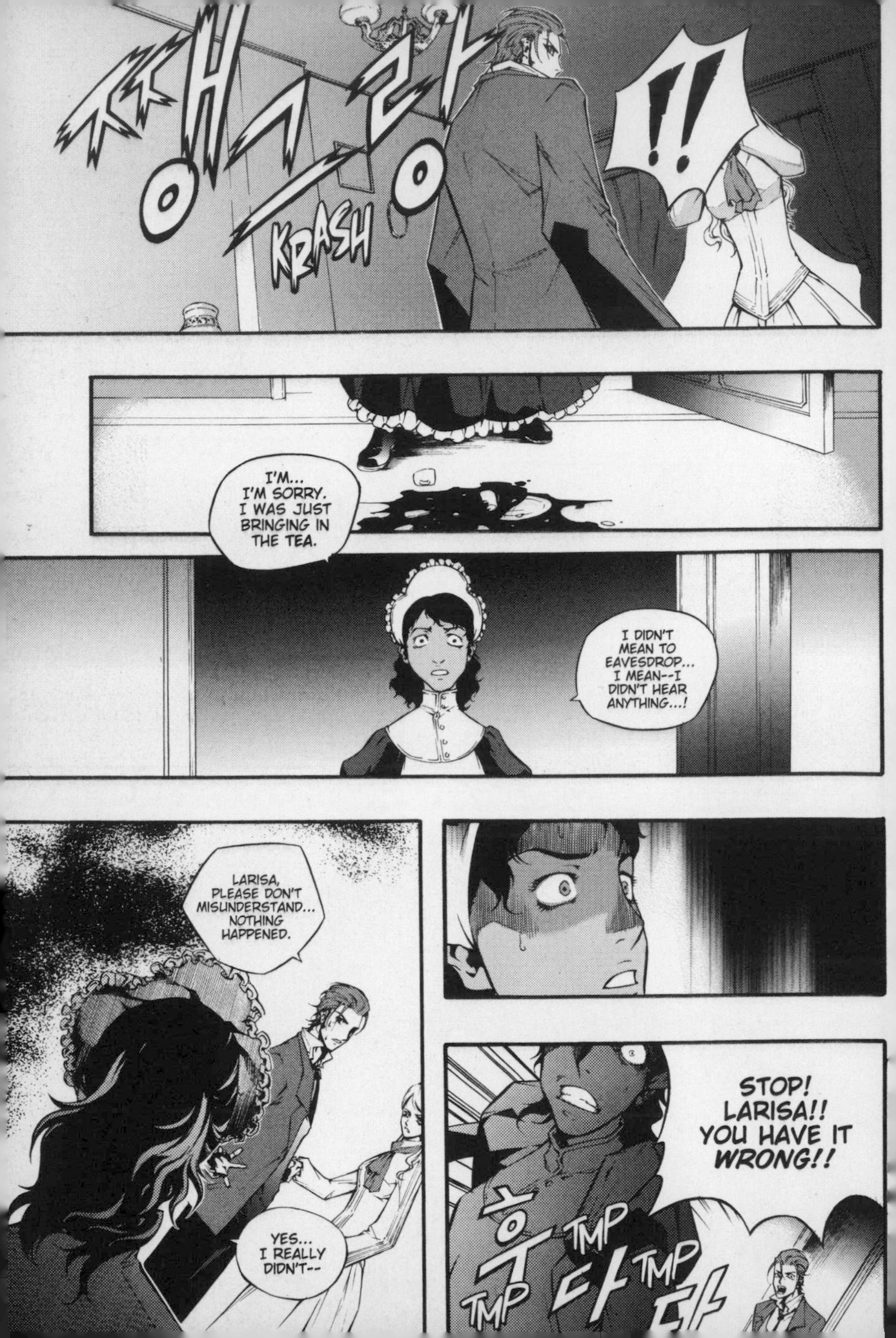
KRASH
!!
I'M... I'M SORRY. I WAS JUST BRINGING IN THE TEA.
I DIDN'T MEAN TO EAVESDROP... I MEAN--I DIDN'T HEAR ANYTHING...!
LARISA, PLEASE DON'T MISUNDERSTAND... NOTHING HAPPENED.
YES... I REALLY DIDN'T--
STOP! LARISA!! YOU HAVE IT WRONG!!
TMP TMP TMP TMP

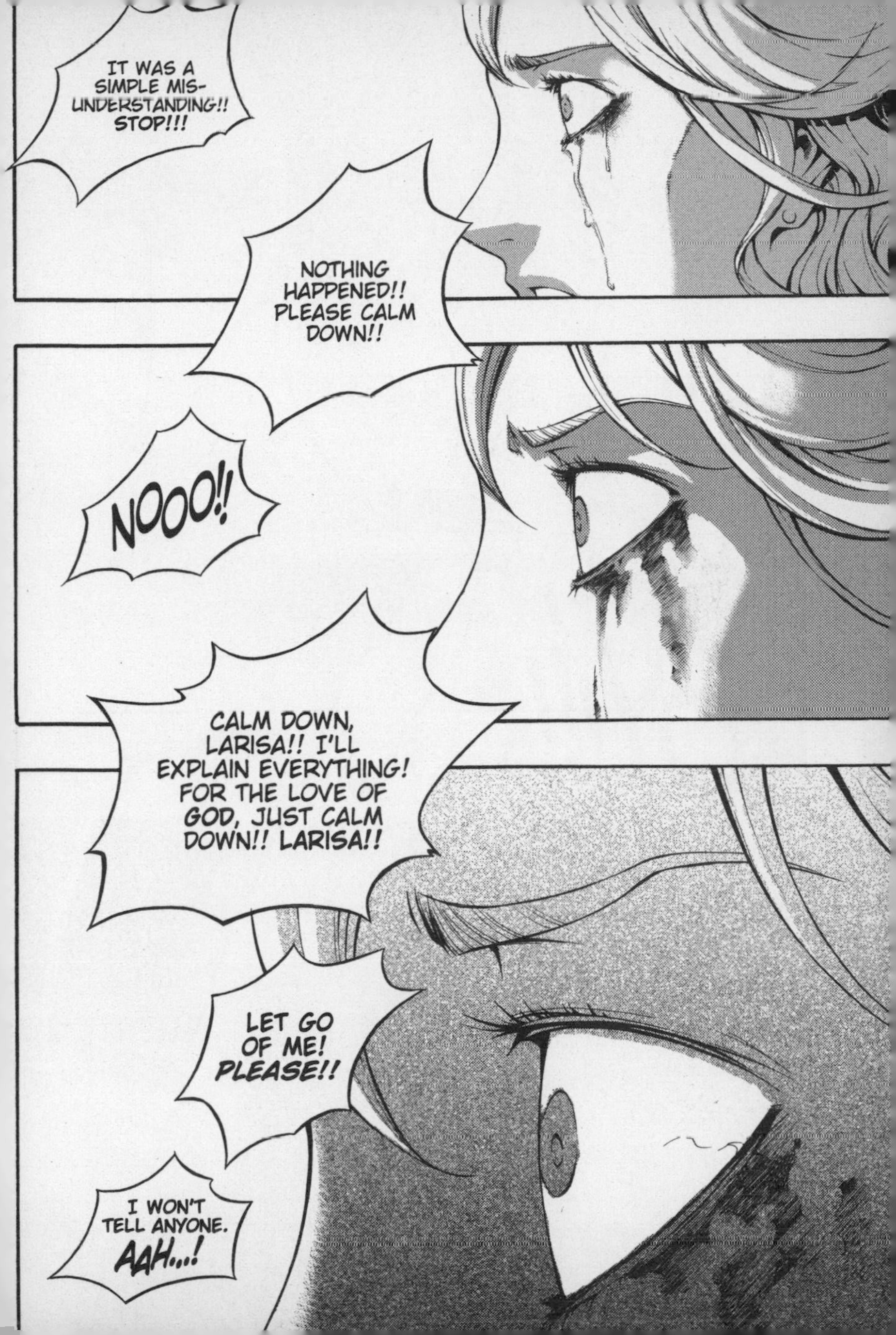
IT WAS A SIMPLE MIS-UNDERSTANDING!! STOP!!!
NOTHING HAPPENED!! PLEASE CALM DOWN!!
NOOO!!
CALM DOWN, LARISA!! I'LL EXPLAIN EVERYTHING! FOR THE LOVE OF GOD, JUST CALM DOWN!! LARISA!!
LET GO OF ME! PLEASE!!
I WON'T TELL ANYONE. AAH...!

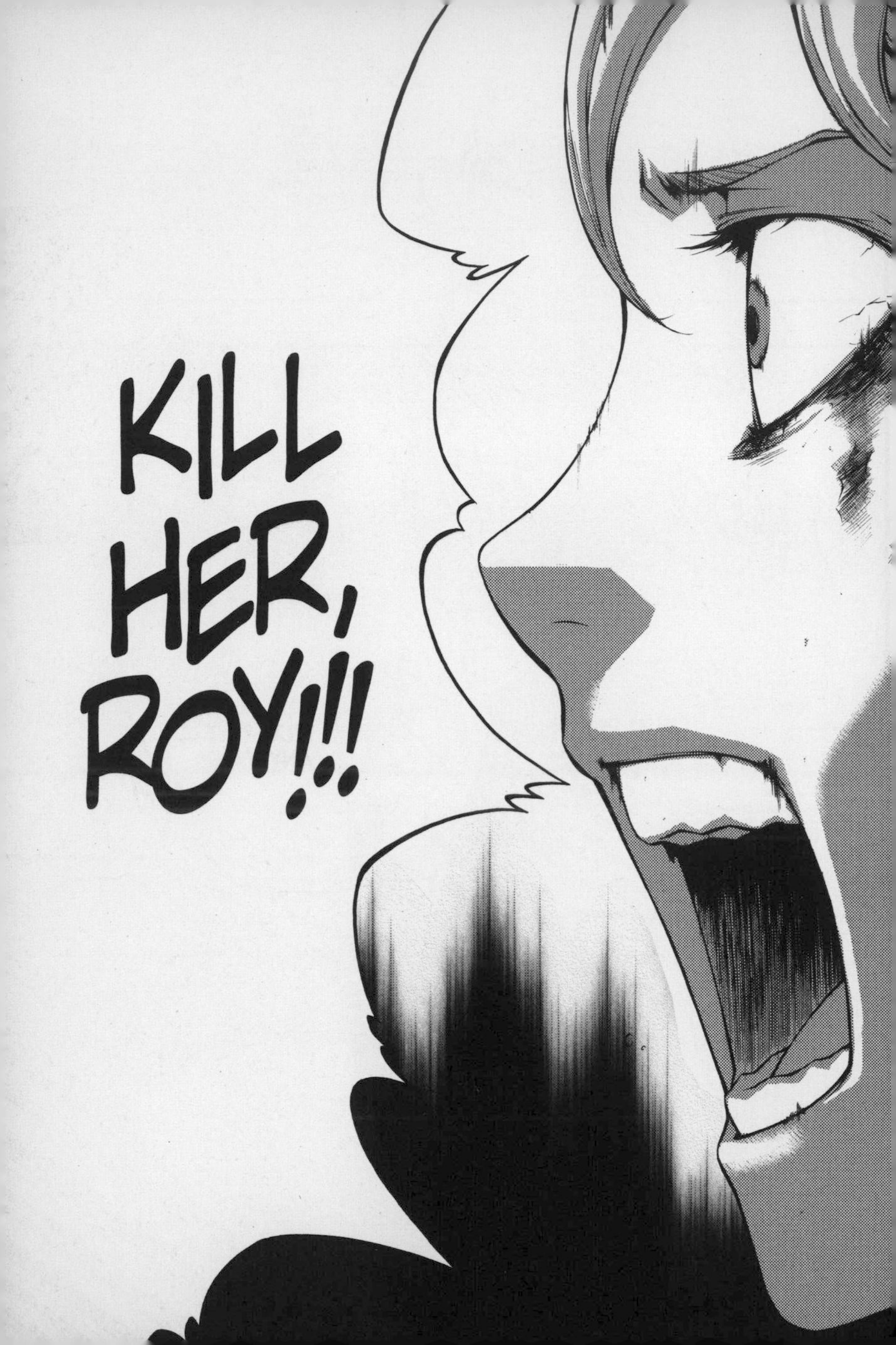
KILL HER, ROY!!!

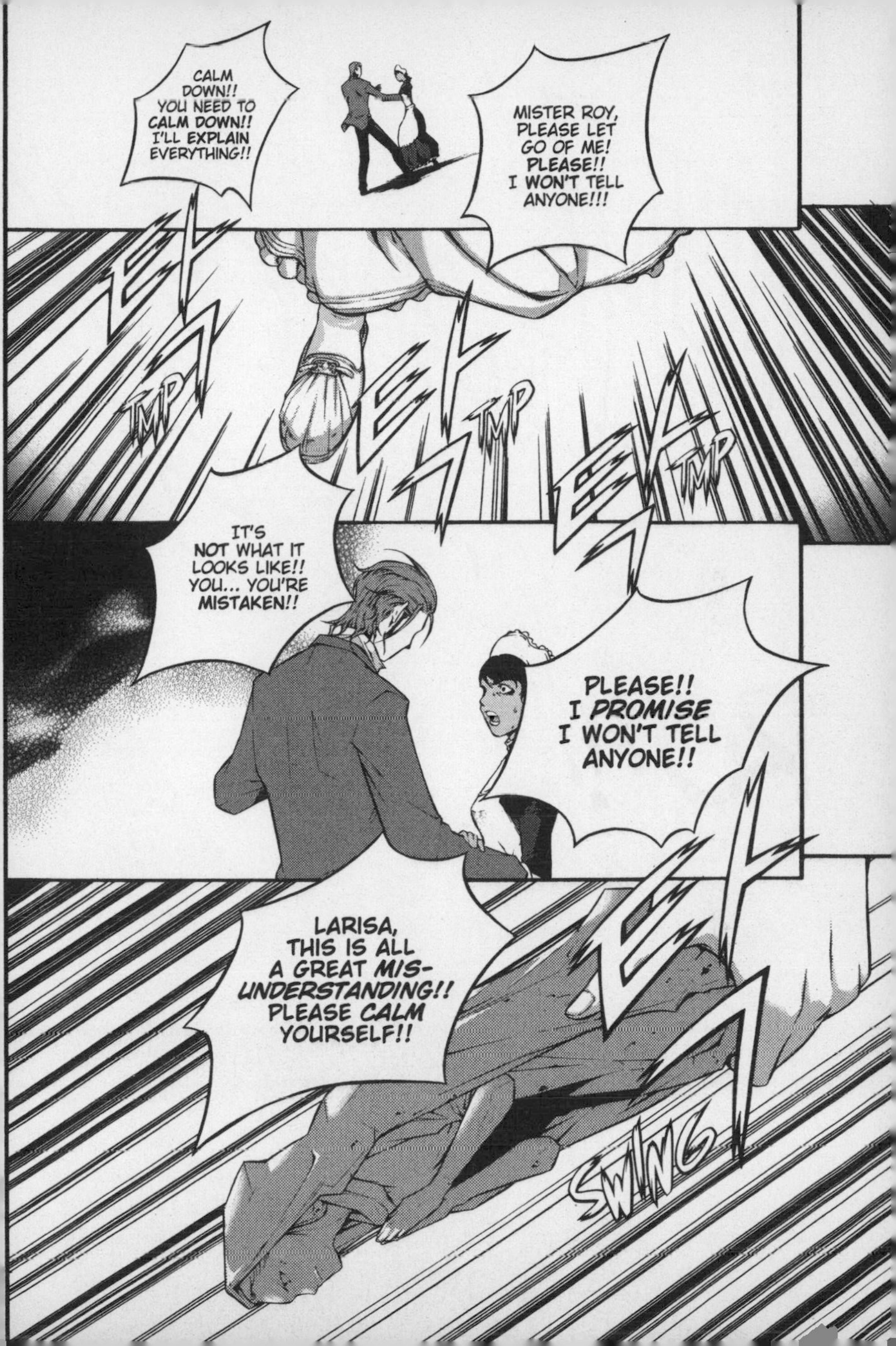
CALM DOWN!! YOU NEED TO CALM DOWN!! I'LL EXPLAIN EVERYTHING!!
MISTER ROY, PLEASE LET GO OF ME! PLEASE!! I WON'T TELL ANYONE!!!
TMP
TMP
TMP
IT'S NOT WHAT IT LOOKS LIKE!! YOU... YOU'RE MISTAKEN!!
PLEASE!! I *PROMISE* I WON'T TELL ANYONE!!
LARISA, THIS IS ALL A GREAT *MIS-UNDERSTANDING!!* PLEASE *CALM* YOURSELF!!
SWING

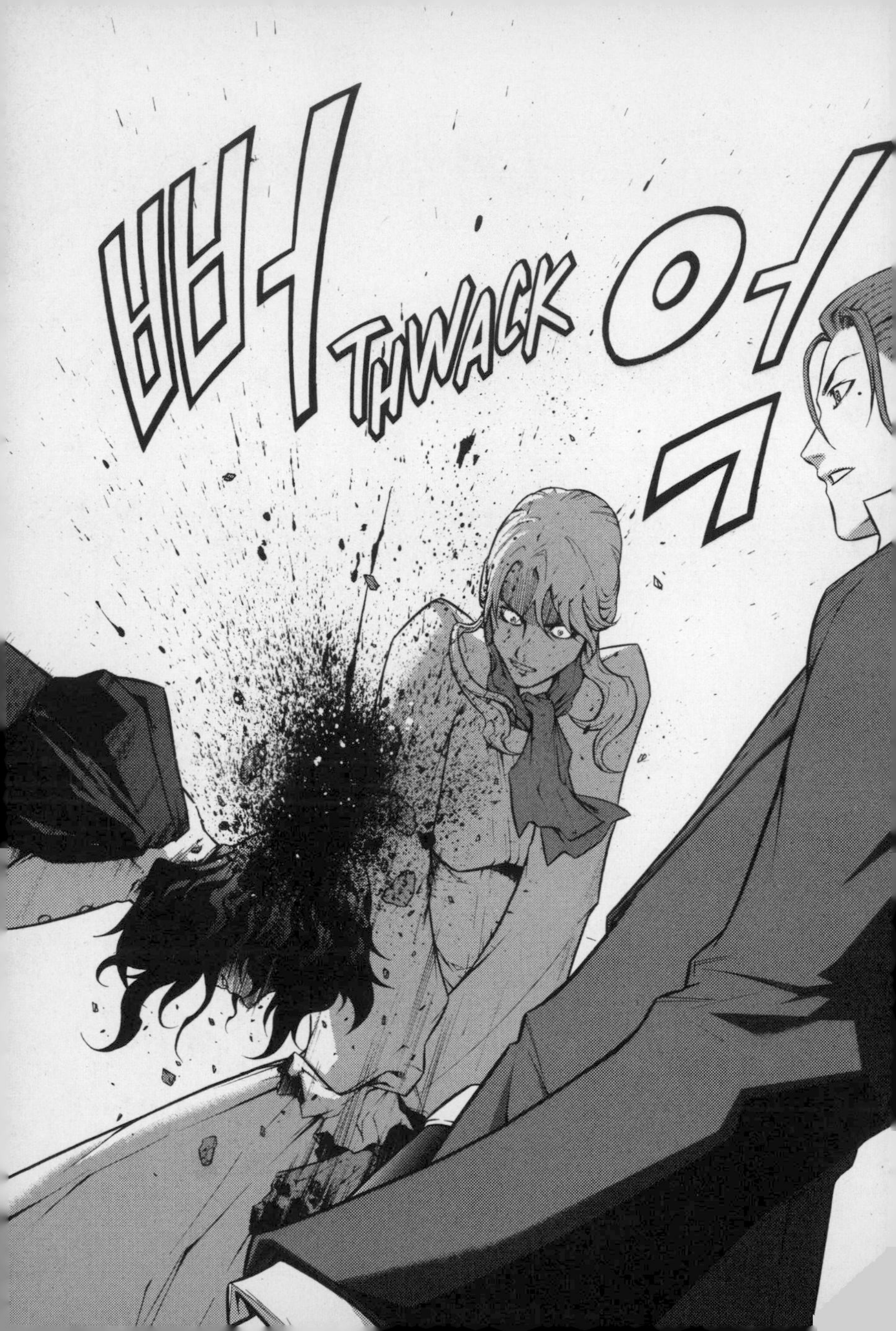
THWACK

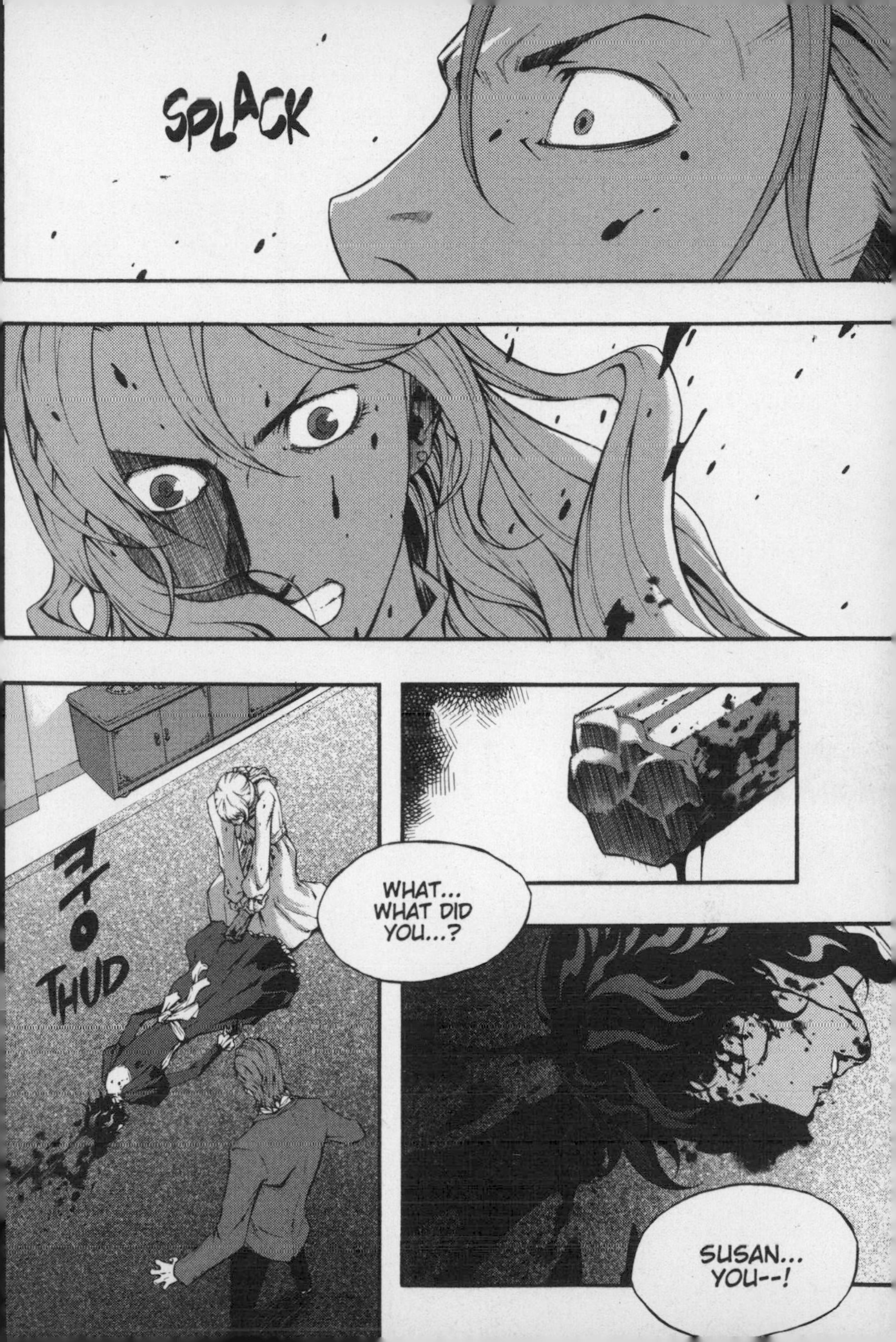
SPLACK
쿵
THUD
WHAT... WHAT DID YOU...?
SUSAN... YOU--!

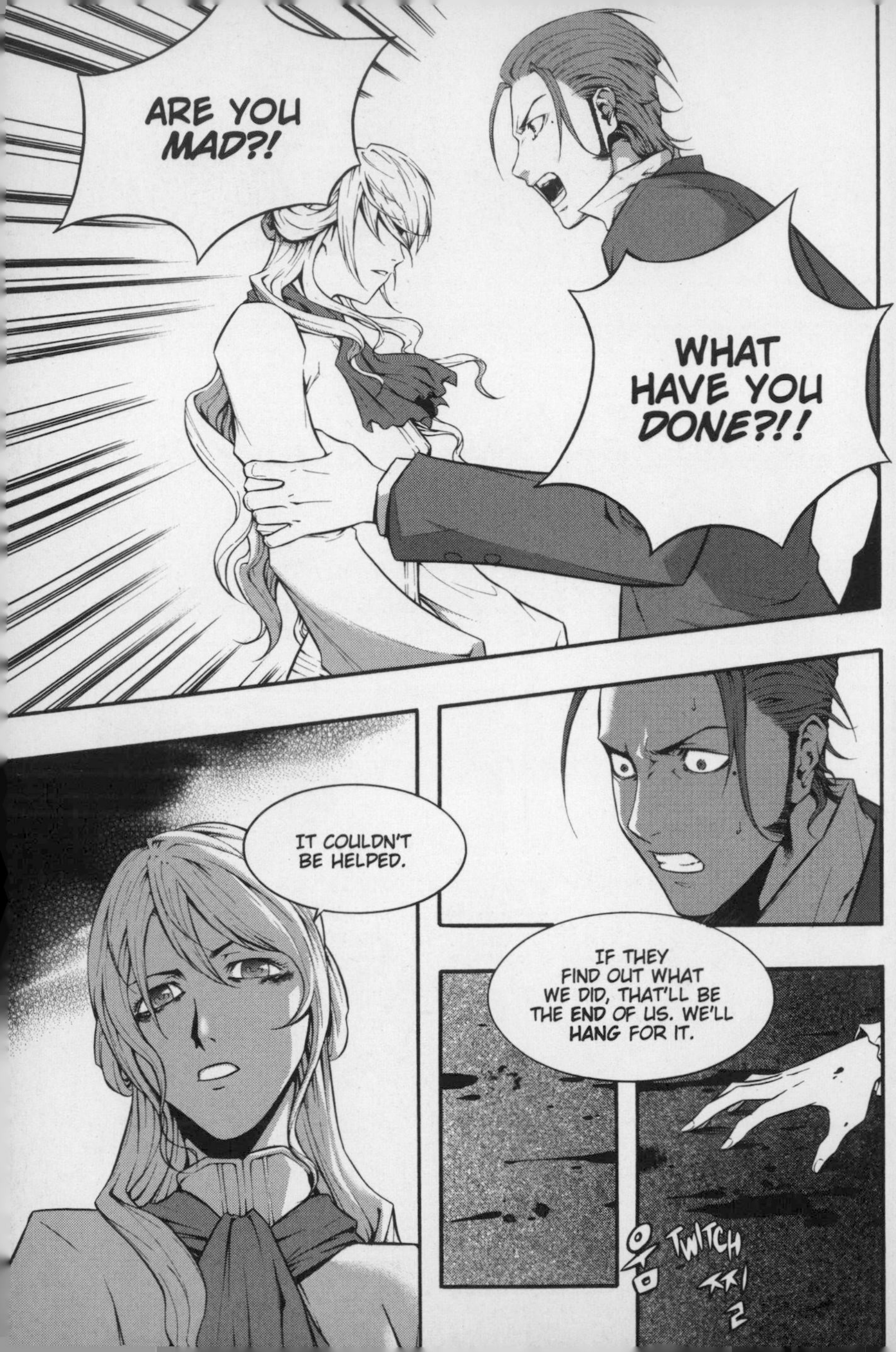
ARE YOU MAD?!
WHAT HAVE YOU DONE?!!
IT COULDN'T BE HELPED.
IF THEY FIND OUT WHAT WE DID, THAT'LL BE THE END OF US. WE'LL HANG FOR IT.
TWITCH

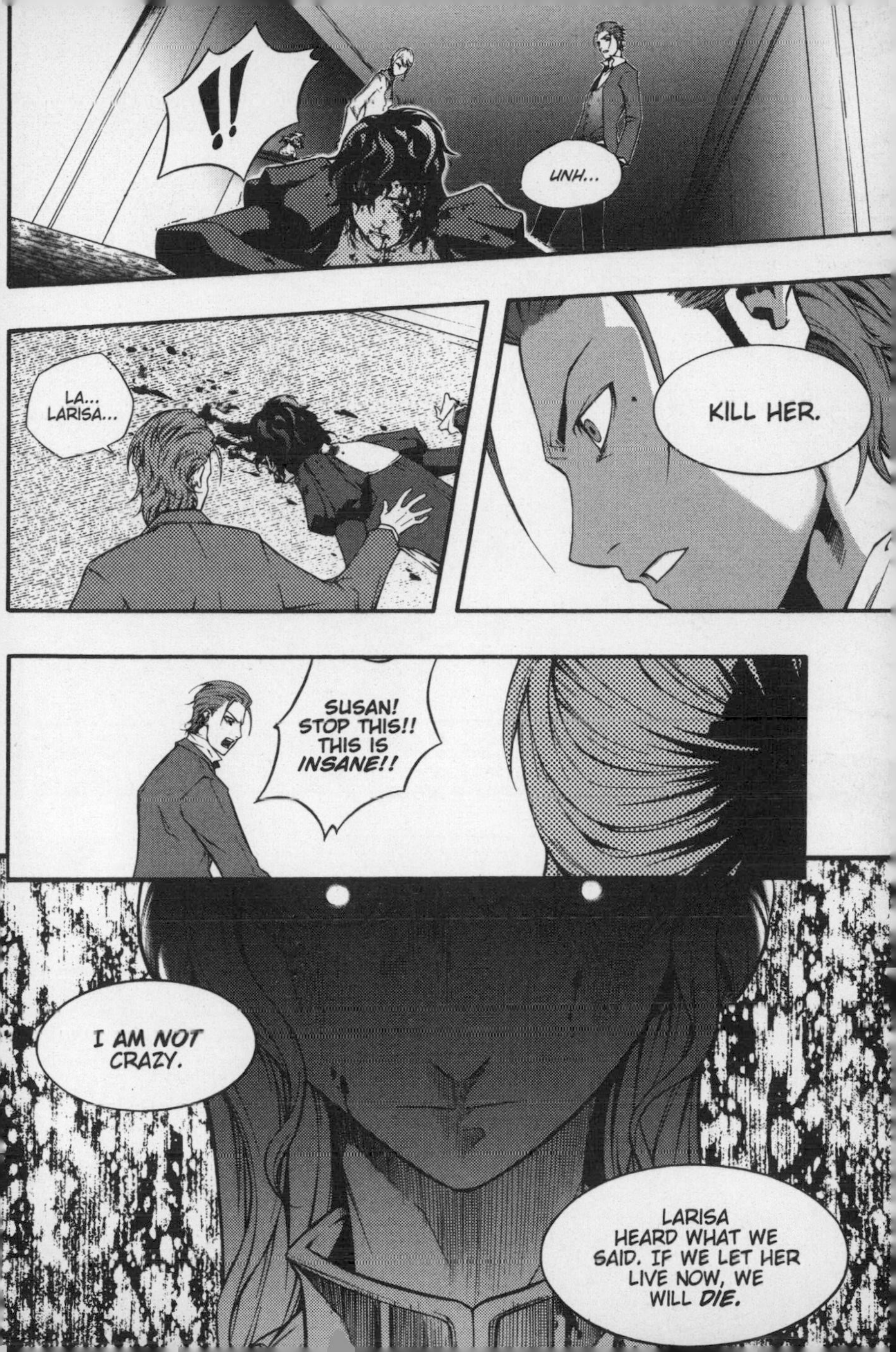
!!
UNH...
LA... LARISA...
KILL HER.
SUSAN! STOP THIS!! THIS IS *INSANE!!*
I AM *NOT* CRAZY.
LARISA HEARD WHAT WE SAID. IF WE LET HER LIVE NOW, WE WILL *DIE.*

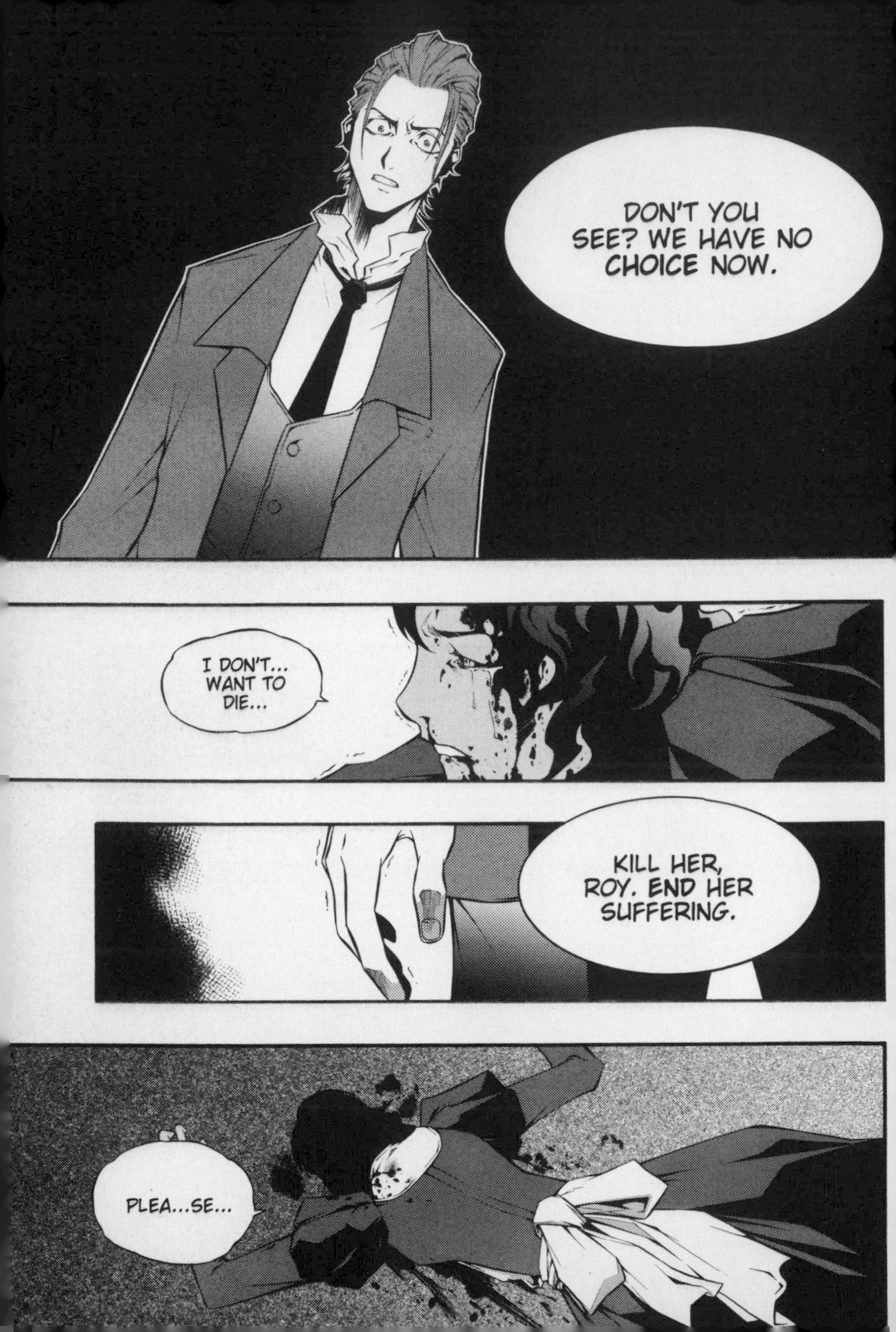
DON'T YOU SEE? WE HAVE NO CHOICE NOW.
I DON'T... WANT TO DIE...
KILL HER, ROY. END HER SUFFERING.
PLEA...SE...

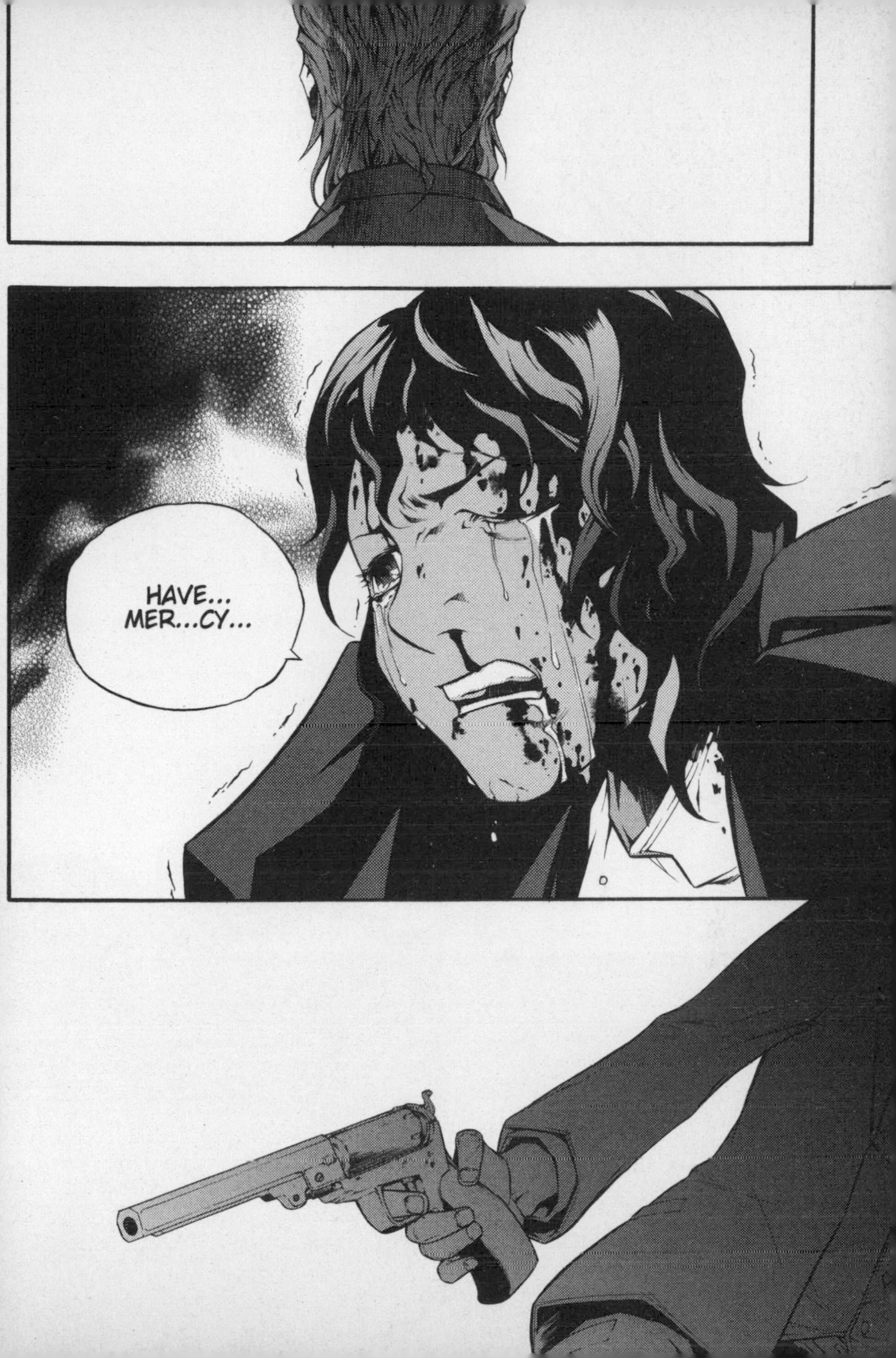
HAVE...
MER...CY...

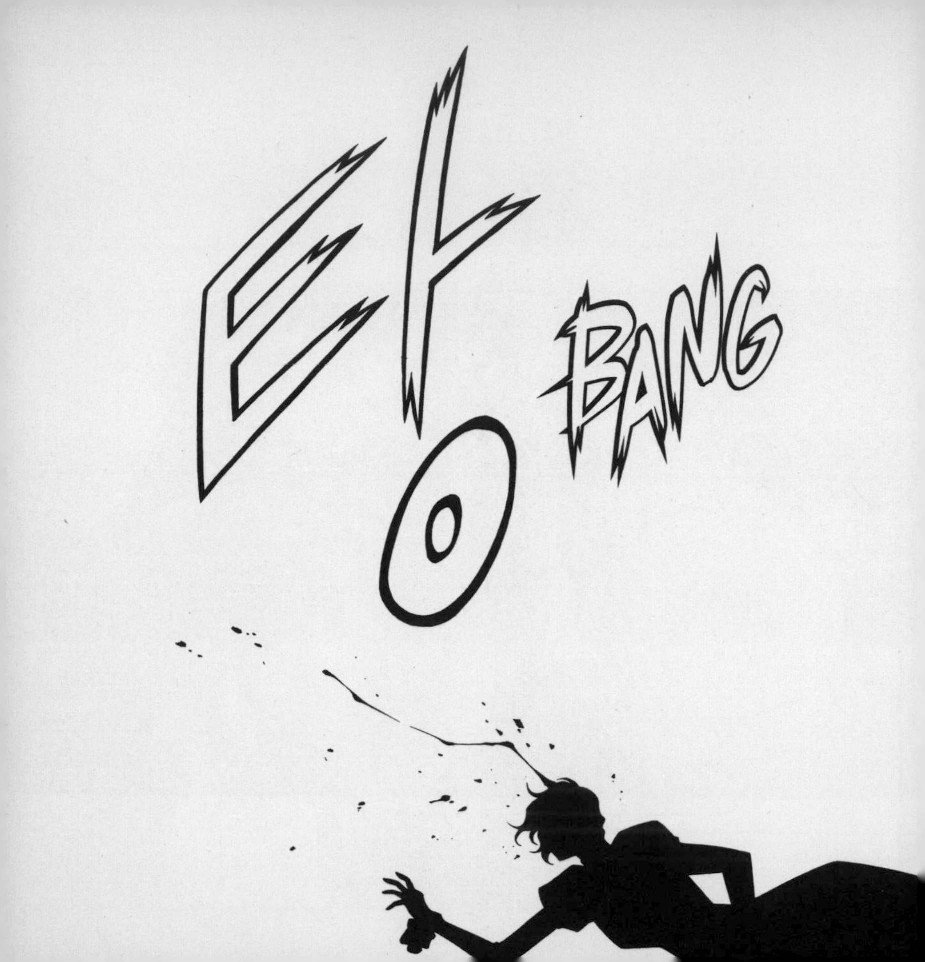
탕
BANG

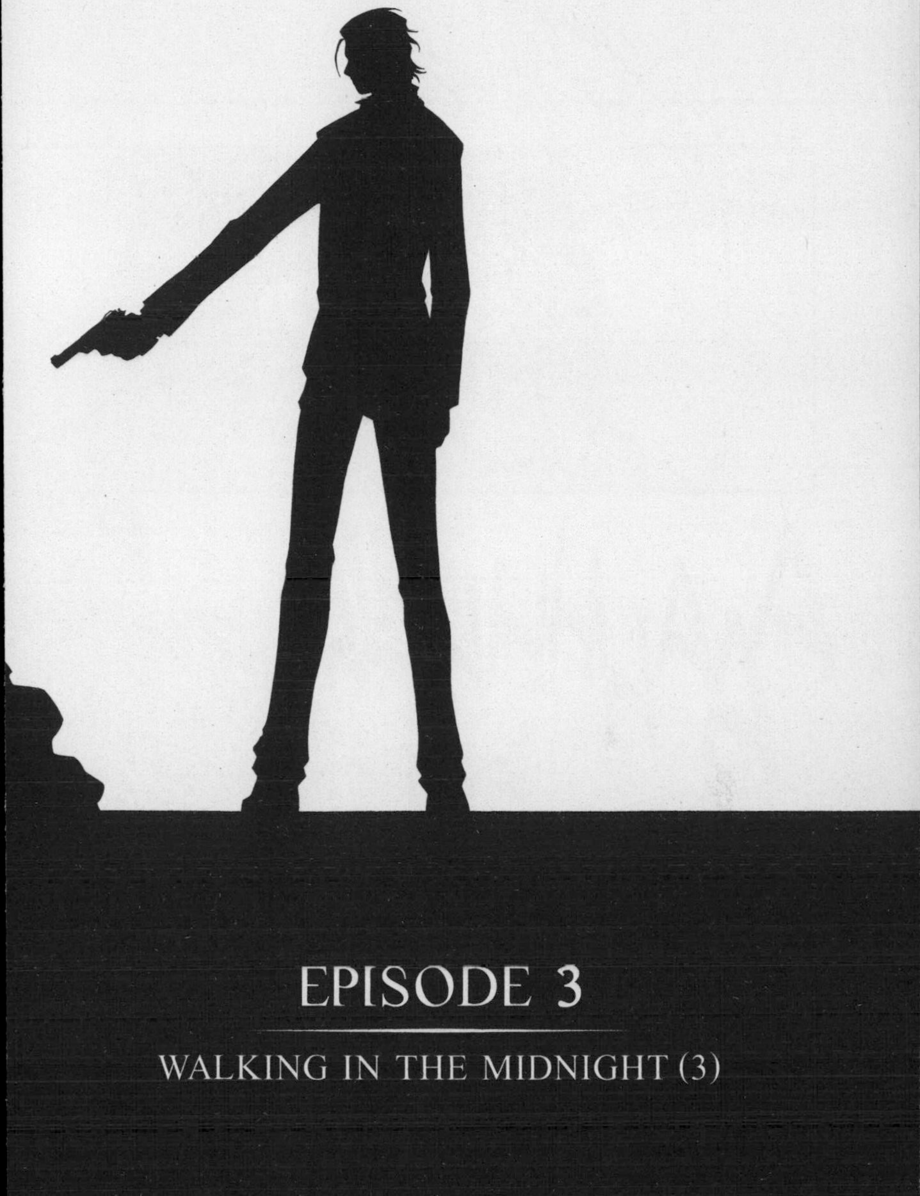

EPISODE 3

WALKING IN THE MIDNIGHT (3)

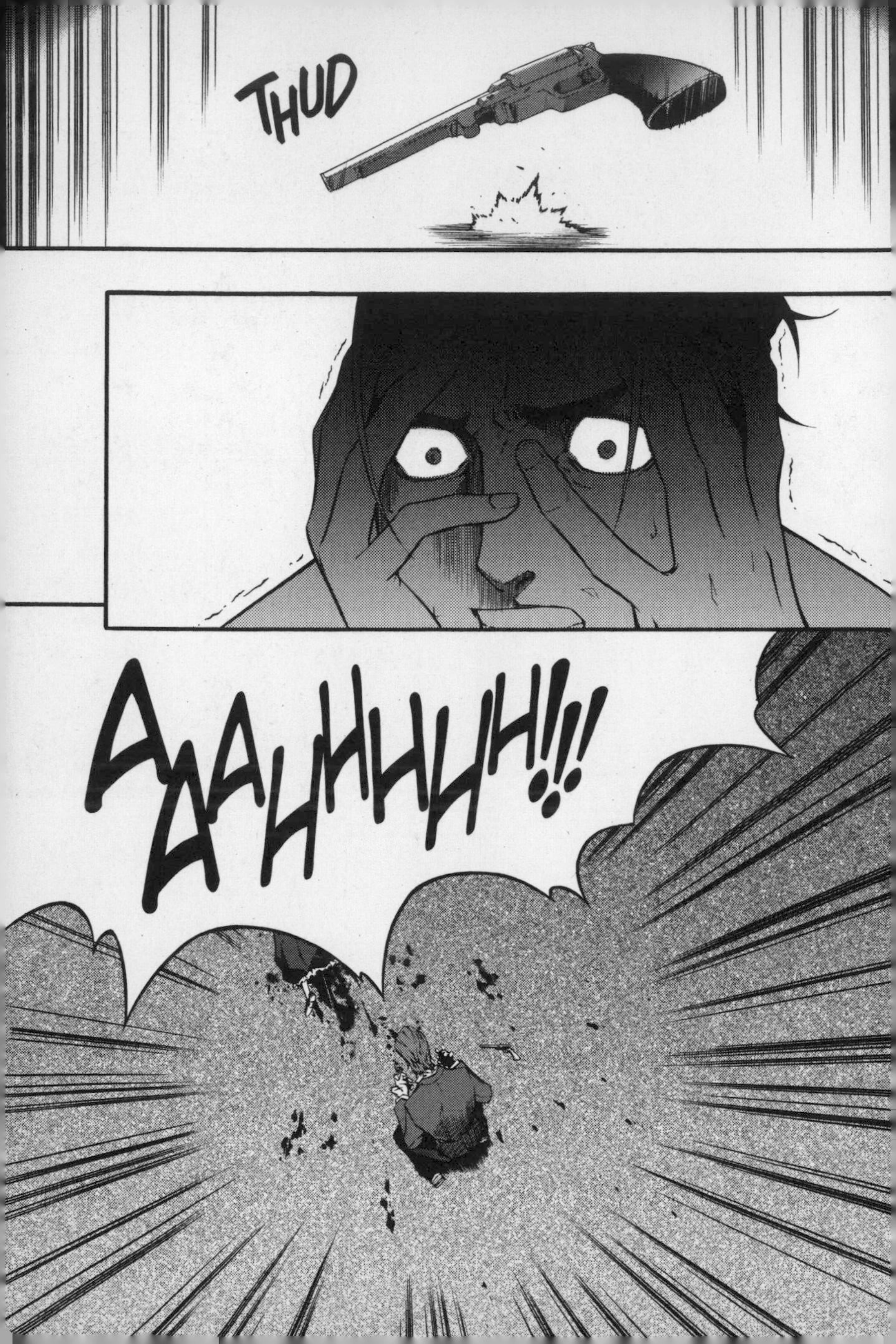
THUD
AAAHHHHH!!!

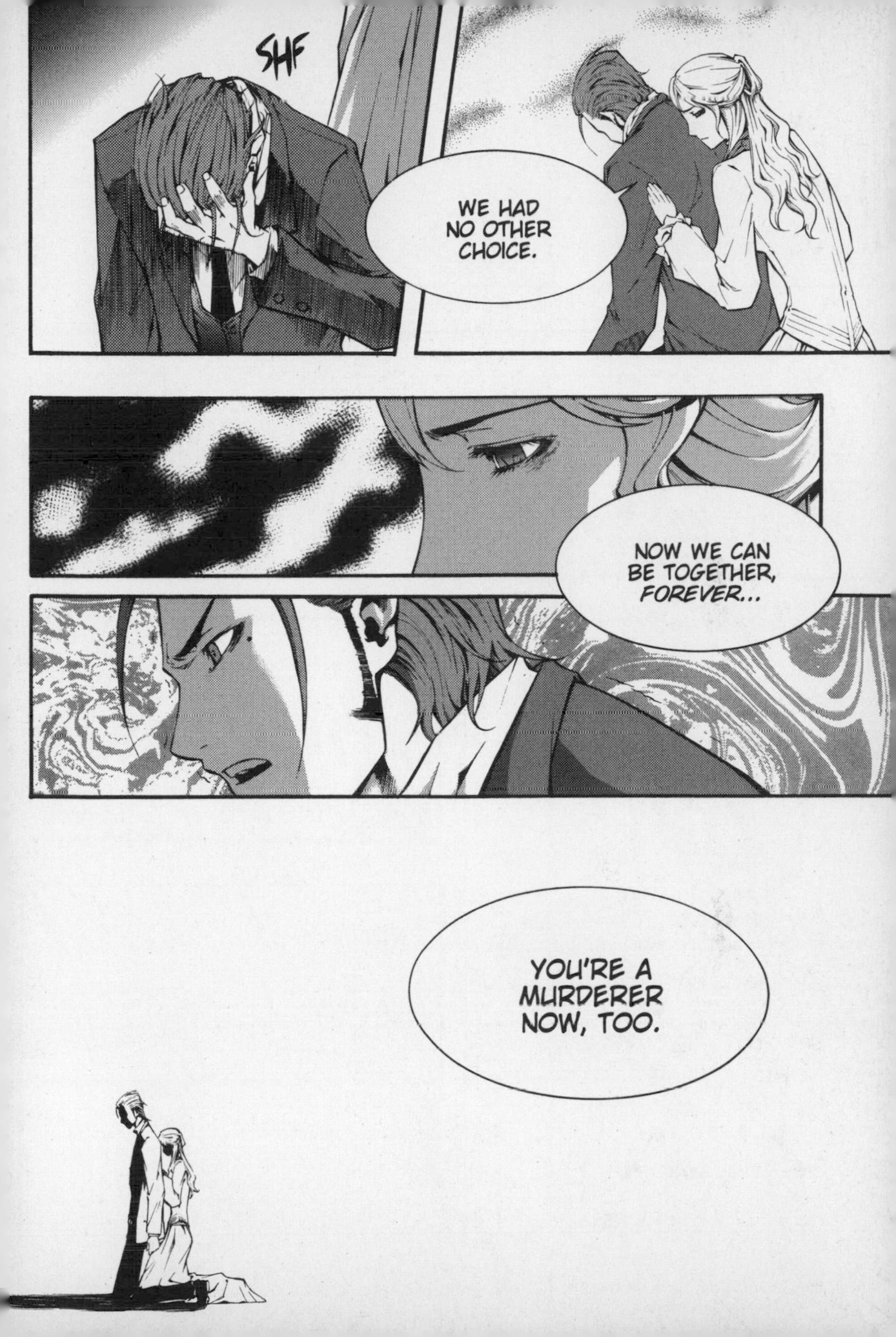
SHF
WE HAD NO OTHER CHOICE.
NOW WE CAN BE TOGETHER, FOREVER...
YOU'RE A MURDERER NOW, TOO.

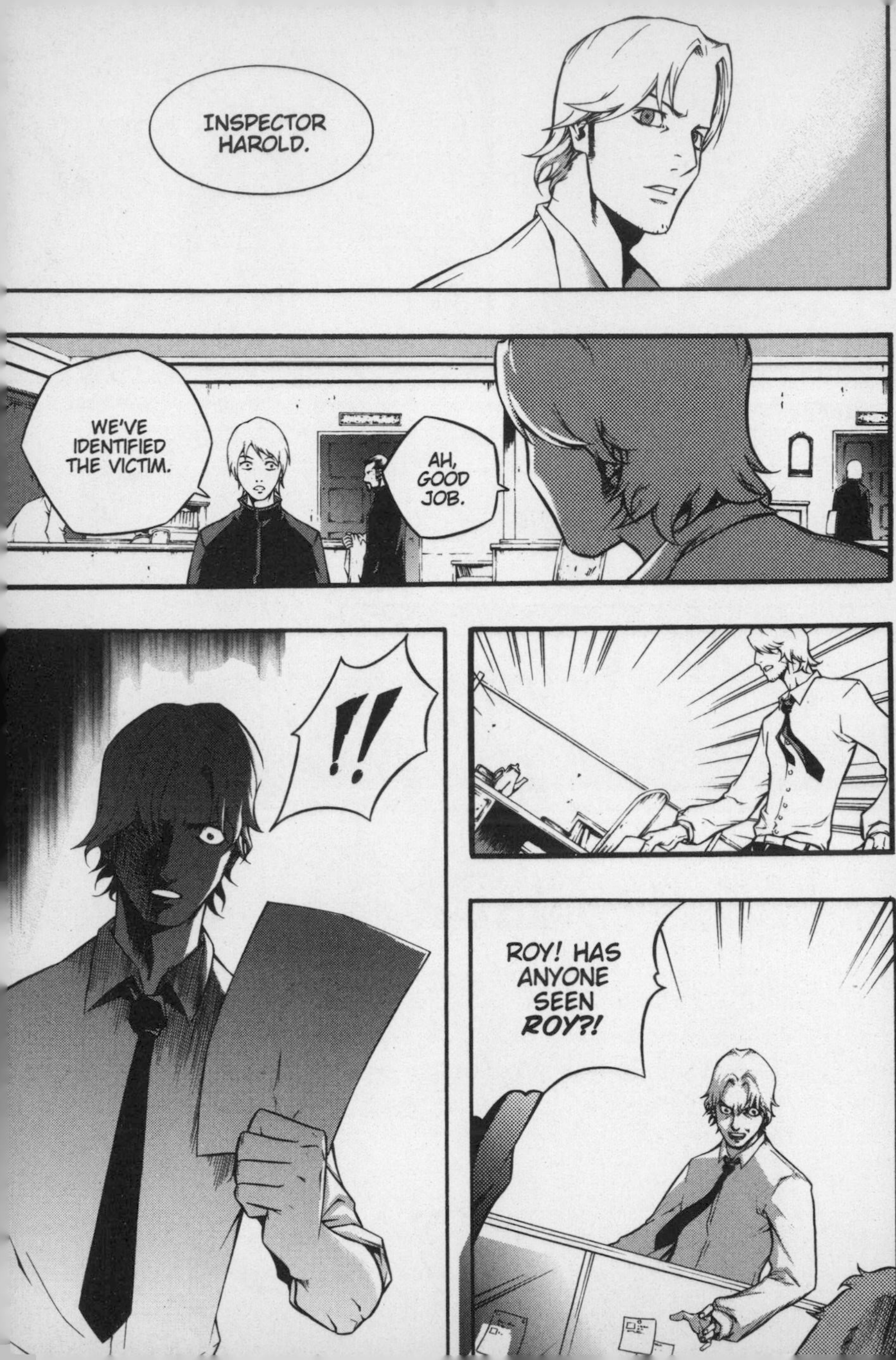
INSPECTOR HAROLD.
WE'VE IDENTIFIED THE VICTIM.
AH, GOOD JOB.
!!
ROY! HAS ANYONE SEEN ROY?!

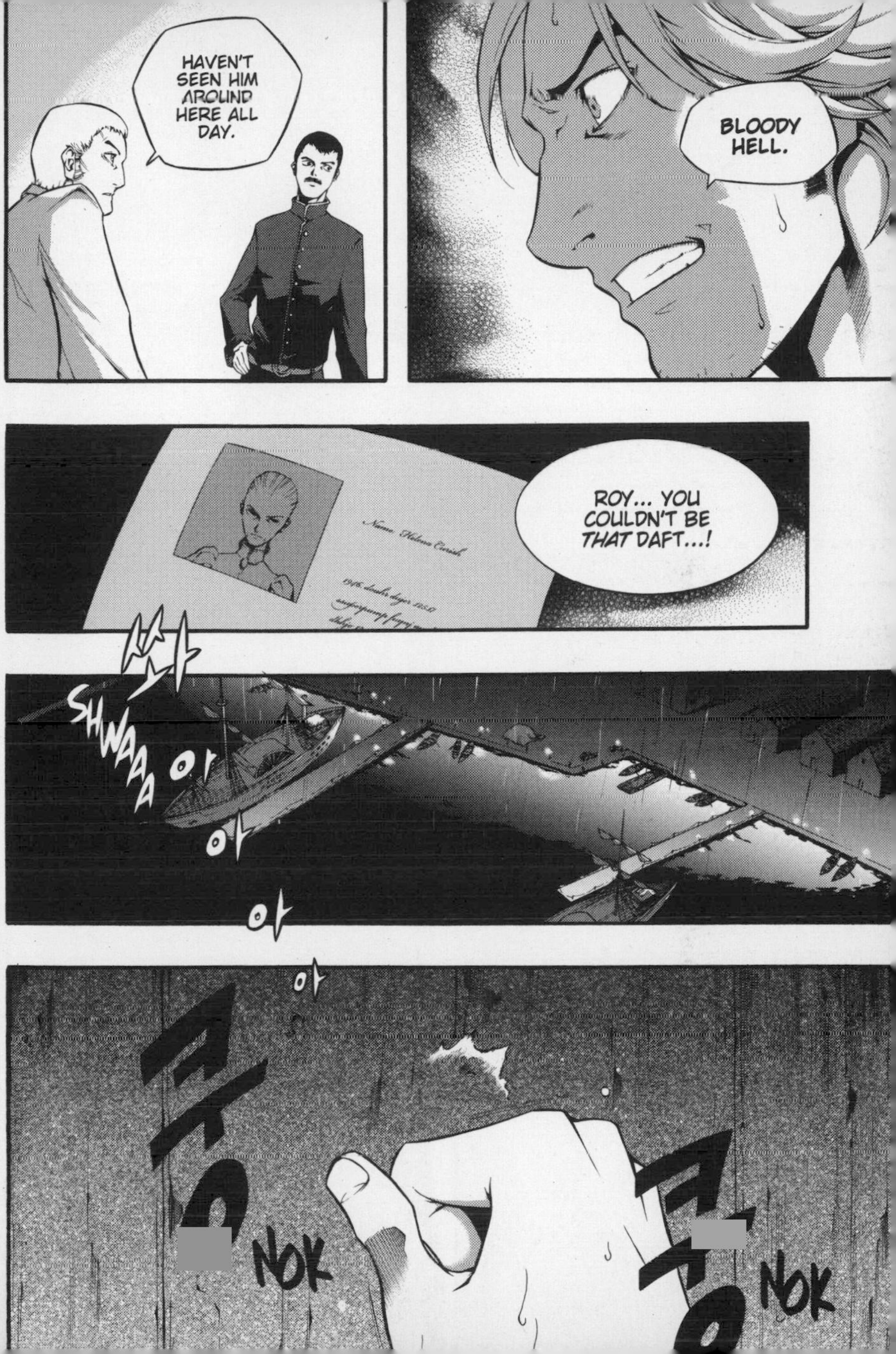
HAVEN'T SEEN HIM AROUND HERE ALL DAY.
BLOODY HELL.
ROY... YOU COULDN'T BE *THAT* DAFT...!
SHWAAA
NOK
NOK

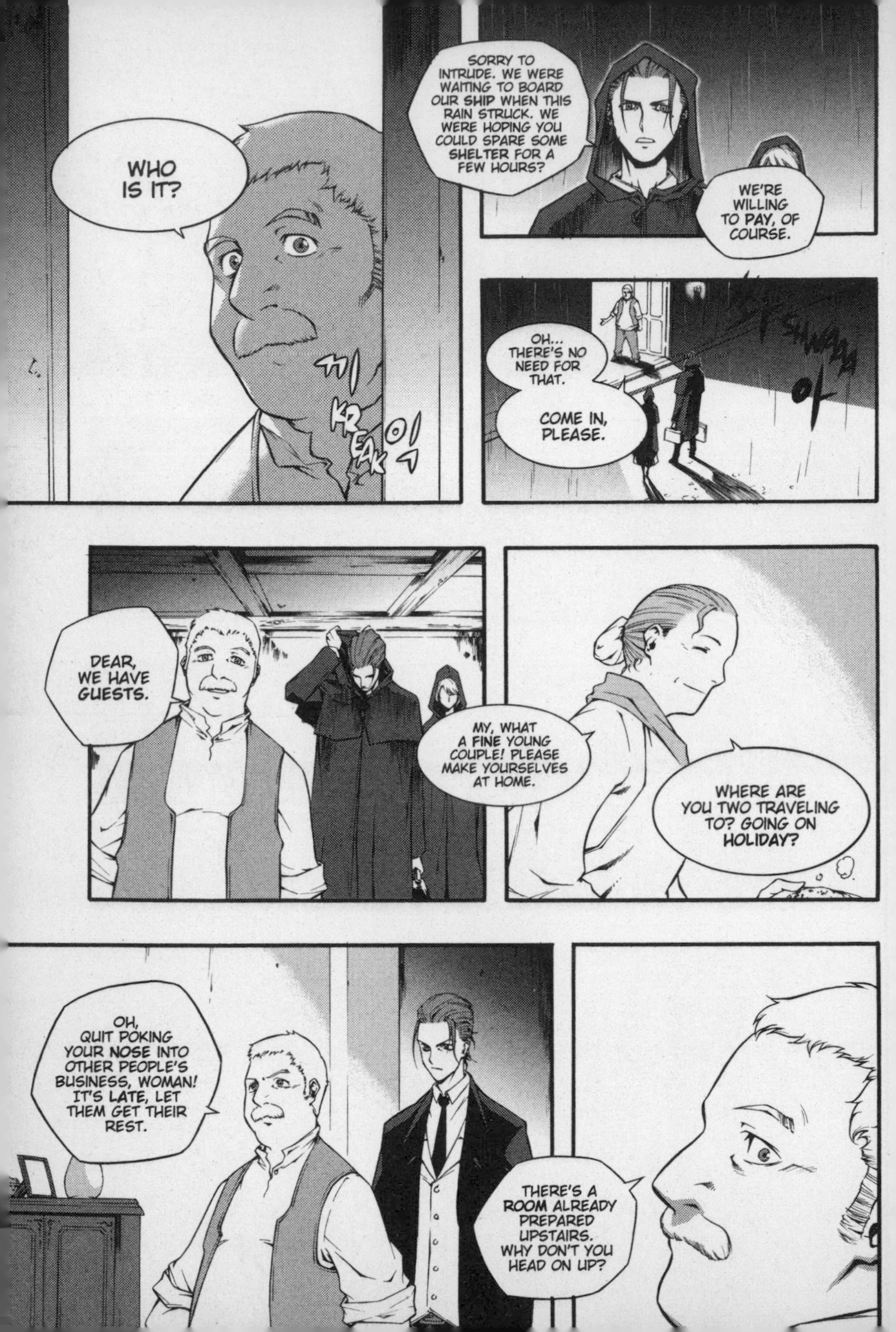
WHO IS IT?
KREAK
SORRY TO INTRUDE. WE WERE WAITING TO BOARD OUR SHIP WHEN THIS RAIN STRUCK. WE WERE HOPING YOU COULD SPARE SOME SHELTER FOR A FEW HOURS?
WE'RE WILLING TO PAY, OF COURSE.
OH... THERE'S NO NEED FOR THAT.
COME IN, PLEASE.
DEAR, WE HAVE GUESTS.
MY, WHAT A FINE YOUNG COUPLE! PLEASE MAKE YOURSELVES AT HOME.
WHERE ARE YOU TWO TRAVELING TO? GOING ON HOLIDAY?
OH, QUIT POKING YOUR NOSE INTO OTHER PEOPLE'S BUSINESS, WOMAN! IT'S LATE, LET THEM GET THEIR REST.
THERE'S A ROOM ALREADY PREPARED UPSTAIRS. WHY DON'T YOU HEAD ON UP?

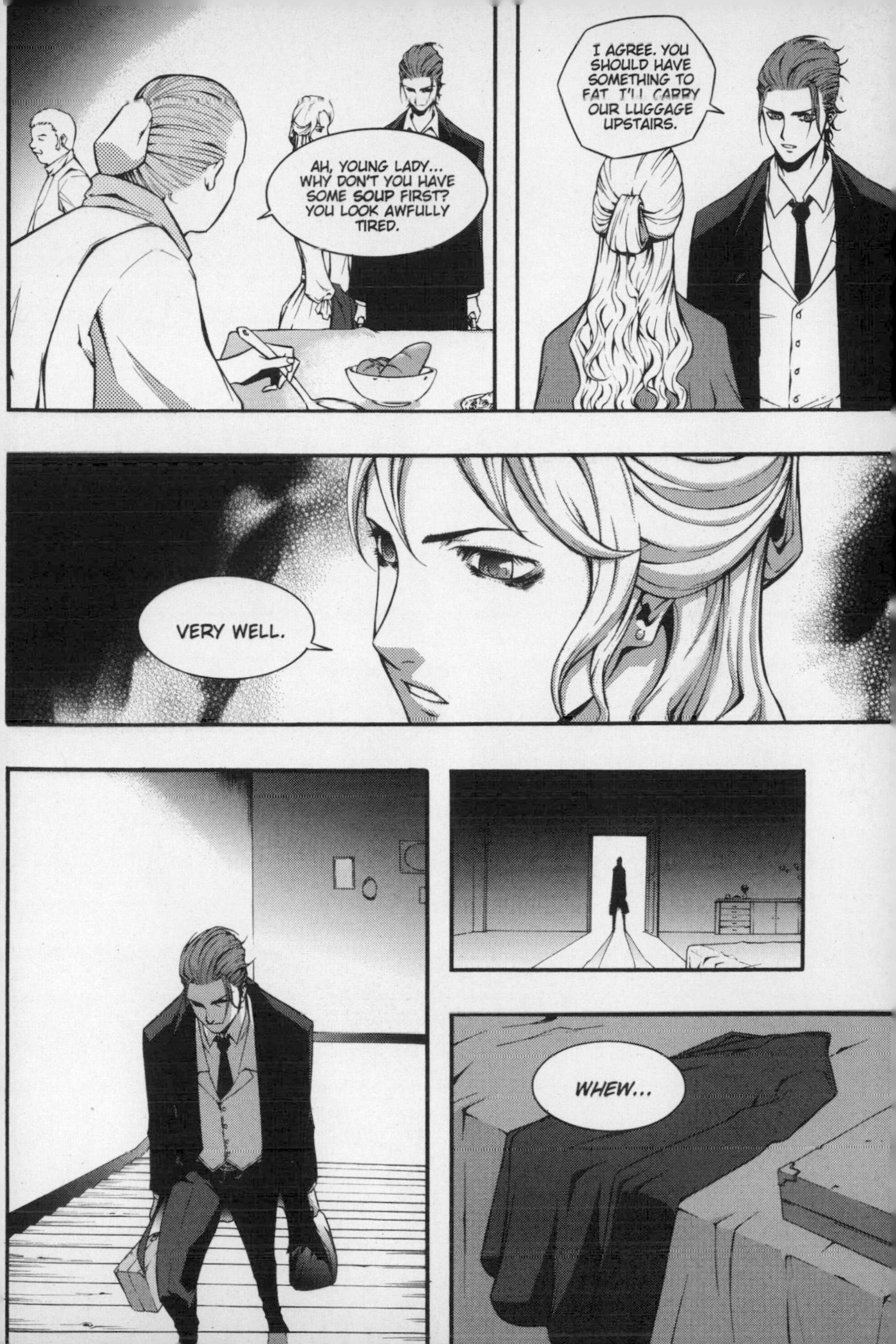
AH, YOUNG LADY... WHY DON'T YOU HAVE SOME SOUP FIRST? YOU LOOK AWFULLY TIRED.
I AGREE. YOU SHOULD HAVE SOMETHING TO EAT. I'LL CARRY OUR LUGGAGE UPSTAIRS.
VERY WELL.
WHEW...

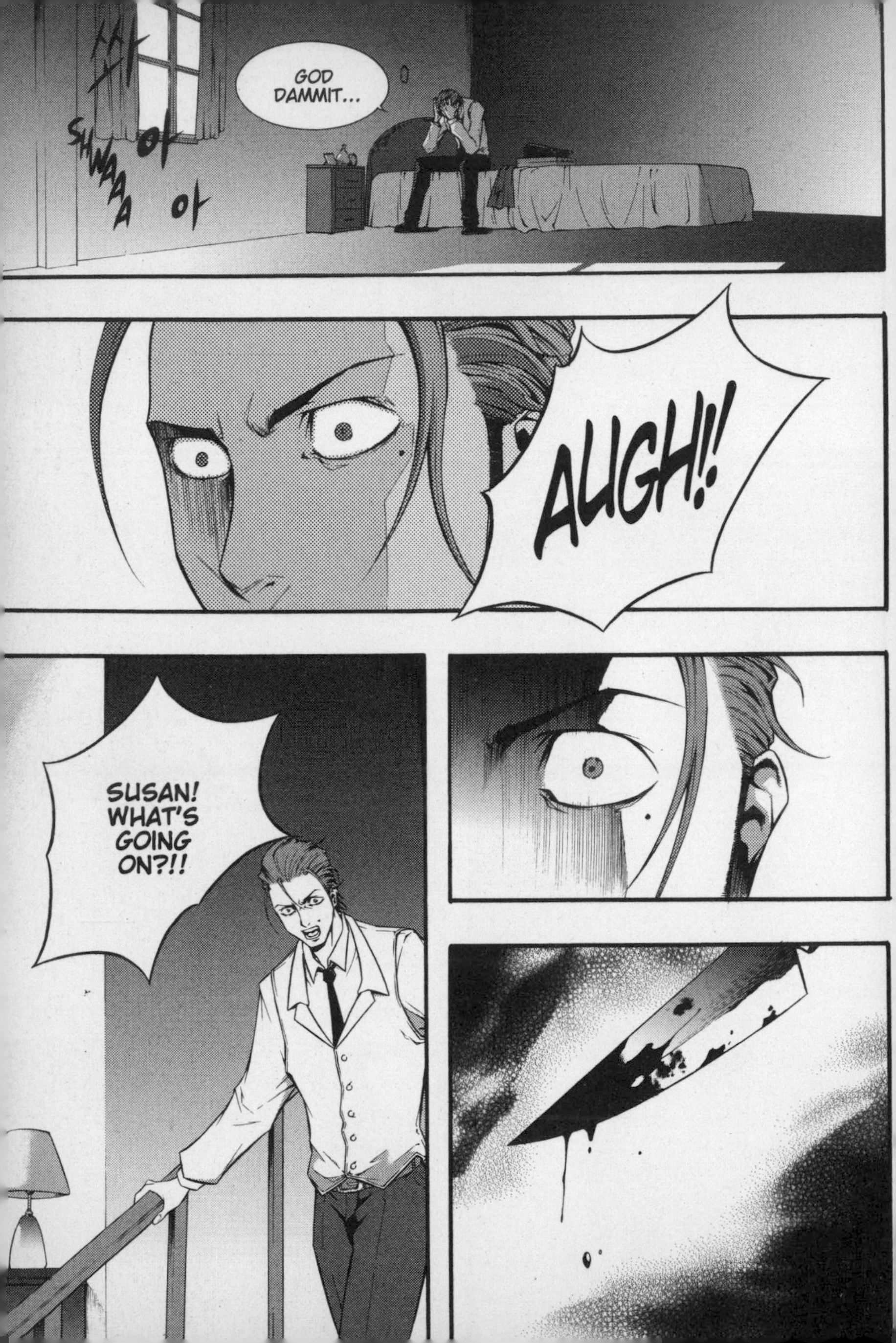

쏴아아
SHWAAAA
GOD DAMMIT...
AUGH!!
SUSAN! WHAT'S GOING ON?!!

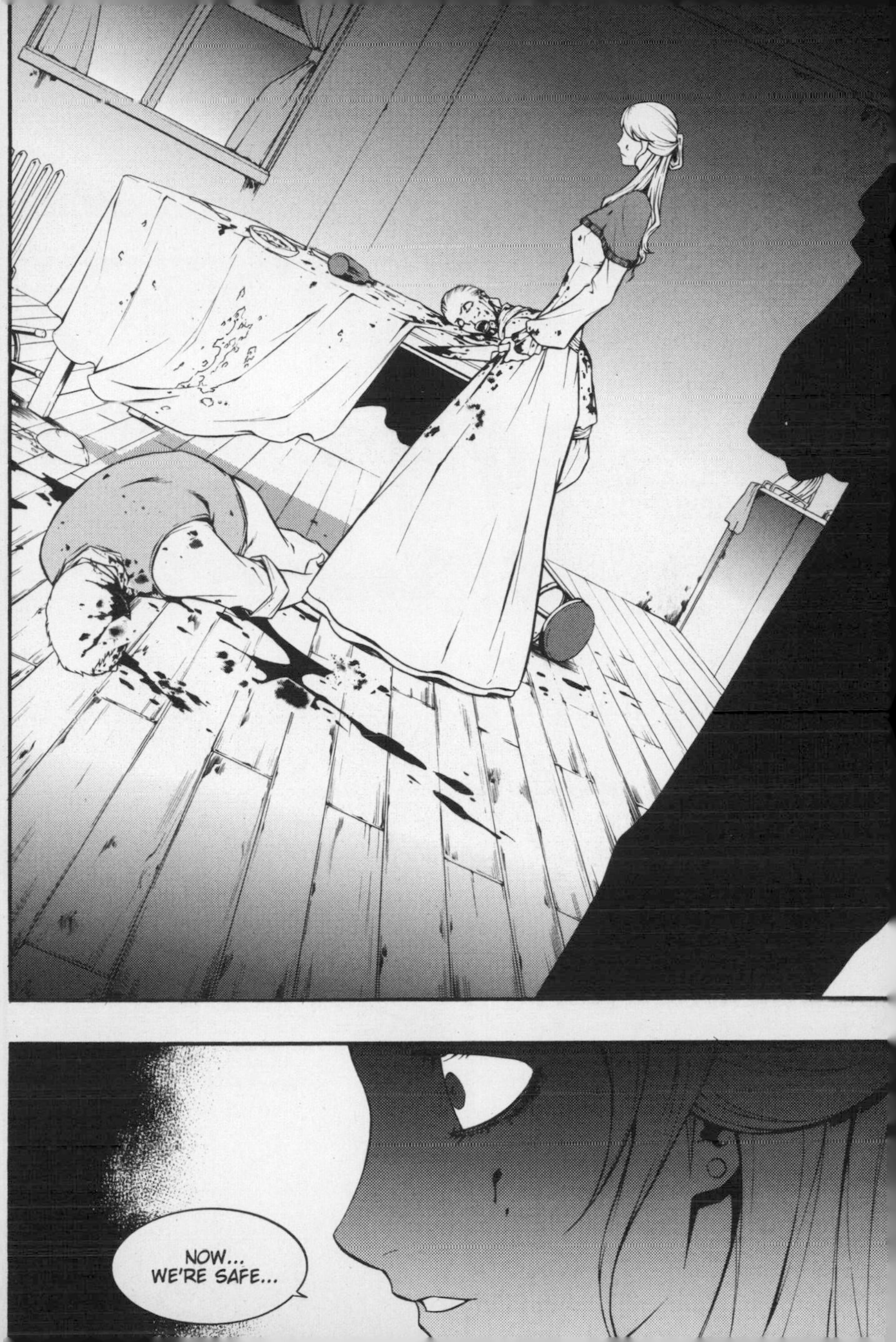
NOW... WE'RE SAFE...

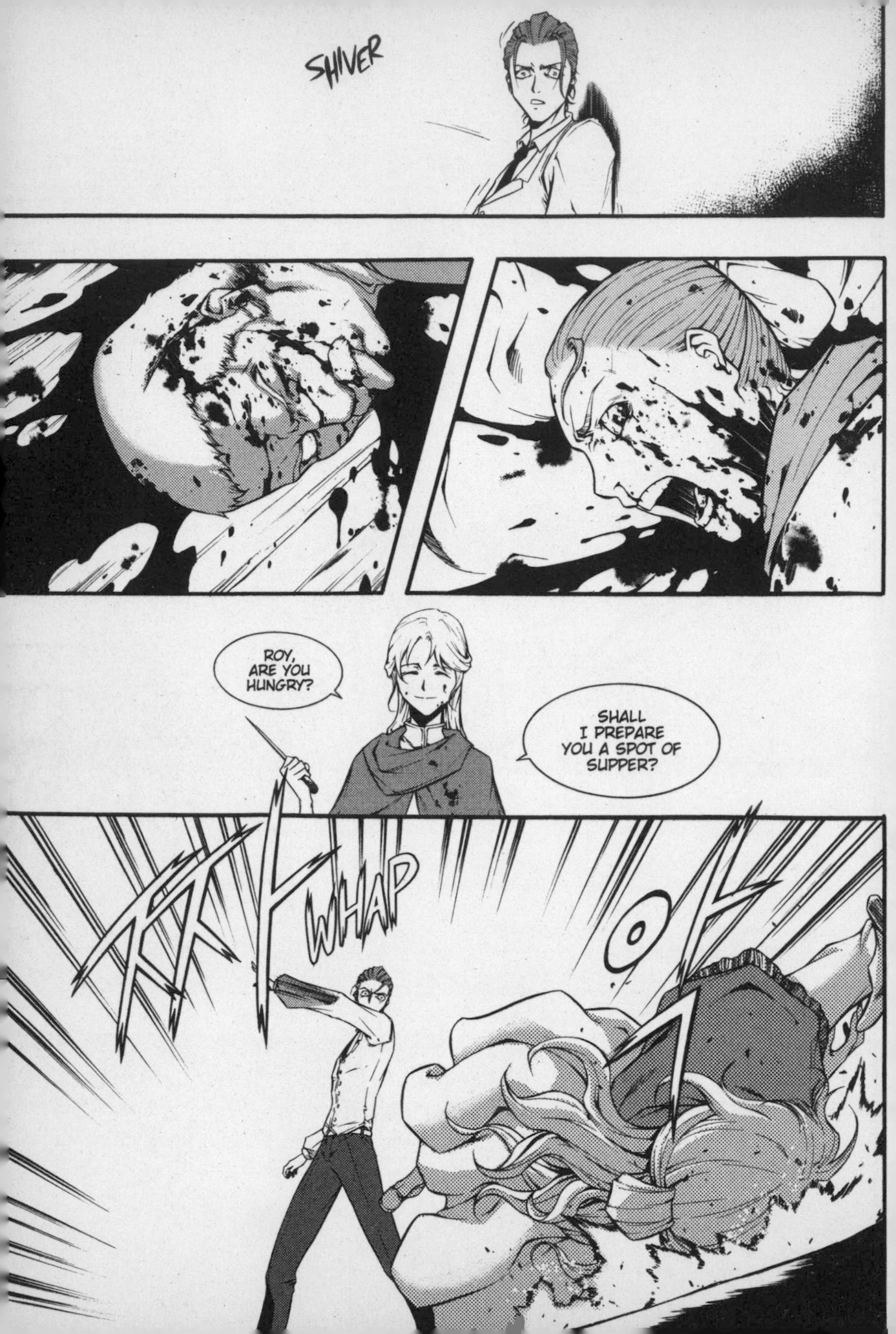
SHIVER
ROY, ARE YOU HUNGRY?
SHALL I PREPARE YOU A SPOT OF SUPPER?
WHAP

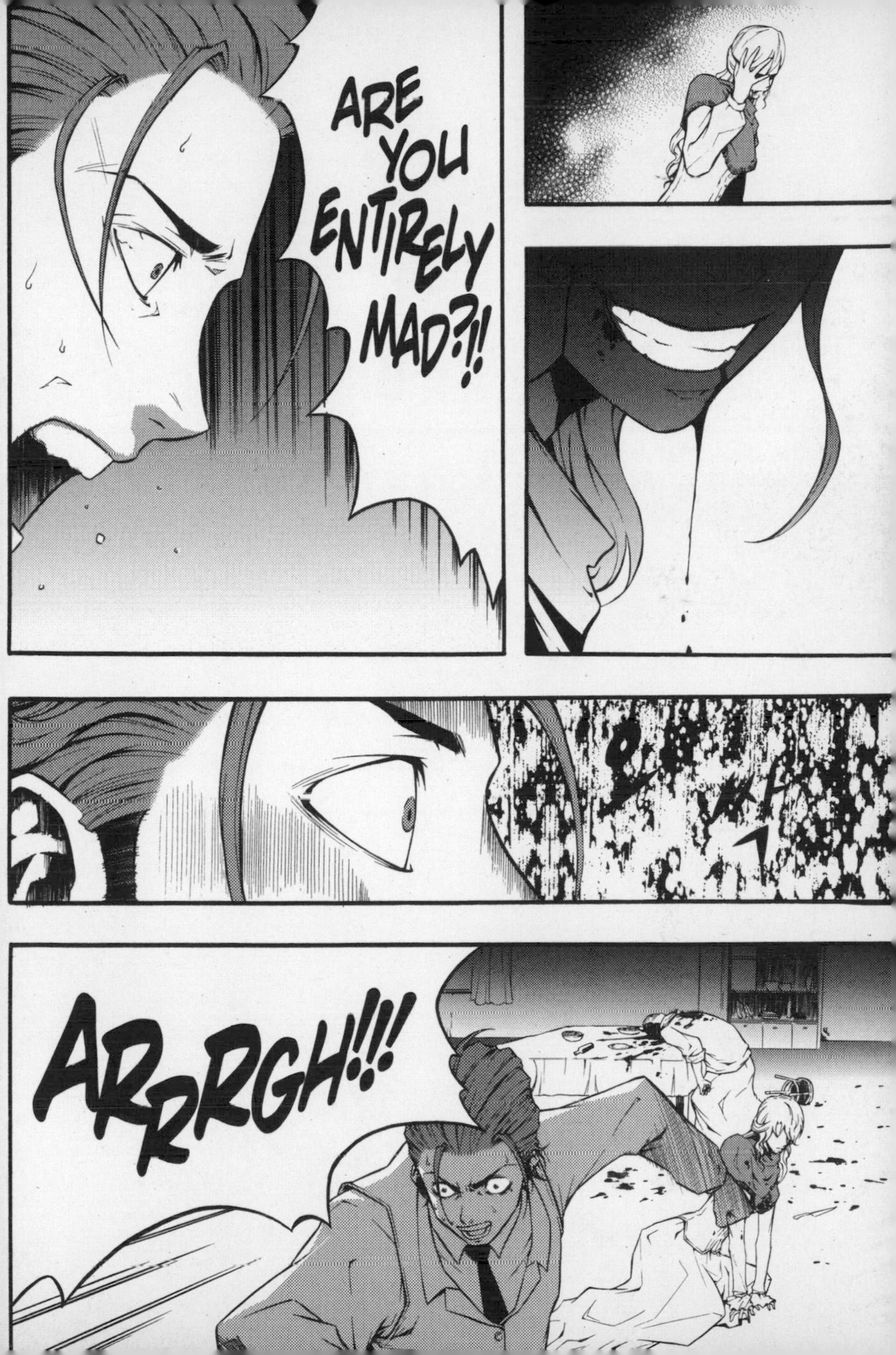
ARE YOU ENTIRELY MAD?!!
ARRRGH!!!

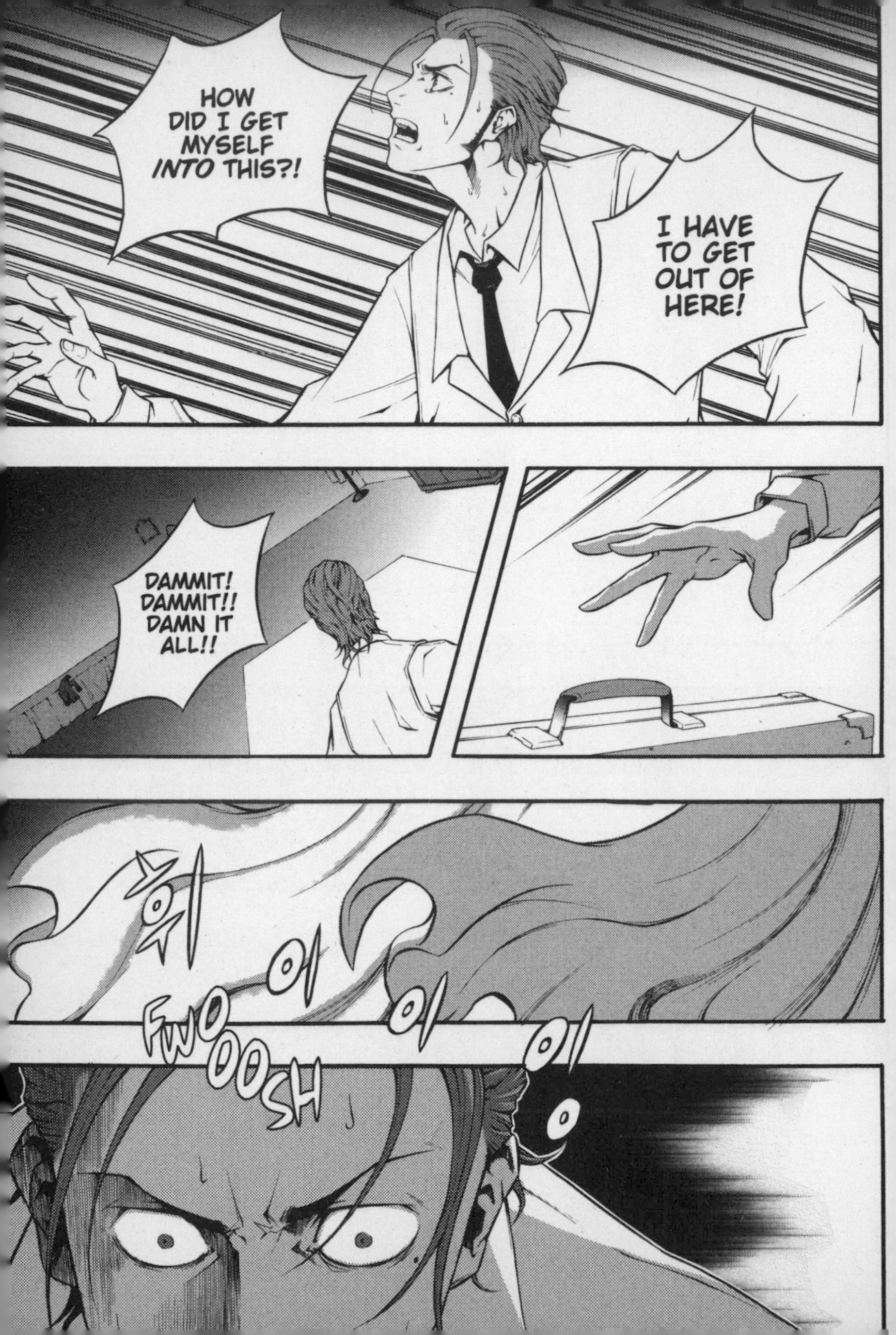
HOW DID I GET MYSELF *INTO* THIS?!
I HAVE TO GET OUT OF HERE!
DAMMIT! DAMMIT!! DAMN IT ALL!!
FWOOOSH

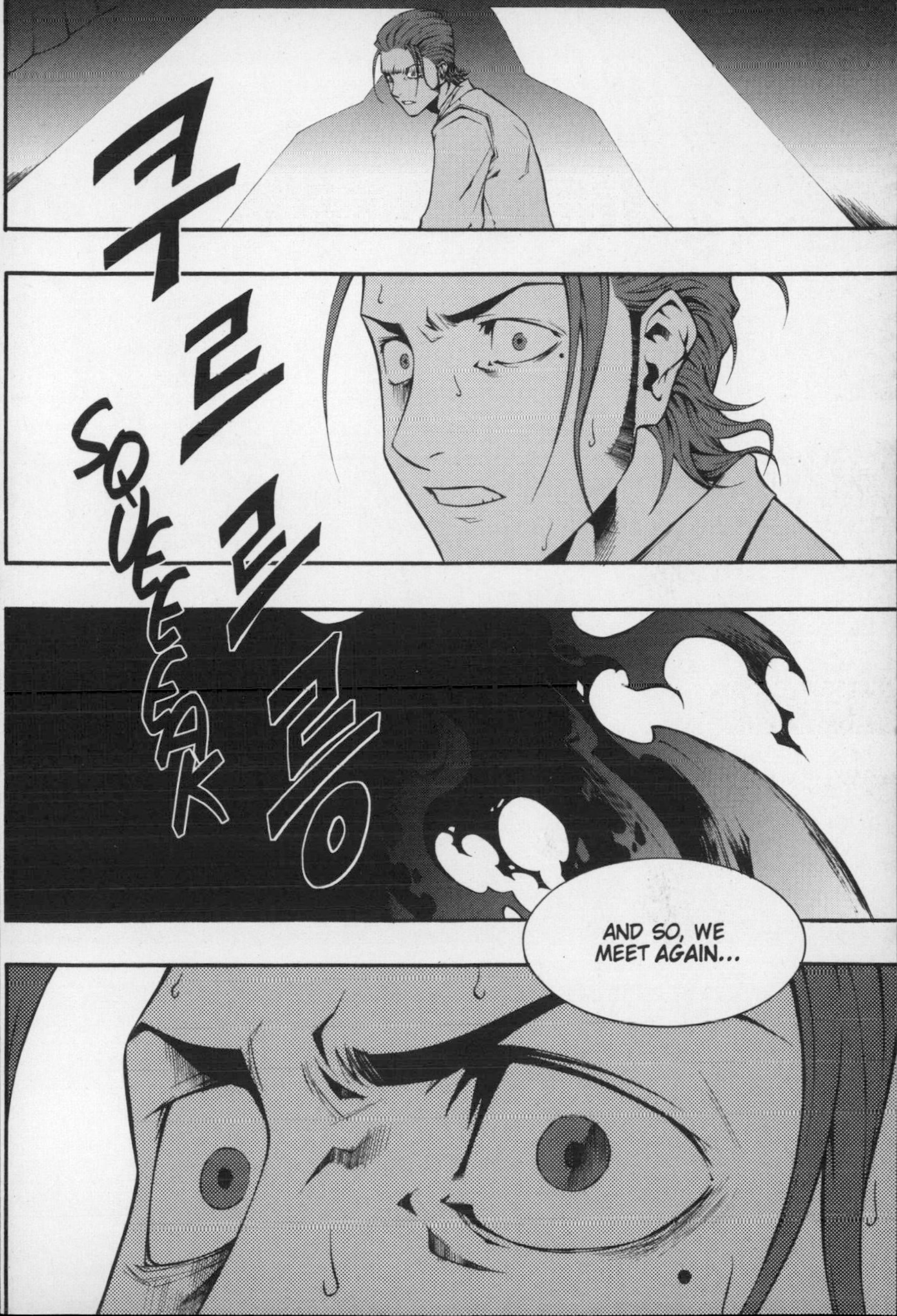
SQUEEEAK
AND SO, WE MEET AGAIN...

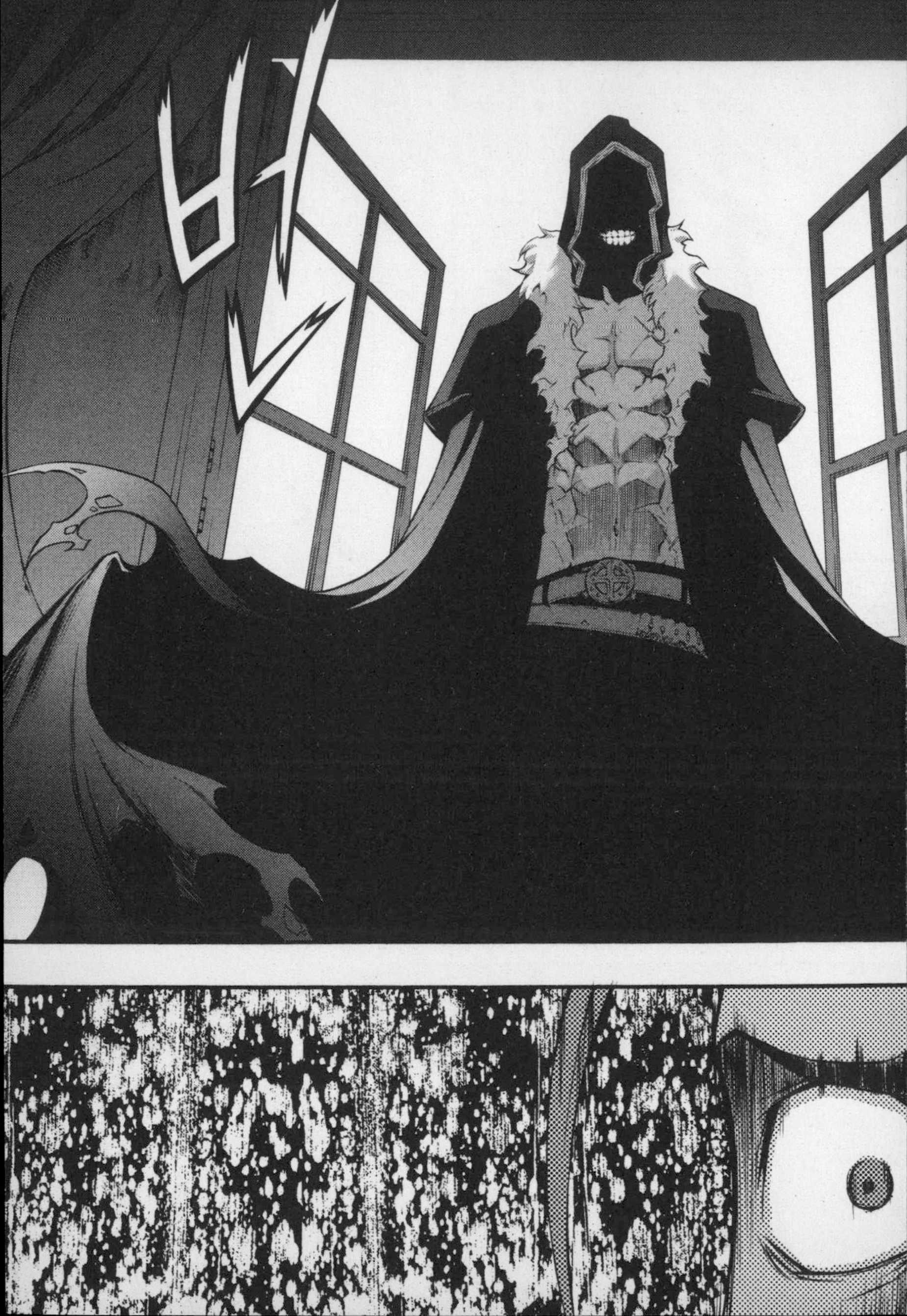

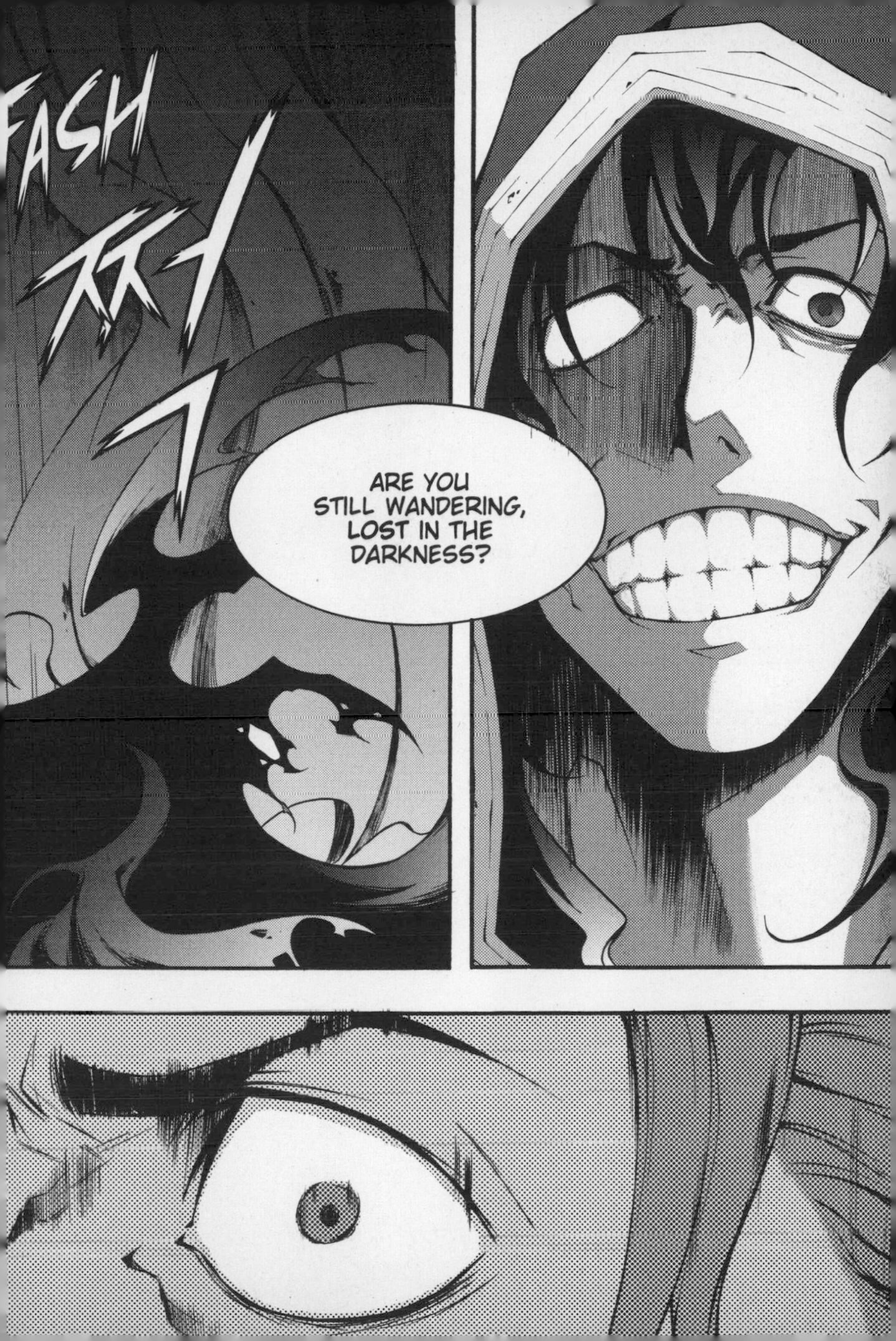
FASH
ARE YOU STILL WANDERING, LOST IN THE DARKNESS?

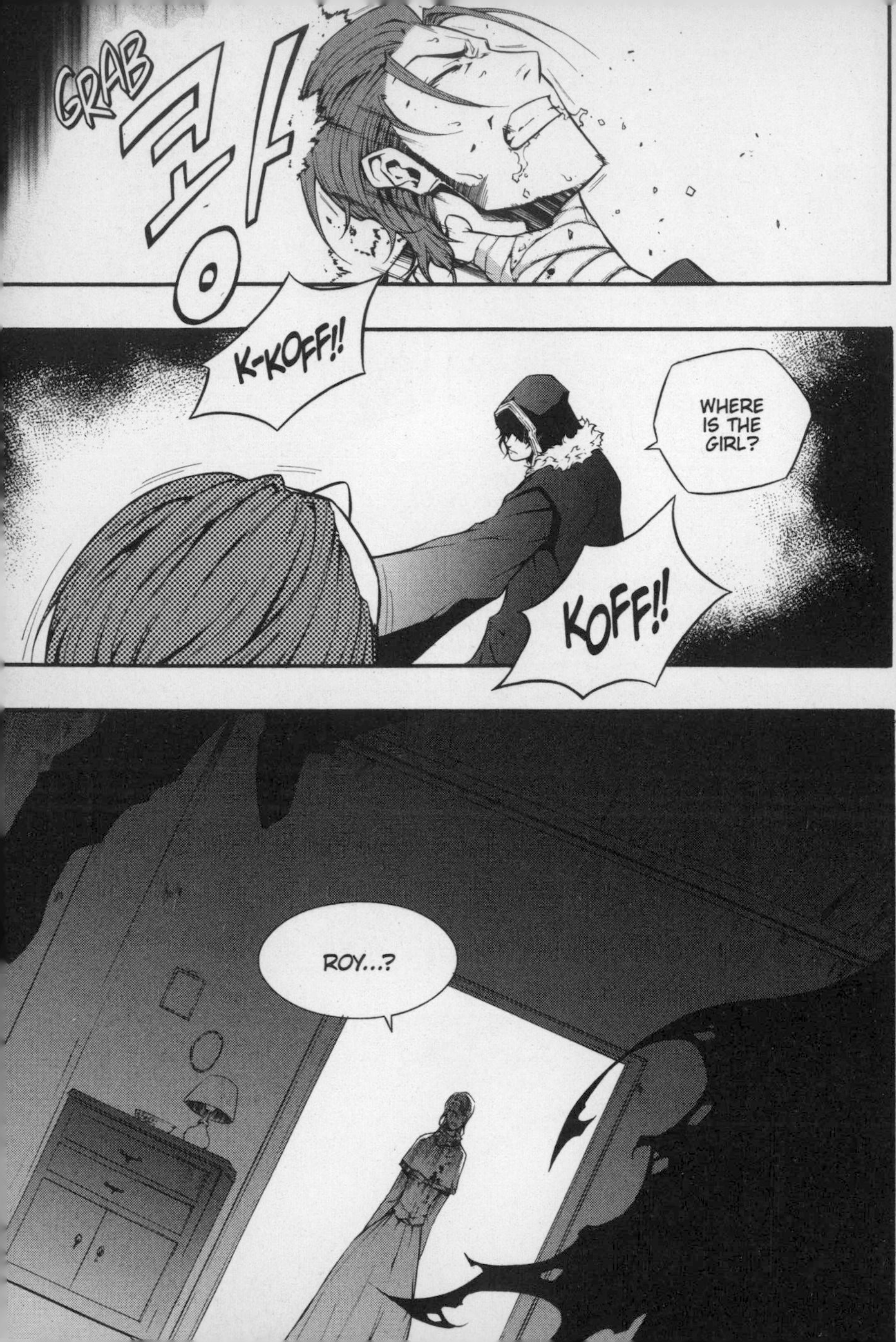
GRAB
K-KOFF!!
WHERE IS THE GIRL?
KOFF!!
ROY...?

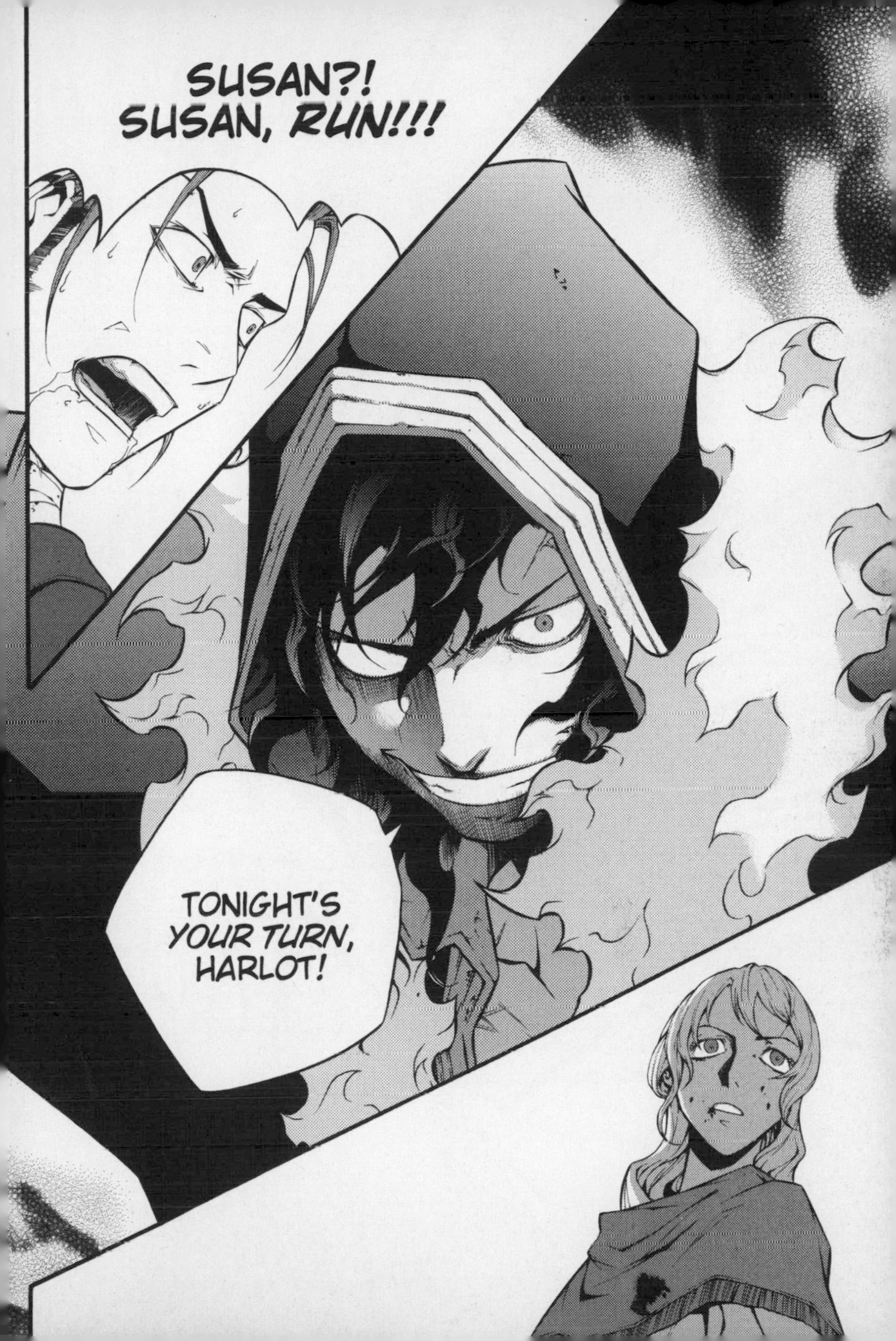
SUSAN?! SUSAN, RUN!!!
TONIGHT'S YOUR TURN, HARLOT!

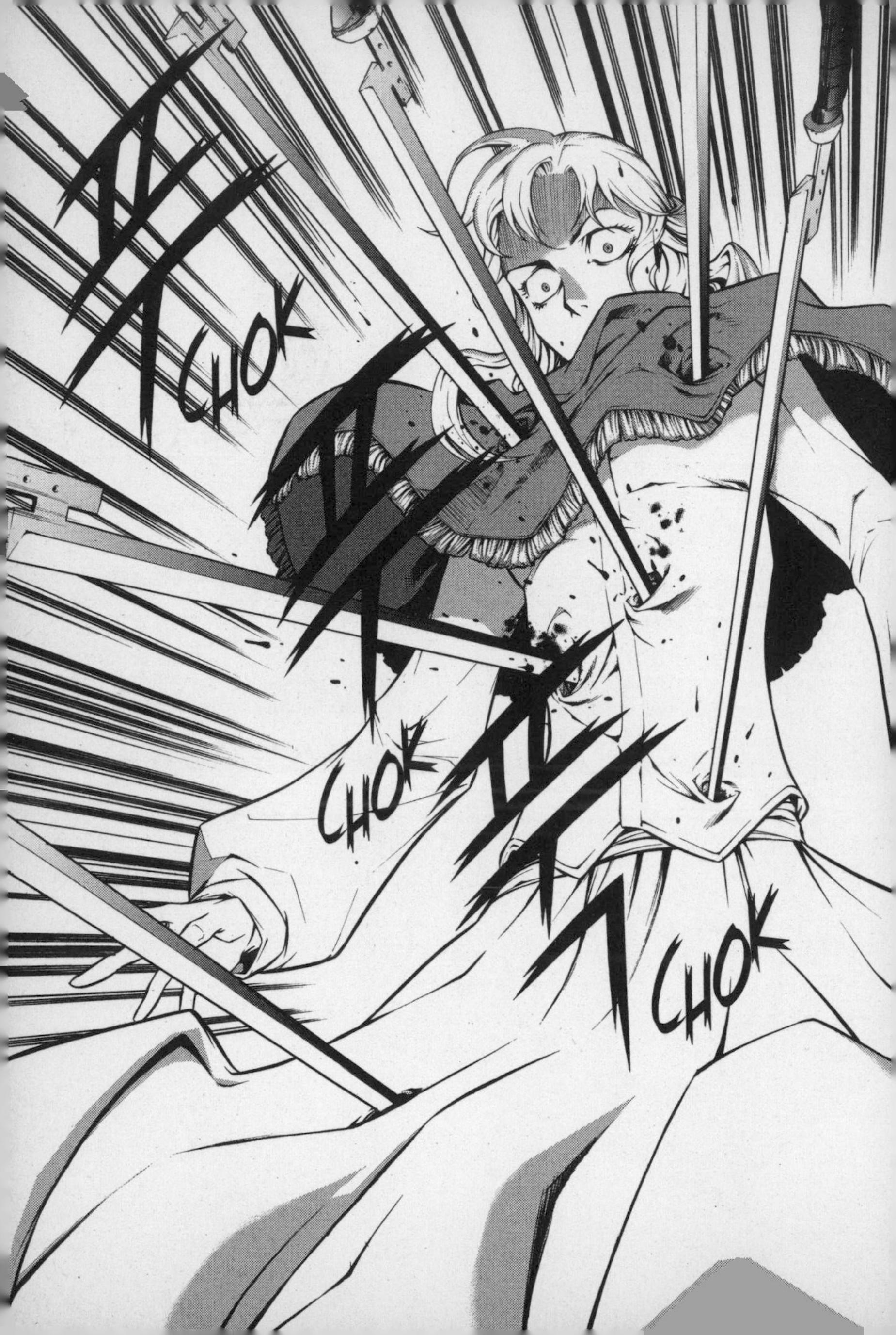
CHOK
CHOK
CHOK

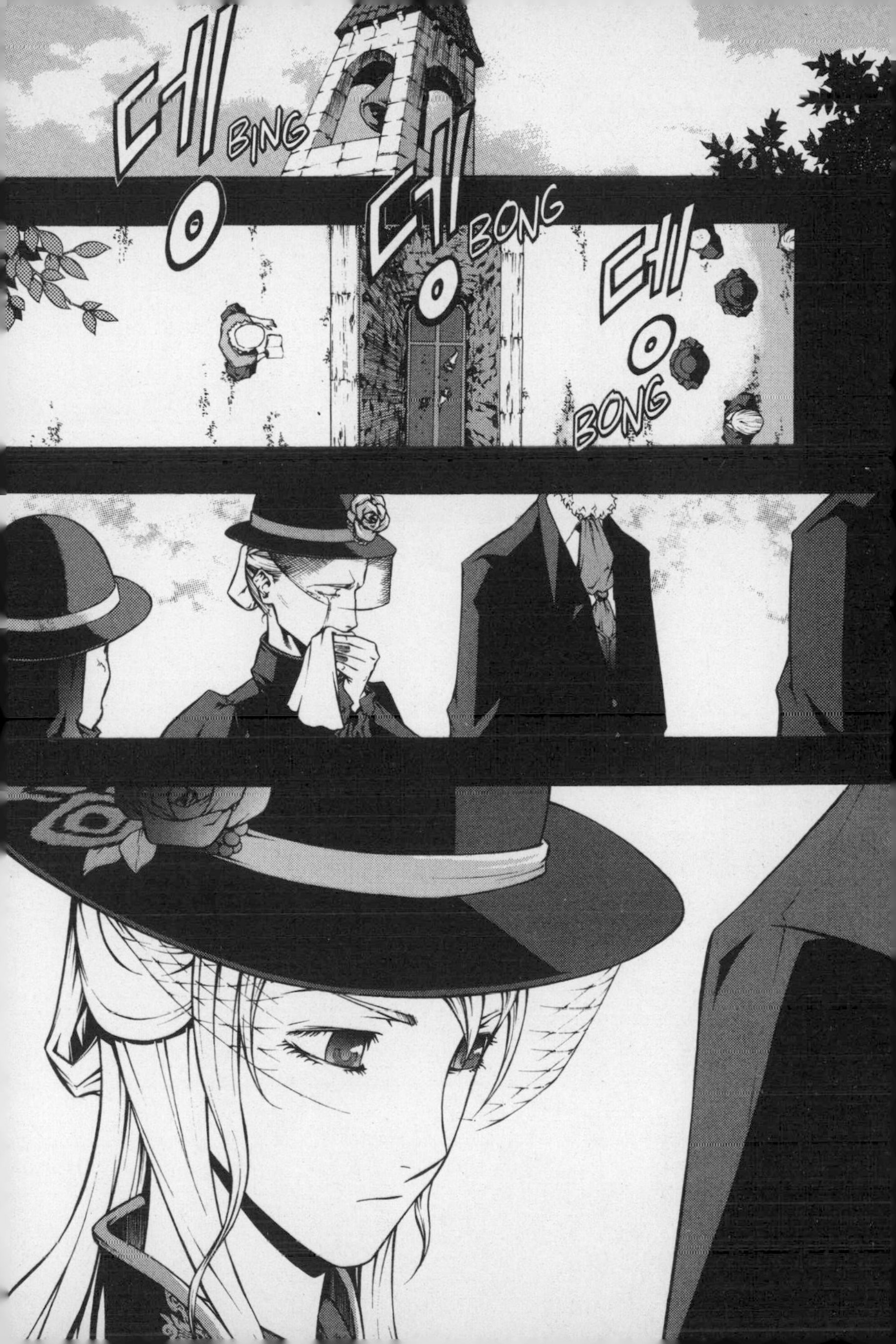

딩
BING
딩
BONG
딩
BONG

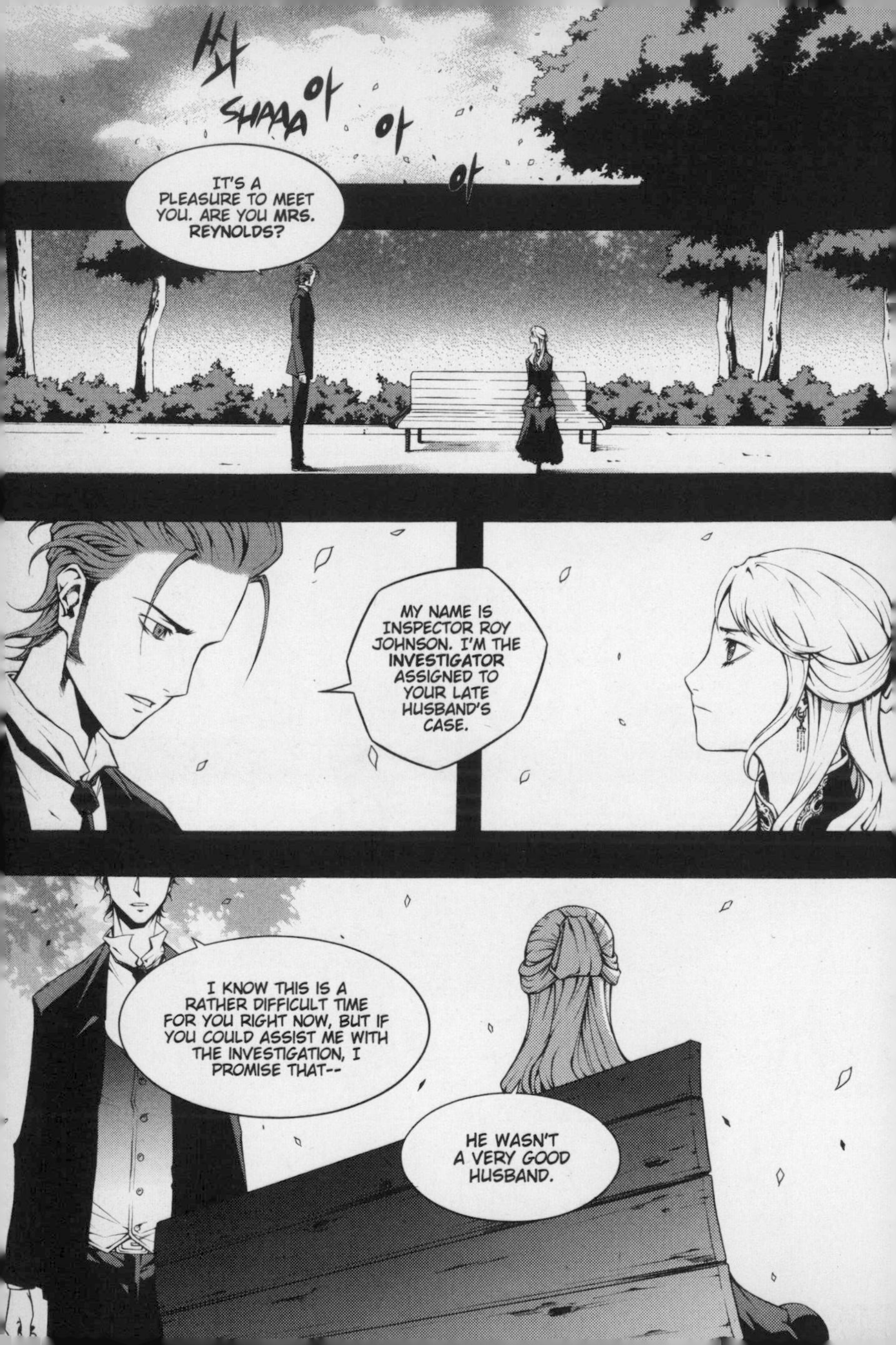
싸
SHAAA
아
아
아
IT'S A PLEASURE TO MEET YOU. ARE YOU MRS. REYNOLDS?
MY NAME IS INSPECTOR ROY JOHNSON. I'M THE INVESTIGATOR ASSIGNED TO YOUR LATE HUSBAND'S CASE.
I KNOW THIS IS A RATHER DIFFICULT TIME FOR YOU RIGHT NOW, BUT IF YOU COULD ASSIST ME WITH THE INVESTIGATION, I PROMISE THAT--
HE WASN'T A VERY GOOD HUSBAND.

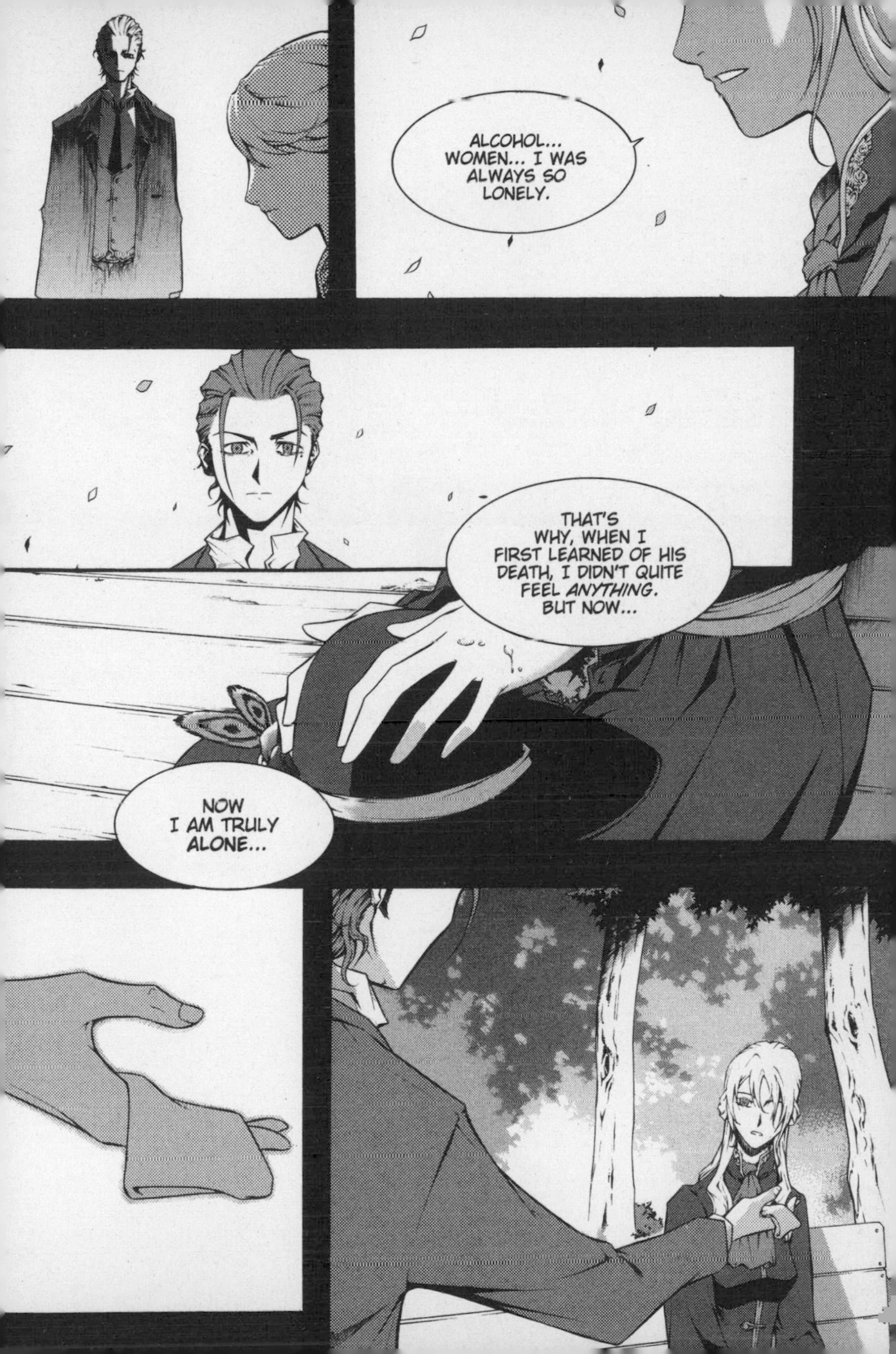
ALCOHOL... WOMEN... I WAS ALWAYS SO LONELY.
THAT'S WHY, WHEN I FIRST LEARNED OF HIS DEATH, I DIDN'T QUITE FEEL *ANYTHING*. BUT NOW...
NOW I AM TRULY ALONE...

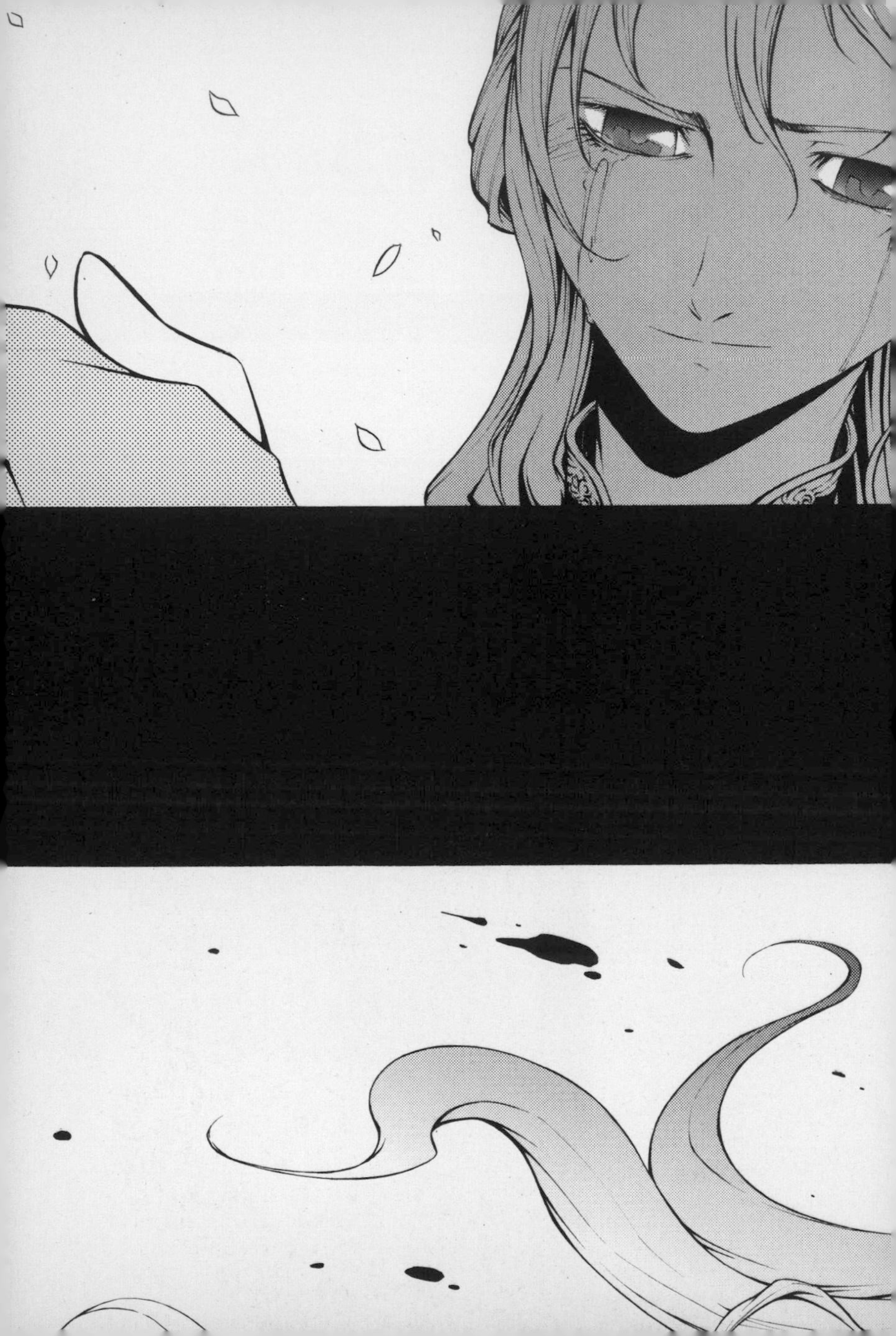

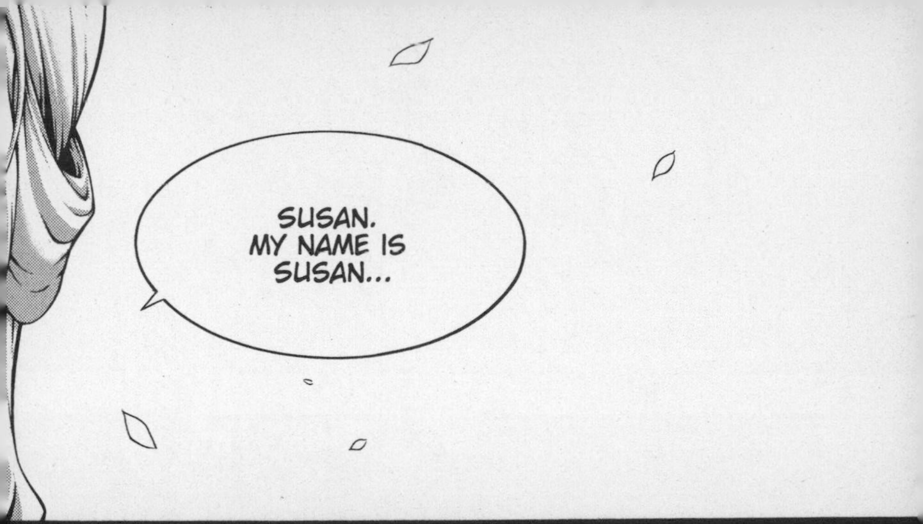
SUSAN. MY NAME IS SUSAN...

EPISODE 4

WALKING IN THE MIDNIGHT (4)

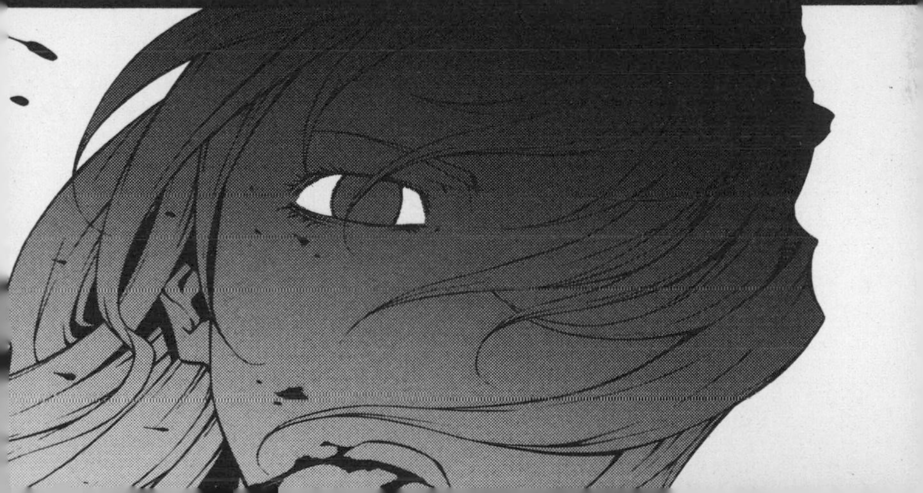

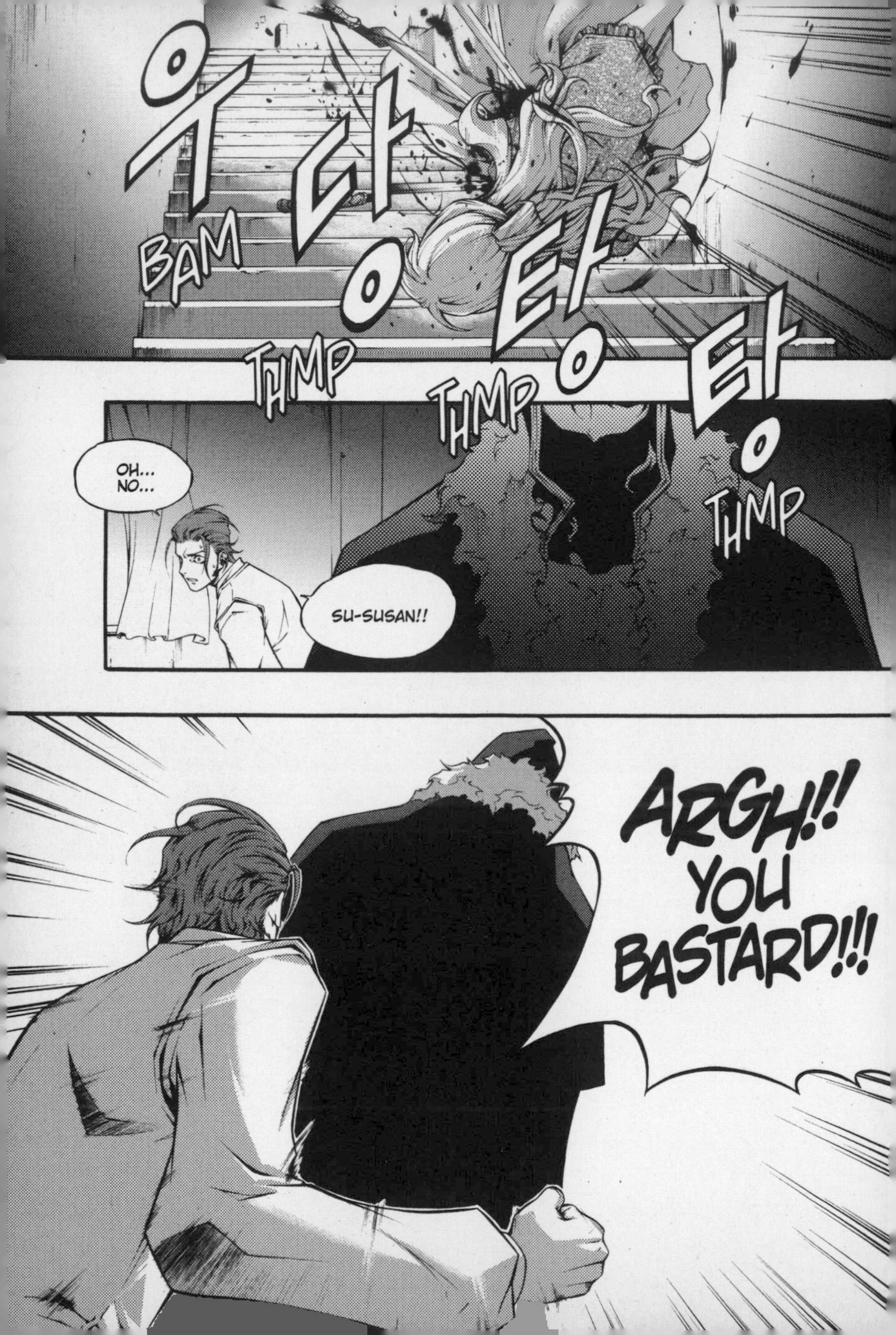
BAM
THMP
THMP
THMP
OH... NO...
SU-SUSAN!!
ARGH!! YOU BASTARD!!!

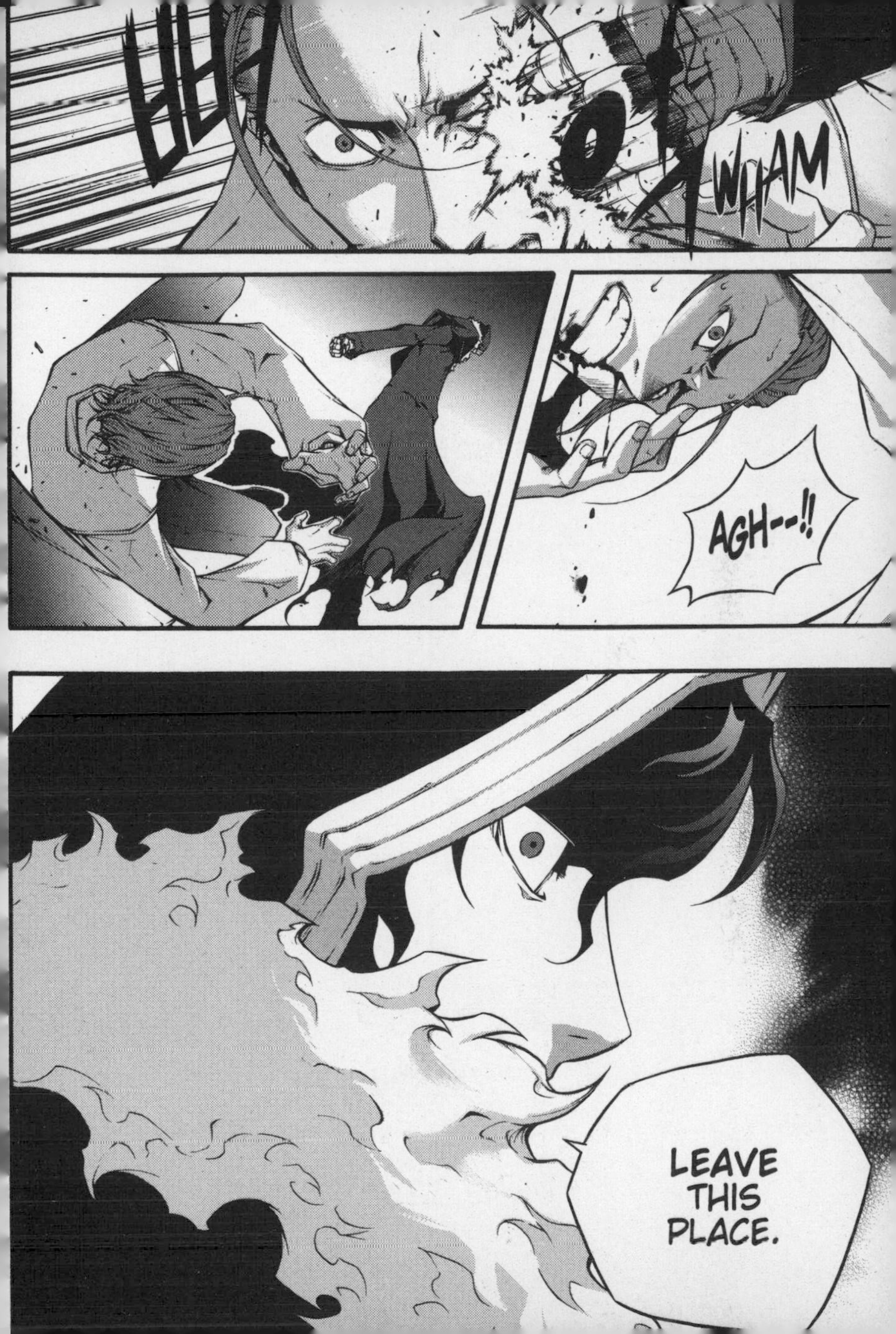
WHAM
AGH--!!
LEAVE THIS PLACE.

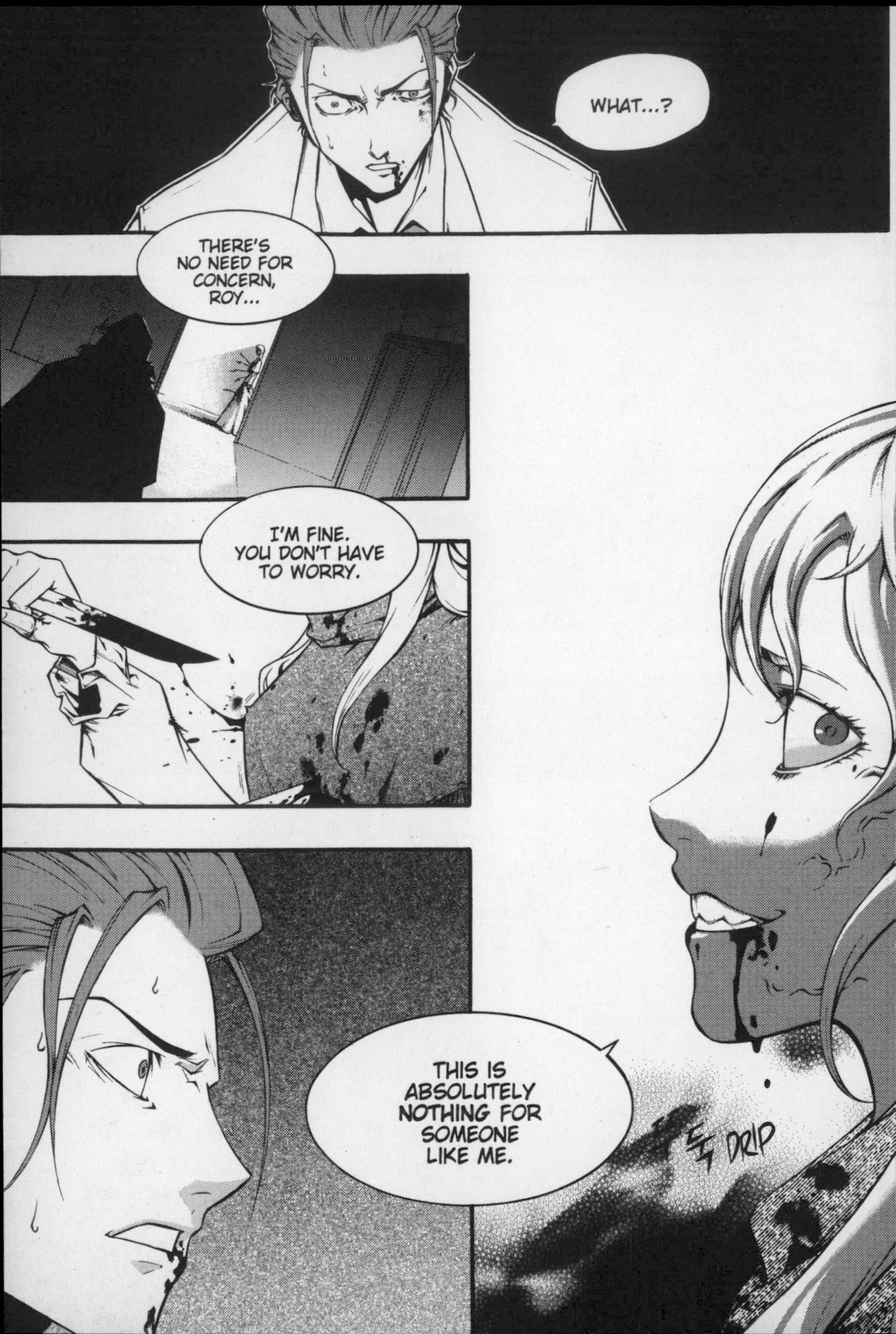
WHAT...?
THERE'S NO NEED FOR CONCERN, ROY...
I'M FINE. YOU DON'T HAVE TO WORRY.
THIS IS ABSOLUTELY NOTHING FOR SOMEONE LIKE ME.
DRIP

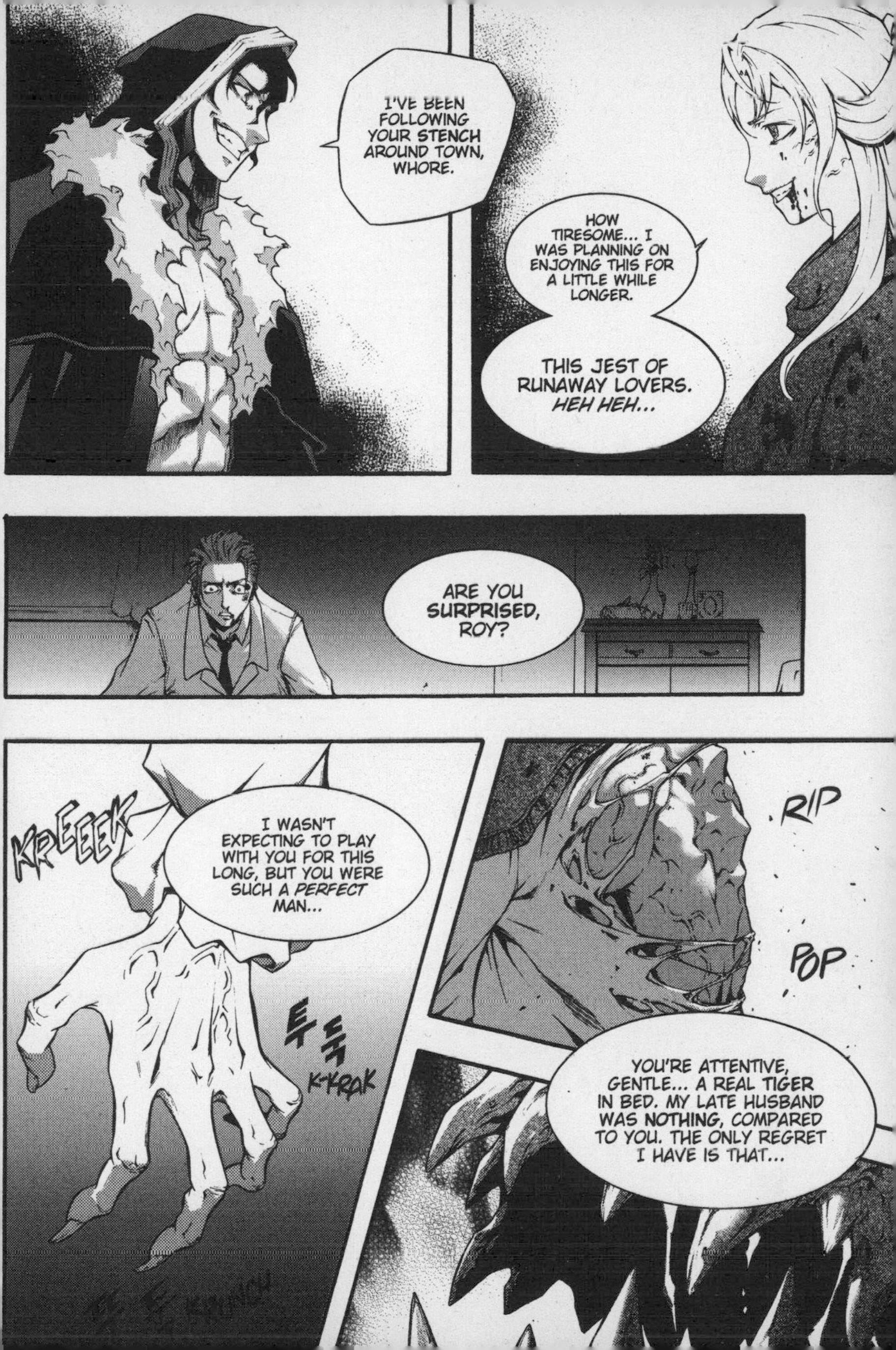
I'VE BEEN FOLLOWING YOUR STENCH AROUND TOWN, WHORE.
HOW TIRESOME... I WAS PLANNING ON ENJOYING THIS FOR A LITTLE WHILE LONGER.
THIS JEST OF RUNAWAY LOVERS. *HEH HEH...*
ARE YOU SURPRISED, ROY?
KREEEK
I WASN'T EXPECTING TO PLAY WITH YOU FOR THIS LONG, BUT YOU WERE SUCH A *PERFECT* MAN...
K-KRAK
RIP
POP
YOU'RE ATTENTIVE, GENTLE... A REAL TIGER IN BED. MY LATE HUSBAND WAS NOTHING, COMPARED TO YOU. THE ONLY REGRET I HAVE IS THAT...

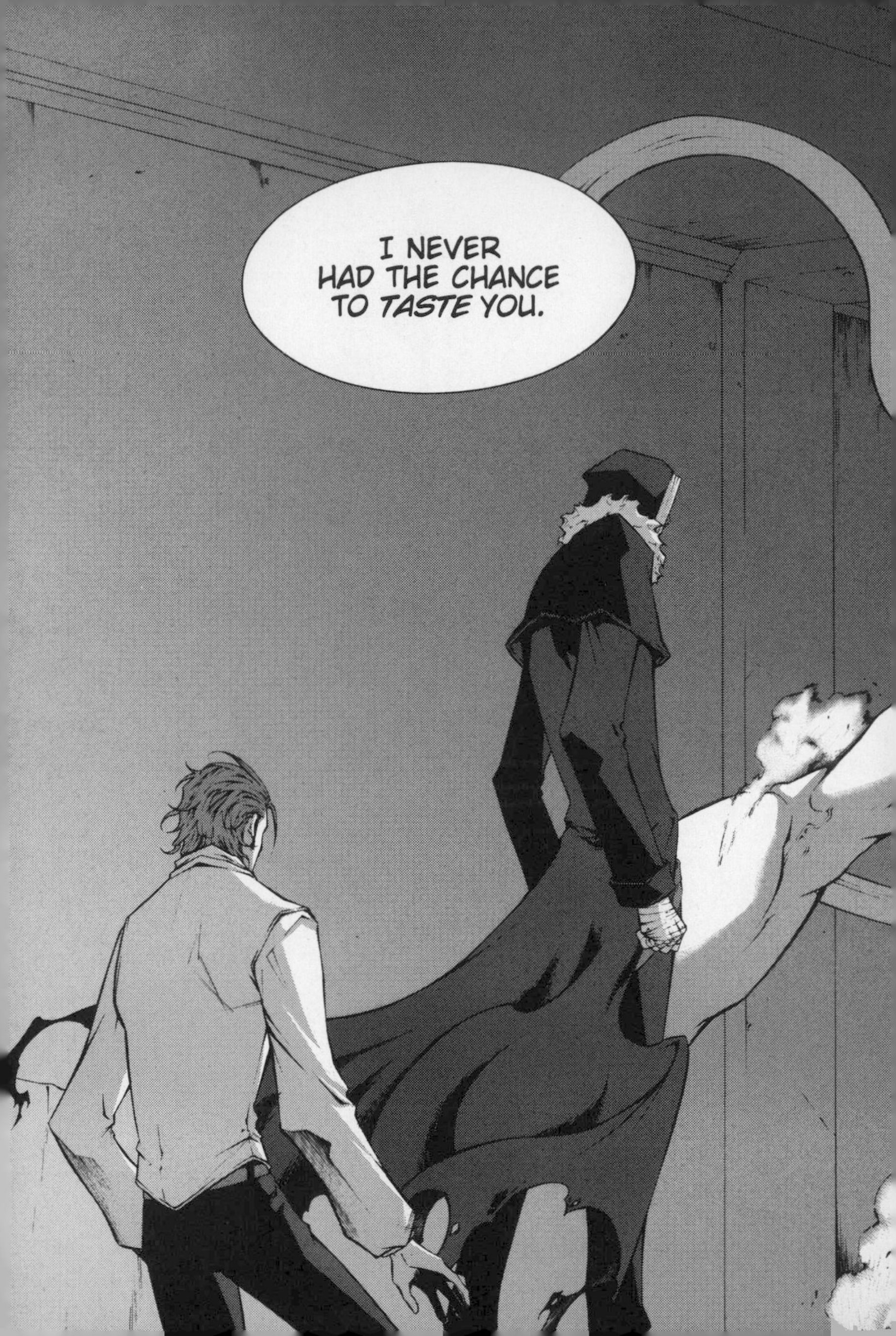
I NEVER HAD THE CHANCE TO *TASTE* YOU.

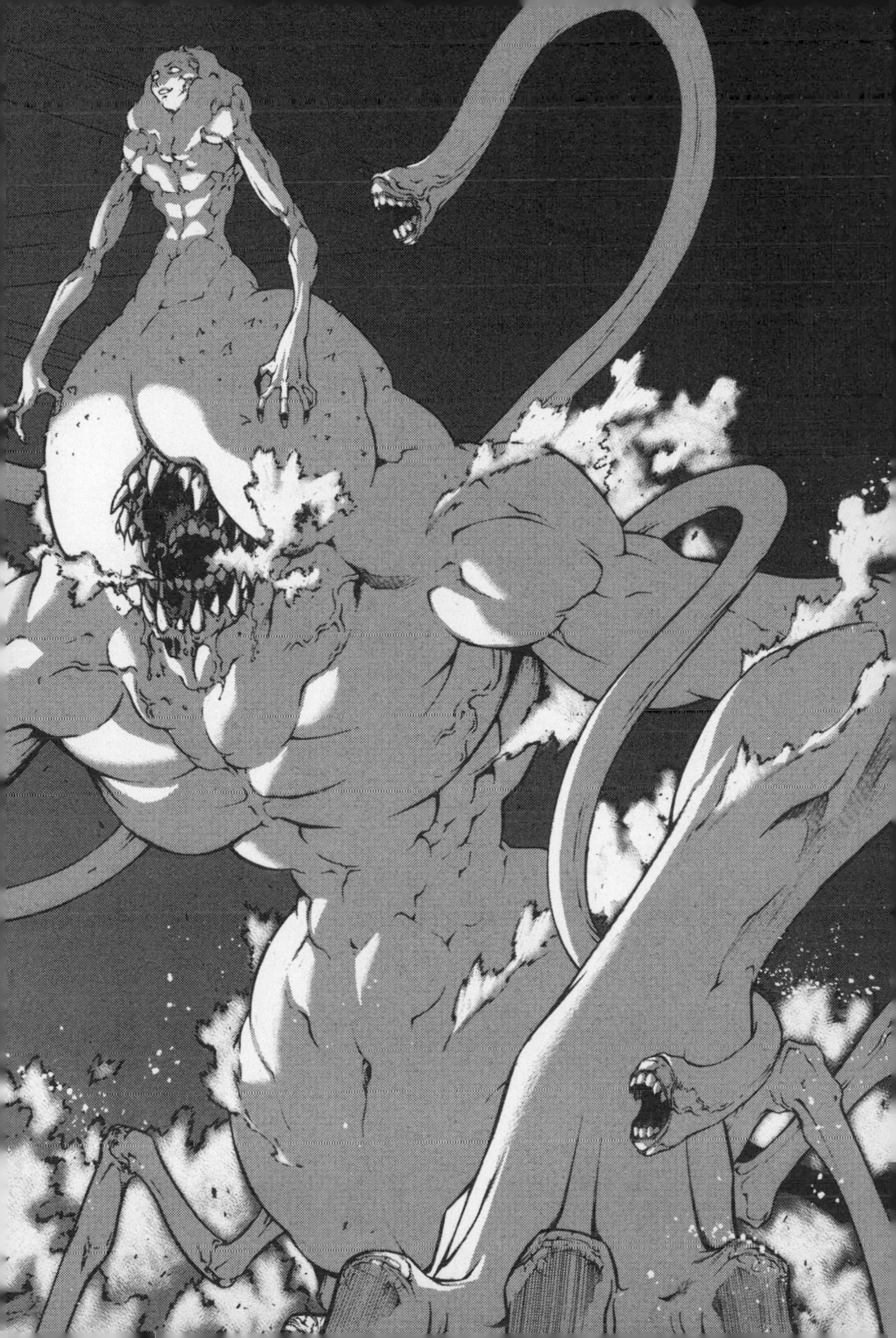

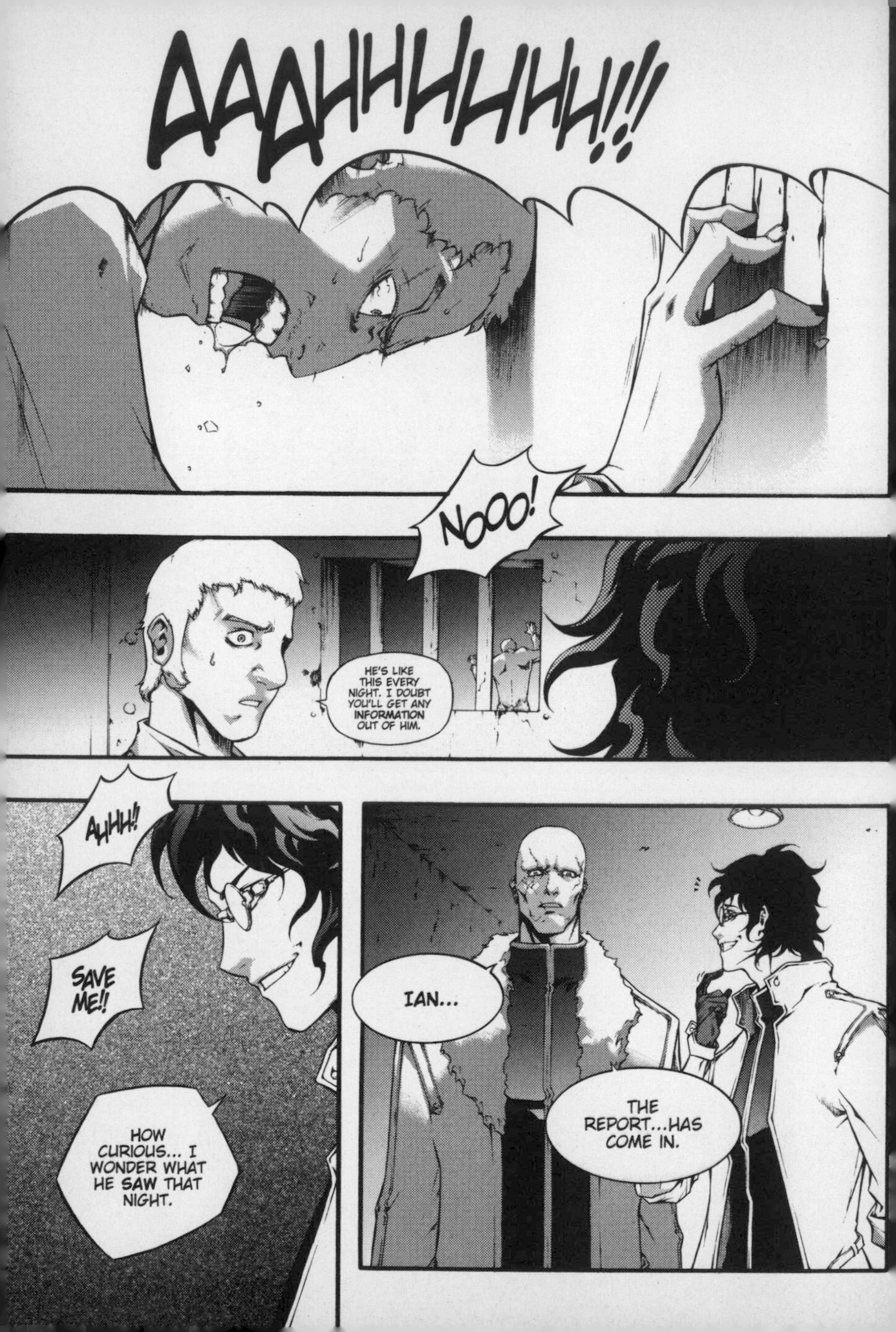
AAAHHHHHH!!!
NOOO!
HE'S LIKE THIS EVERY NIGHT. I DOUBT YOU'LL GET ANY INFORMATION OUT OF HIM.
AHHH!!
SAVE ME!!
HOW CURIOUS... I WONDER WHAT HE SAW THAT NIGHT.
IAN...
THE REPORT...HAS COME IN.

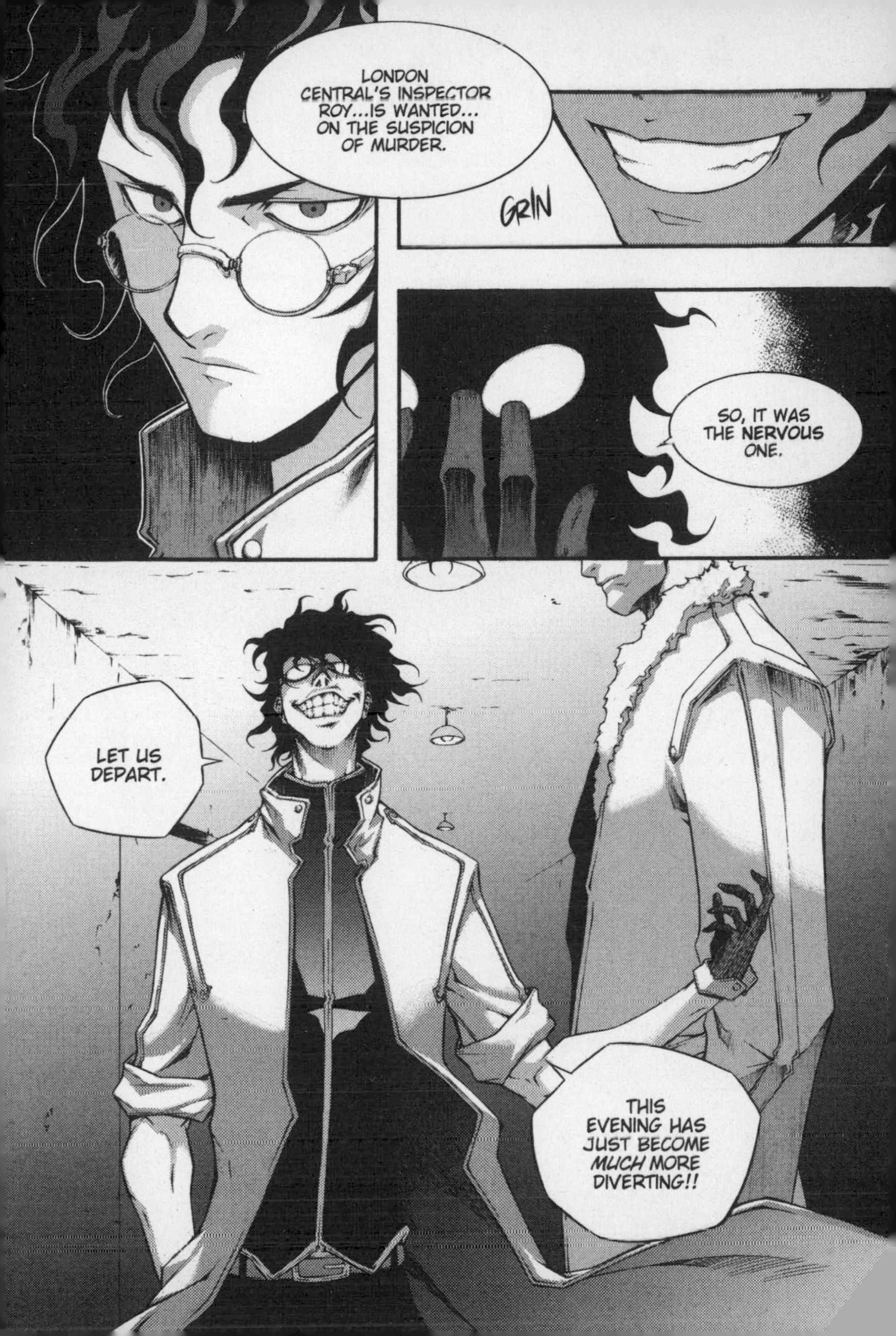
LONDON CENTRAL'S INSPECTOR ROY...IS WANTED... ON THE SUSPICION OF MURDER.
GRIN
SO, IT WAS THE NERVOUS ONE.
LET US DEPART.
THIS EVENING HAS JUST BECOME *MUCH* MORE DIVERTING!!

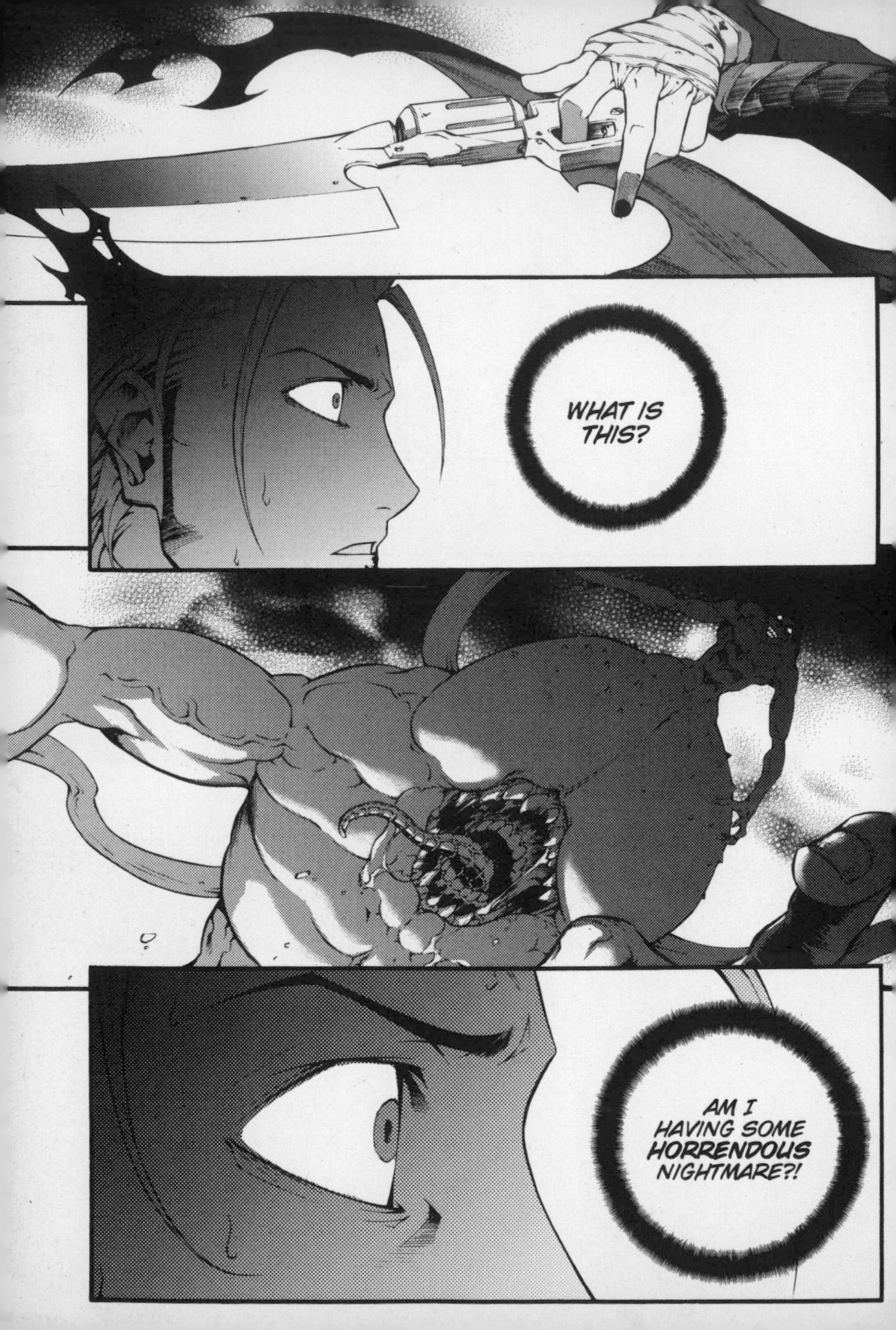
WHAT IS THIS?
AM I HAVING SOME HORRENDOUS NIGHTMARE?!

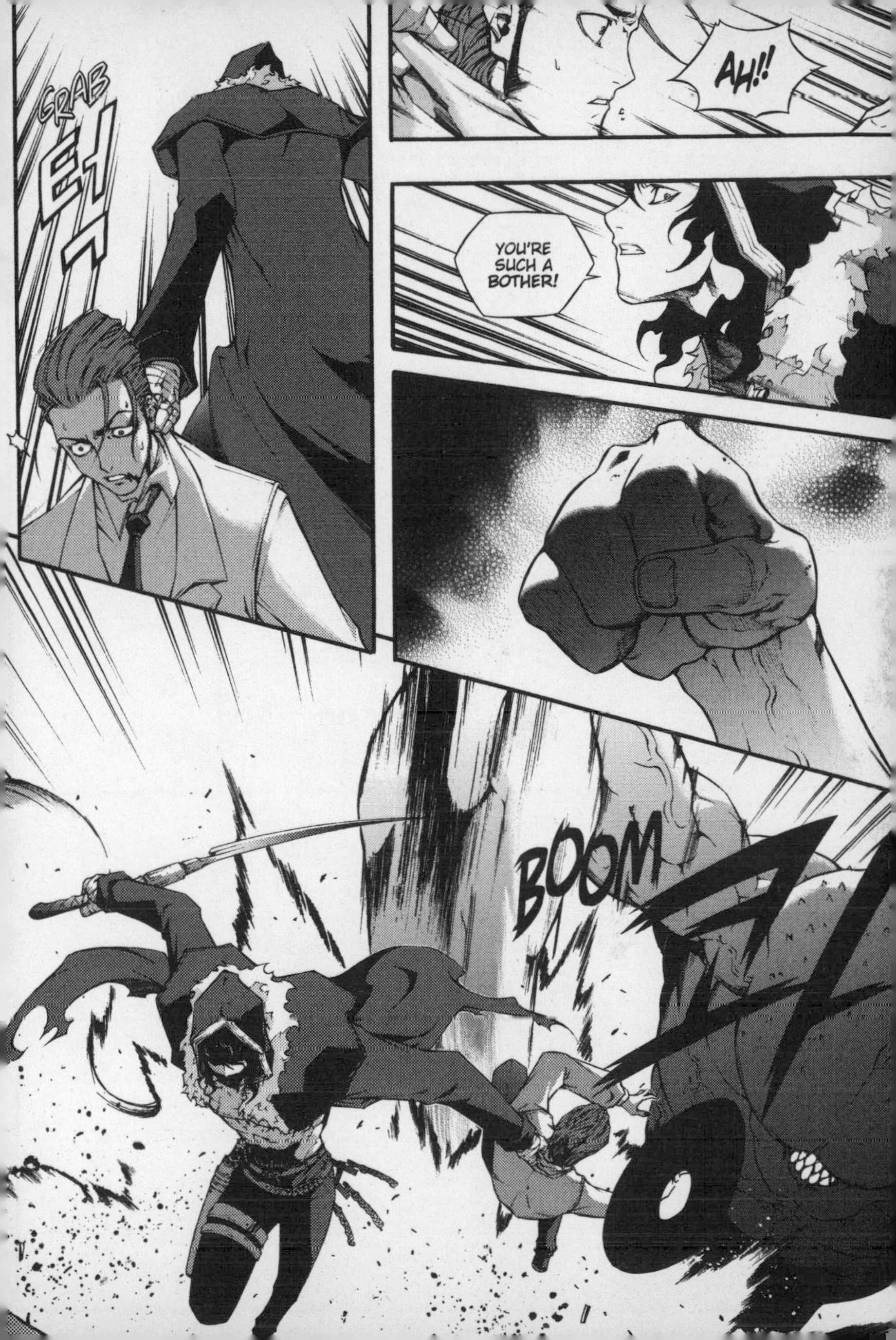
GRAB
AH!!
YOU'RE SUCH A BOTHER!
BOOM

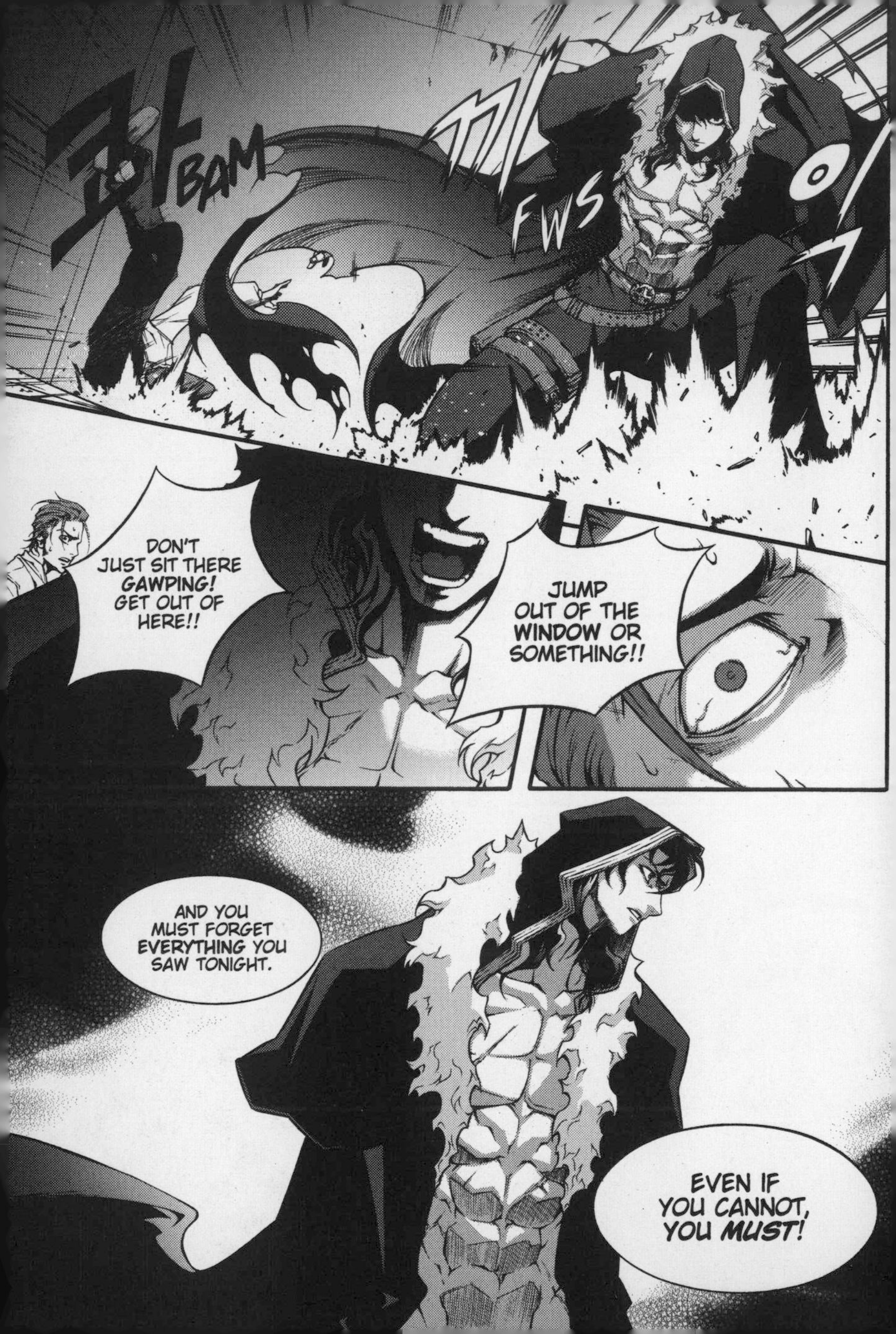
BAM
FWS
DON'T JUST SIT THERE GAWPING! GET OUT OF HERE!!
JUMP OUT OF THE WINDOW OR SOMETHING!!
AND YOU MUST FORGET EVERYTHING YOU SAW TONIGHT.
EVEN IF YOU CANNOT, YOU *MUST*!

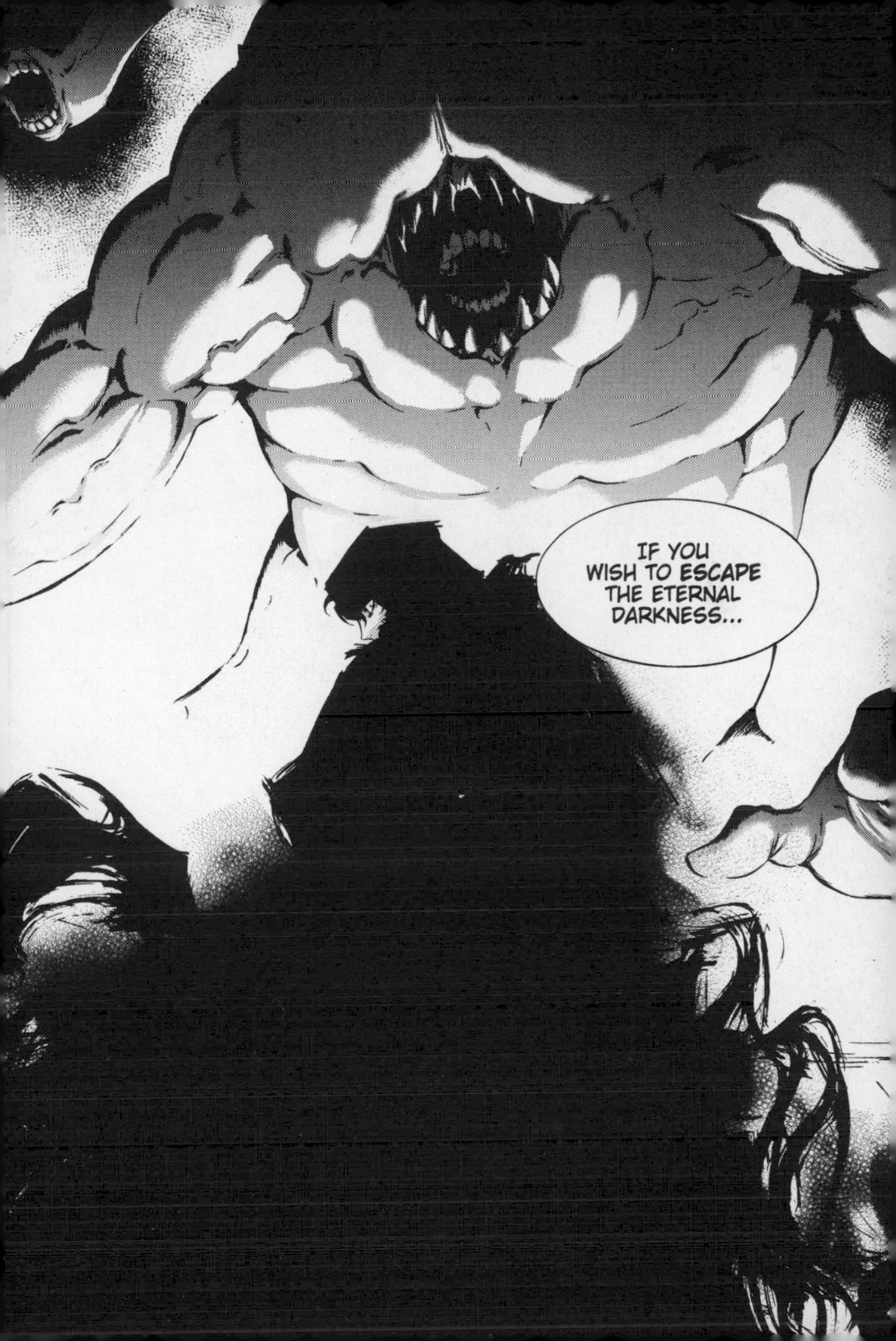
IF YOU WISH TO ESCAPE THE ETERNAL DARKNESS...

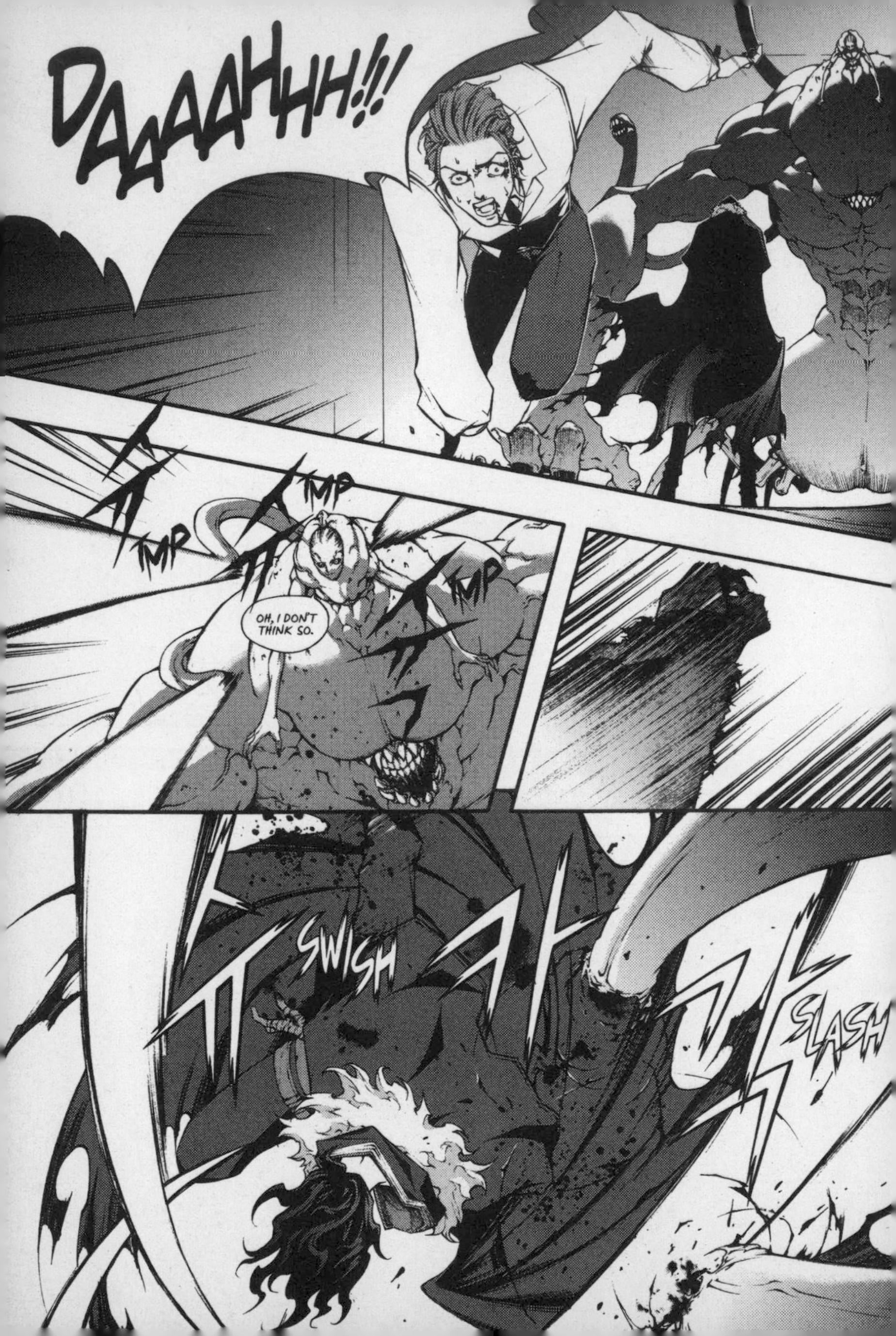
DAAAAHHH!!!
TMP
TMP
OH, I DON'T THINK SO.
TMP
SWISH
SLASH

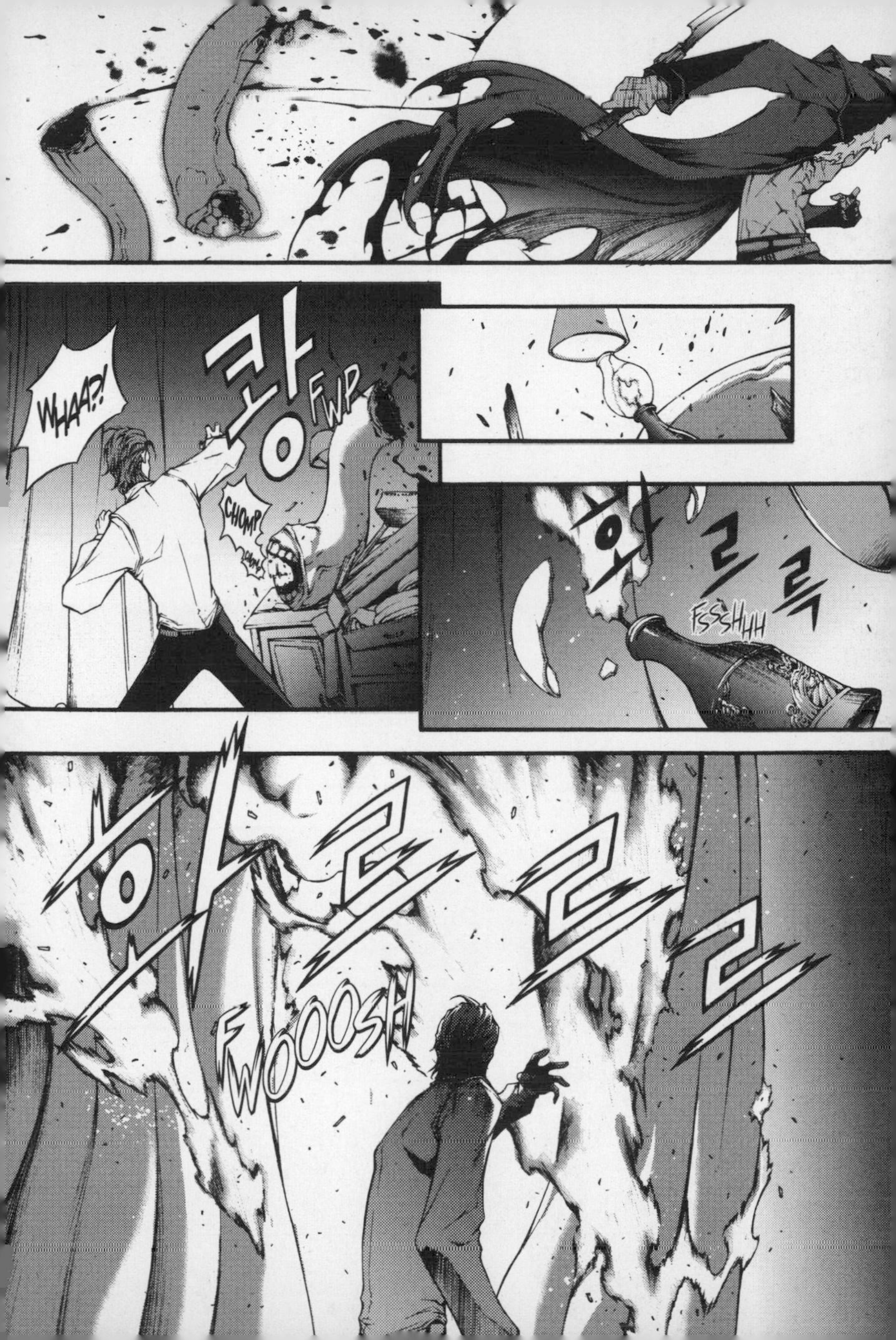
WHAA?!
쾅
FWP
CHOMP
CHOMP
화르륵
FSSHHH
화르르르
FWOOOSH

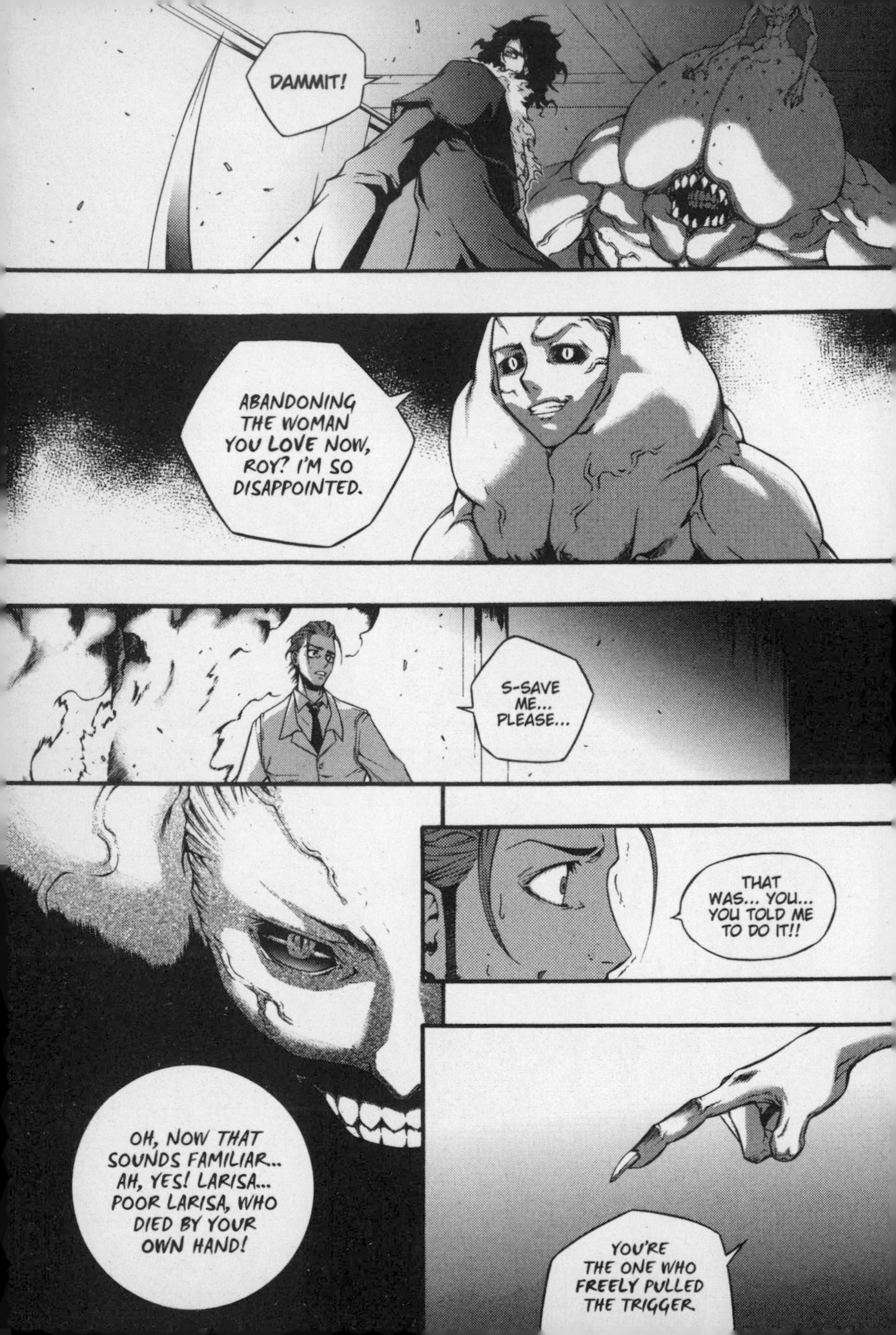
DAMMIT!
ABANDONING THE WOMAN YOU LOVE NOW, ROY? I'M SO DISAPPOINTED.
S-SAVE ME... PLEASE...
THAT WAS... YOU... YOU TOLD ME TO DO IT!!
OH, NOW THAT SOUNDS FAMILIAR... AH, YES! LARISA... POOR LARISA, WHO DIED BY YOUR OWN HAND!
YOU'RE THE ONE WHO FREELY PULLED THE TRIGGER

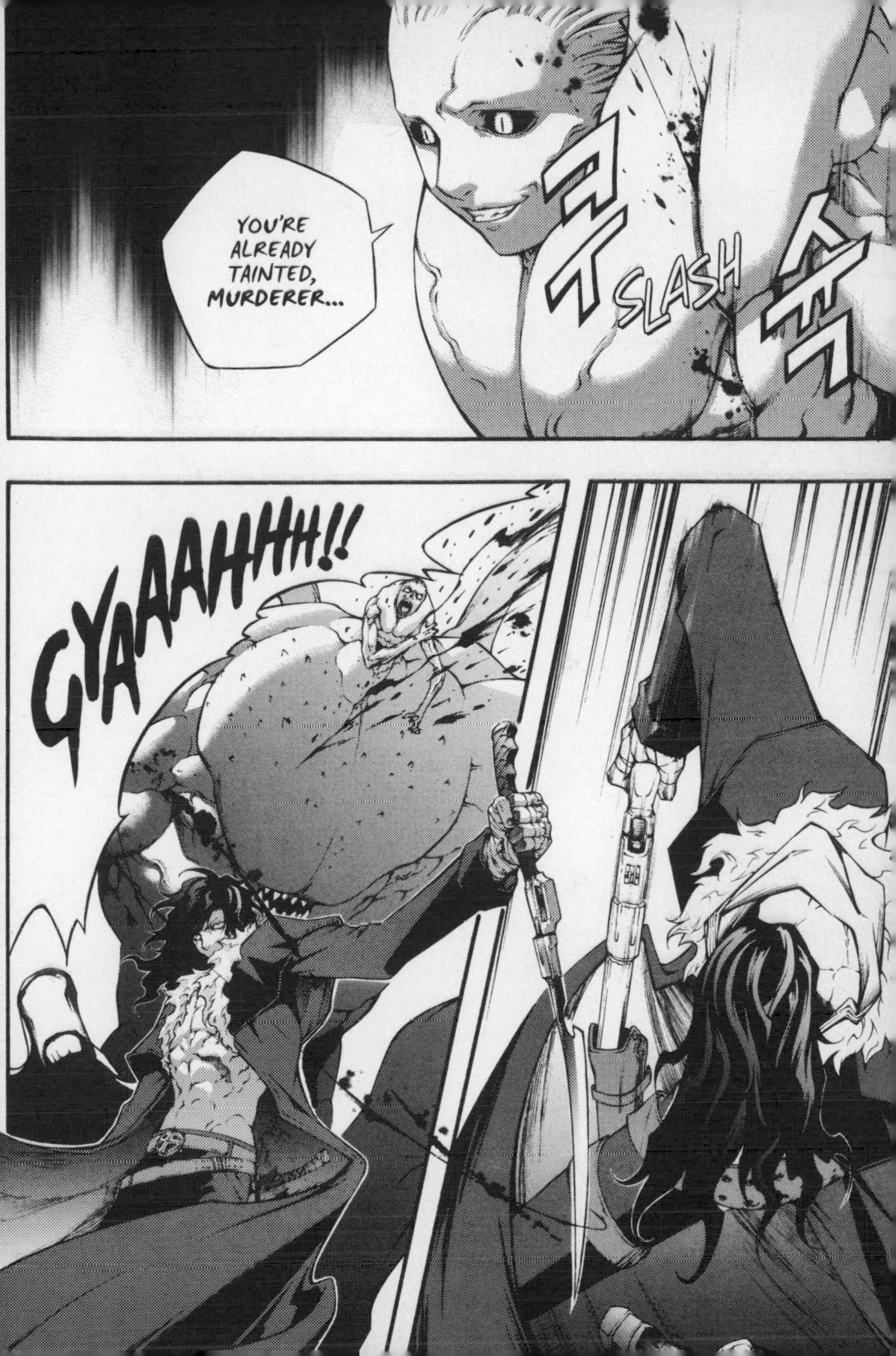
YOU'RE ALREADY TAINTED, MURDERER...
SLASH
GYAAAHHH!!

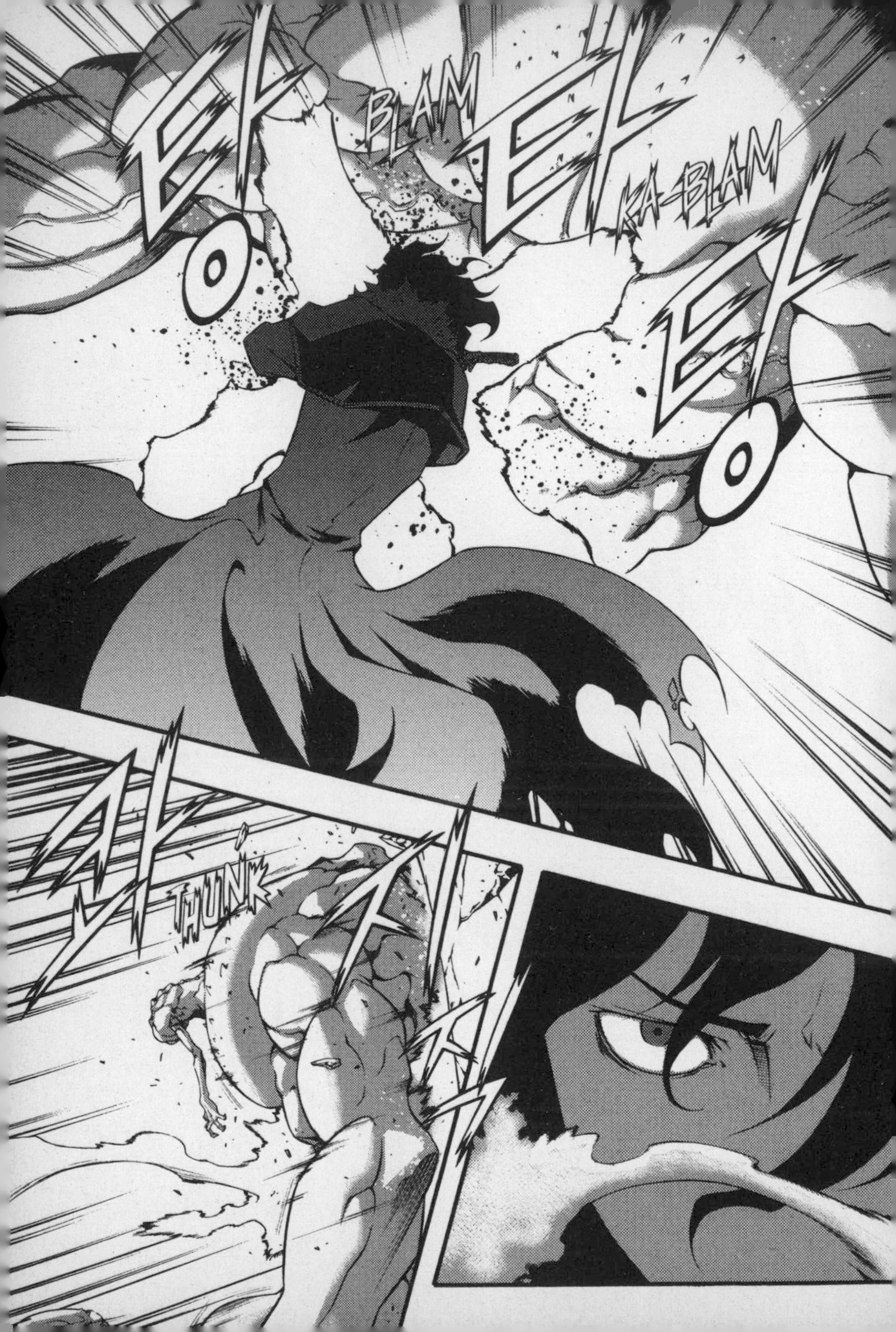
BLAM
KA-BLAM
THUNK

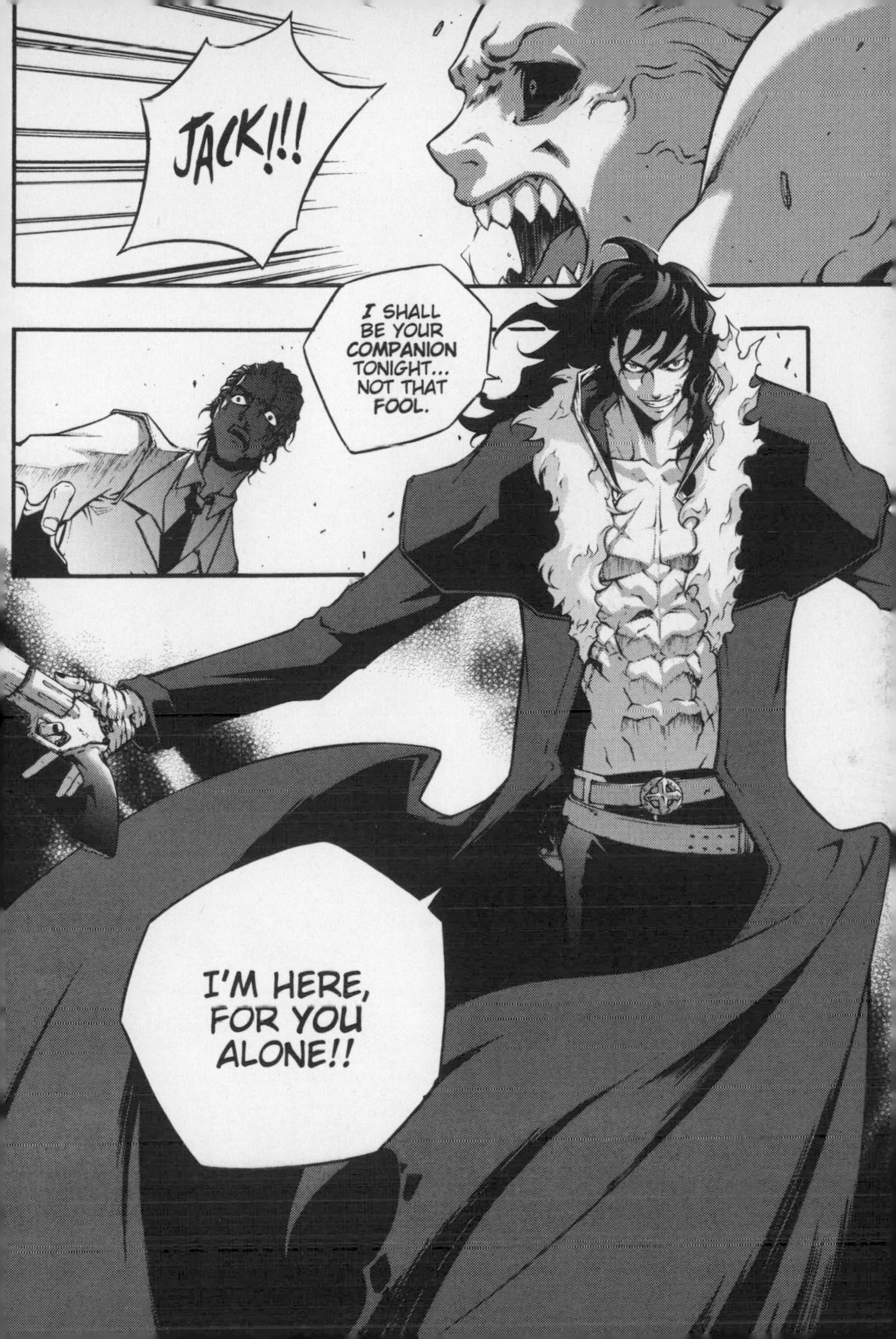
JACK!!!
I SHALL BE YOUR COMPANION TONIGHT... NOT THAT FOOL.
I'M HERE, FOR YOU ALONE!!

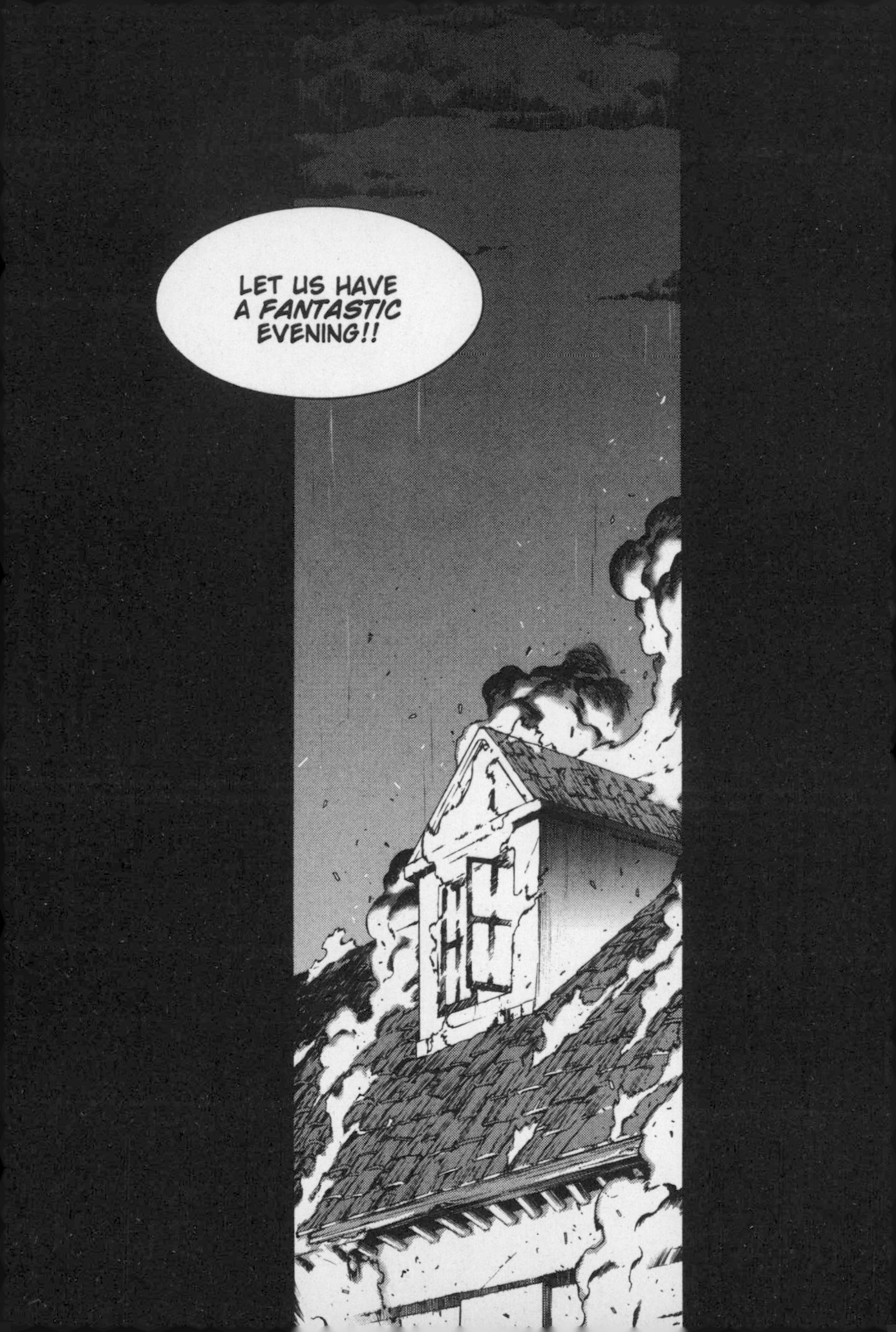
LET US HAVE A *FANTASTIC* EVENING!!

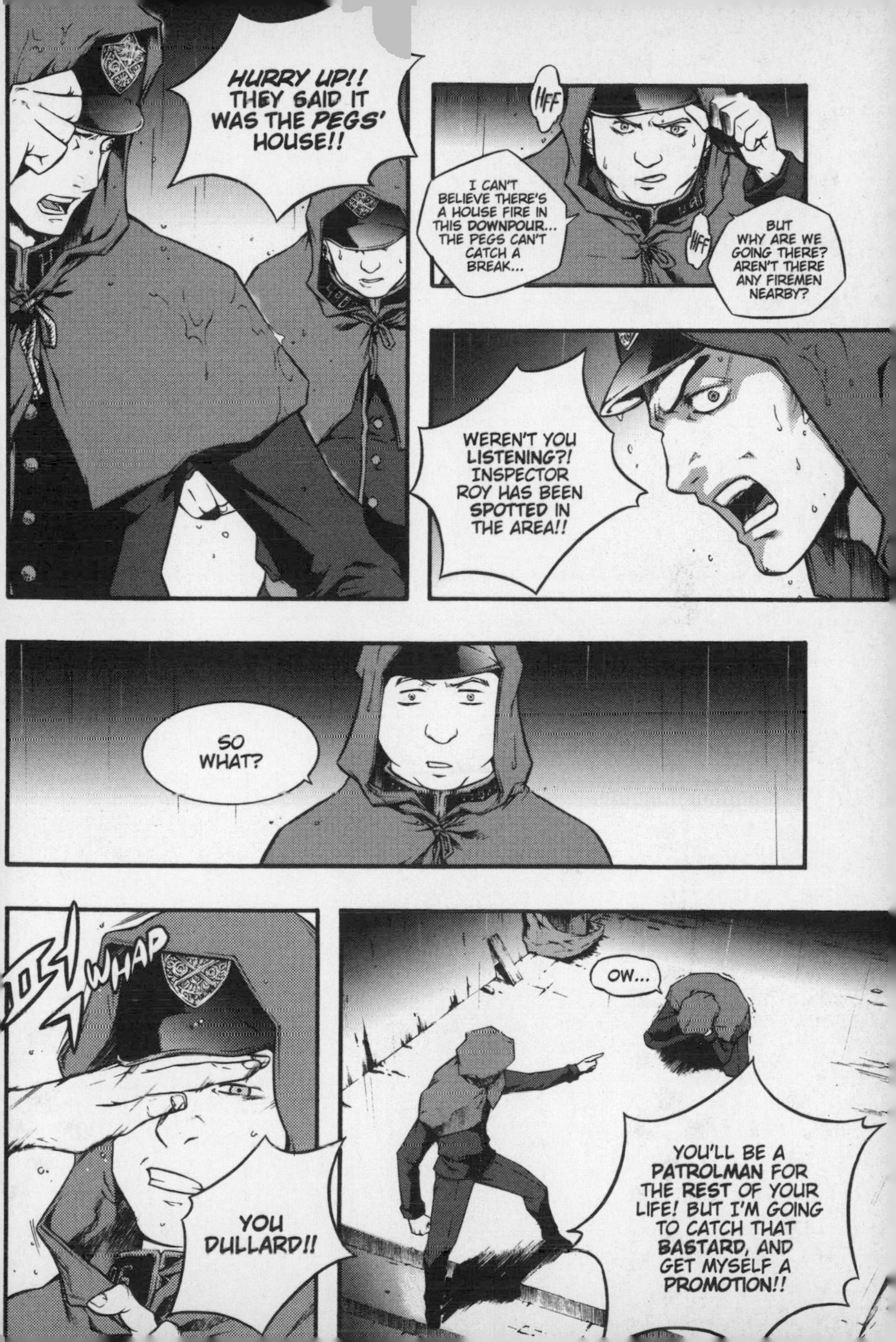
HURRY UP!! THEY SAID IT WAS THE PEGS' HOUSE!!
HFF
I CAN'T BELIEVE THERE'S A HOUSE FIRE IN THIS DOWNPOUR... THE PEGS CAN'T CATCH A BREAK...
HFF
BUT WHY ARE WE GOING THERE? AREN'T THERE ANY FIREMEN NEARBY?
WEREN'T YOU LISTENING?! INSPECTOR ROY HAS BEEN SPOTTED IN THE AREA!!
SO WHAT?
WHAP
YOU DULLARD!!
OW...
YOU'LL BE A PATROLMAN FOR THE REST OF YOUR LIFE! BUT I'M GOING TO CATCH THAT BASTARD, AND GET MYSELF A PROMOTION!!

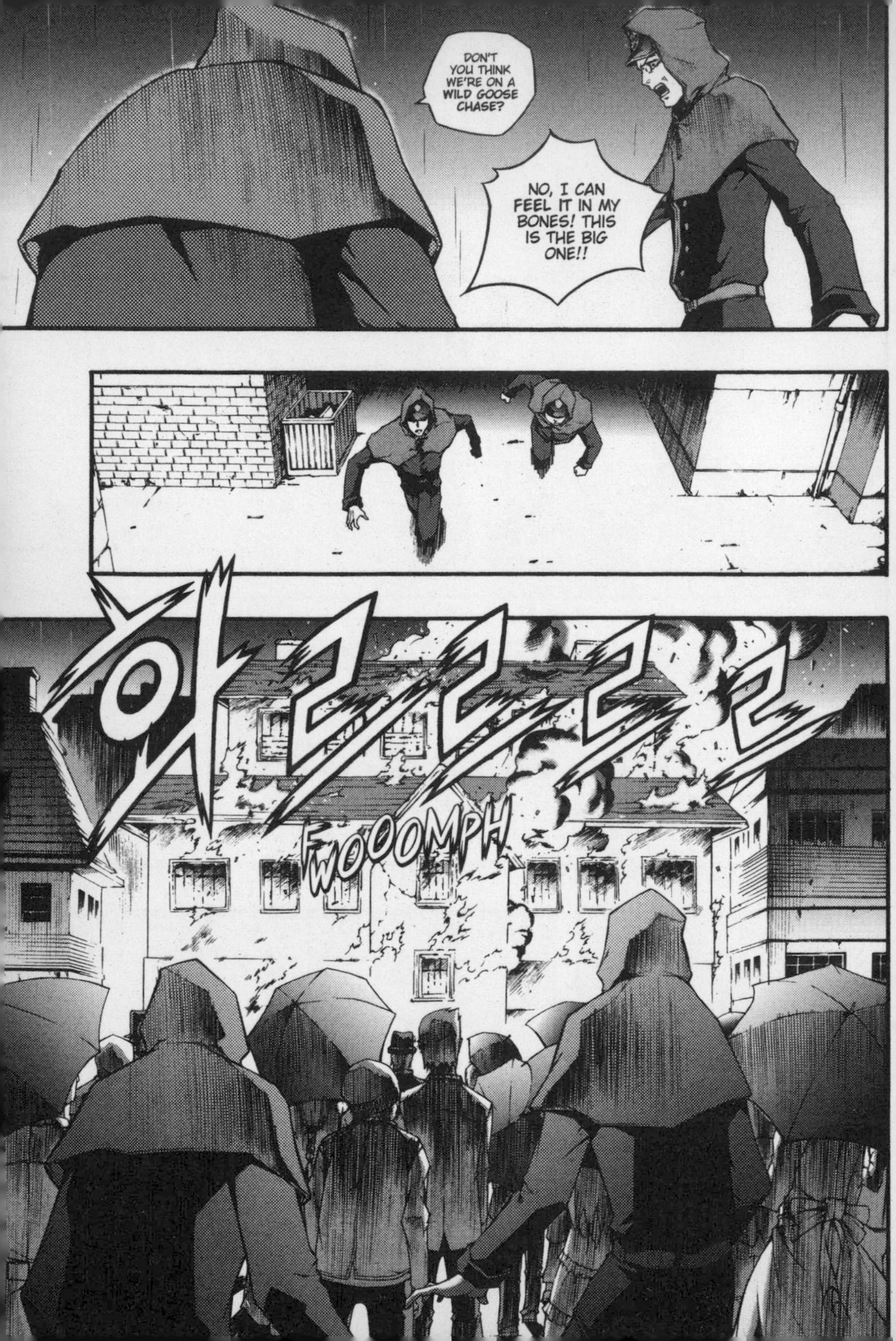
DON'T YOU THINK WE'RE ON A WILD GOOSE CHASE?
NO, I CAN FEEL IT IN MY BONES! THIS IS THE BIG ONE!!
화르르르
FWOOOMPH

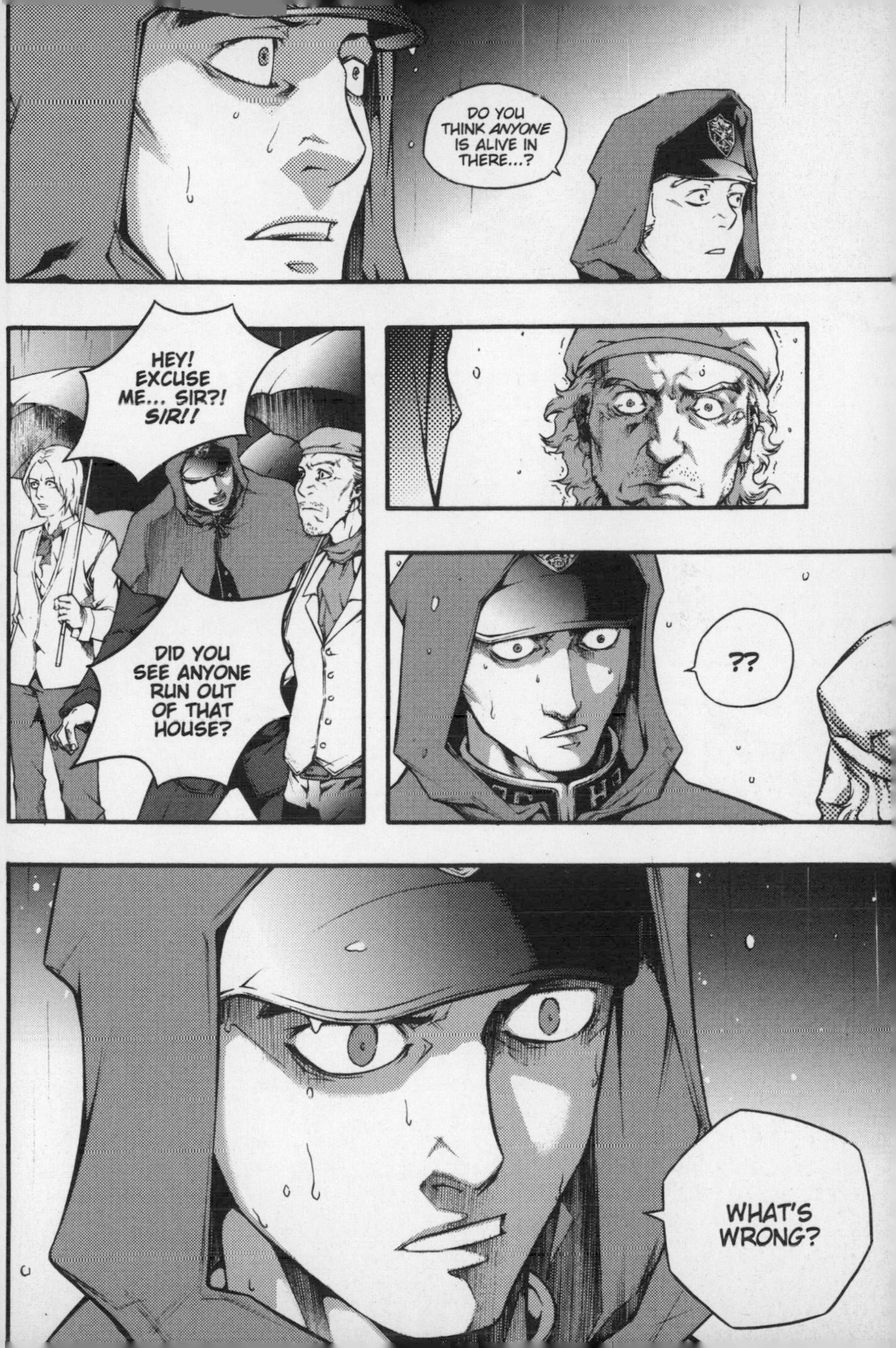
DO YOU THINK *ANYONE* IS ALIVE IN THERE...?
HEY! EXCUSE ME... SIR?! *SIR!!*
DID YOU SEE ANYONE RUN OUT OF THAT HOUSE?
??
WHAT'S WRONG?

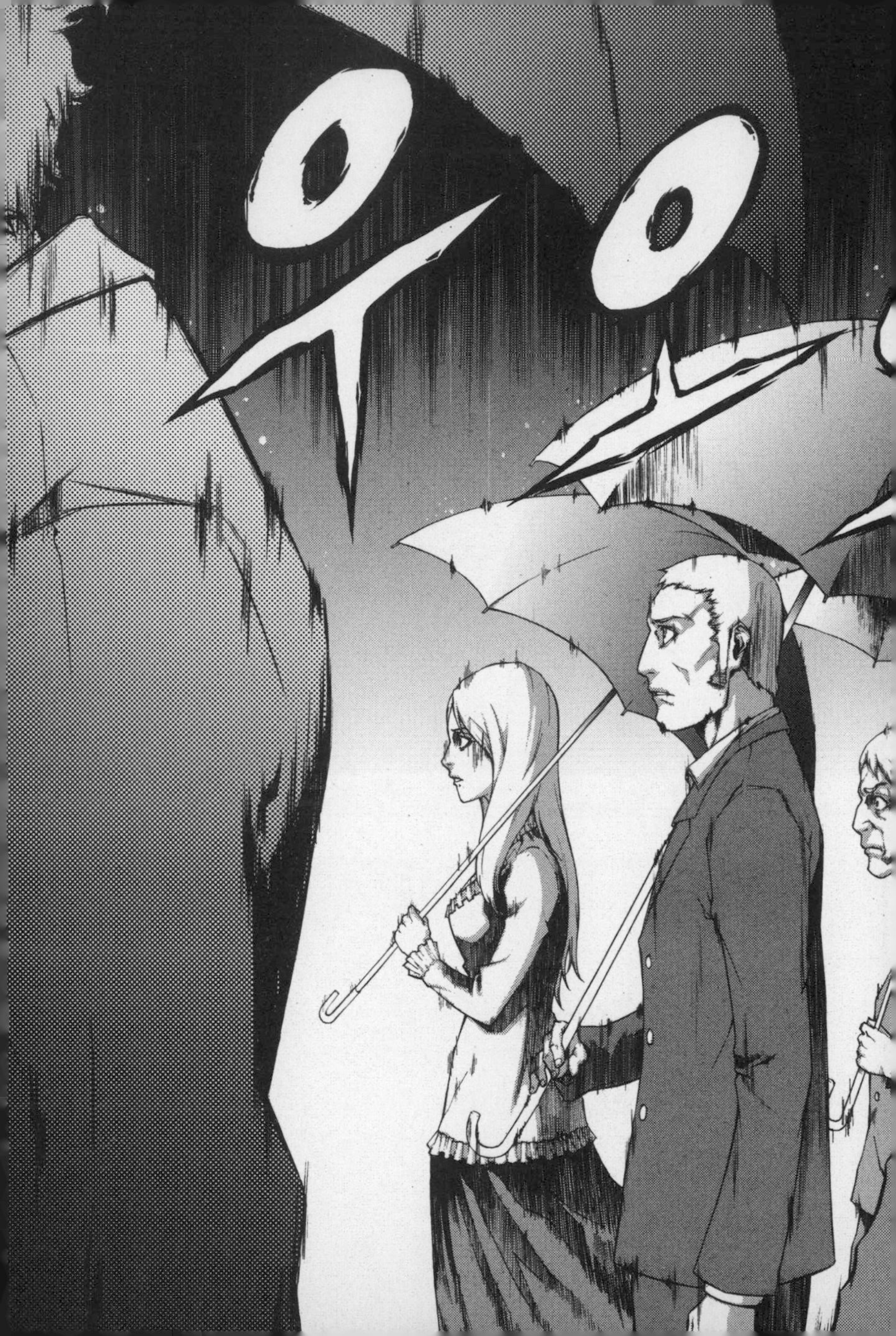

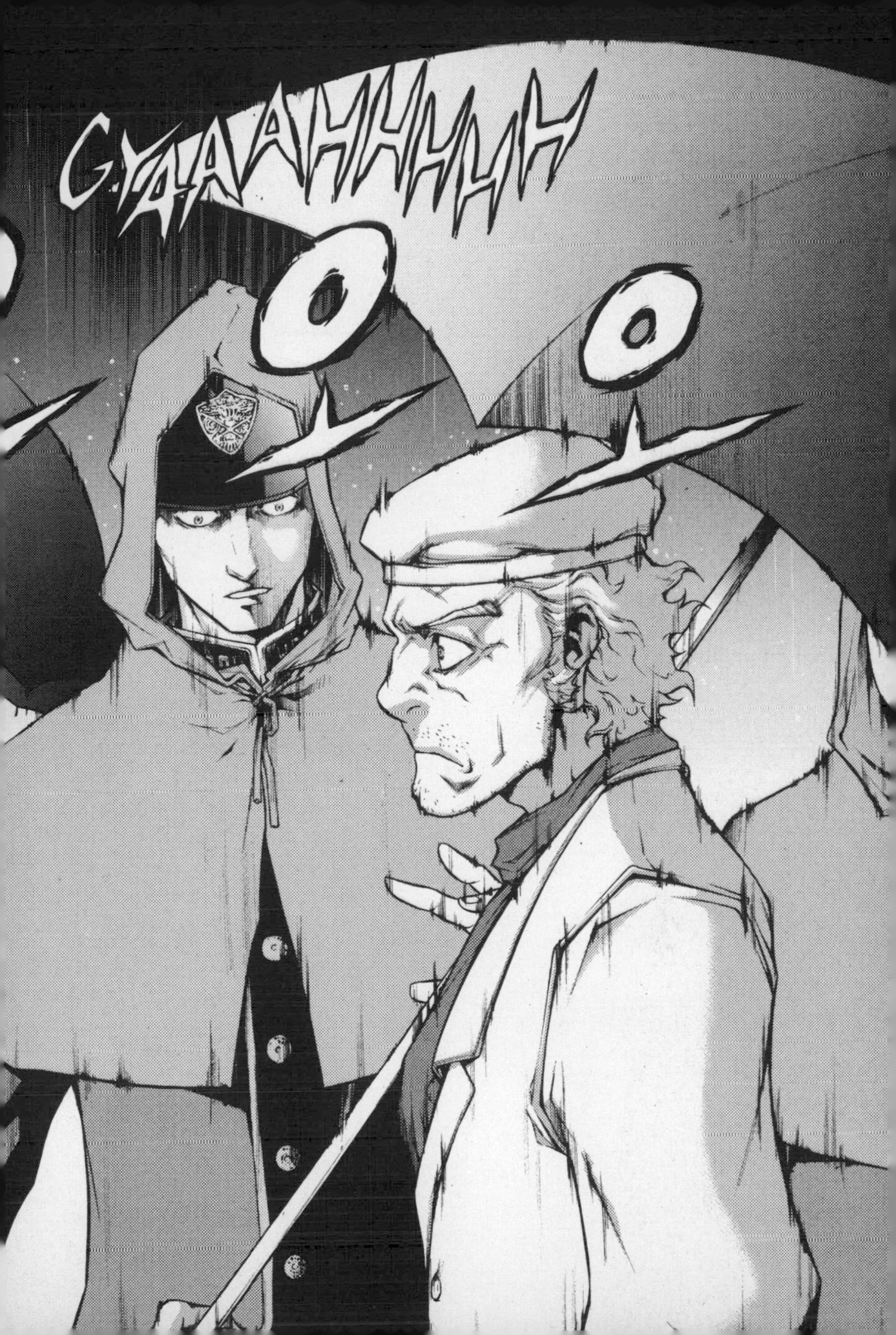
GYAAHHHHH

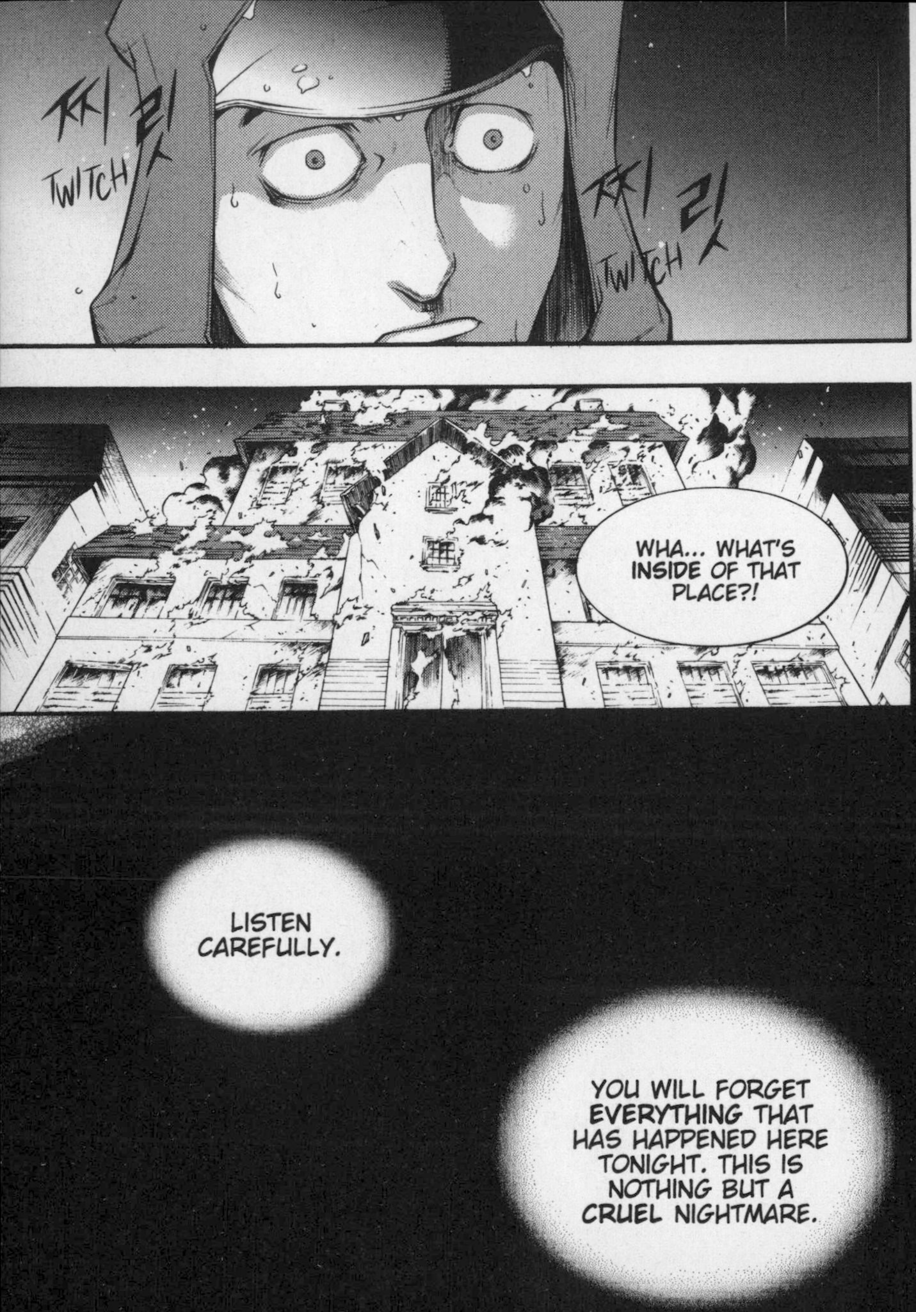
찌릿
TWITCH
찌릿
TWITCH
WHA... WHAT'S INSIDE OF THAT PLACE?!
LISTEN CAREFULLY.
YOU WILL FORGET EVERYTHING THAT HAS HAPPENED HERE TONIGHT. THIS IS NOTHING BUT A CRUEL NIGHTMARE.

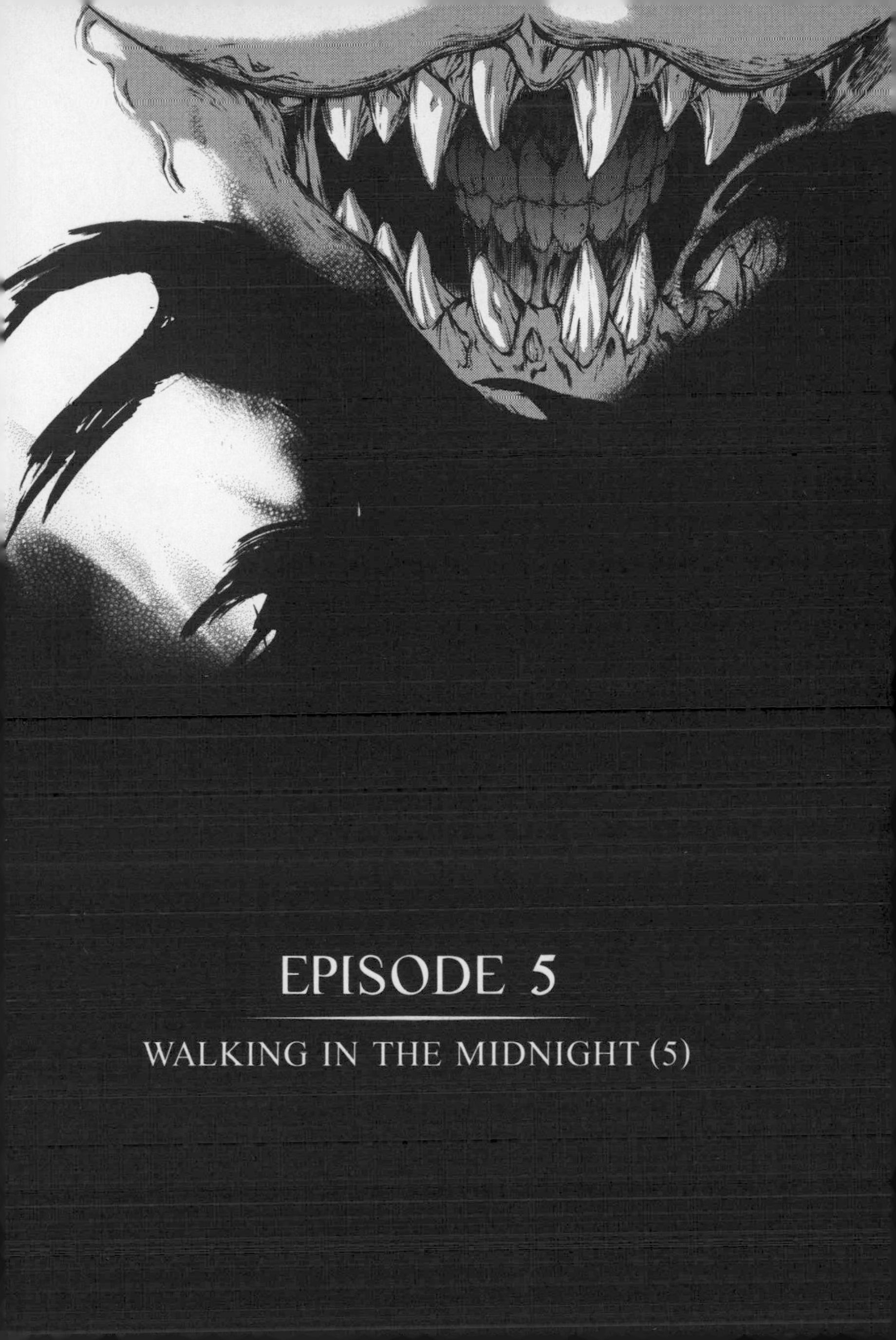

EPISODE 5

WALKING IN THE MIDNIGHT (5)

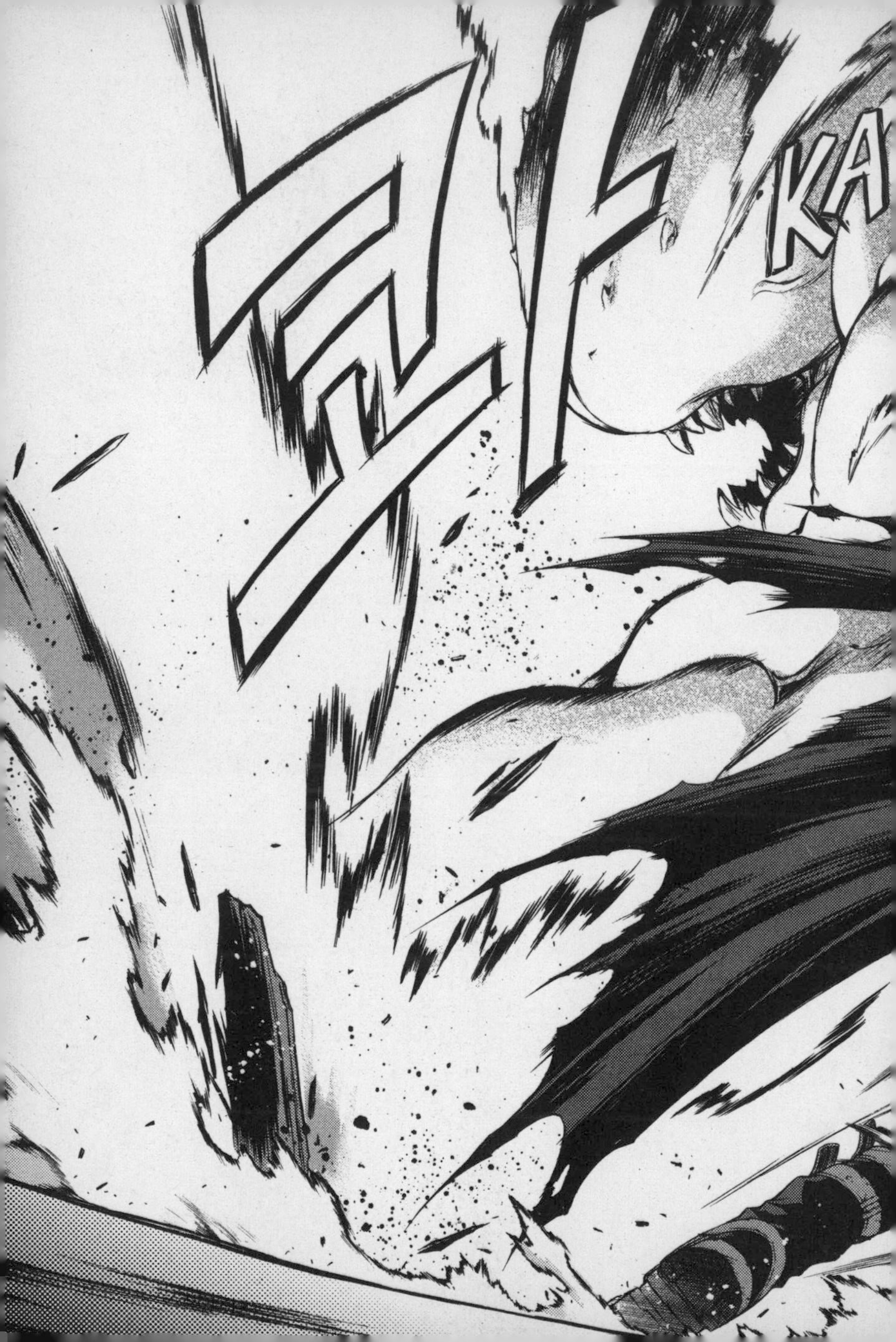
KA

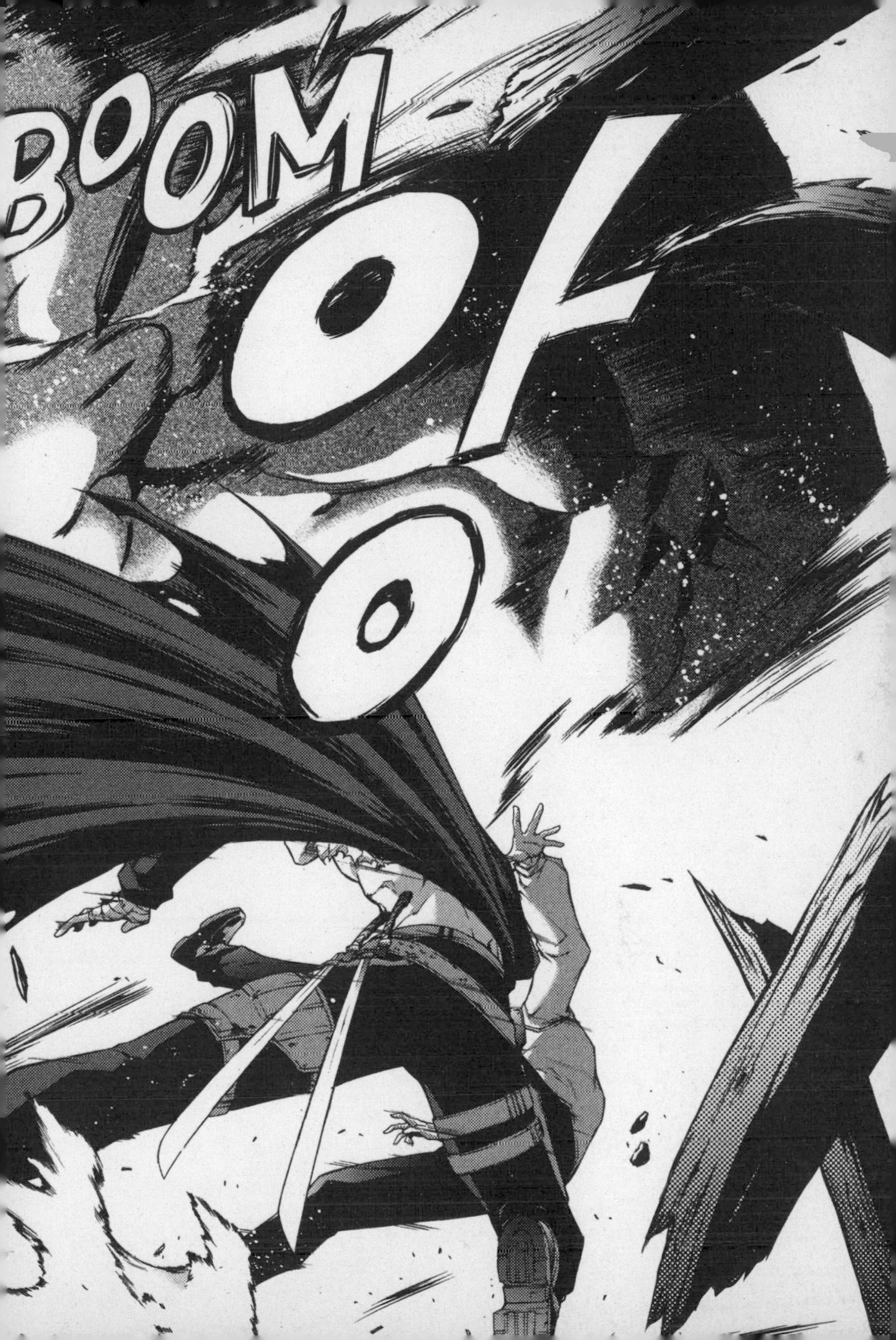
BOOM

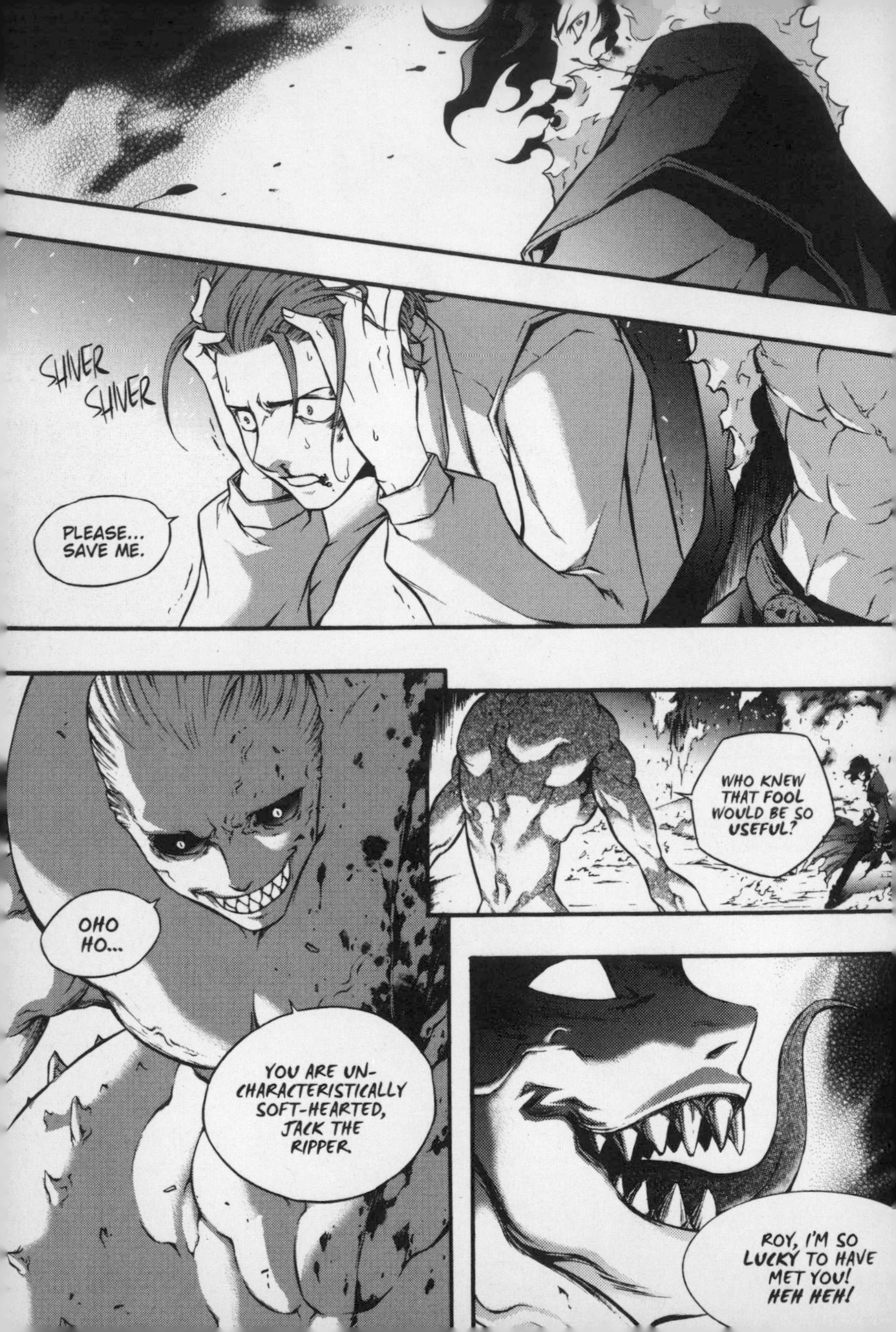
SHIVER SHIVER
PLEASE... SAVE ME.
OHO HO...
YOU ARE UN-CHARACTERISTICALLY SOFT-HEARTED, JACK THE RIPPER
WHO KNEW THAT FOOL WOULD BE SO USEFUL?
ROY, I'M SO LUCKY TO HAVE MET YOU! HEH HEH!

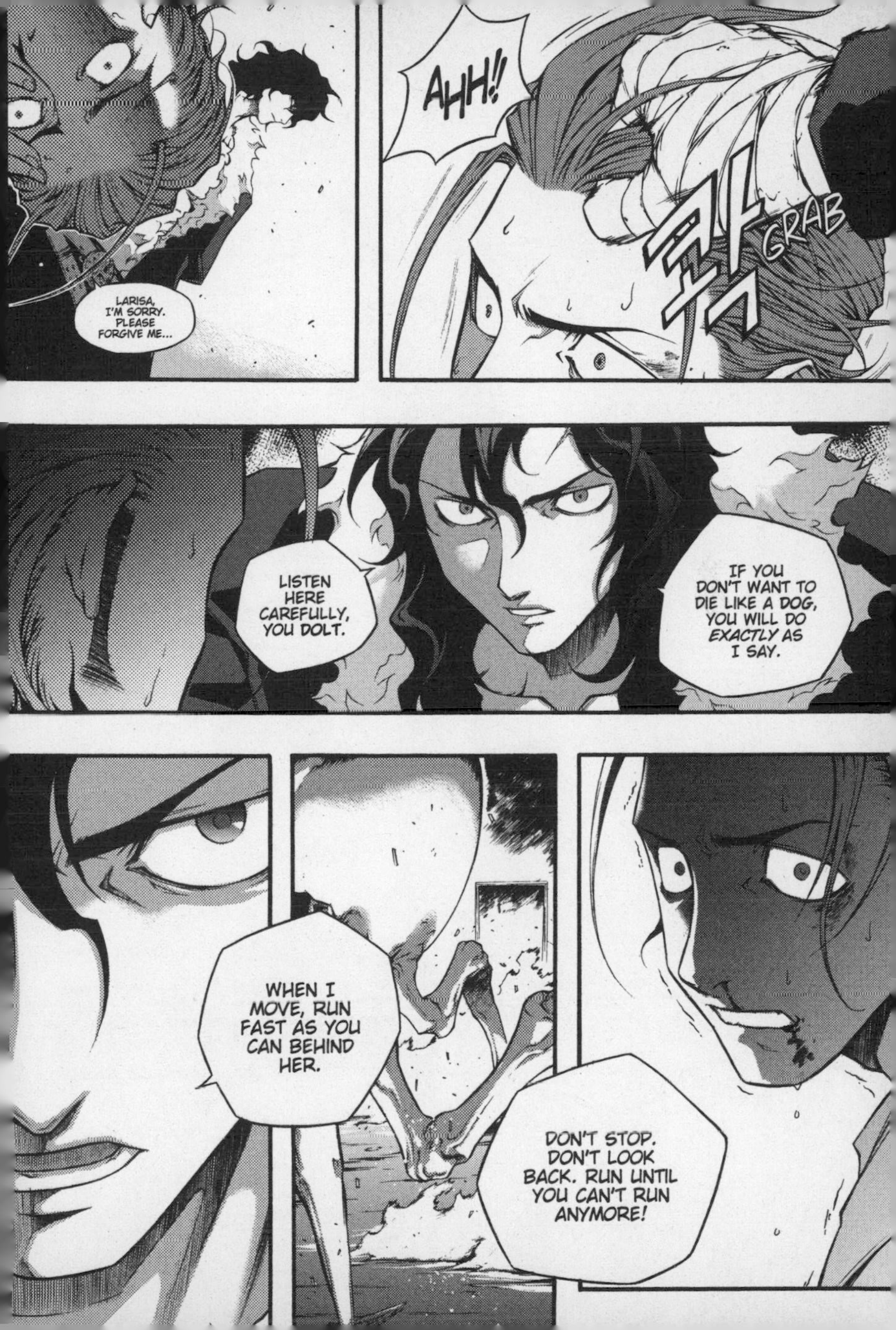
LARISA, I'M SORRY. PLEASE FORGIVE ME...
AHH!!
GRAB
LISTEN HERE CAREFULLY, YOU DOLT.
IF YOU DON'T WANT TO DIE LIKE A DOG, YOU WILL DO *EXACTLY* AS I SAY.
WHEN I MOVE, RUN FAST AS YOU CAN BEHIND HER.
DON'T STOP. DON'T LOOK BACK. RUN UNTIL YOU CAN'T RUN ANYMORE!

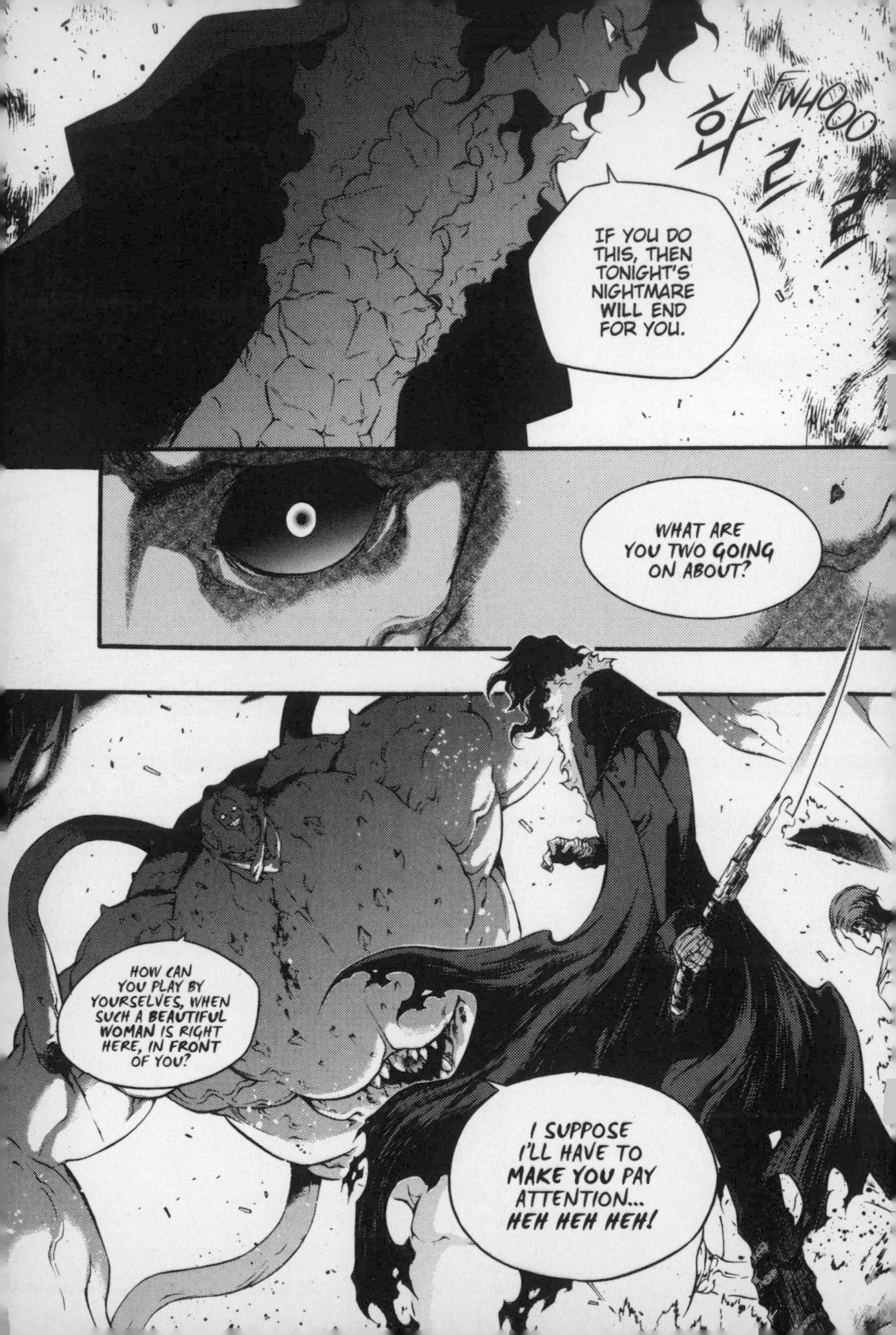

FWHOOO
화르르
IF YOU DO THIS, THEN TONIGHT'S NIGHTMARE WILL END FOR YOU.
WHAT ARE YOU TWO GOING ON ABOUT?
HOW CAN YOU PLAY BY YOURSELVES, WHEN SUCH A BEAUTIFUL WOMAN IS RIGHT HERE, IN FRONT OF YOU?
I SUPPOSE I'LL HAVE TO MAKE YOU PAY ATTENTION... HEH HEH HEH!

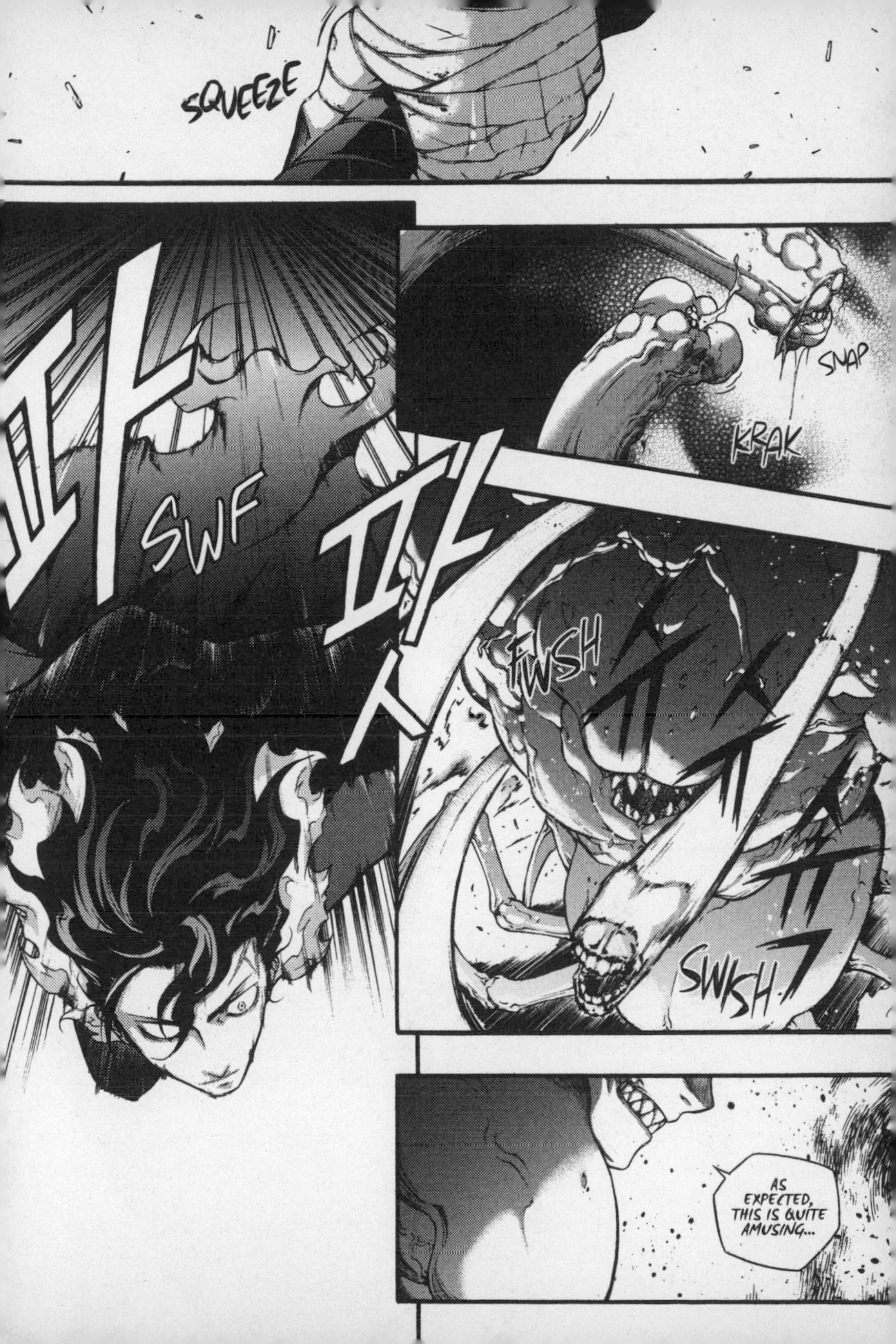
SQUEEZE
SWF
SNAP
KRAK
FWSH
SWISH
AS EXPECTED, THIS IS QUITE AMUSING...

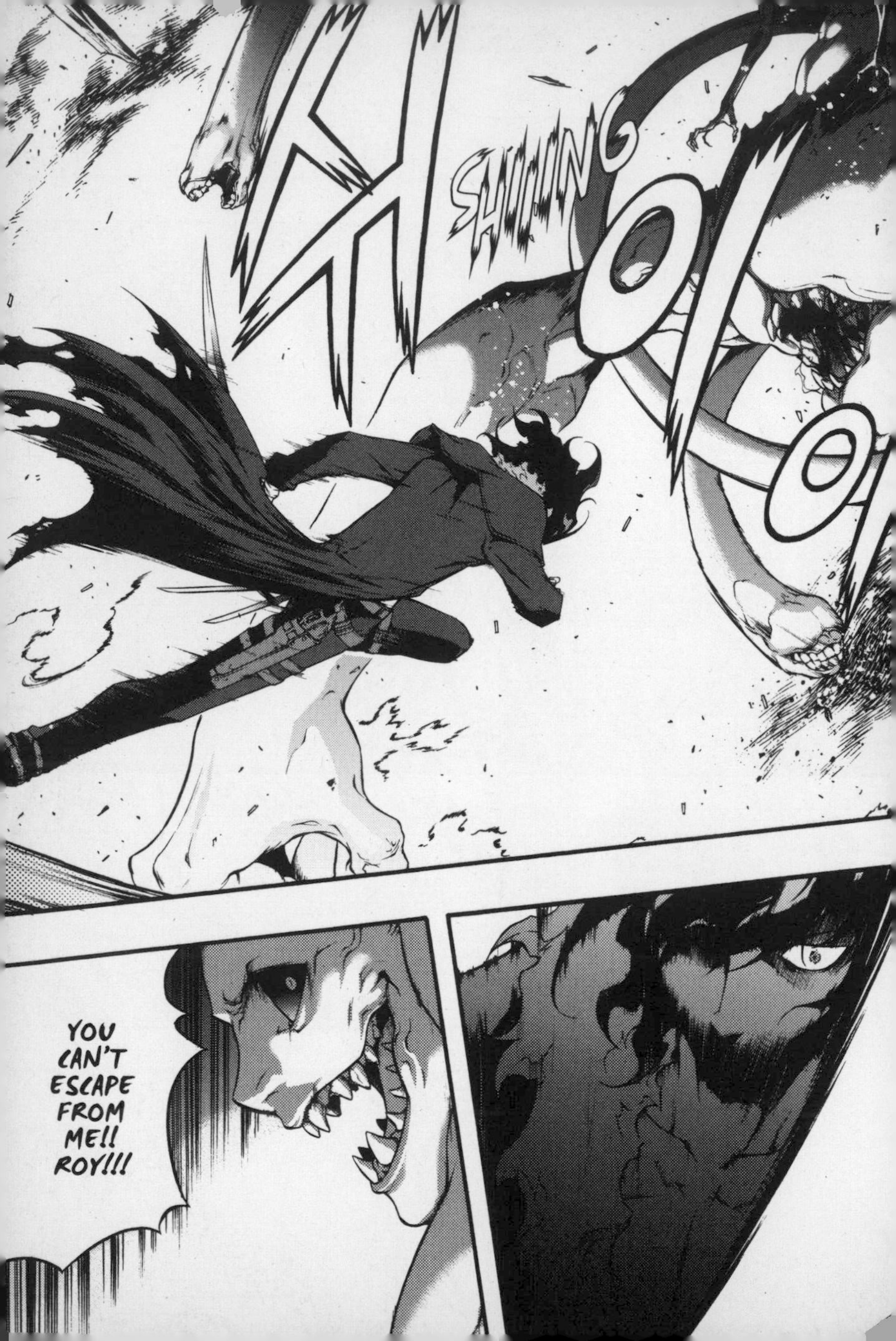
SHOO
YOU CAN'T ESCAPE FROM ME!! ROY!!!

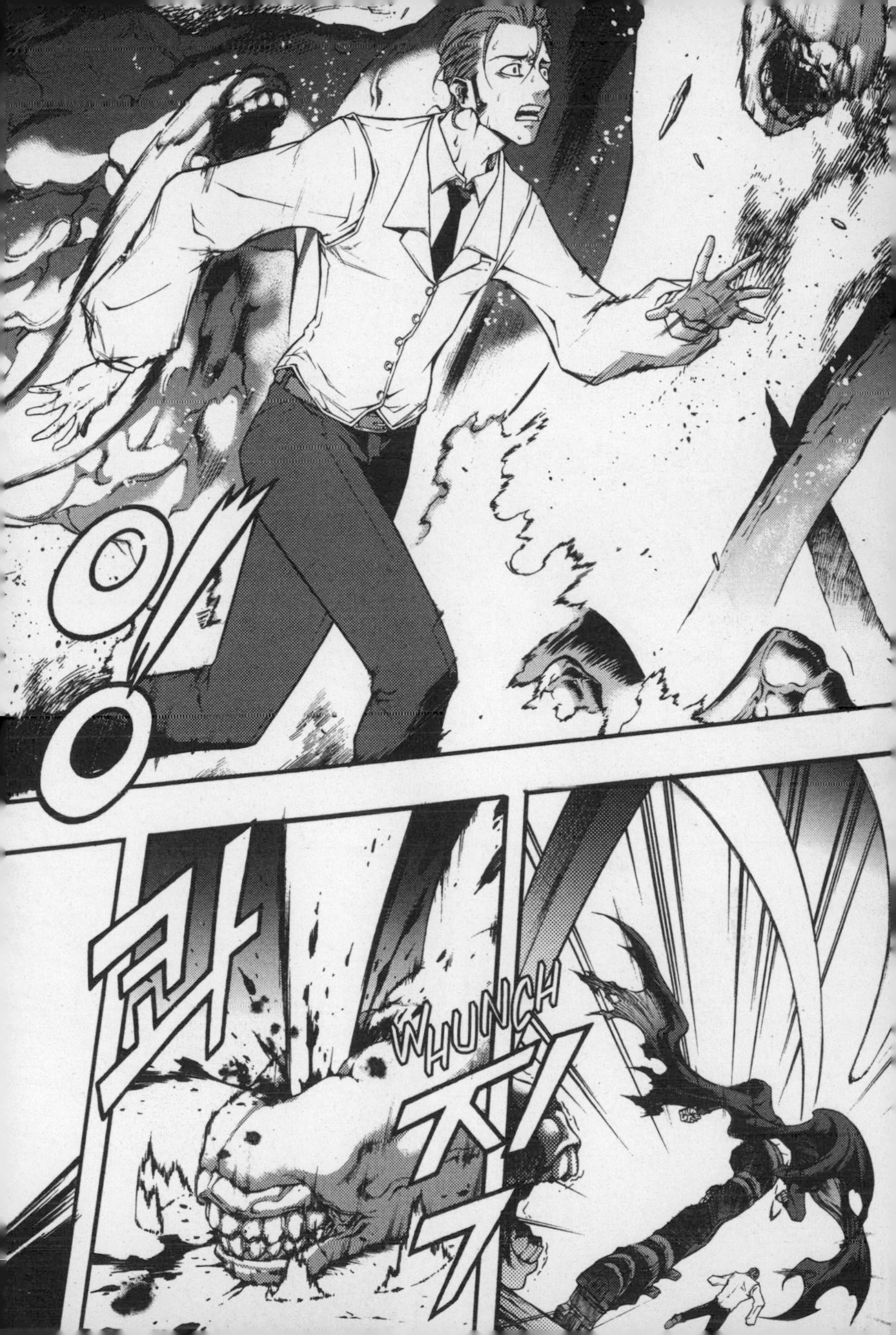
WHUNCH

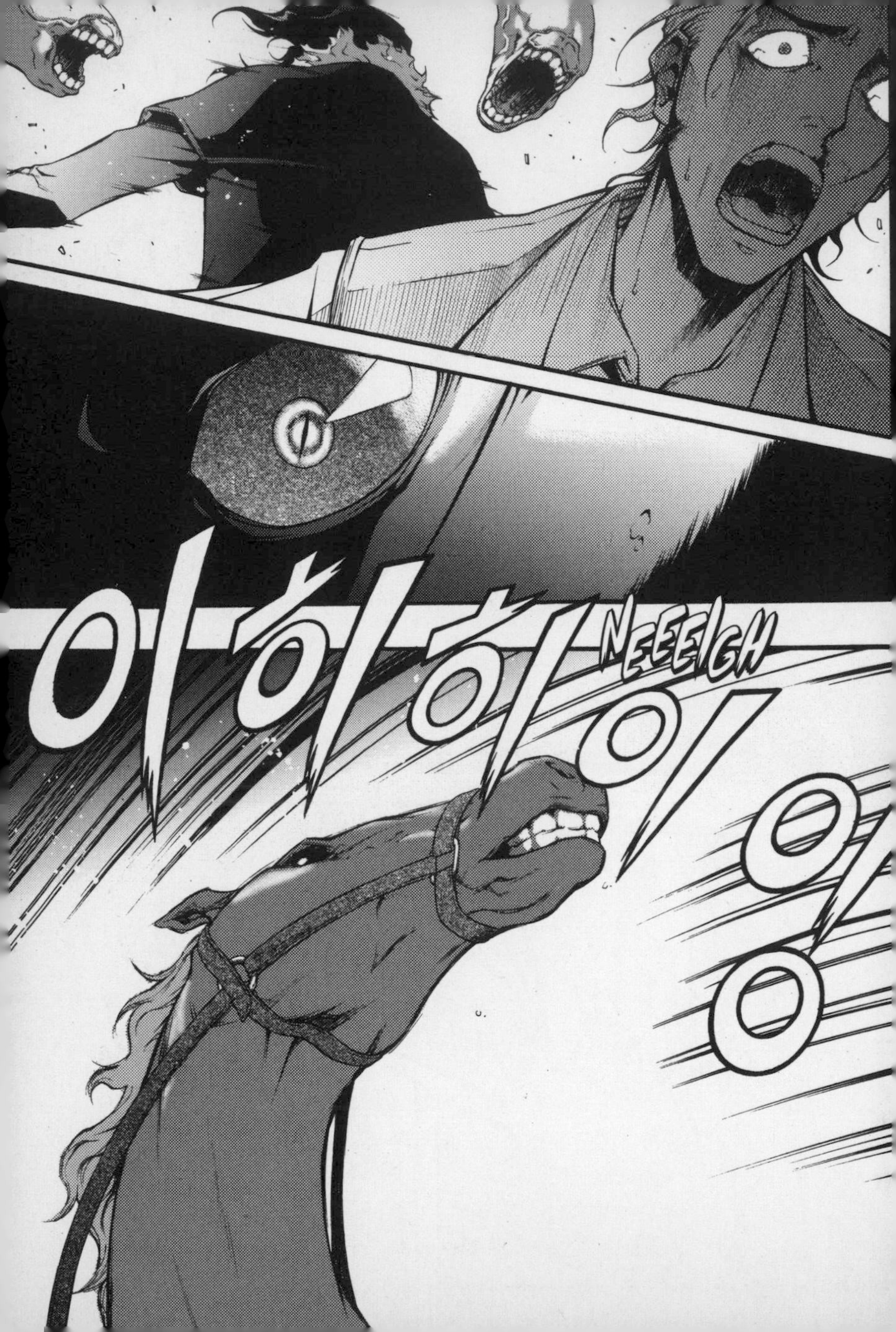
이히히이잉
NEEEIGH

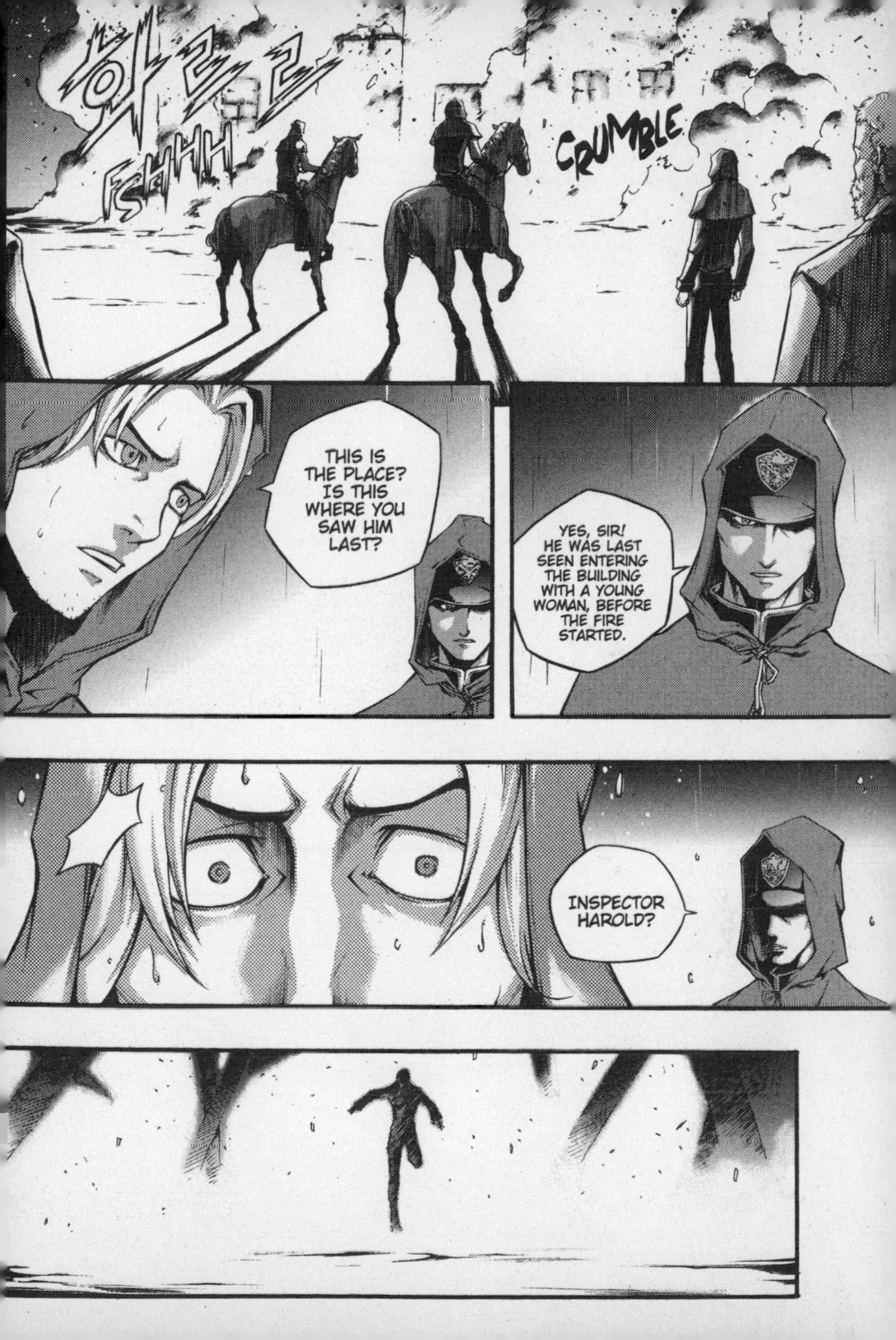
화르르
FSHHH
CRUMBLE
THIS IS THE PLACE? IS THIS WHERE YOU SAW HIM LAST?
YES, SIR! HE WAS LAST SEEN ENTERING THE BUILDING WITH A YOUNG WOMAN, BEFORE THE FIRE STARTED.
INSPECTOR HAROLD?

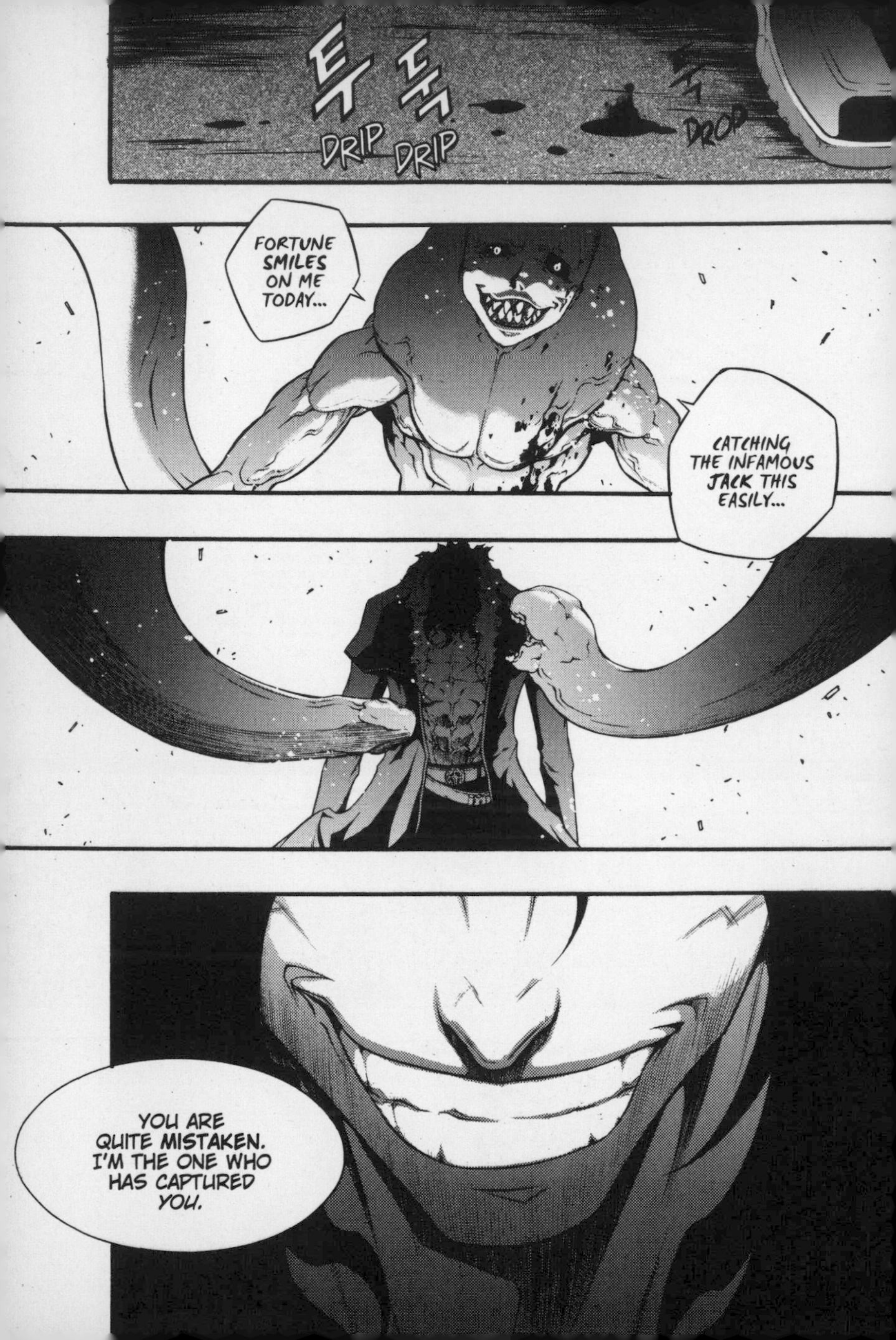
DRIP DRIP
DROP
FORTUNE SMILES ON ME TODAY...
CATCHING THE INFAMOUS JACK THIS EASILY...
YOU ARE QUITE MISTAKEN. I'M THE ONE WHO HAS CAPTURED YOU.

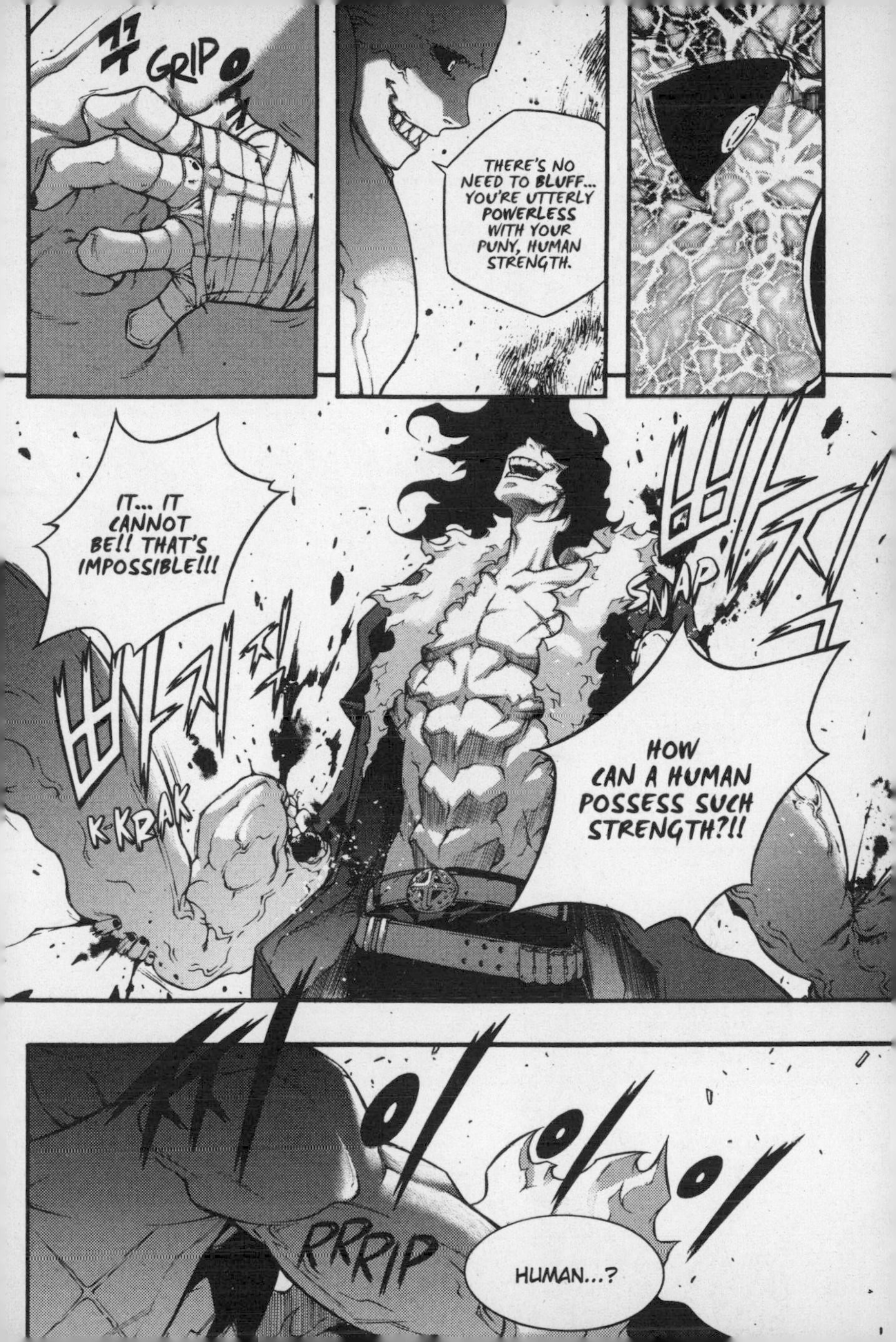
GRIP
THERE'S NO NEED TO BLUFF... YOU'RE UTTERLY POWERLESS WITH YOUR PUNY, HUMAN STRENGTH.
IT... IT CANNOT BE!! THAT'S IMPOSSIBLE!!!
SNAP
HOW CAN A HUMAN POSSESS SUCH STRENGTH?!!
K-KRAK
RRRIP
HUMAN...?

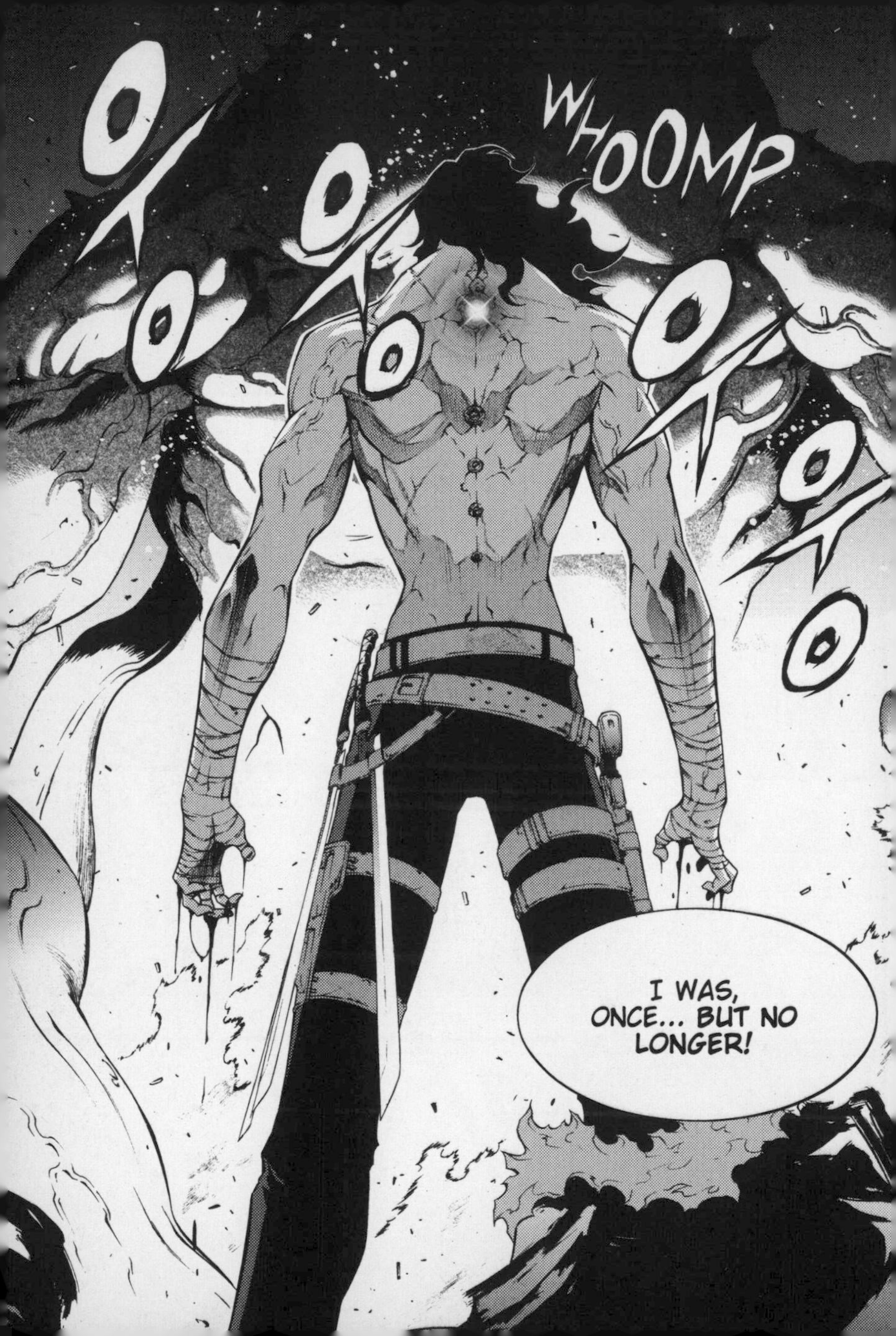
WHOOMP
OOOO
OOOO
I WAS, ONCE... BUT NO LONGER!

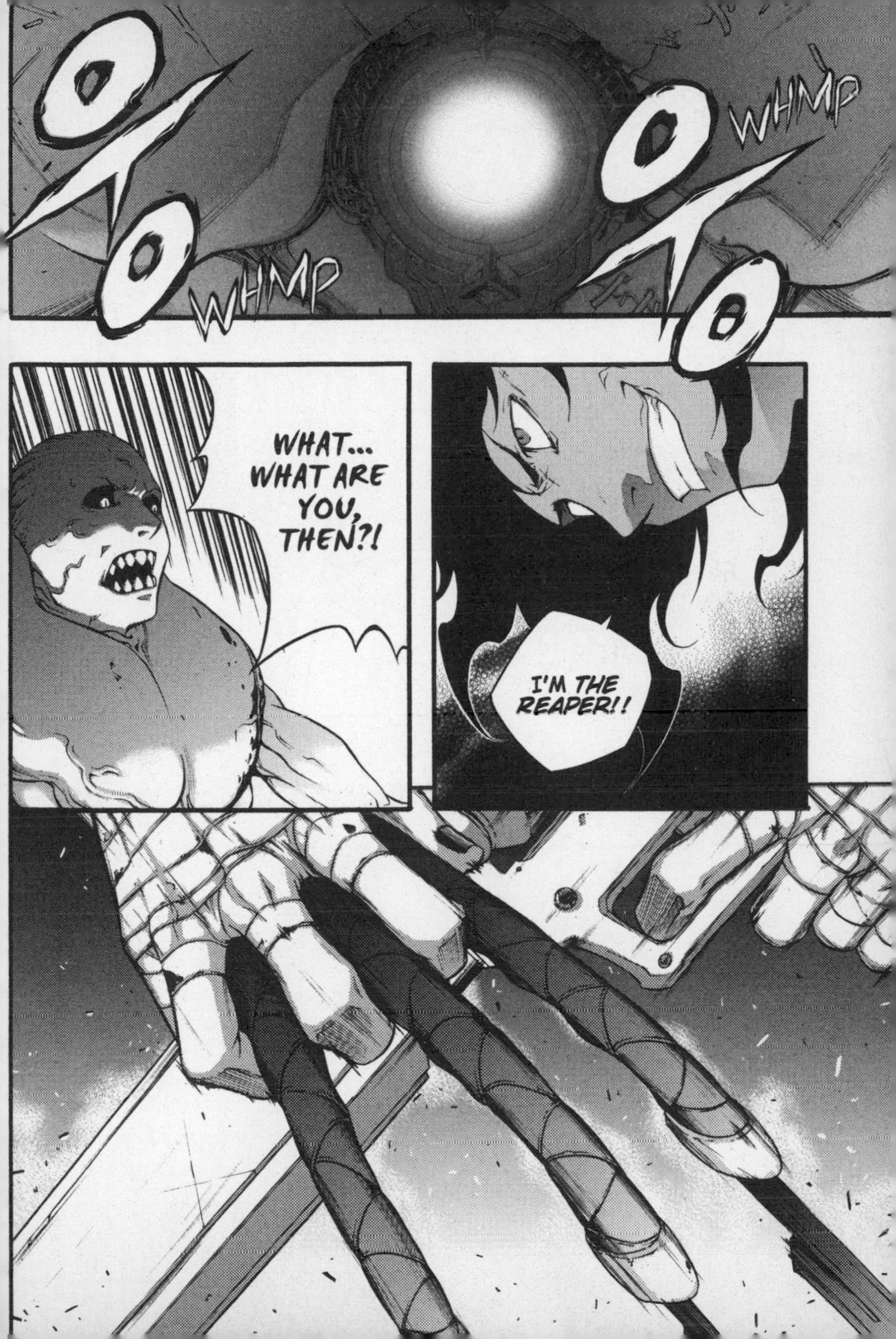
WHMP
WHMP
WHAT... WHAT ARE YOU, THEN?!
I'M THE REAPER!!

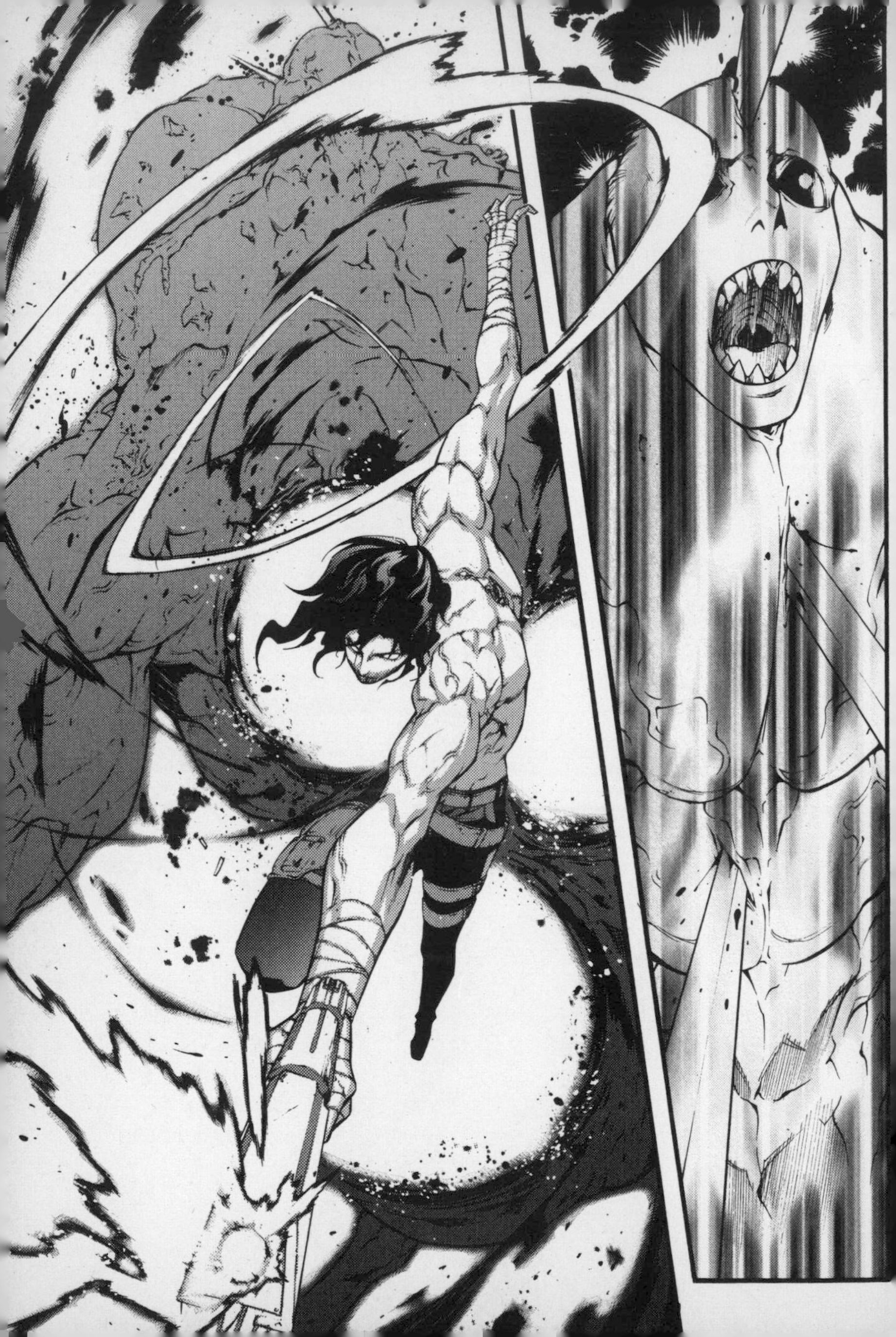

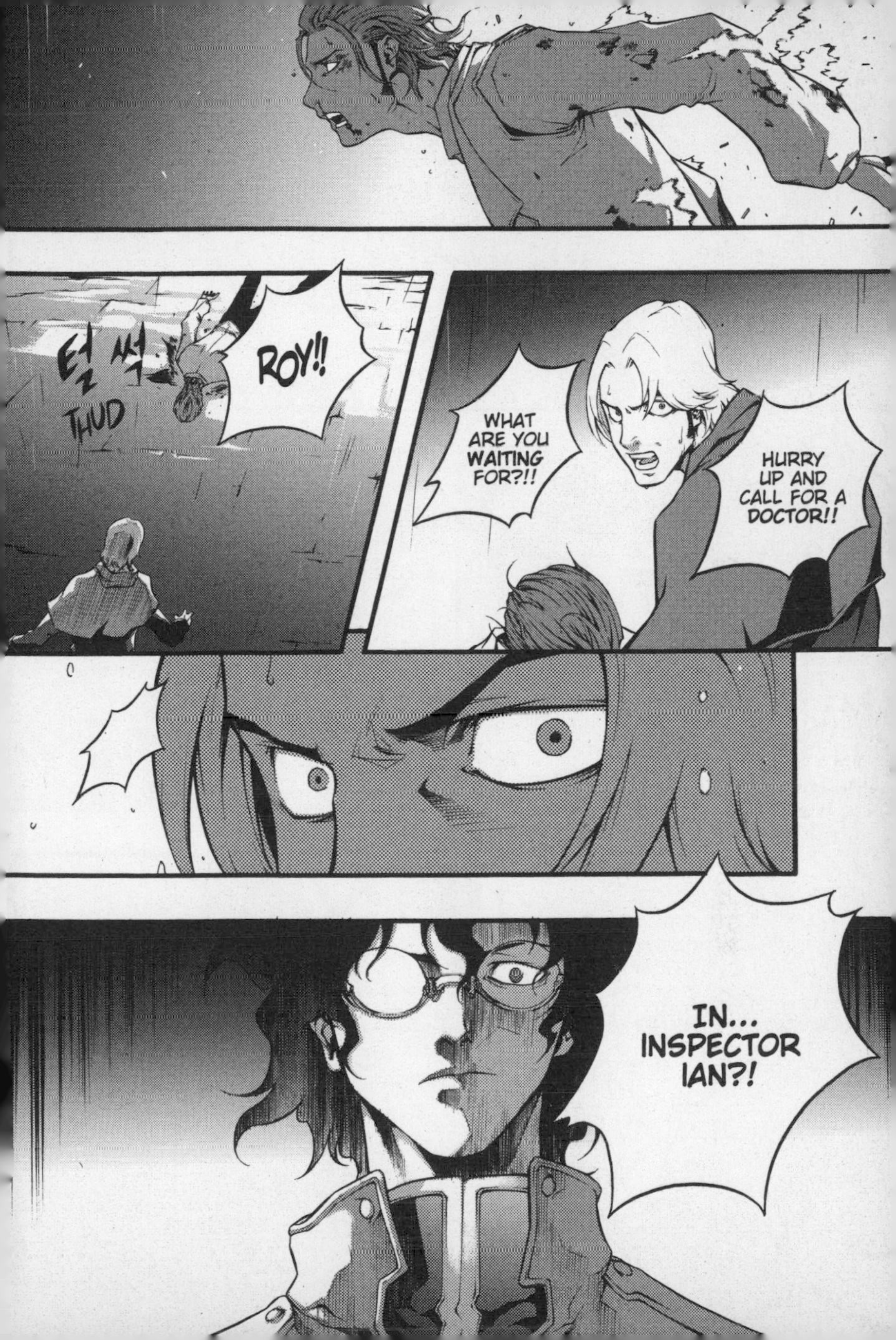
털썩
THUD
ROY!!
WHAT ARE YOU WAITING FOR?!!
HURRY UP AND CALL FOR A DOCTOR!!
IN... INSPECTOR IAN?!

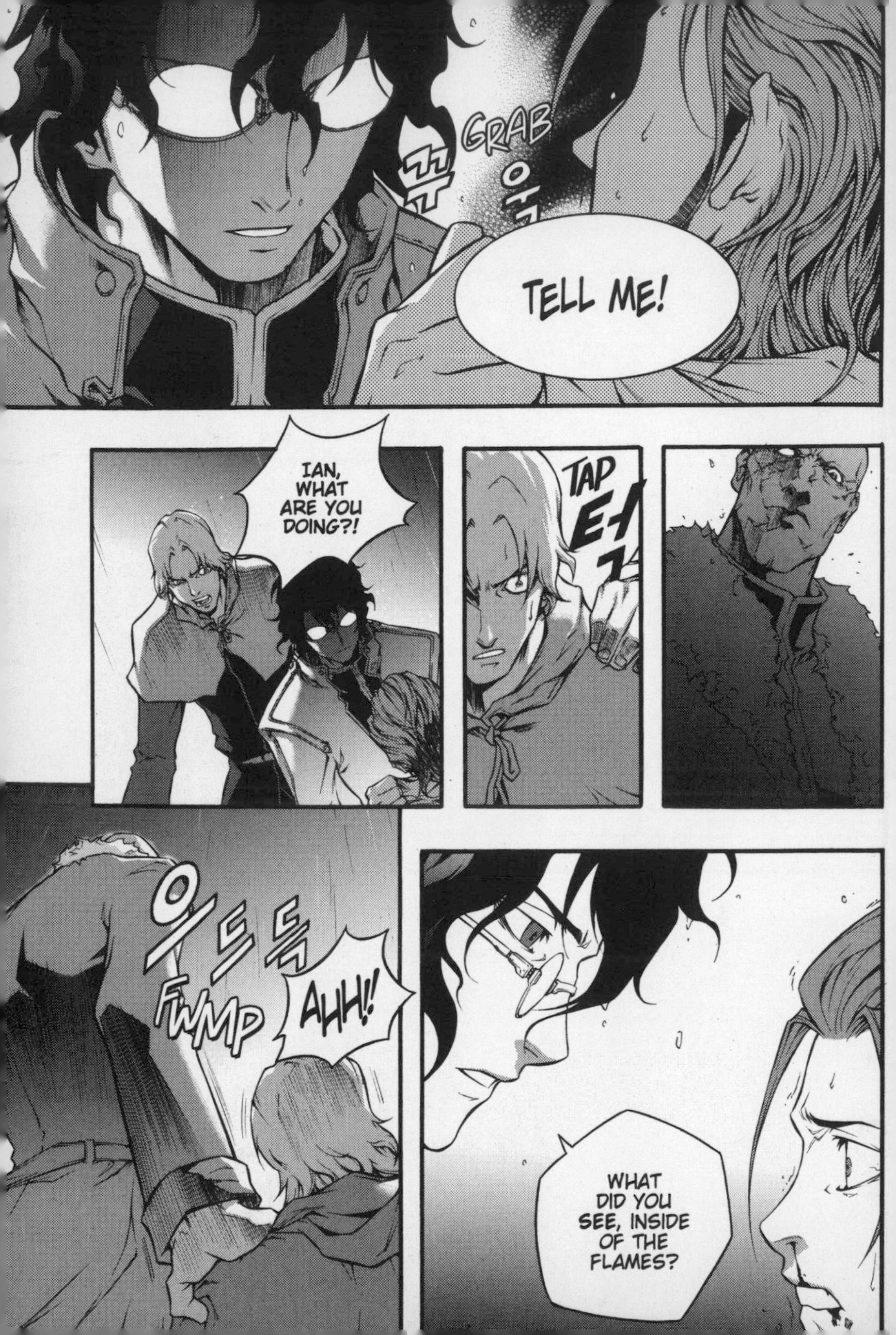
GRAB
TELL ME!
IAN, WHAT ARE YOU DOING?!
TAP
FWMP
AHH!!
WHAT DID YOU SEE, INSIDE OF THE FLAMES?

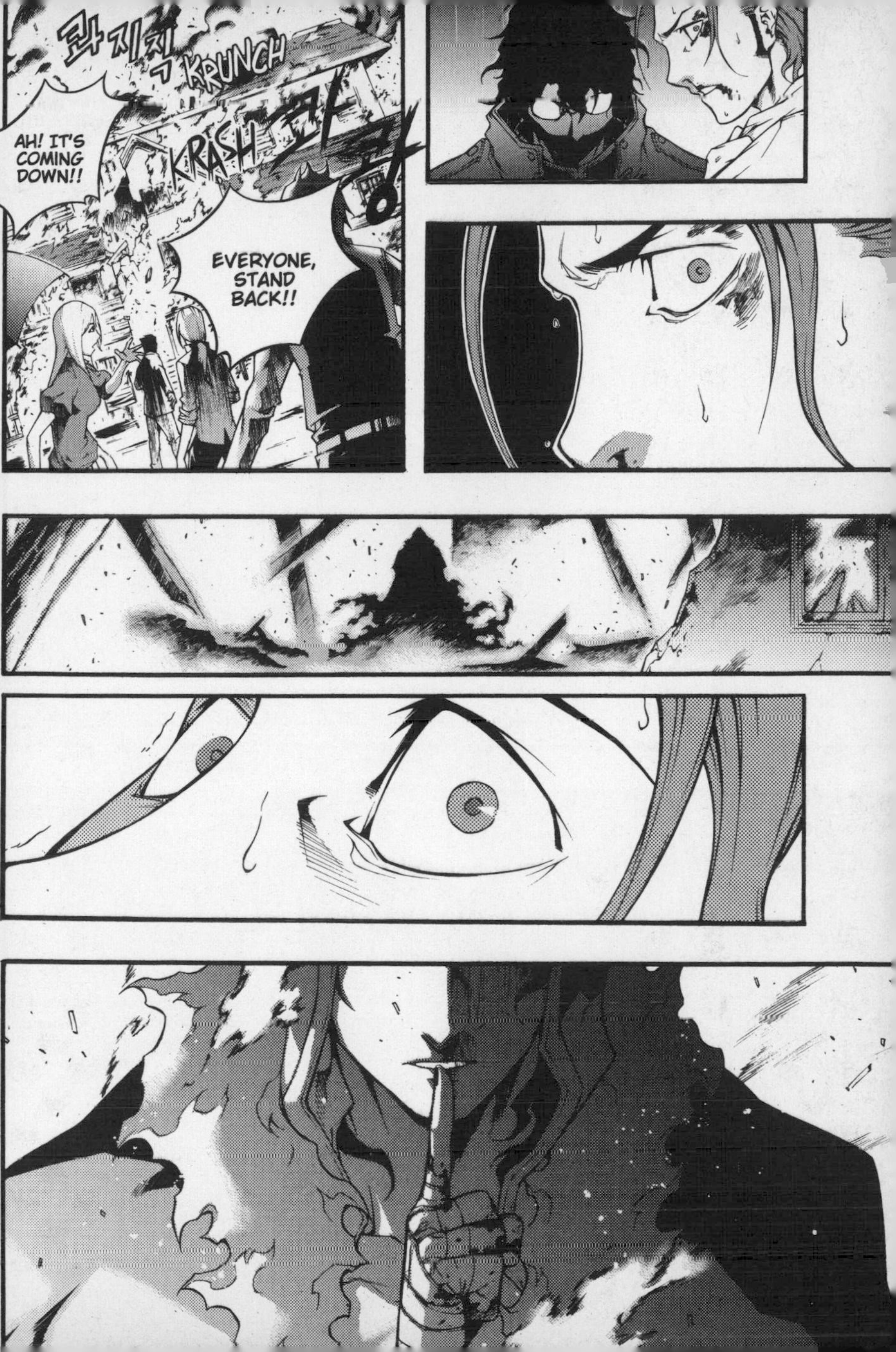

콰지직
KRUNCH
KRASH
콰앙
AH! IT'S COMING DOWN!!
EVERYONE, STAND BACK!!

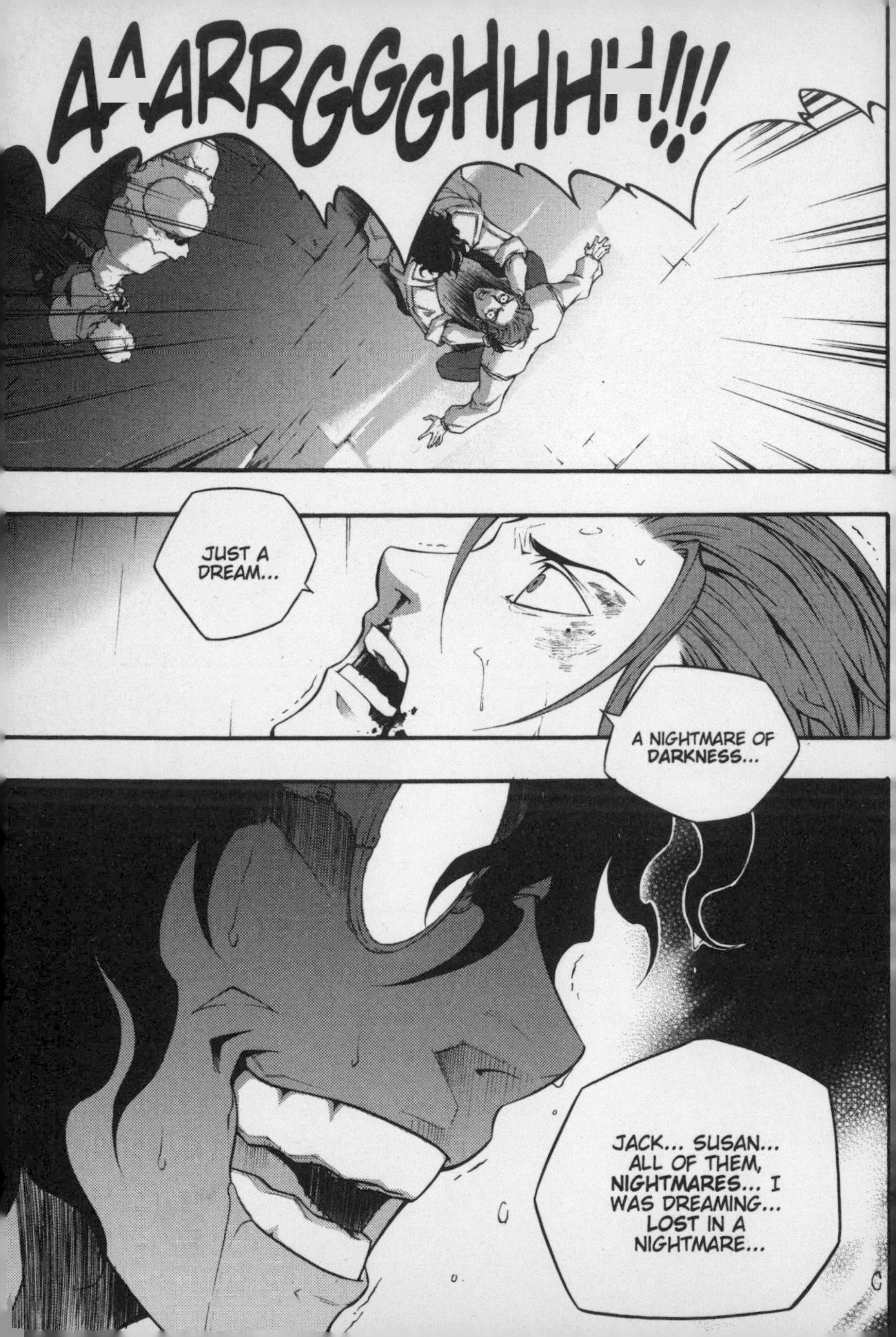
AAARRGGGHHHH!!!
JUST A DREAM...
A NIGHTMARE OF DARKNESS...
JACK... SUSAN... ALL OF THEM, NIGHTMARES... I WAS DREAMING... LOST IN A NIGHTMARE...

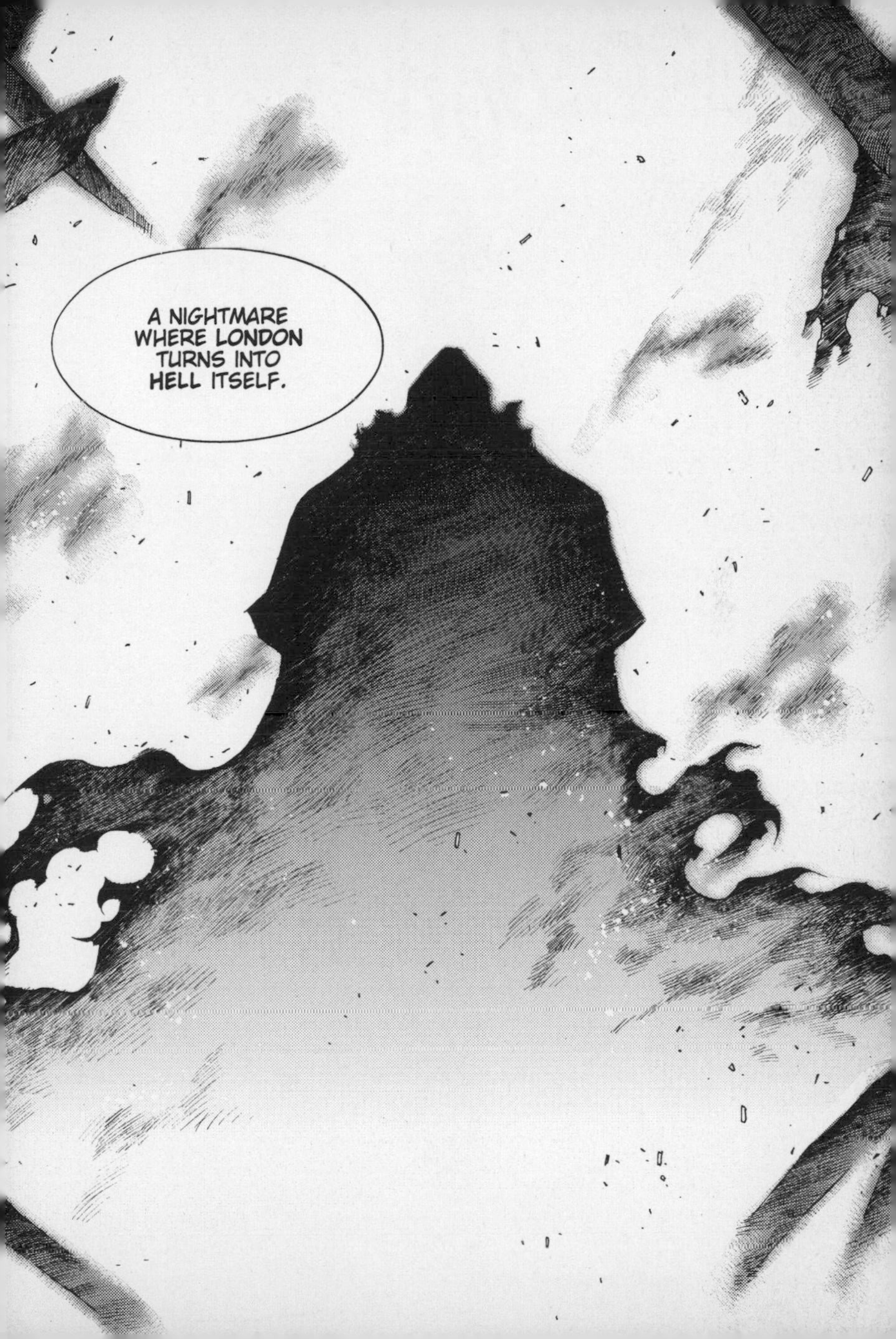
A NIGHTMARE WHERE LONDON TURNS INTO HELL ITSELF.

JACK THE RIPPER
Hell Blade

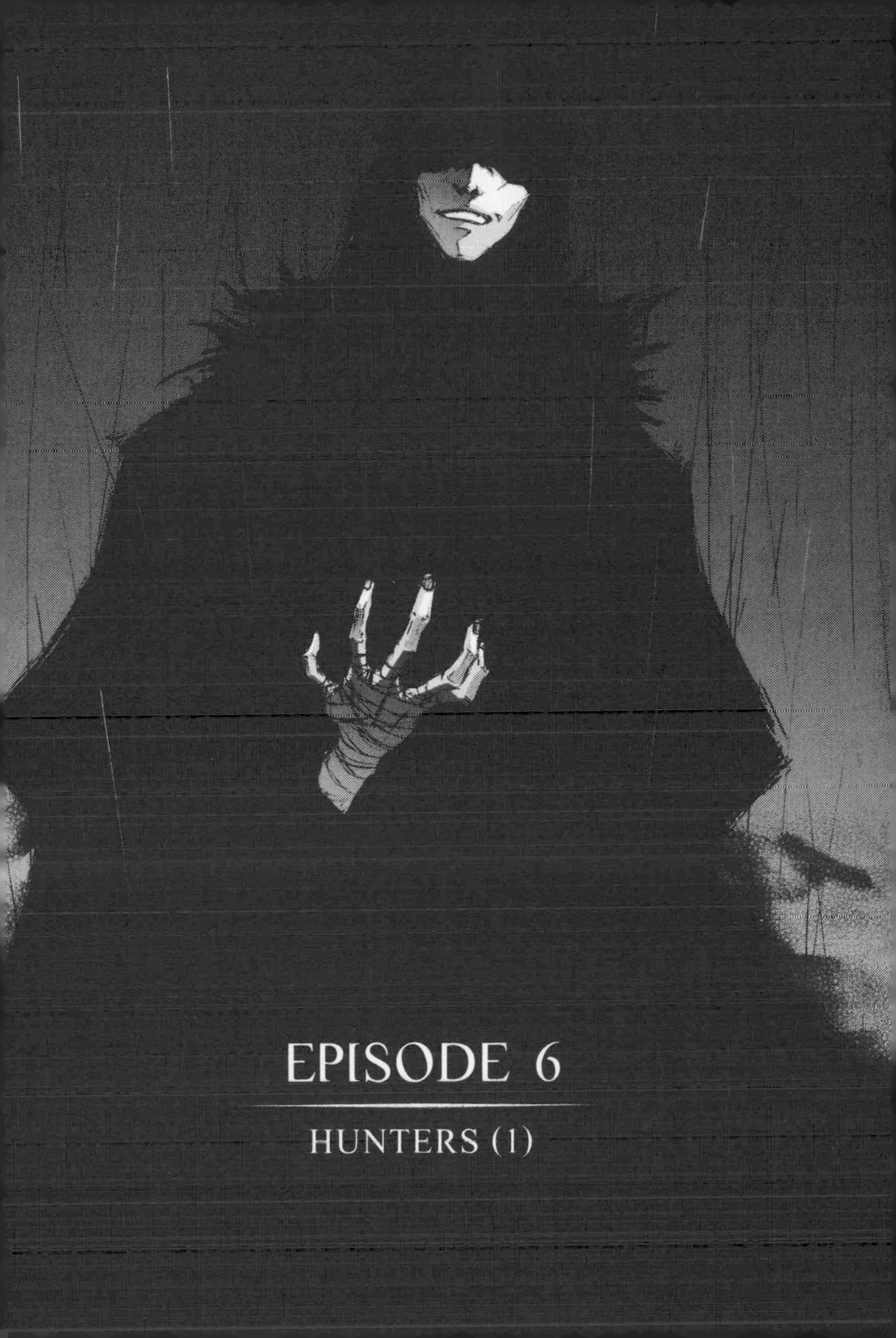

EPISODE 6

HUNTERS (1)

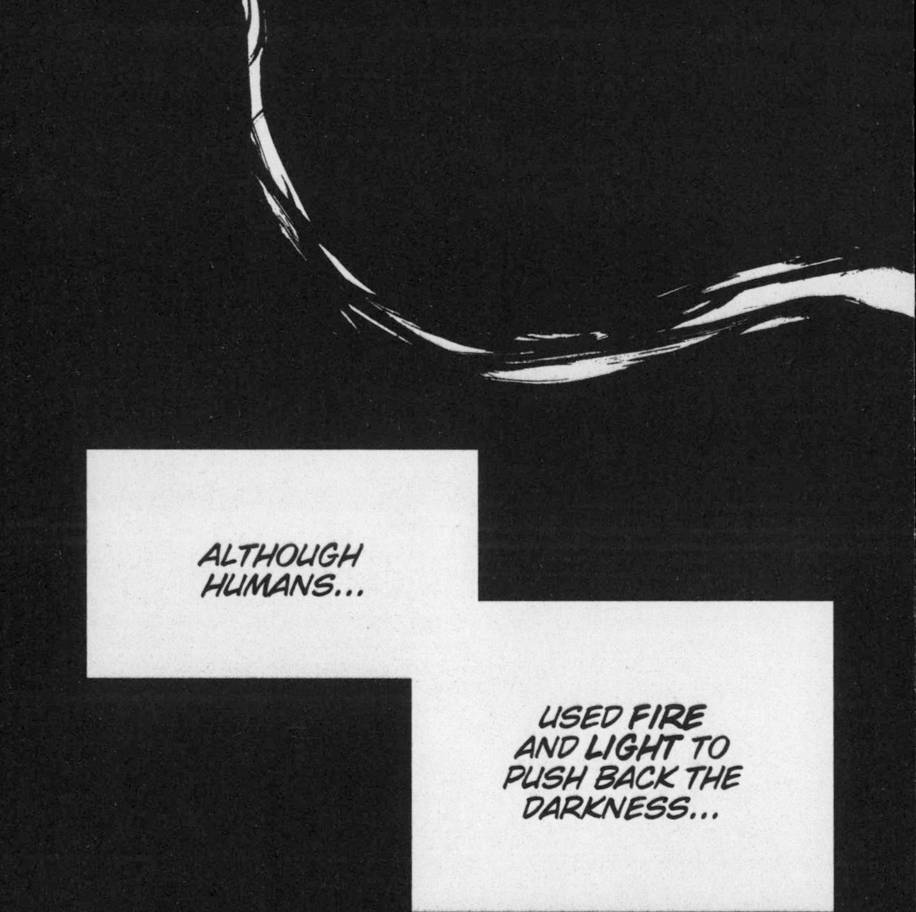
ALTHOUGH HUMANS...
USED **FIRE** AND **LIGHT** TO PUSH BACK THE DARKNESS...

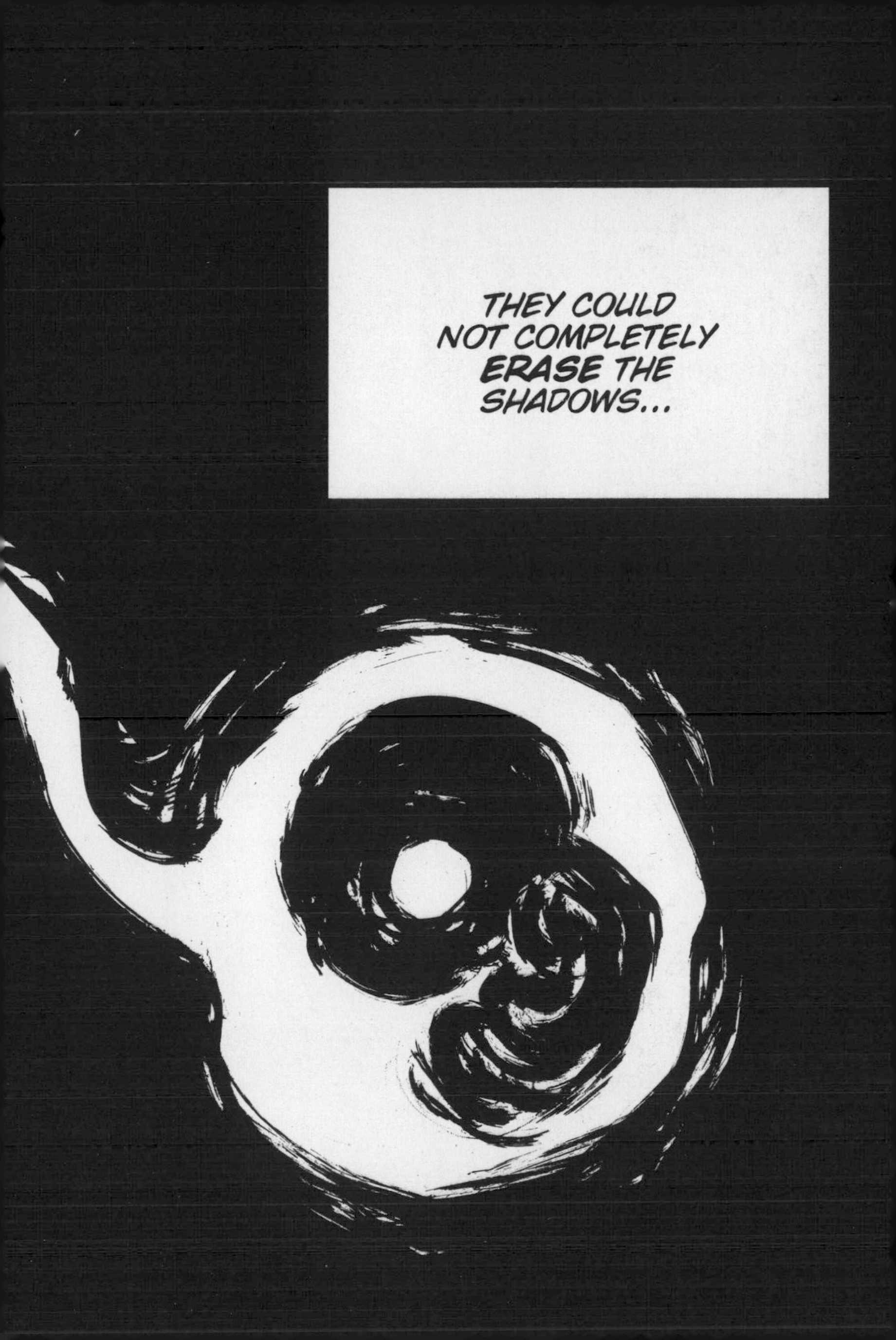
THEY COULD NOT COMPLETELY ERASE THE SHADOWS...

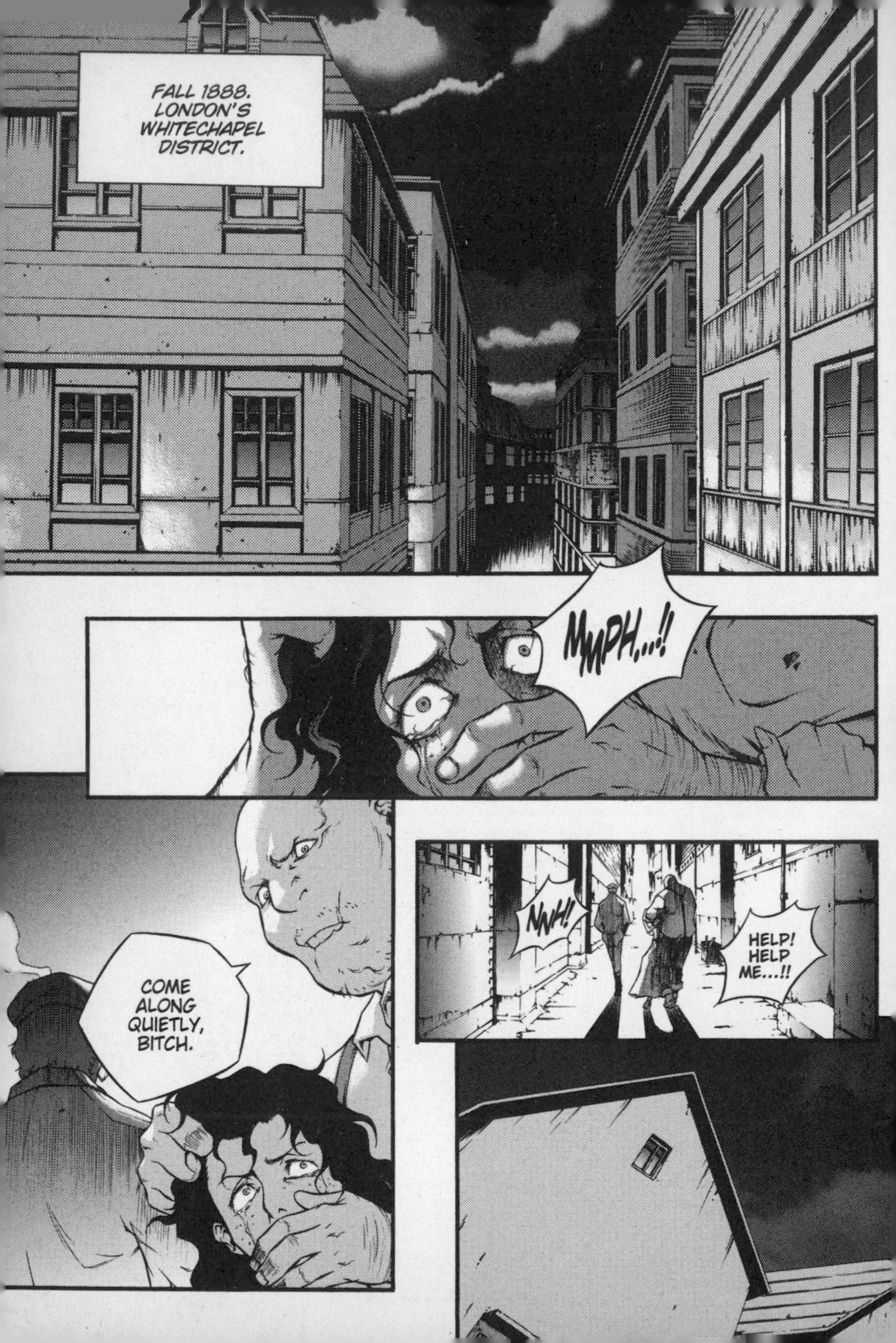
FALL 1888. LONDON'S WHITECHAPEL DISTRICT.
MMPH...!!
COME ALONG QUIETLY, BITCH.
NNH!
HELP! HELP ME...!!

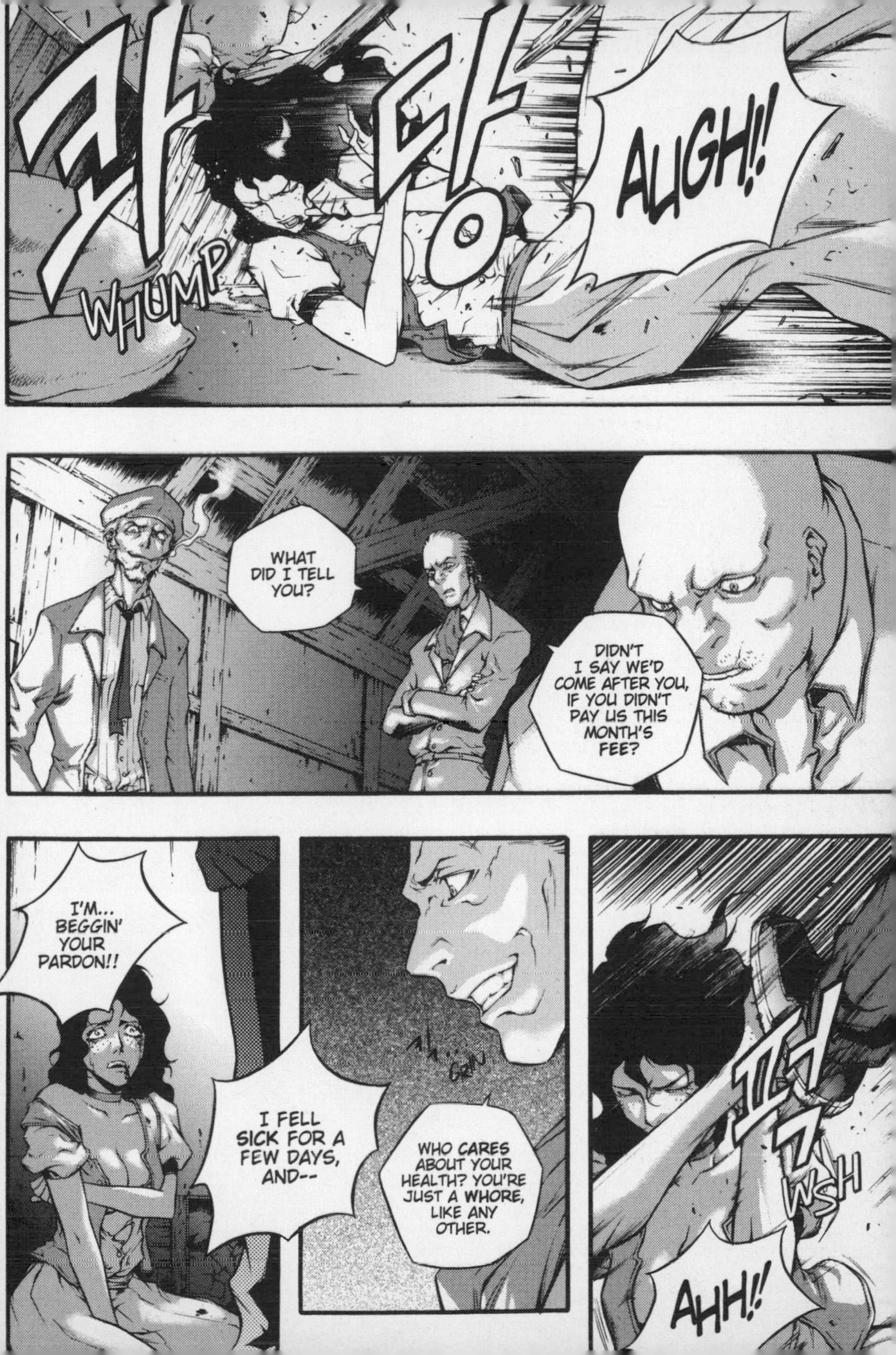
WHUMP
AUGH!!
WHAT DID I TELL YOU?
DIDN'T I SAY WE'D COME AFTER YOU, IF YOU DIDN'T PAY US THIS MONTH'S FEE?
I'M... BEGGIN' YOUR PARDON!!
I FELL SICK FOR A FEW DAYS, AND--
WHO CARES ABOUT YOUR HEALTH? YOU'RE JUST A WHORE, LIKE ANY OTHER.
WSH
AHH!!

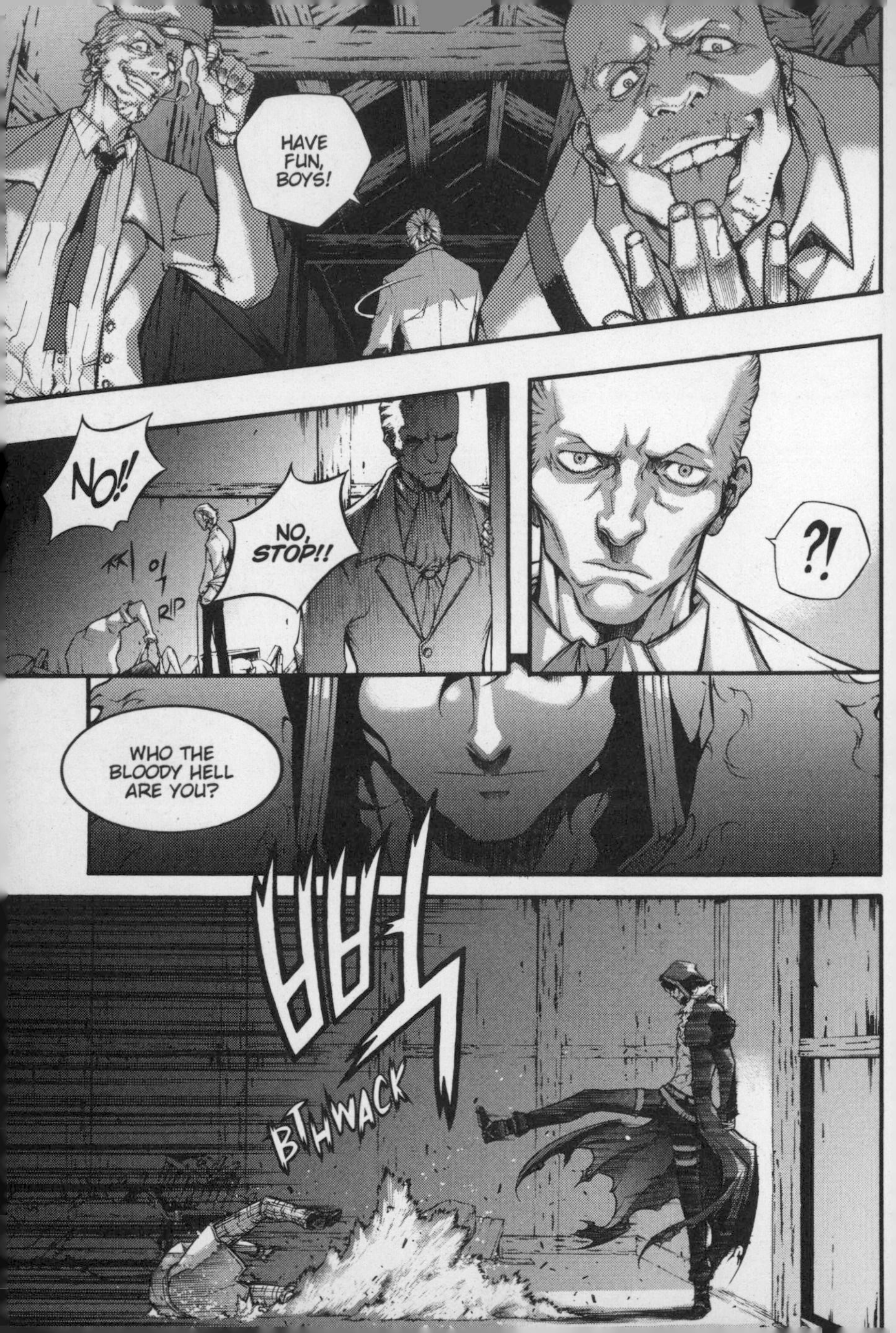
HAVE FUN, BOYS!
NO!!
RIP
NO, STOP!!
?!
WHO THE BLOODY HELL ARE YOU?
BTHWACK

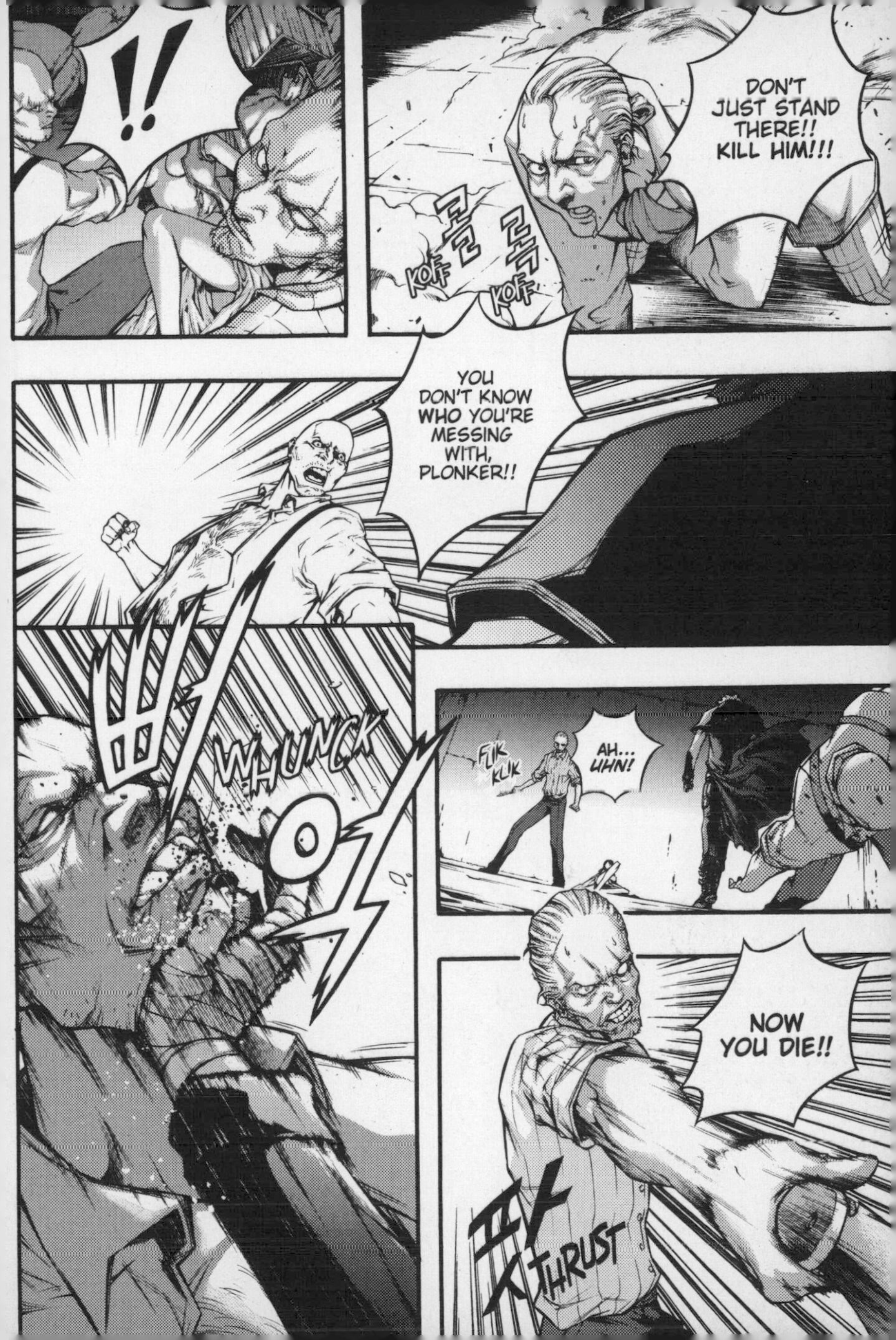
!!
DON'T JUST STAND THERE!! KILL HIM!!!
KOFF
KOFF
YOU DON'T KNOW WHO YOU'RE MESSING WITH, PLONKER!!
WHUNCK
FLIK KLIK
AH... UHN!
NOW YOU DIE!!
THRUST

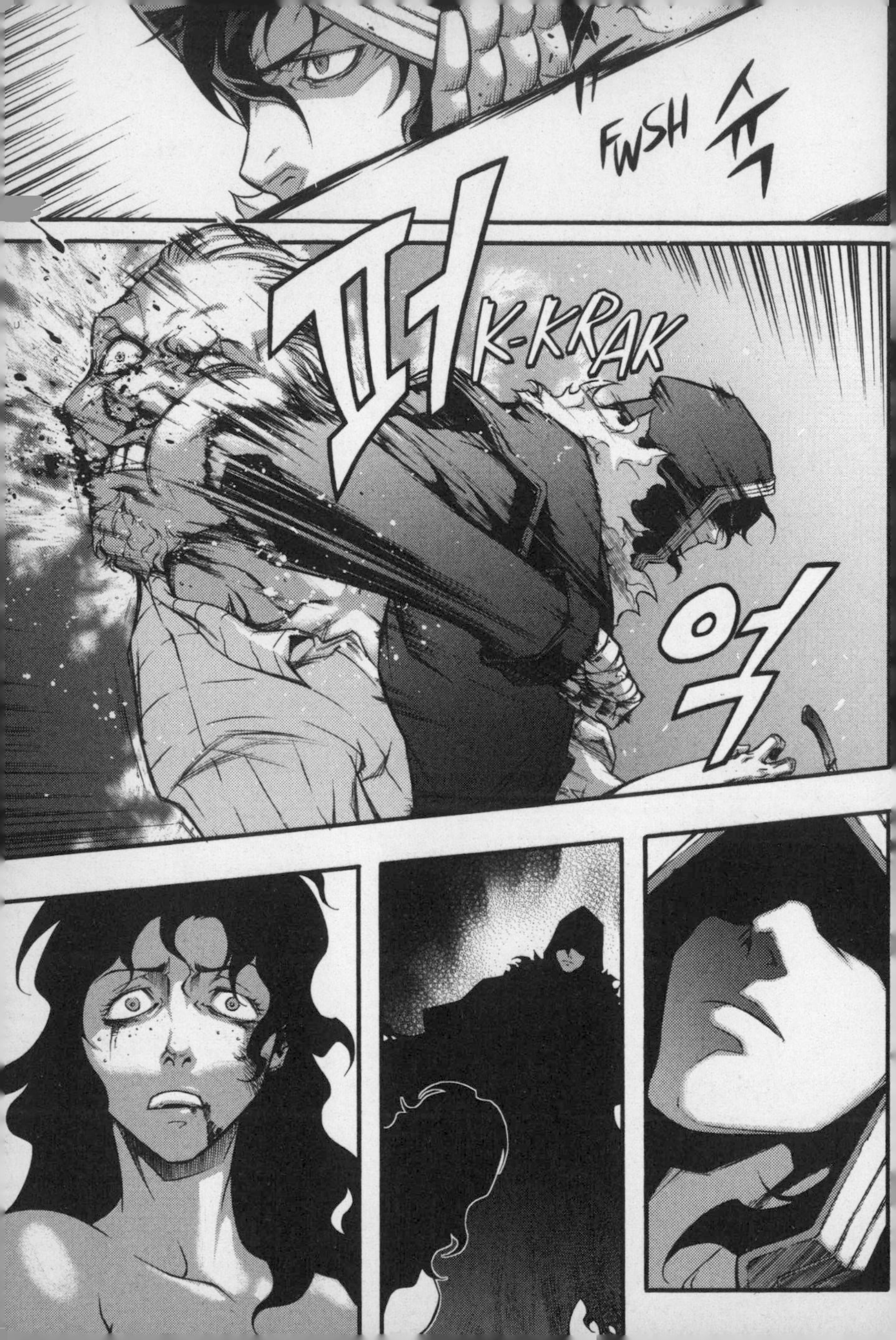
FWSH
슈
K-KRAK
퍽
억

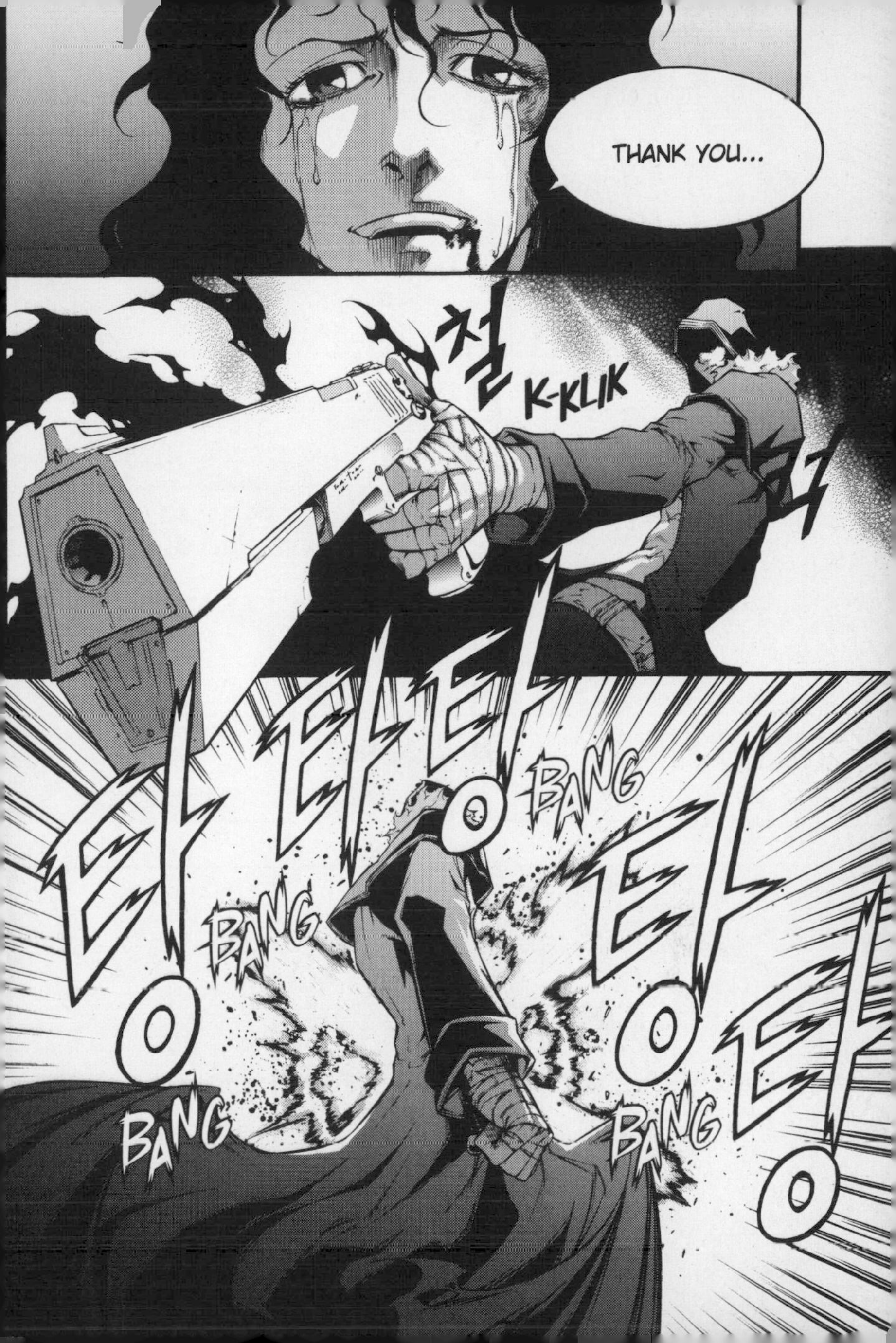
THANK YOU...
철
K-KLIK
탕
탕
BANG
BANG
탕
BANG
탕
BANG

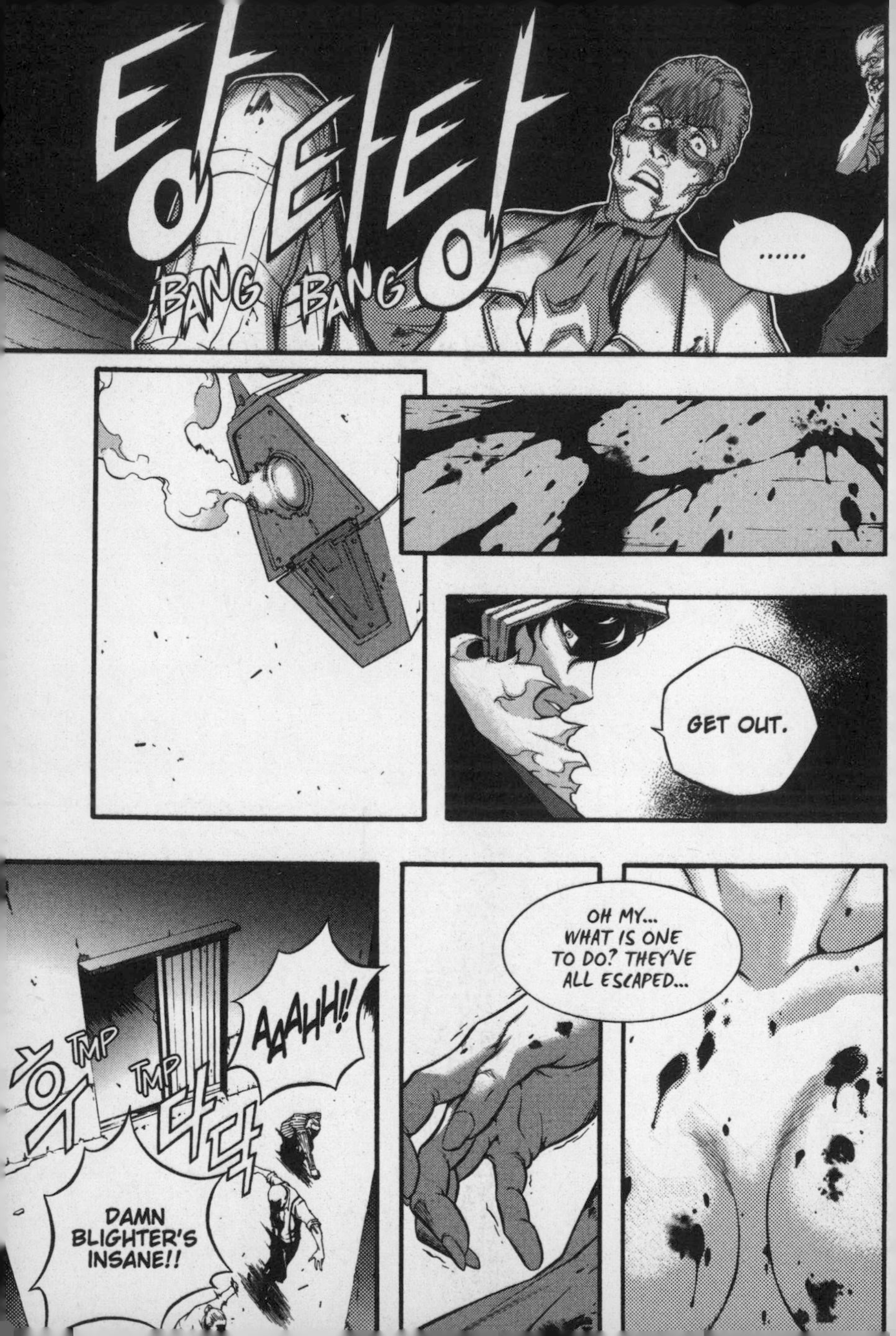
BANG BANG
......
GET OUT.
TMP TMP
AAAHH!!
DAMN BLIGHTER'S INSANE!!
OH MY... WHAT IS ONE TO DO? THEY'VE ALL ESCAPED...

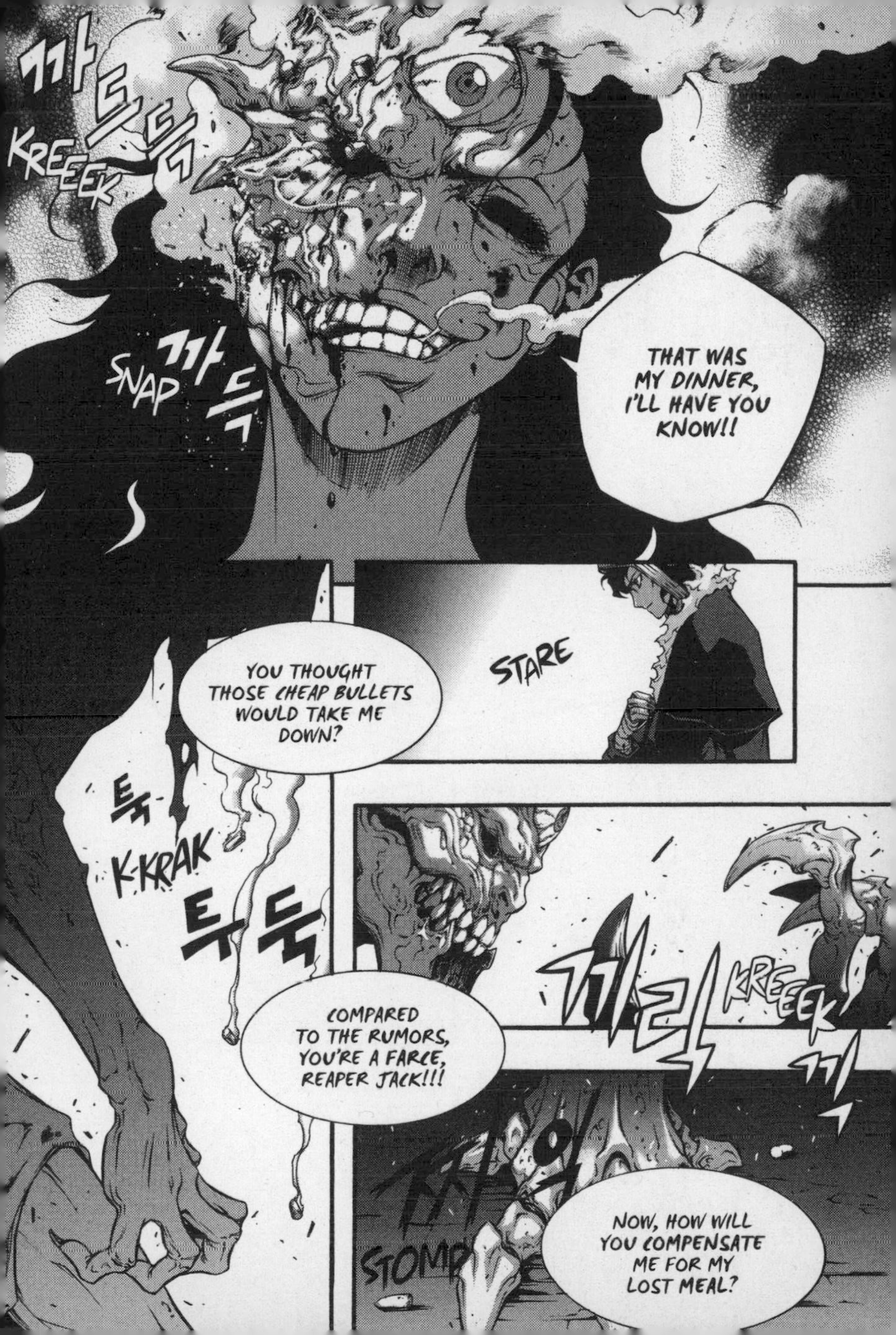
까드득
KREEEK
까득
SNAP
THAT WAS MY DINNER, I'LL HAVE YOU KNOW!!
YOU THOUGHT THOSE CHEAP BULLETS WOULD TAKE ME DOWN?
툭
K-KRAK
투둑
COMPARED TO THE RUMORS, YOU'RE A FARCE, REAPER JACK!!!
STARE
KREEEK
STOMP
NOW, HOW WILL YOU COMPENSATE ME FOR MY LOST MEAL?

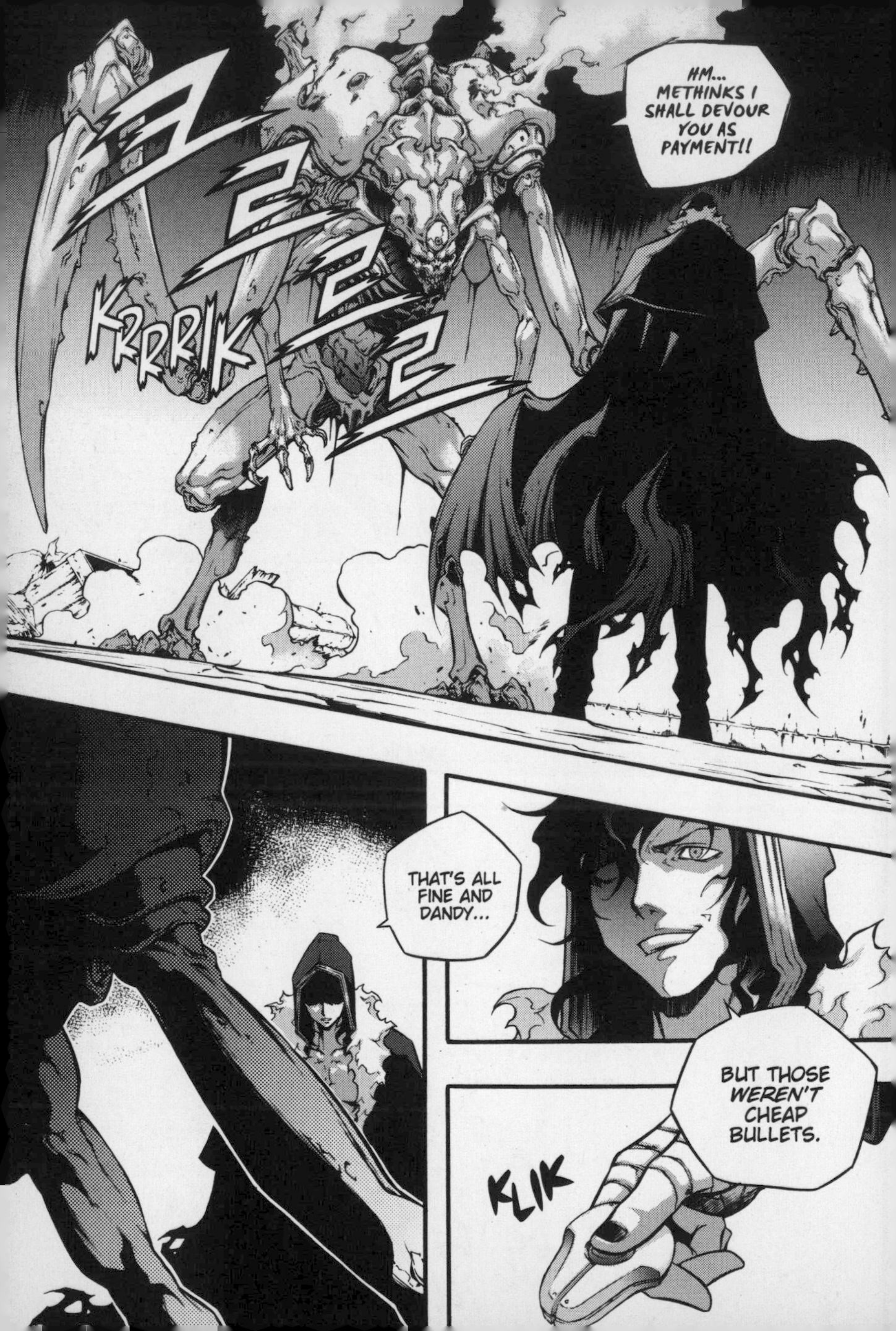
HM... METHINKS I SHALL DEVOUR YOU AS PAYMENT!!
KRRRIK
THAT'S ALL FINE AND DANDY...
BUT THOSE WEREN'T CHEAP BULLETS.
KLIK

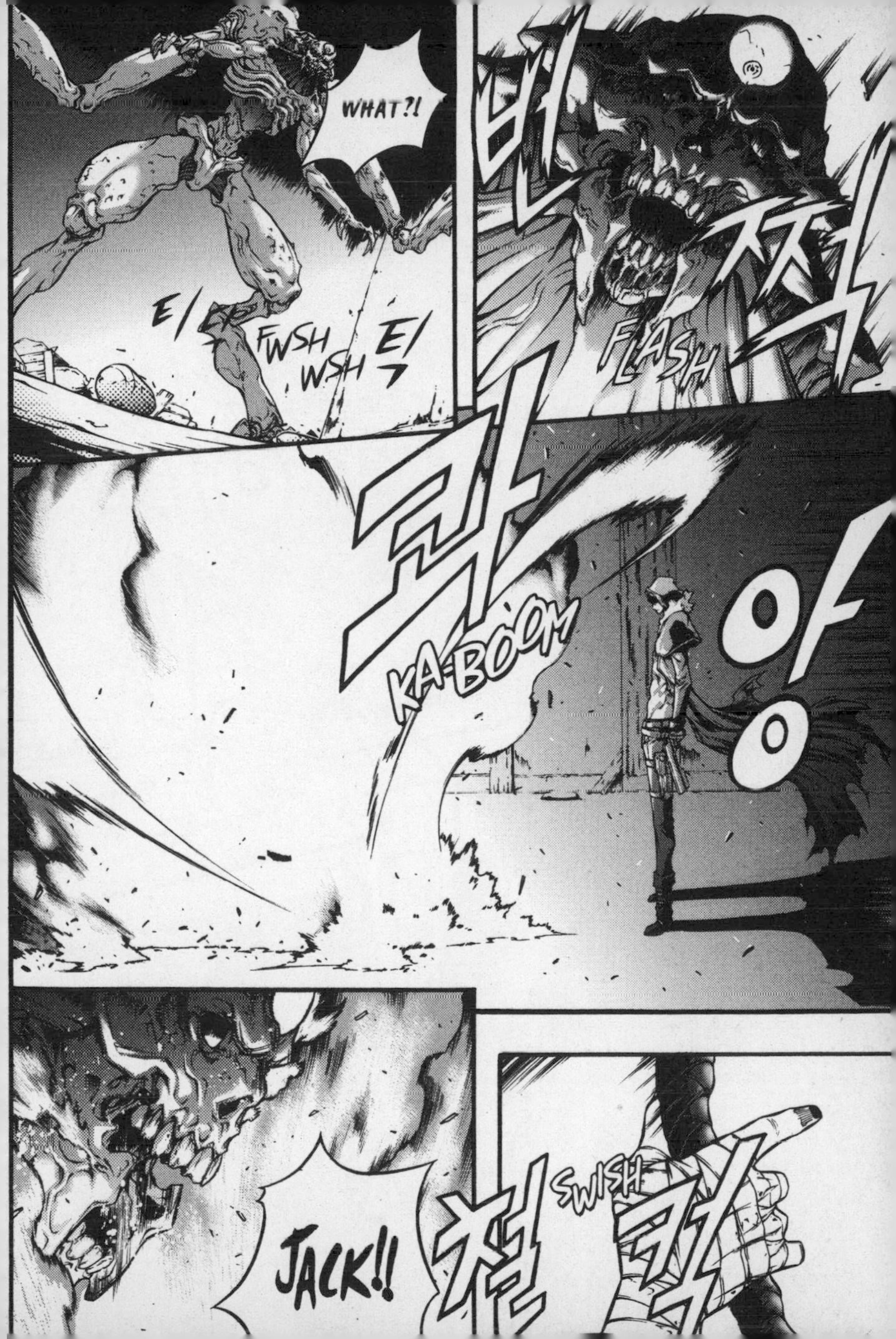
WHAT?!
FWSH
WSH
FLASH
KA-BOOM
JACK!!
SWISH

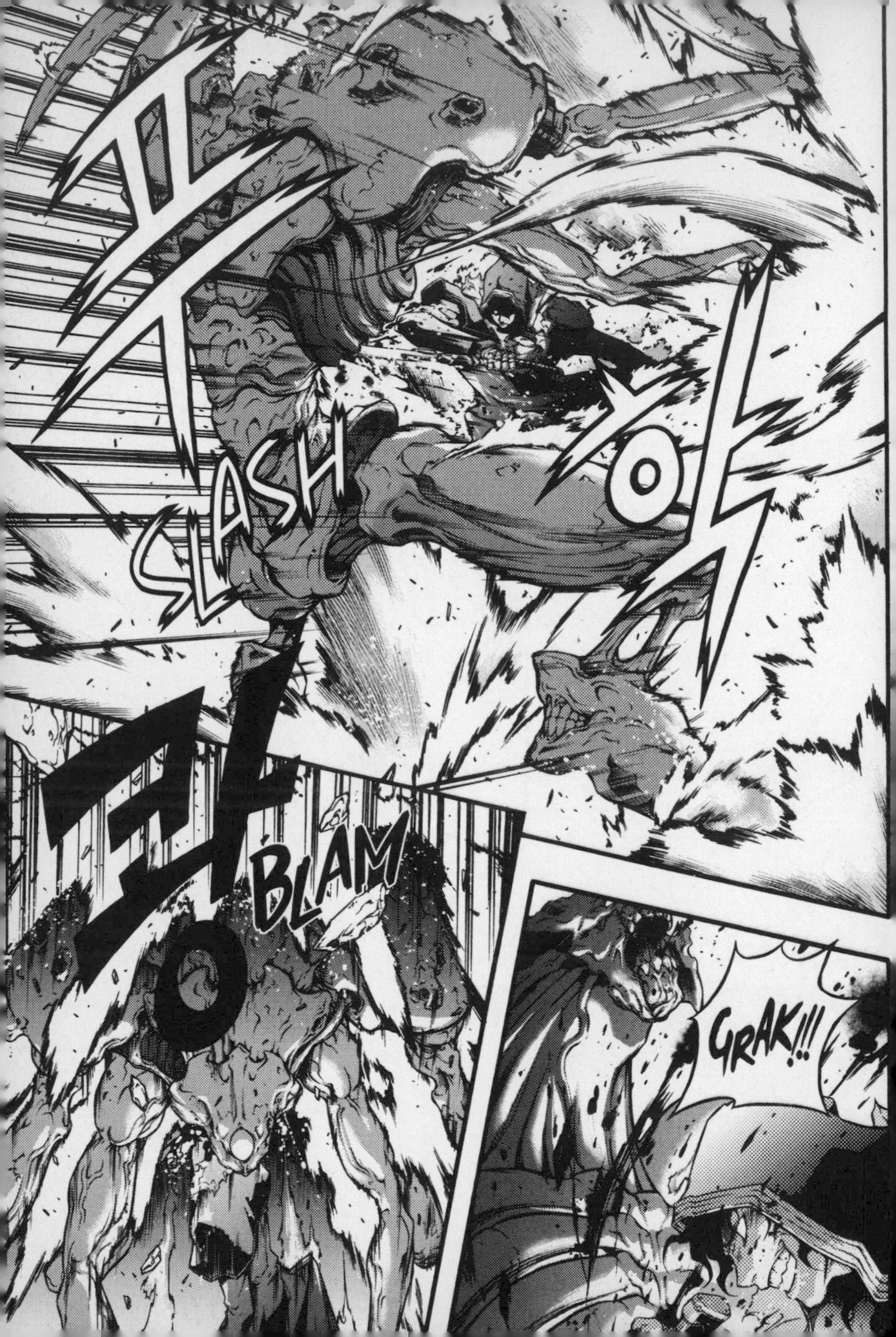
SLASH
BLAM
GRAK!!!

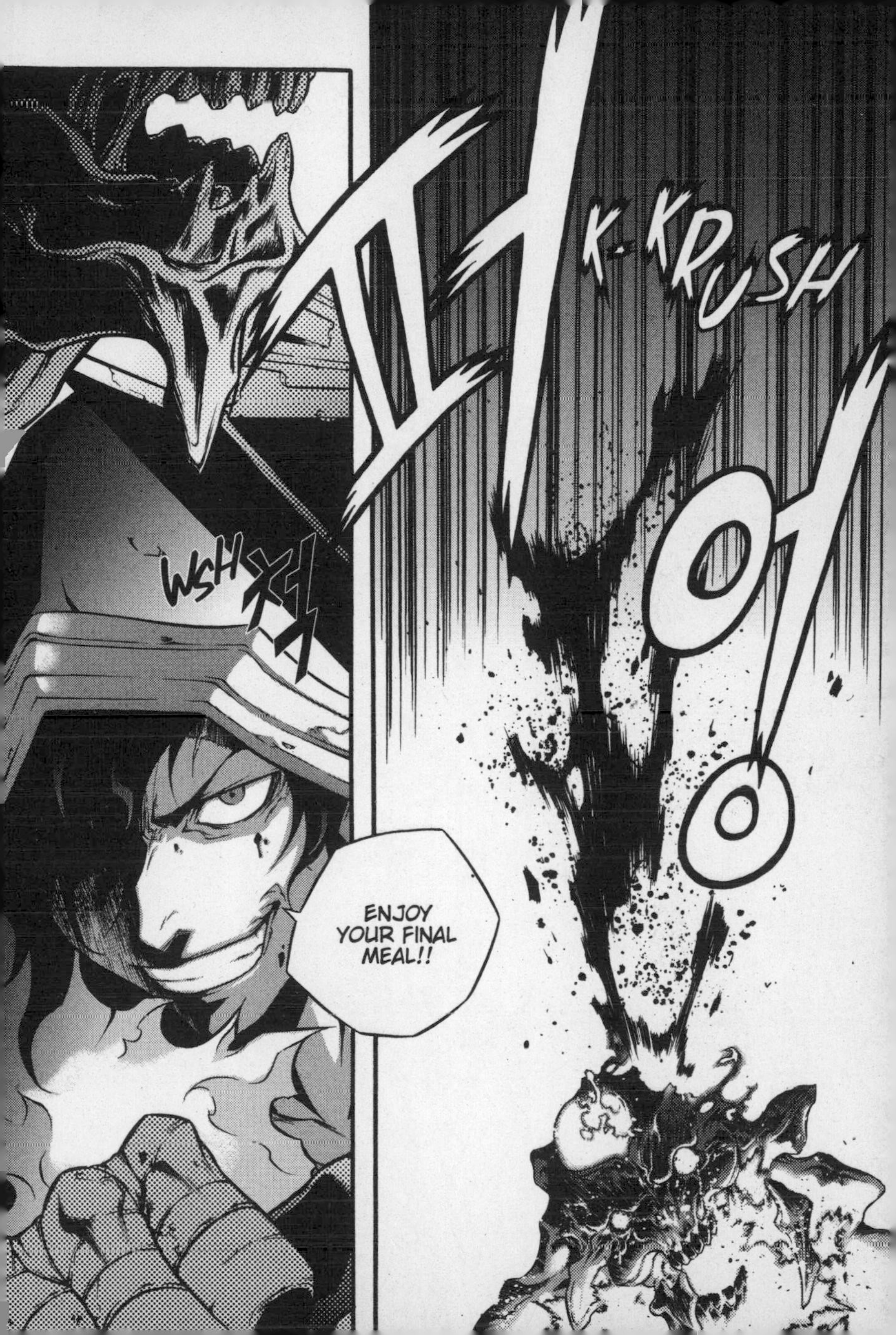
WSH
ENJOY YOUR FINAL MEAL!!
K-KRUSH

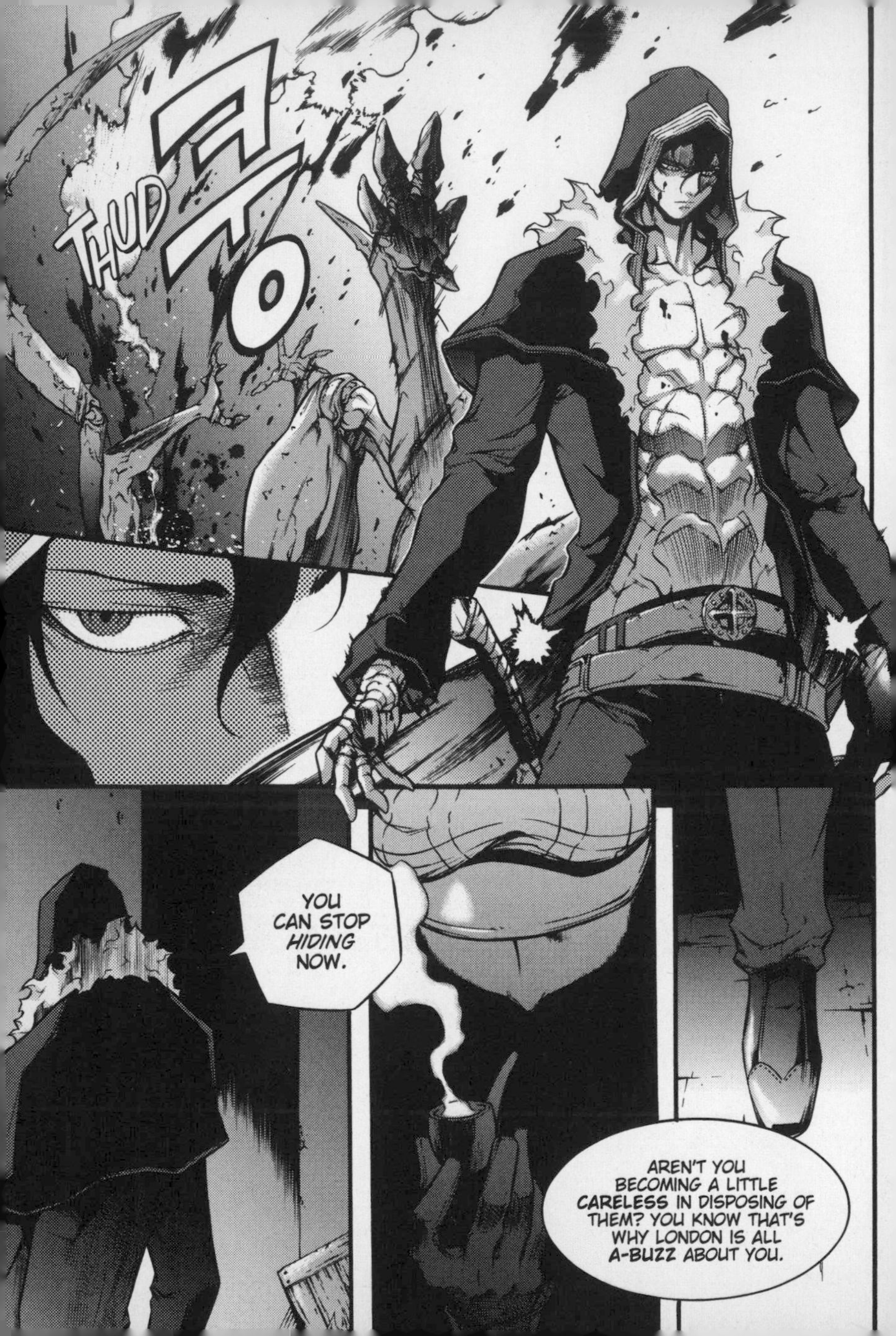
THUD
YOU CAN STOP HIDING NOW.
AREN'T YOU BECOMING A LITTLE CARELESS IN DISPOSING OF THEM? YOU KNOW THAT'S WHY LONDON IS ALL A-BUZZ ABOUT YOU.

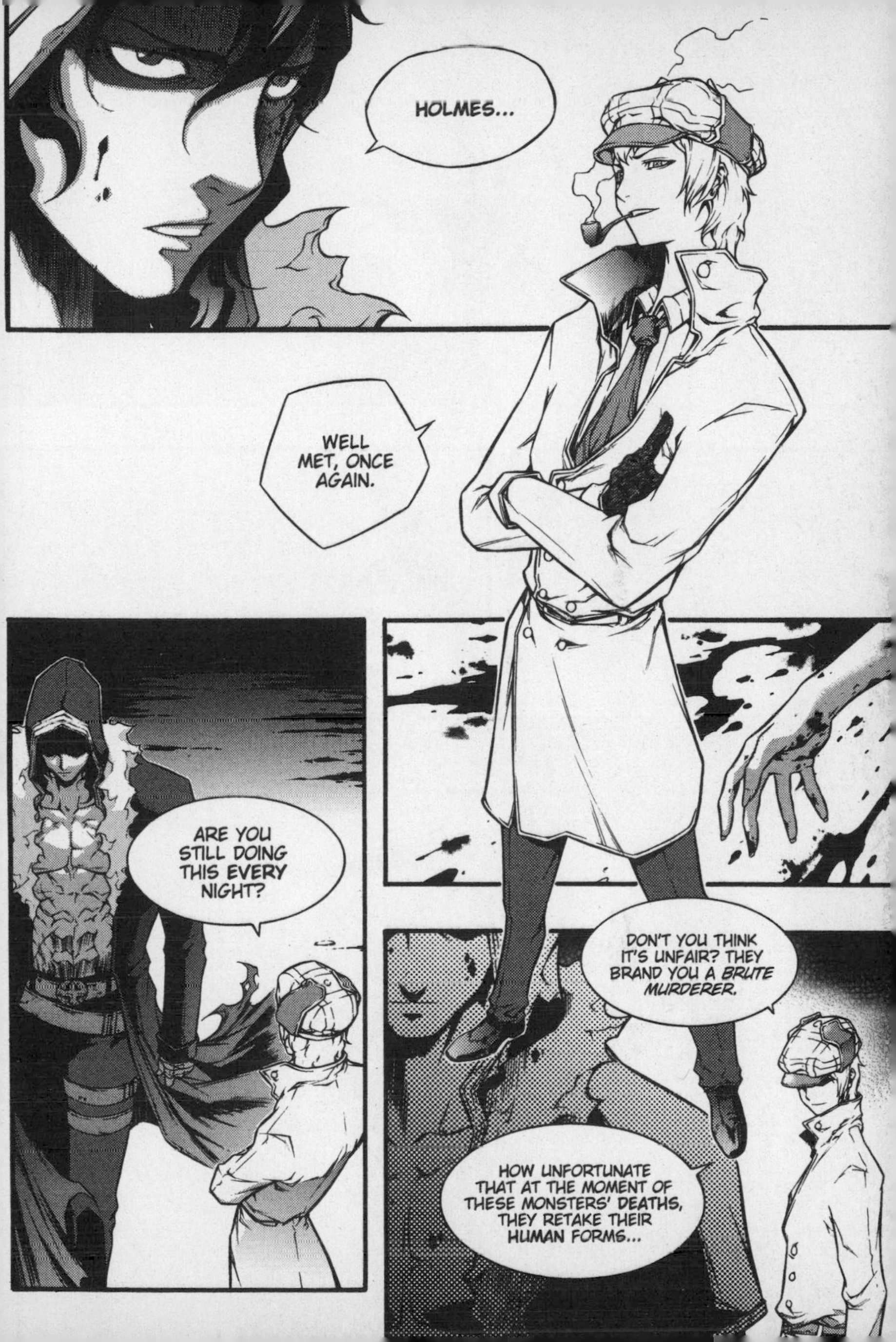
HOLMES...
WELL MET, ONCE AGAIN.
ARE YOU STILL DOING THIS EVERY NIGHT?
DON'T YOU THINK IT'S UNFAIR? THEY BRAND YOU A *BRUTE MURDERER*.
HOW UNFORTUNATE THAT AT THE MOMENT OF THESE MONSTERS' DEATHS, THEY RETAKE THEIR HUMAN FORMS...

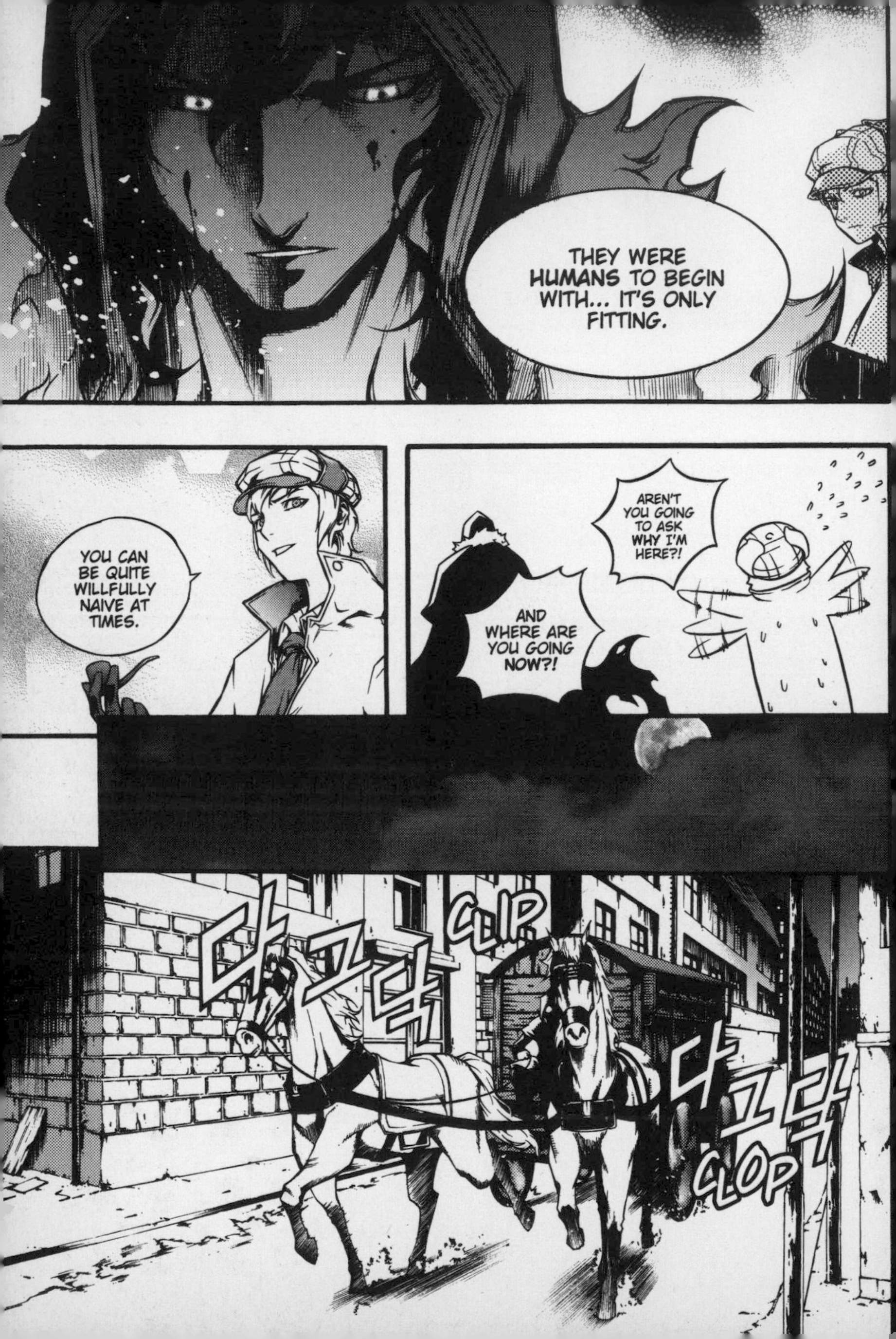
THEY WERE HUMANS TO BEGIN WITH... IT'S ONLY FITTING.
YOU CAN BE QUITE WILLFULLY NAIVE AT TIMES.
AREN'T YOU GOING TO ASK WHY I'M HERE?!
AND WHERE ARE YOU GOING NOW?!
CLIP
CLOP

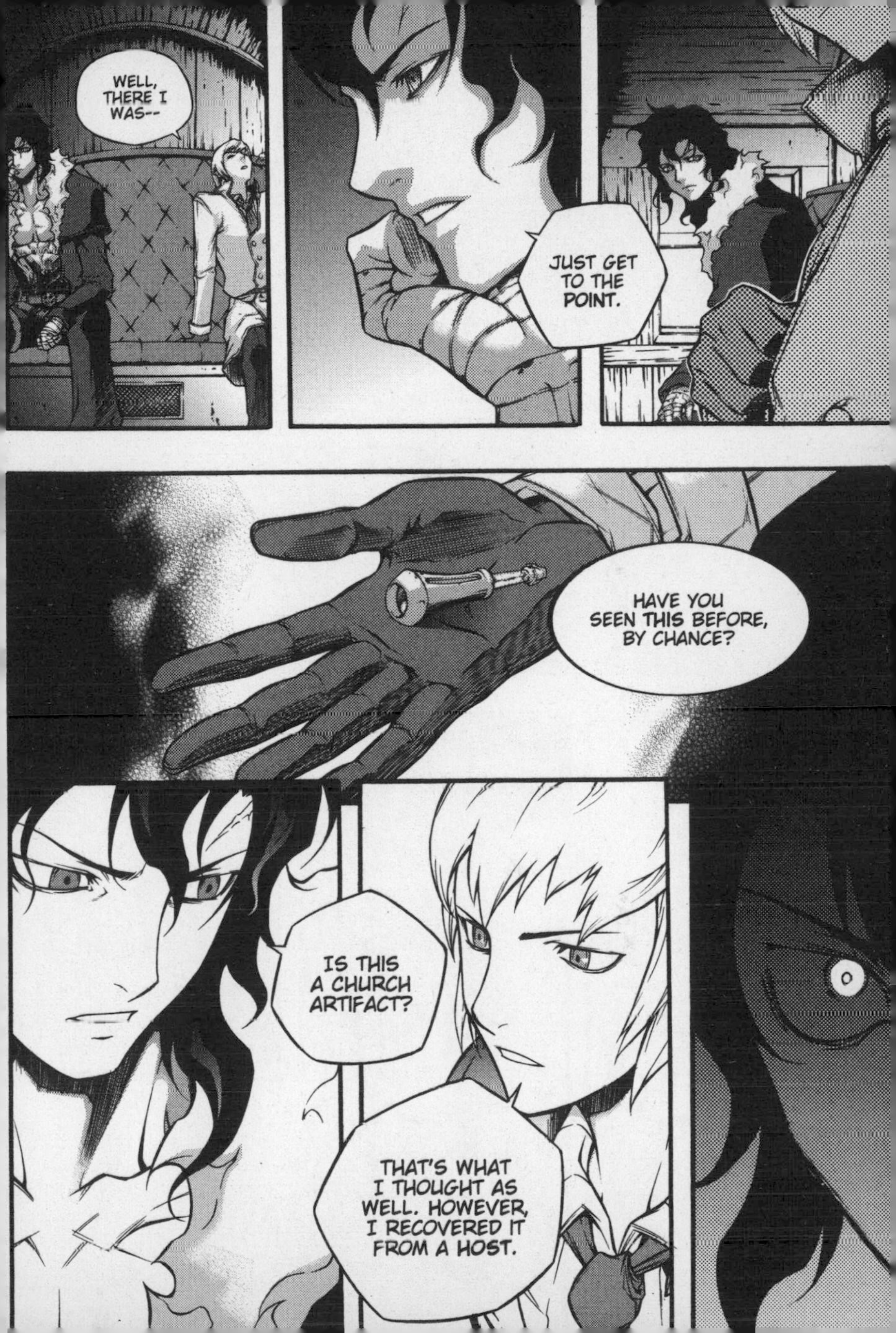
WELL, THERE I WAS--
JUST GET TO THE POINT.
HAVE YOU SEEN THIS BEFORE, BY CHANCE?
IS THIS A CHURCH ARTIFACT?
THAT'S WHAT I THOUGHT AS WELL. HOWEVER, I RECOVERED IT FROM A HOST.

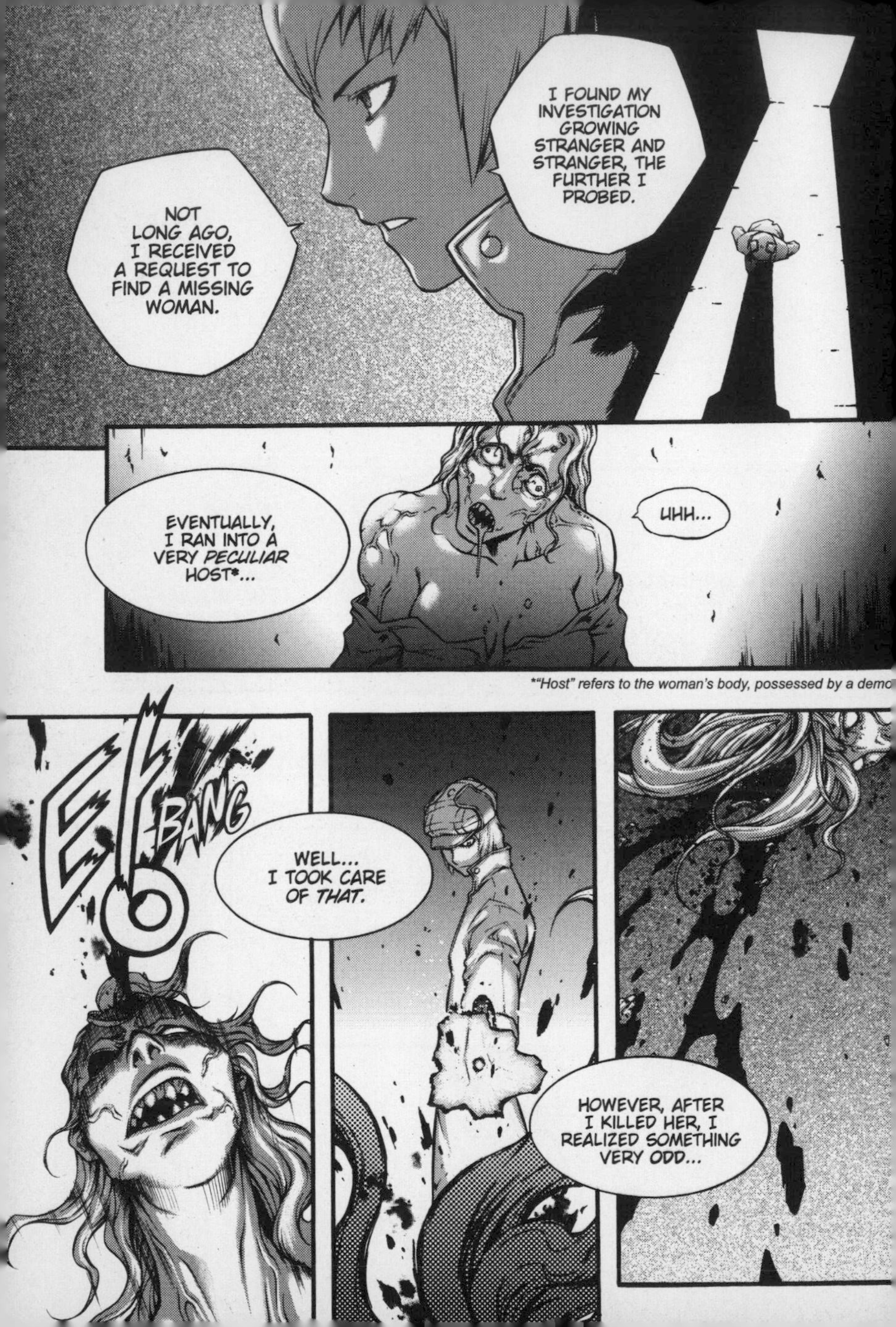
NOT LONG AGO, I RECEIVED A REQUEST TO FIND A MISSING WOMAN.
I FOUND MY INVESTIGATION GROWING STRANGER AND STRANGER, THE FURTHER I PROBED.
EVENTUALLY, I RAN INTO A VERY *PECULIAR* HOST*...
UHH...
BANG
WELL... I TOOK CARE OF *THAT*.
HOWEVER, AFTER I KILLED HER, I REALIZED SOMETHING VERY ODD...

*"Host" refers to the woman's body, possessed by a demo

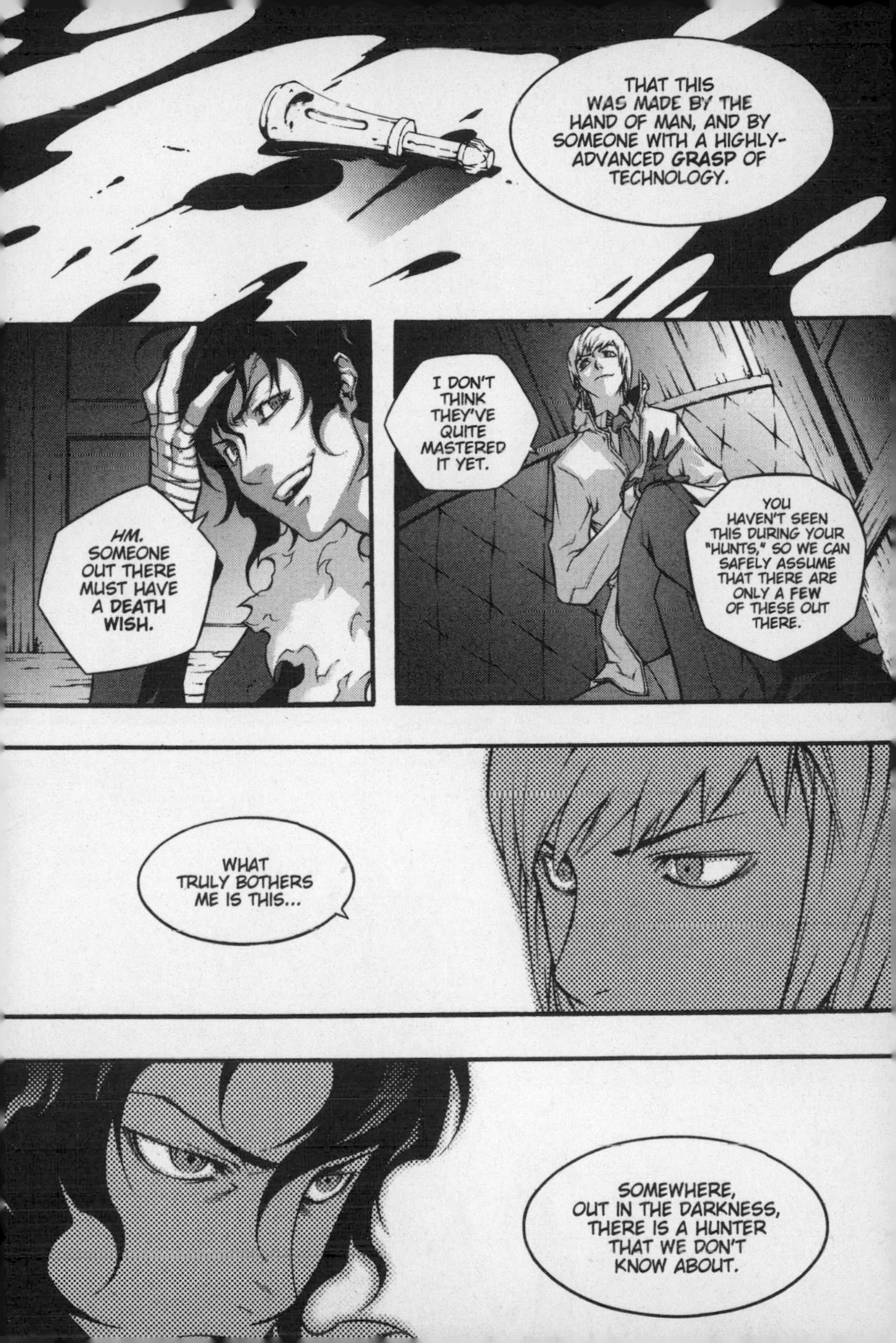
THAT THIS WAS MADE BY THE HAND OF MAN, AND BY SOMEONE WITH A HIGHLY-ADVANCED GRASP OF TECHNOLOGY.
HM. SOMEONE OUT THERE MUST HAVE A DEATH WISH.
I DON'T THINK THEY'VE QUITE MASTERED IT YET.
YOU HAVEN'T SEEN THIS DURING YOUR "HUNTS," SO WE CAN SAFELY ASSUME THAT THERE ARE ONLY A FEW OF THESE OUT THERE.
WHAT TRULY BOTHERS ME IS THIS...
SOMEWHERE, OUT IN THE DARKNESS, THERE IS A HUNTER THAT WE DON'T KNOW ABOUT.

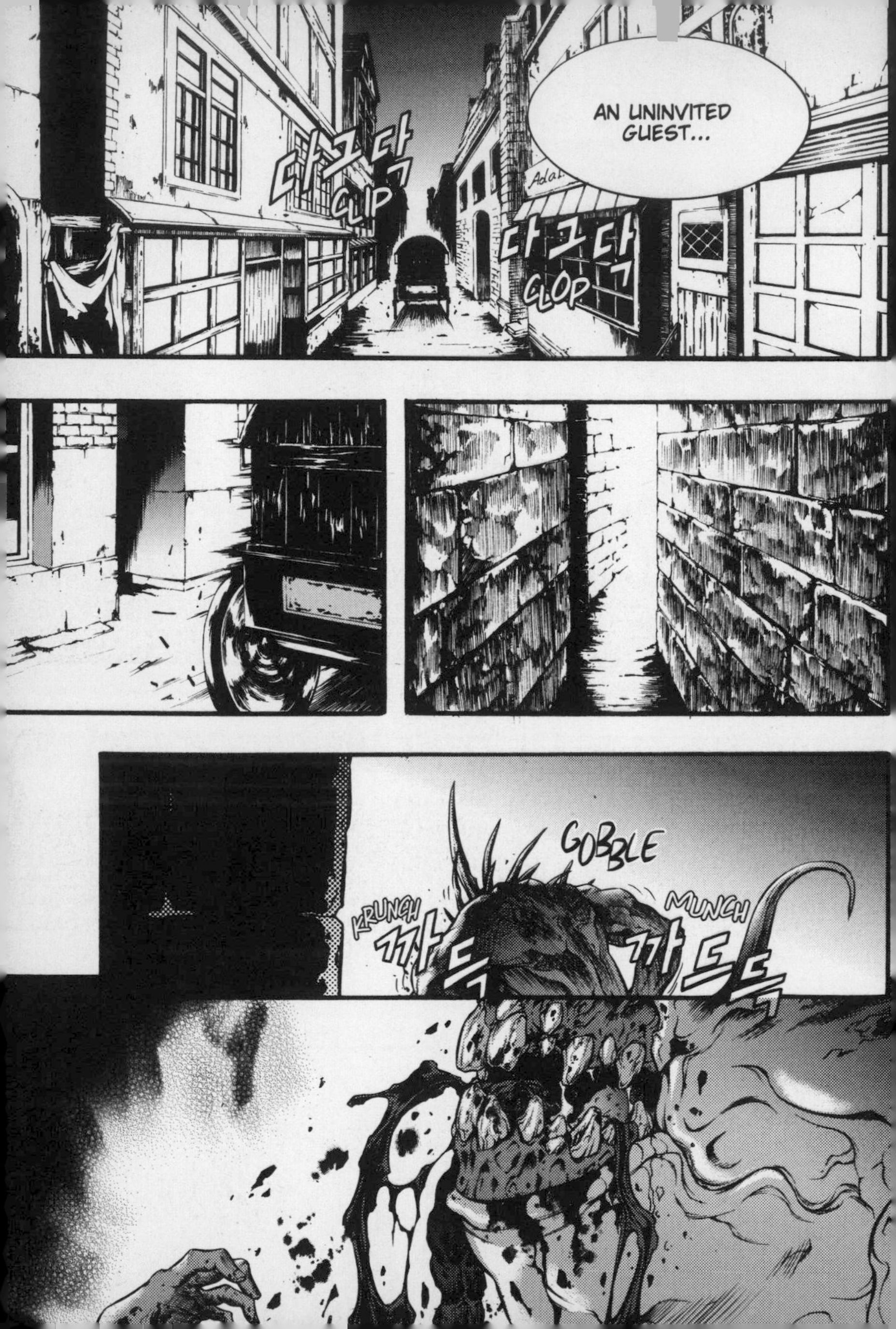

AN UNINVITED GUEST...
CLIP
CLOP
GOBBLE
KRUNCH
MUNCH

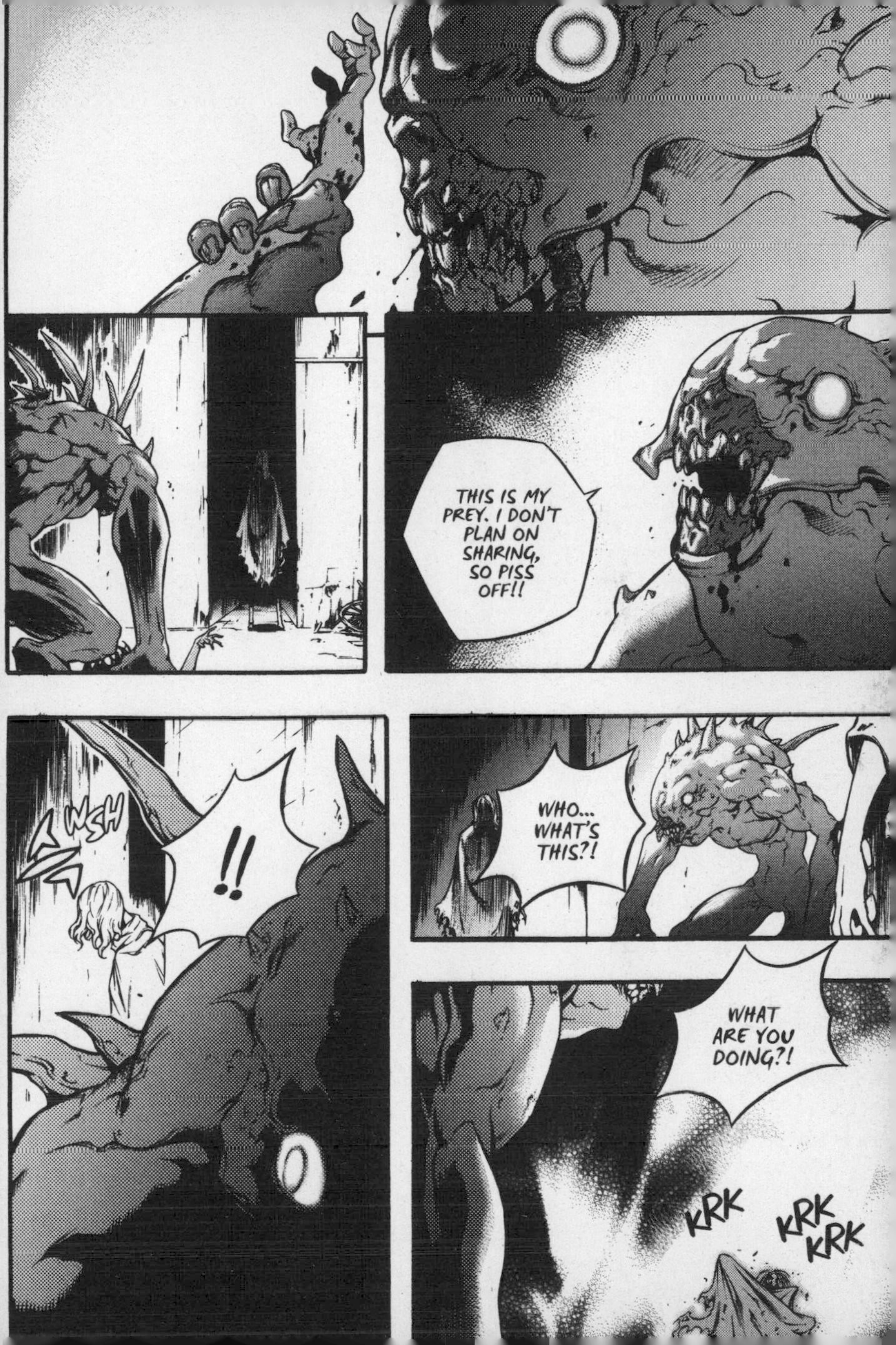
THIS IS MY PREY. I DON'T PLAN ON SHARING, SO PISS OFF!!
WSH
!!
WHO... WHAT'S THIS?!
WHAT ARE YOU DOING?!
KRK
KRK KRK

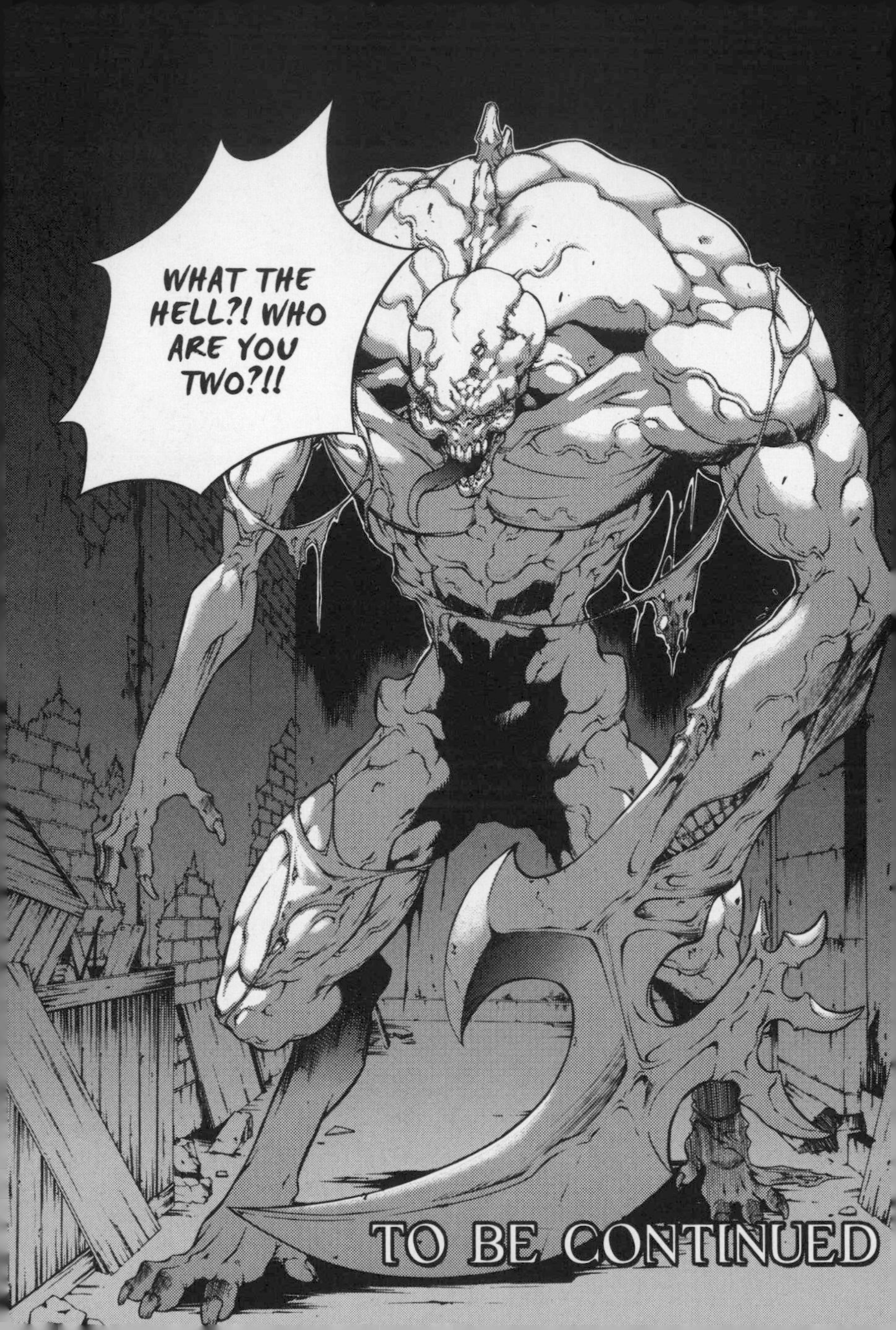
WHAT THE HELL?! WHO ARE YOU TWO?!!
TO BE CONTINUED

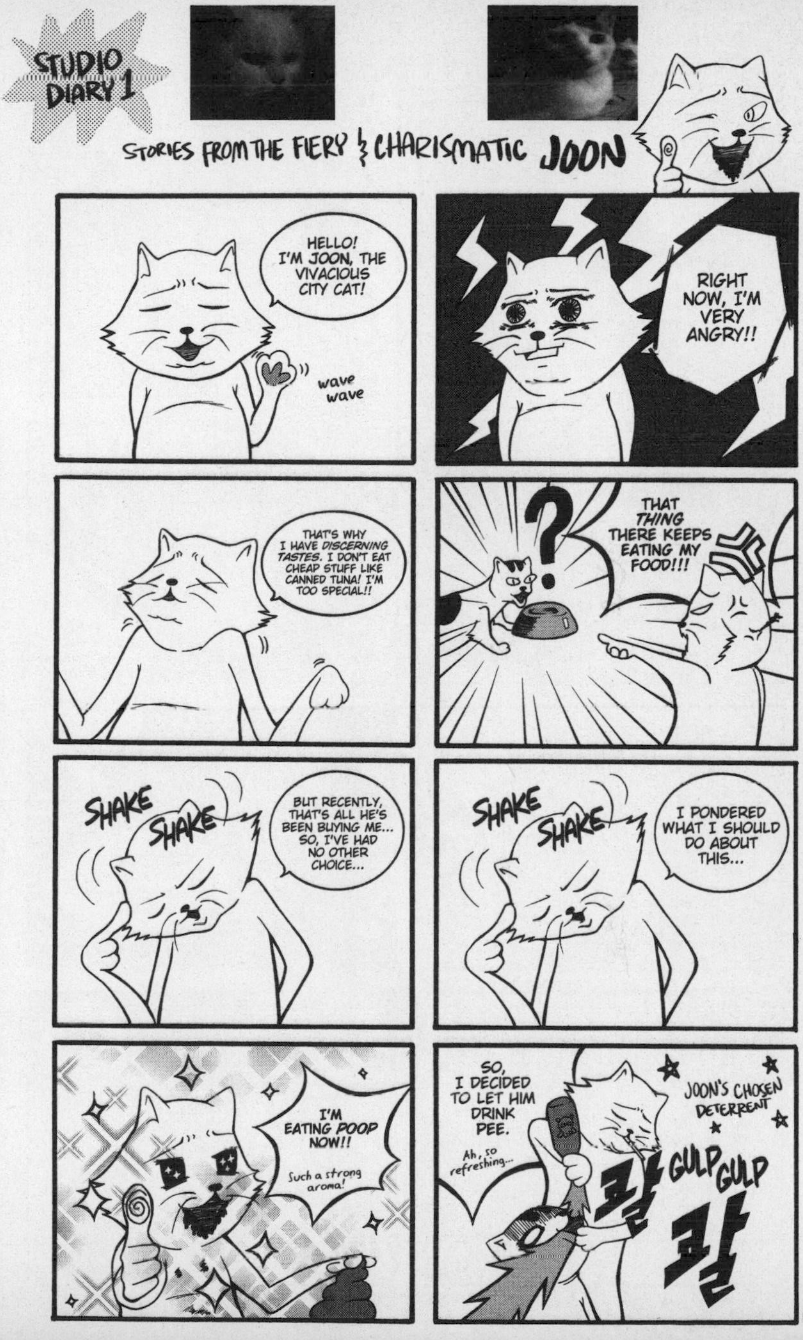
STUDIO DIARY 1
STORIES FROM THE FIERY & CHARISMATIC JOON
HELLO! I'M JOON, THE VIVACIOUS CITY CAT!
wave wave
RIGHT NOW, I'M VERY ANGRY!!
THAT'S WHY I HAVE DISCERNING TASTES. I DON'T EAT CHEAP STUFF LIKE CANNED TUNA! I'M TOO SPECIAL!!
?
THAT THING THERE KEEPS EATING MY FOOD!!!
SHAKE SHAKE
BUT RECENTLY, THAT'S ALL HE'S BEEN BUYING ME... SO, I'VE HAD NO OTHER CHOICE...
SHAKE SHAKE
I PONDERED WHAT I SHOULD DO ABOUT THIS...
I'M EATING POOP NOW!!
Such a strong aroma!
SO, I DECIDED TO LET HIM DRINK PEE.
Ah, so refreshing...
JOON'S CHOSEN DETERRENT
GULP GULP

By Joon

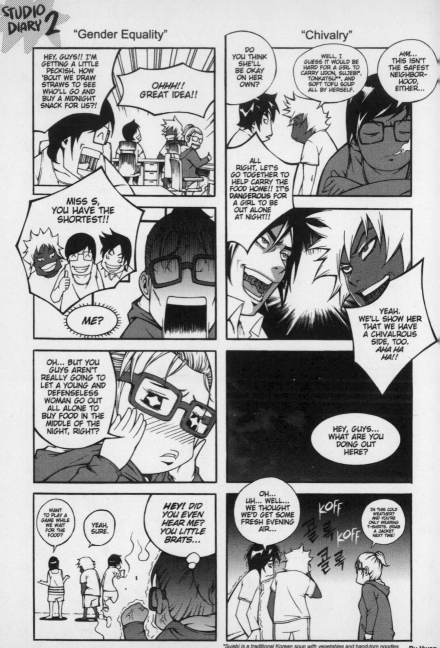

STUDIO DIARY 2

"Gender Equality"

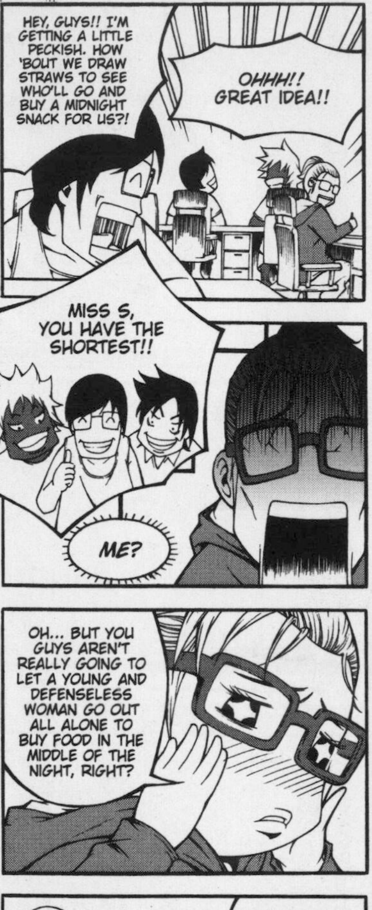
HEY, GUYS!! I'M GETTING A LITTLE PECKISH. HOW 'BOUT WE DRAW STRAWS TO SEE WHO'LL GO AND BUY A MIDNIGHT SNACK FOR US?!
OHHH!! GREAT IDEA!!
MISS S, YOU HAVE THE SHORTEST!!
ME?
OH... BUT YOU GUYS AREN'T REALLY GOING TO LET A YOUNG AND DEFENSELESS WOMAN GO OUT ALL ALONE TO BUY FOOD IN THE MIDDLE OF THE NIGHT, RIGHT?
WANT TO PLAY A GAME WHILE WE WAIT FOR THE FOOD?
YEAH, SURE.
HEY! DID YOU EVEN HEAR ME? YOU LITTLE BRATS...

"Chivalry"

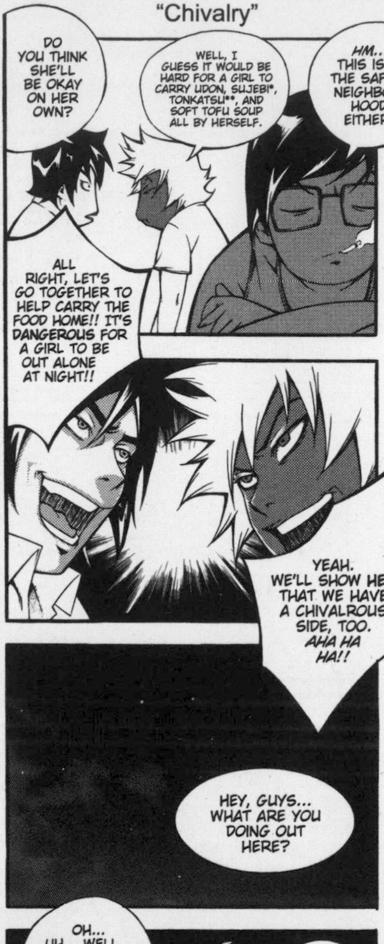
DO YOU THINK SHE'LL BE OKAY ON HER OWN?
WELL, I GUESS IT WOULD BE HARD FOR A GIRL TO CARRY UDON, SUJEBI*, TONKATSU**, AND SOFT TOFU SOUP ALL BY HERSELF.
HM... THIS ISN'T THE SAFEST NEIGHBORHOOD, EITHER...
ALL RIGHT, LET'S GO TOGETHER TO HELP CARRY THE FOOD HOME!! IT'S DANGEROUS FOR A GIRL TO BE OUT ALONE AT NIGHT!!
YEAH. WE'LL SHOW HER THAT WE HAVE A CHIVALROUS SIDE, TOO. AHA HA HA!!
HEY, GUYS... WHAT ARE YOU DOING OUT HERE?
OH... UH... WELL... WE THOUGHT WE'D GET SOME FRESH EVENING AIR...
KOFF
콜록
KOFF
콜록
IN THIS COLD WEATHER? AND YOU'RE ONLY WEARING T-SHIRTS. GRAB A JACKET NEXT TIME!

*Sujebi is a traditional Korean soup with vegetables and hand-torn noodles.

**Tonkatsu is a Japanese dish, consisting of a deep-fried, breaded pork cutlet, served with cabbage or miso soup.

By Hwan

STUDIO DIARY 3

"Curious"

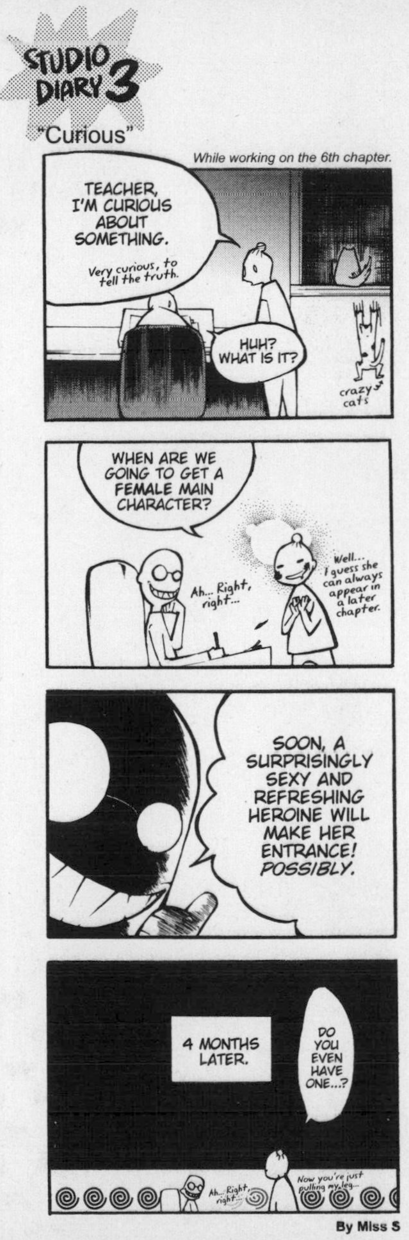
While working on the 6th chapter.
TEACHER, I'M CURIOUS ABOUT SOMETHING.
Very curious, to tell the truth.
HUH? WHAT IS IT?
crazy cats
WHEN ARE WE GOING TO GET A FEMALE MAIN CHARACTER?
Ah... Right, right...
Well... I guess she can always appear in a later chapter.
SOON, A SURPRISINGLY SEXY AND REFRESHING HEROINE WILL MAKE HER ENTRANCE! POSSIBLY.
4 MONTHS LATER.
DO YOU EVEN HAVE ONE...?
Ah... Right, right...
Now you're just pulling my leg...

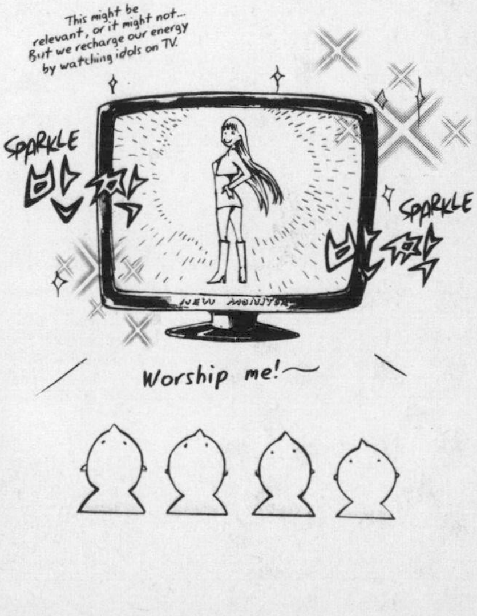
This might be relevant, or it might not... But we recharge our energy by watching idols on TV.
SPARKLE
SPARKLE
NEW MONITER
Worship me!~

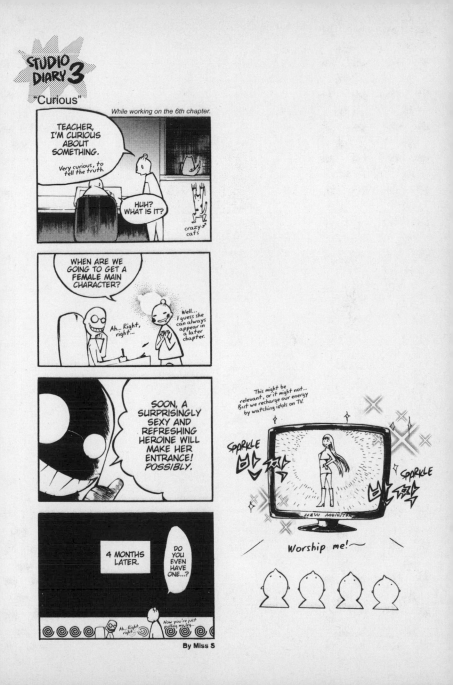

By Miss S

NEXT TIME...

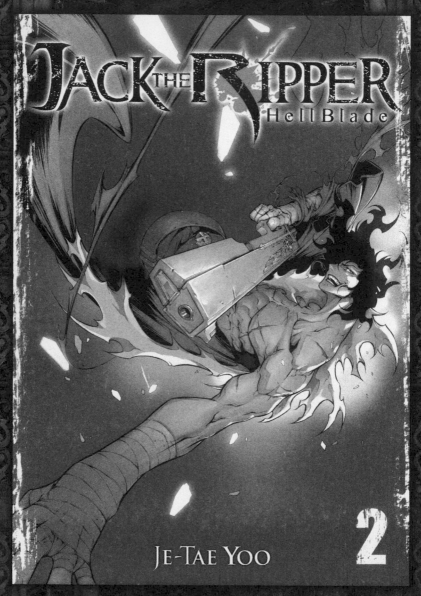

JACK THE RIPPER

HellBlade

2

JE-TAE YOO

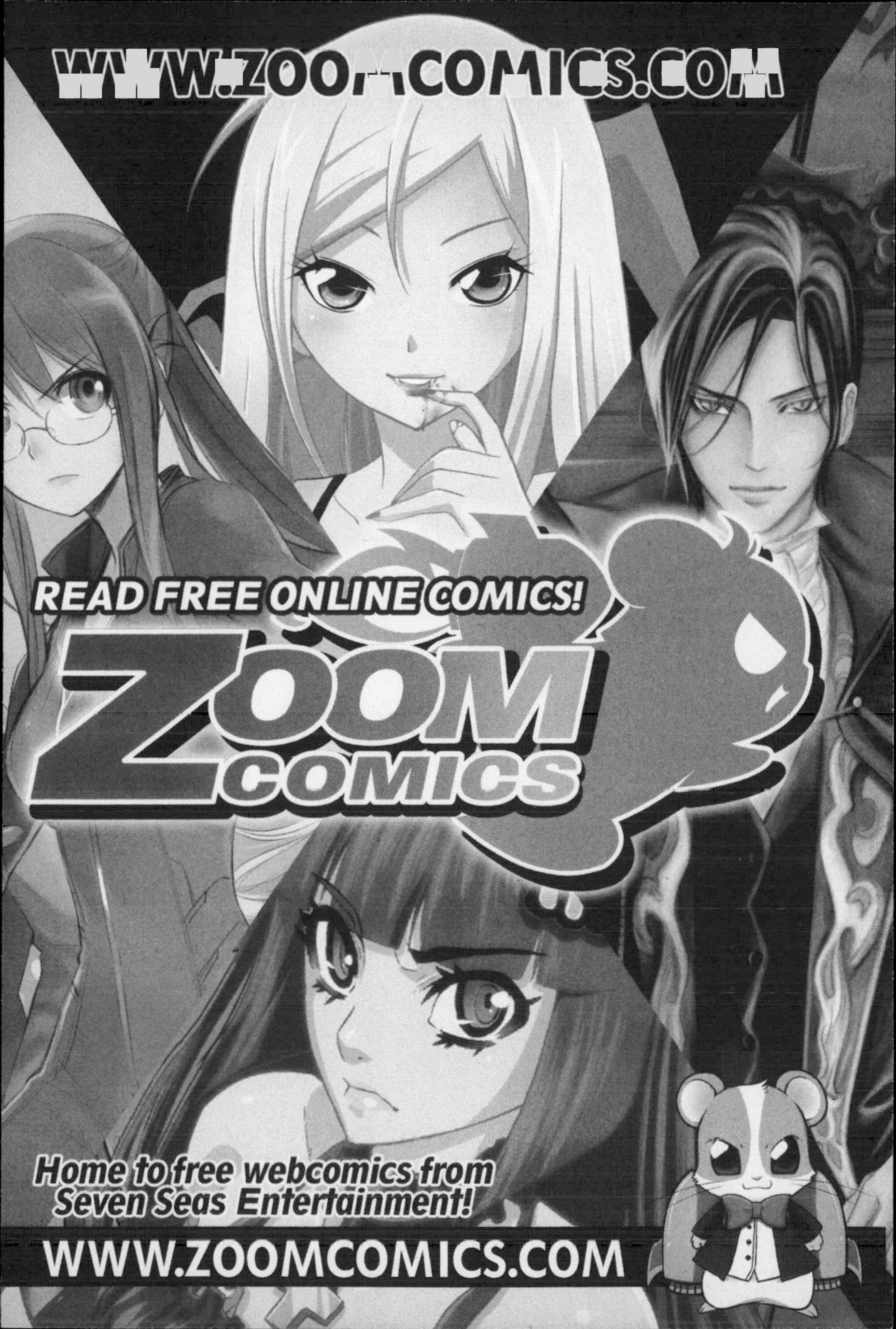
WWW.ZOOMCOMICS.COM
READ FREE ONLINE COMICS!
ZOOM COMICS
Home to free webcomics from Seven Seas Entertainment!
WWW.ZOOMCOMICS.COM

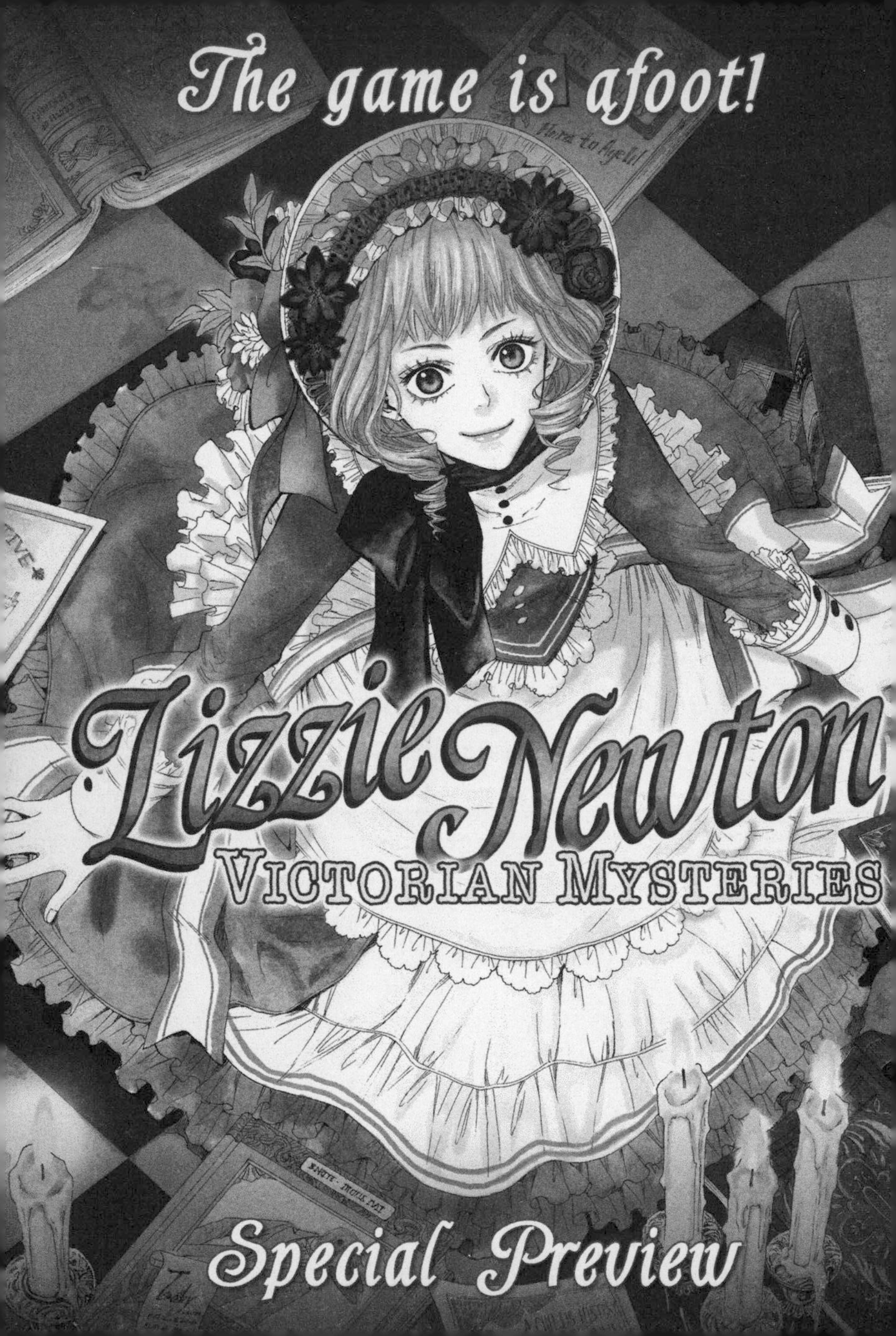
The game is afoot!
Lizzie Newton
VICTORIAN MYSTERIES
Special Preview

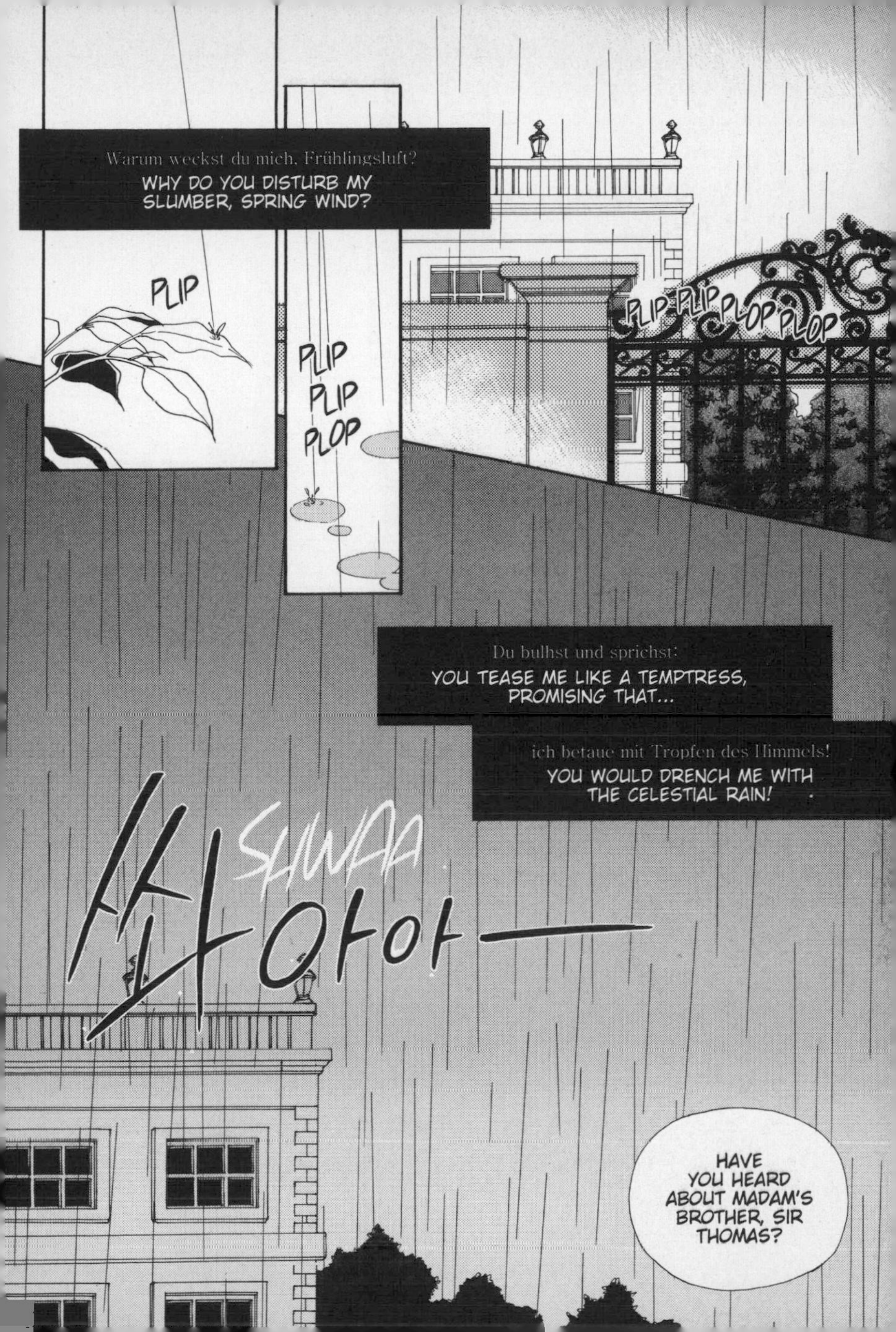
Warum weckst du mich, Frühlingsluft?
WHY DO YOU DISTURB MY SLUMBER, SPRING WIND?
PLIP
PLIP PLIP PLOP
PLIP PLIP PLOP PLOP
Du bulhst und sprichst:
YOU TEASE ME LIKE A TEMPTRESS, PROMISING THAT...
ich betaue mit Tropfen des Himmels!
YOU WOULD DRENCH ME WITH THE CELESTIAL RAIN!
SHWAA
쏴아아—
HAVE YOU HEARD ABOUT MADAM'S BROTHER, SIR THOMAS?

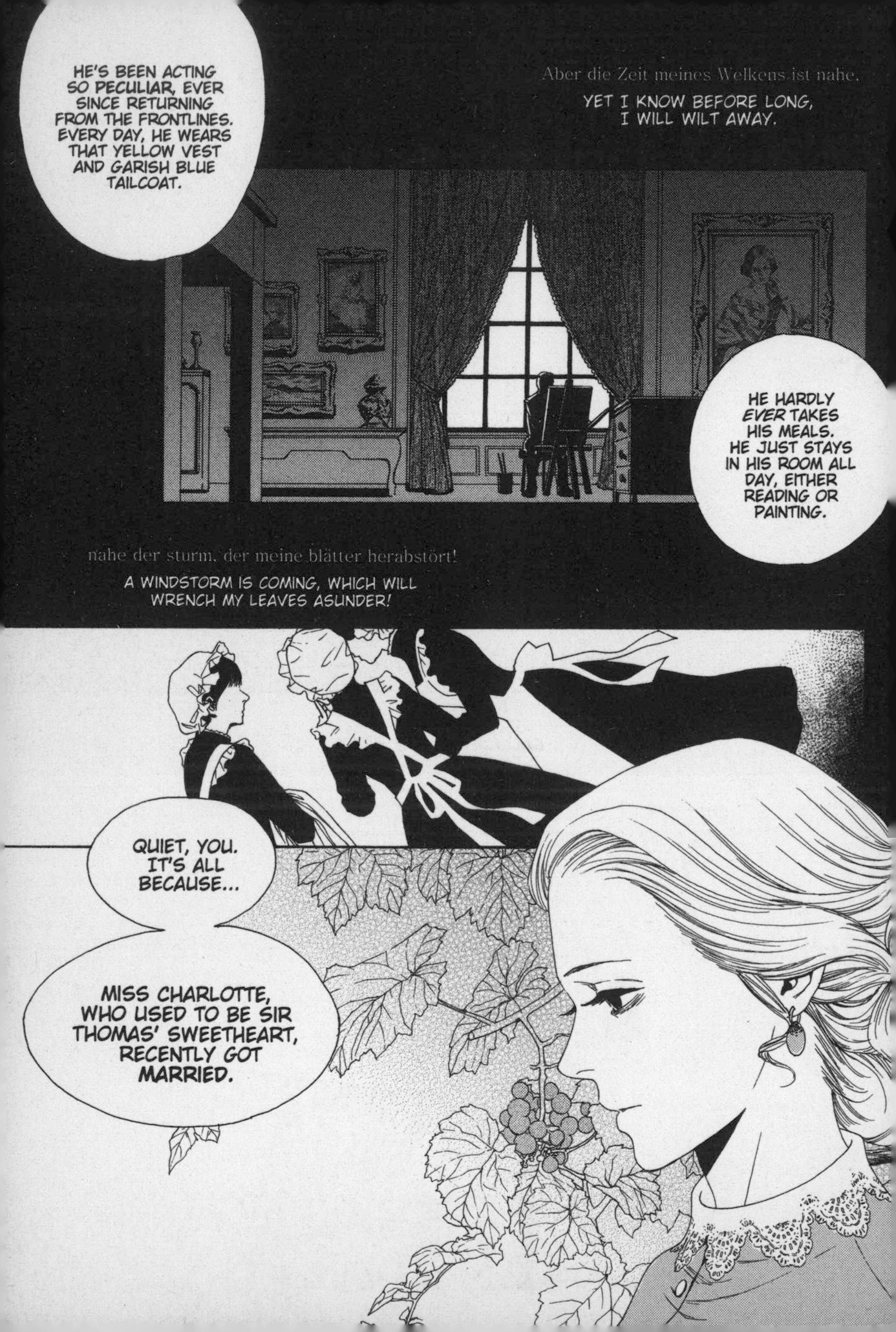
HE'S BEEN ACTING SO PECULIAR, EVER SINCE RETURNING FROM THE FRONTLINES. EVERY DAY, HE WEARS THAT YELLOW VEST AND GARISH BLUE TAILCOAT.
Aber die Zeit meines Welkens ist nahe,
YET I KNOW BEFORE LONG, I WILL WILT AWAY.
HE HARDLY EVER TAKES HIS MEALS. HE JUST STAYS IN HIS ROOM ALL DAY, EITHER READING OR PAINTING.
nahe der sturm, der meine blätter herabstört!
A WINDSTORM IS COMING, WHICH WILL WRENCH MY LEAVES ASUNDER!
QUIET, YOU. IT'S ALL BECAUSE...
MISS CHARLOTTE, WHO USED TO BE SIR THOMAS' SWEETHEART, RECENTLY GOT MARRIED.

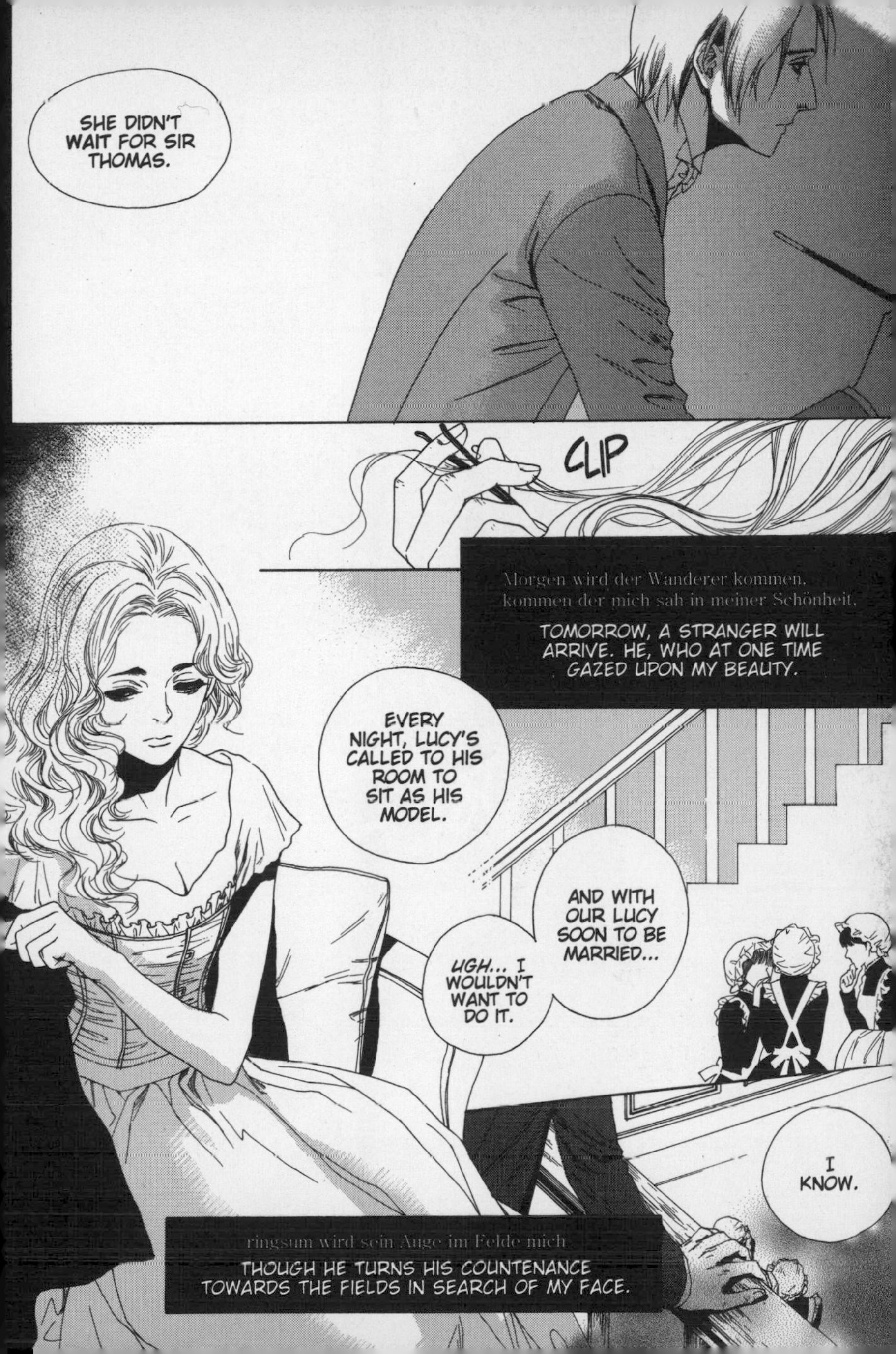
SHE DIDN'T WAIT FOR SIR THOMAS.
CLIP
Morgen wird der Wanderer kommen, kommen der mich sah in meiner Schönheit,
TOMORROW, A STRANGER WILL ARRIVE. HE, WHO AT ONE TIME GAZED UPON MY BEAUTY.
EVERY NIGHT, LUCY'S CALLED TO HIS ROOM TO SIT AS HIS MODEL.
AND WITH OUR LUCY SOON TO BE MARRIED...
UGH... I WOULDN'T WANT TO DO IT.
I KNOW.
ringsum wird sein Auge im Felde mich
THOUGH HE TURNS HIS COUNTENANCE TOWARDS THE FIELDS IN SEARCH OF MY FACE.

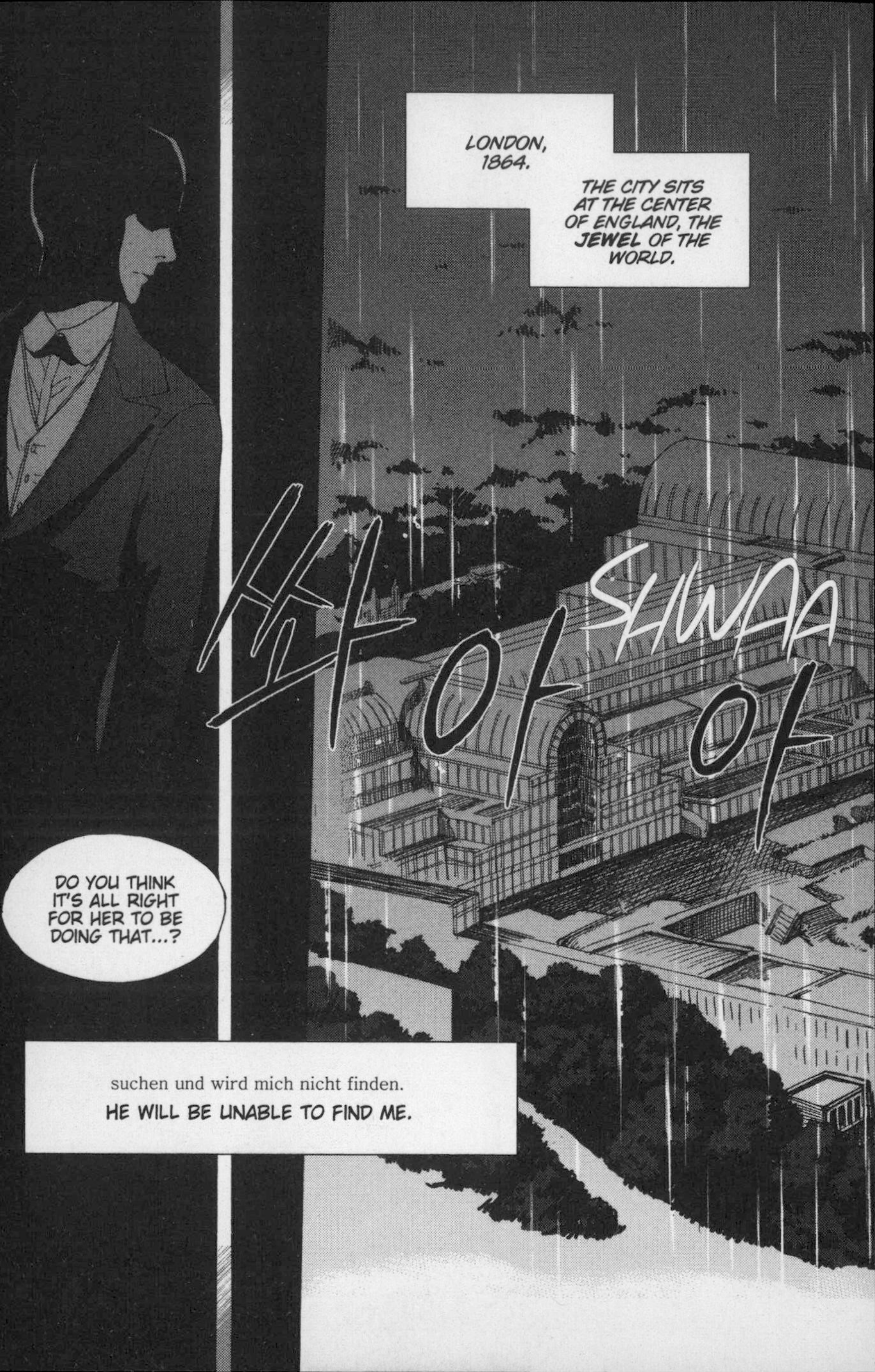
DO YOU THINK IT'S ALL RIGHT FOR HER TO BE DOING THAT...?
suchen und wird mich nicht finden.
HE WILL BE UNABLE TO FIND ME.
LONDON, 1864.
THE CITY SITS AT THE CENTER OF ENGLAND, THE JEWEL OF THE WORLD.
쏴아아
SHWAA

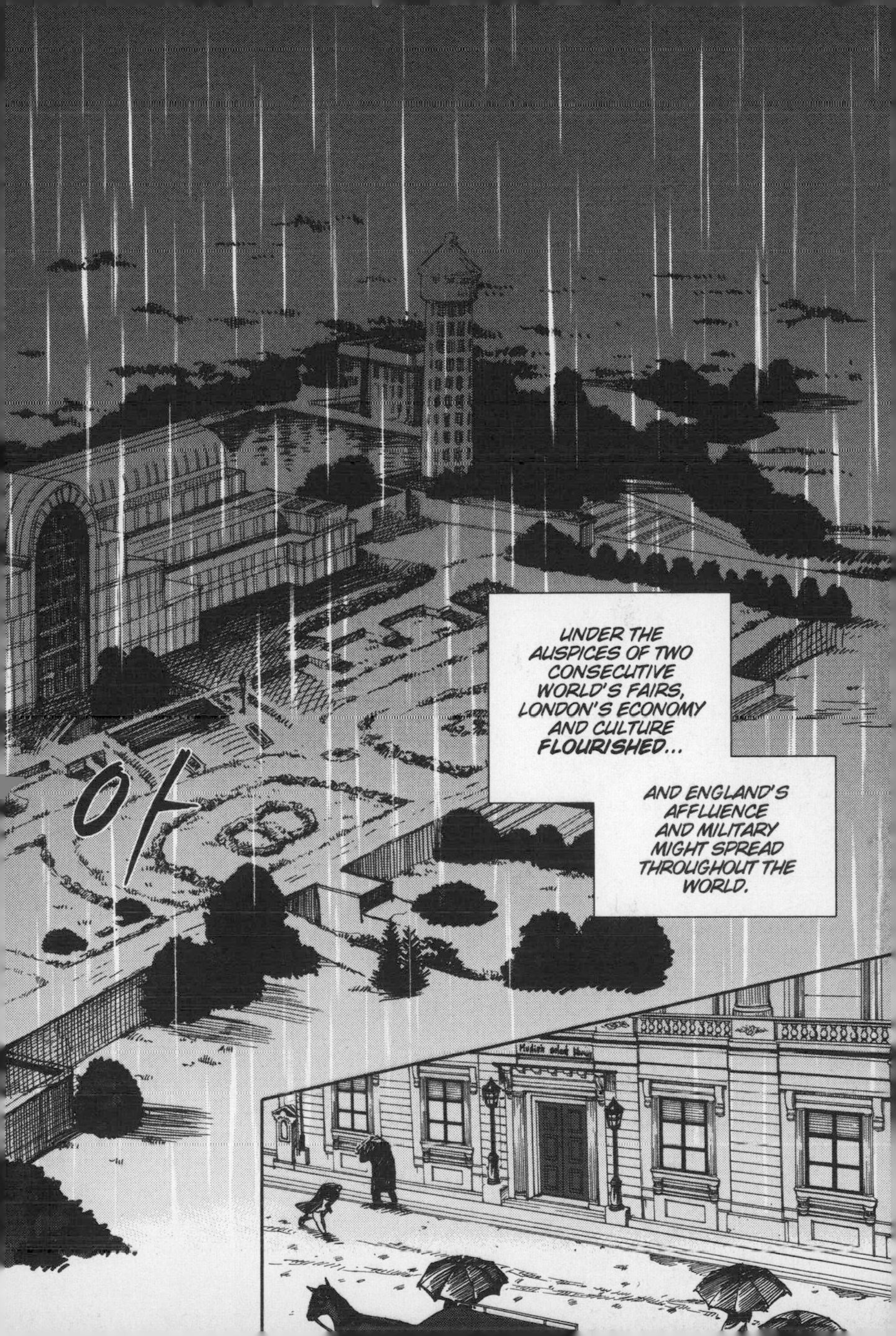
UNDER THE AUSPICES OF TWO CONSECUTIVE WORLD'S FAIRS, LONDON'S ECONOMY AND CULTURE **FLOURISHED...**
AND ENGLAND'S AFFLUENCE AND MILITARY MIGHT SPREAD THROUGHOUT THE WORLD.

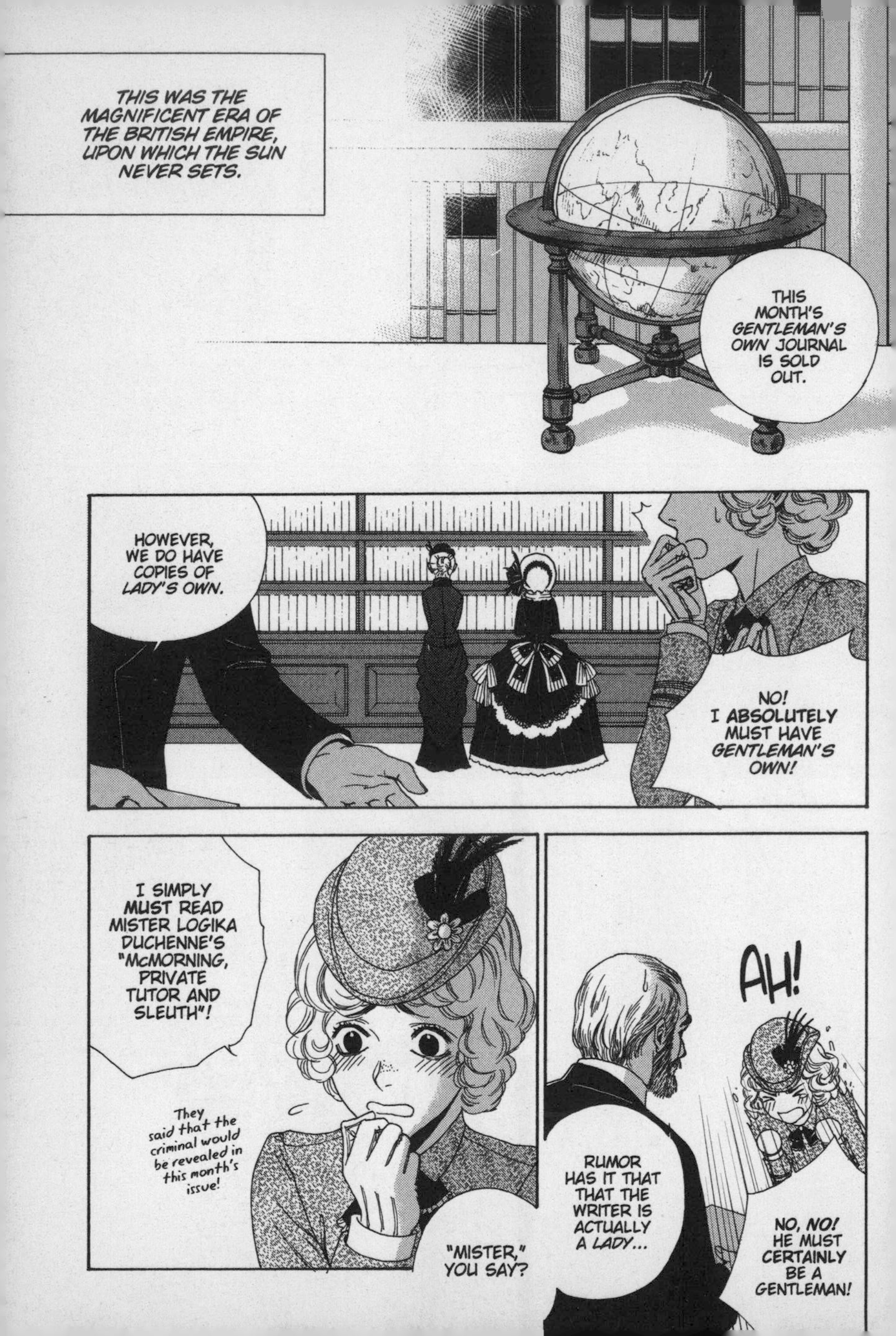

THIS WAS THE MAGNIFICENT ERA OF THE BRITISH EMPIRE, UPON WHICH THE SUN NEVER SETS.
THIS MONTH'S GENTLEMAN'S OWN JOURNAL IS SOLD OUT.
HOWEVER, WE DO HAVE COPIES OF LADY'S OWN.
NO! I ABSOLUTELY MUST HAVE GENTLEMAN'S OWN!
I SIMPLY MUST READ MISTER LOGIKA DUCHENNE'S "McMORNING, PRIVATE TUTOR AND SLEUTH"!
They said that the criminal would be revealed in this month's issue!
"MISTER," YOU SAY?
RUMOR HAS IT THAT THAT THE WRITER IS ACTUALLY A LADY...
AH!
NO, NO! HE MUST CERTAINLY BE A GENTLEMAN!

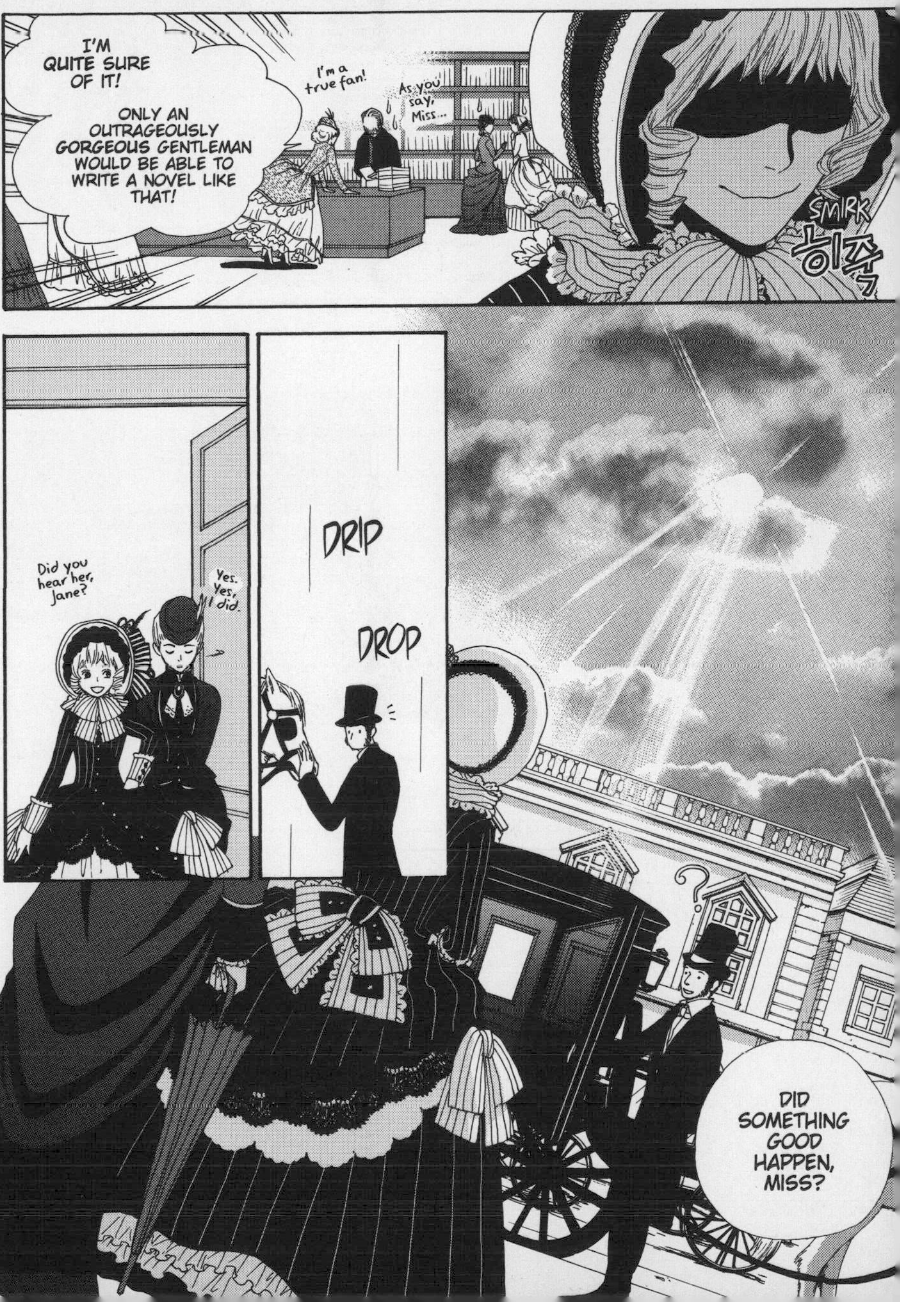
I'M QUITE SURE OF IT!
ONLY AN OUTRAGEOUSLY GORGEOUS GENTLEMAN WOULD BE ABLE TO WRITE A NOVEL LIKE THAT!
I'm a true fan!
As you say, Miss...
SMIRK
히죽
Did you hear her, Jane?
Yes. Yes, I did.
DRIP
DROP
DID SOMETHING GOOD HAPPEN, MISS?

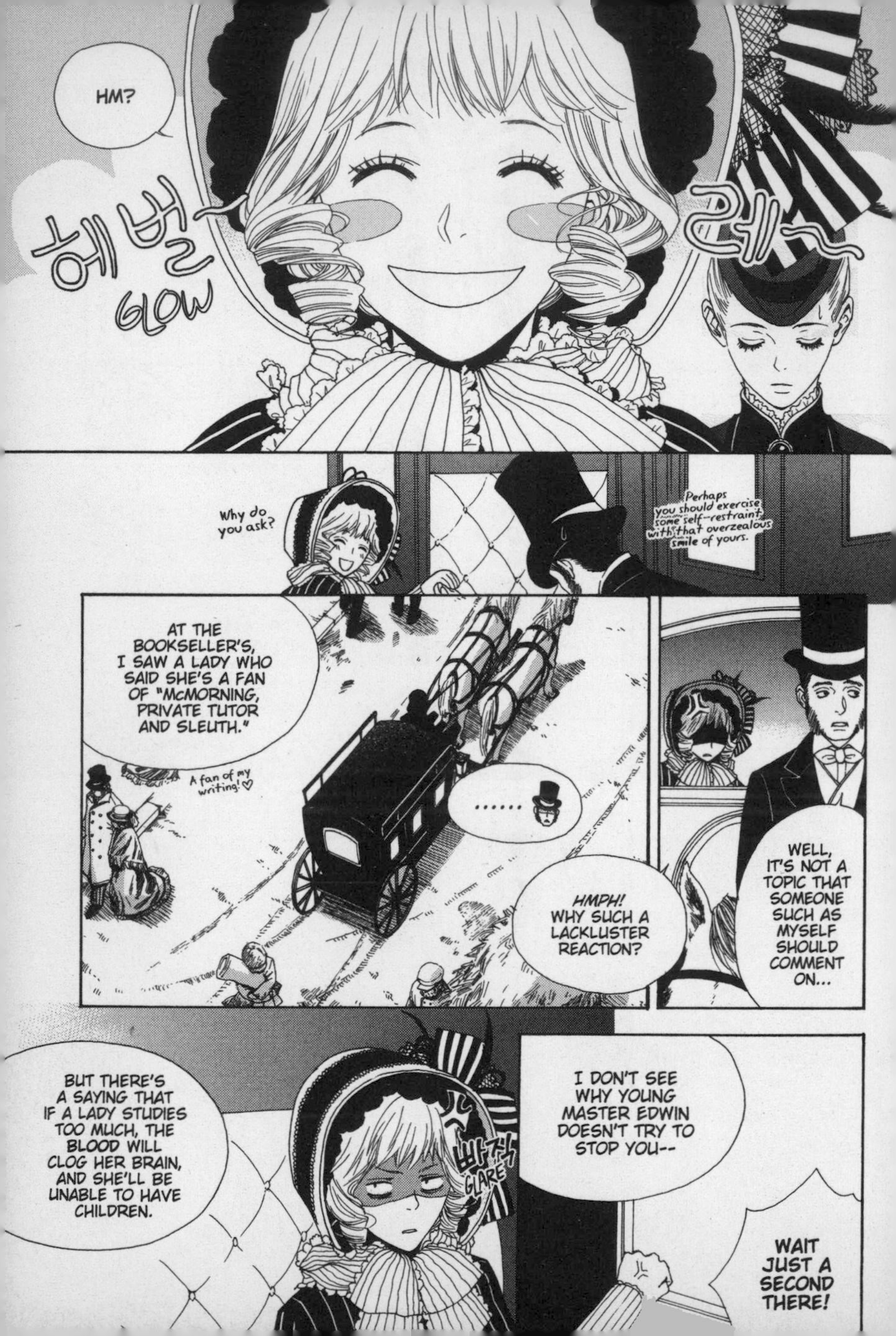
HM?
헤벌~
GLOW
래~
Why do you ask?
Perhaps you should exercise some self-restraint with that overzealous smile of yours.
AT THE BOOKSELLER'S, I SAW A LADY WHO SAID SHE'S A FAN OF "McMORNING, PRIVATE TUTOR AND SLEUTH."
A fan of my writing!♡
......
HMPH! WHY SUCH A LACKLUSTER REACTION?
WELL, IT'S NOT A TOPIC THAT SOMEONE SUCH AS MYSELF SHOULD COMMENT ON...
BUT THERE'S A SAYING THAT IF A LADY STUDIES TOO MUCH, THE BLOOD WILL CLOG HER BRAIN, AND SHE'LL BE UNABLE TO HAVE CHILDREN.
빠직
GLARE
I DON'T SEE WHY YOUNG MASTER EDWIN DOESN'T TRY TO STOP YOU--
WAIT JUST A SECOND THERE!

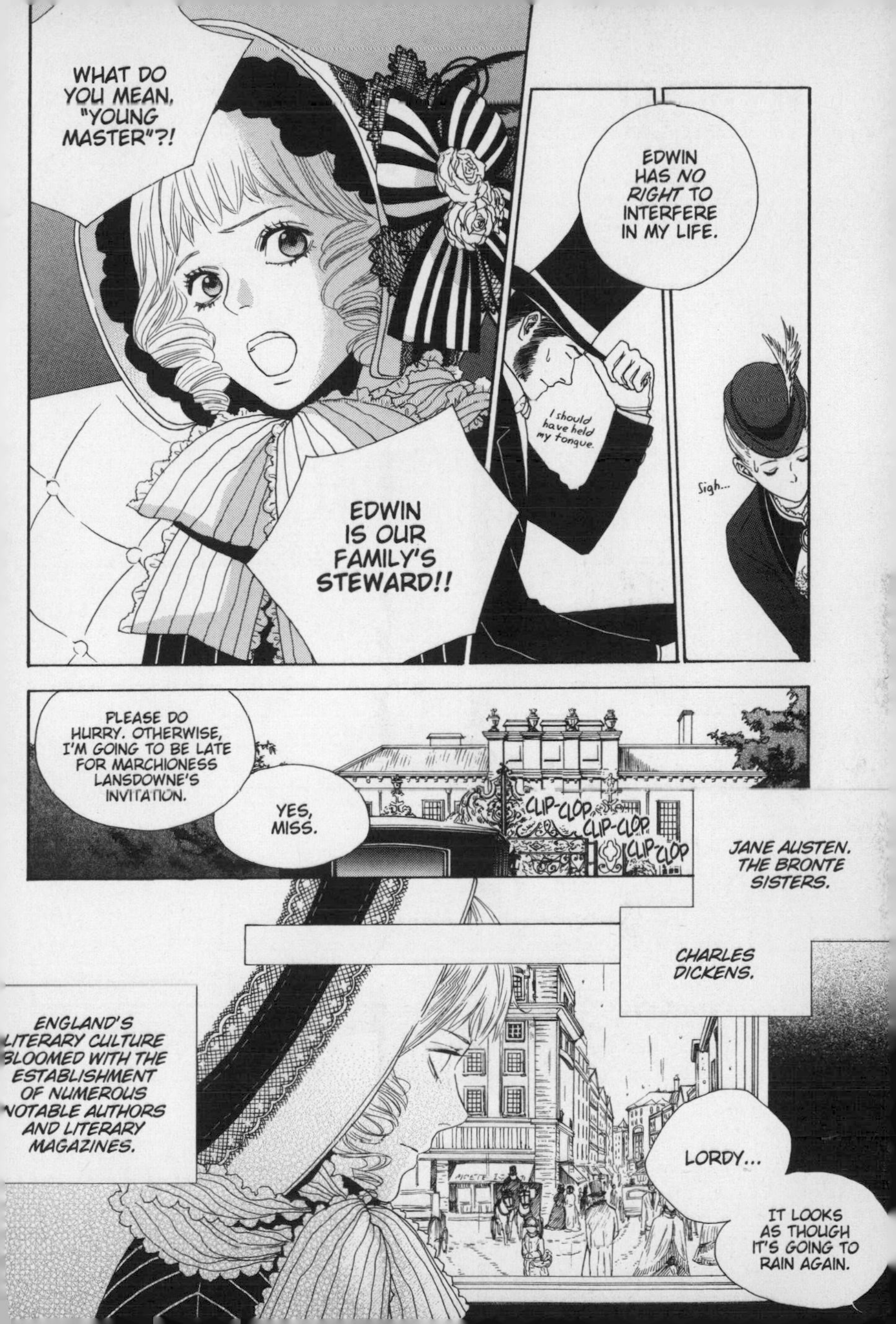
WHAT DO YOU MEAN, "YOUNG MASTER"?!
EDWIN IS OUR FAMILY'S STEWARD!!
EDWIN HAS NO RIGHT TO INTERFERE IN MY LIFE.
I should have held my tongue.
Sigh...
PLEASE DO HURRY. OTHERWISE, I'M GOING TO BE LATE FOR MARCHIONESS LANSDOWNE'S INVITATION.
YES, MISS.
CLIP-CLOP CLIP-CLOP CLIP-CLOP
JANE AUSTEN. THE BRONTE SISTERS.
CHARLES DICKENS.
ENGLAND'S LITERARY CULTURE BLOOMED WITH THE ESTABLISHMENT OF NUMEROUS NOTABLE AUTHORS AND LITERARY MAGAZINES.
LORDY...
IT LOOKS AS THOUGH IT'S GOING TO RAIN AGAIN.

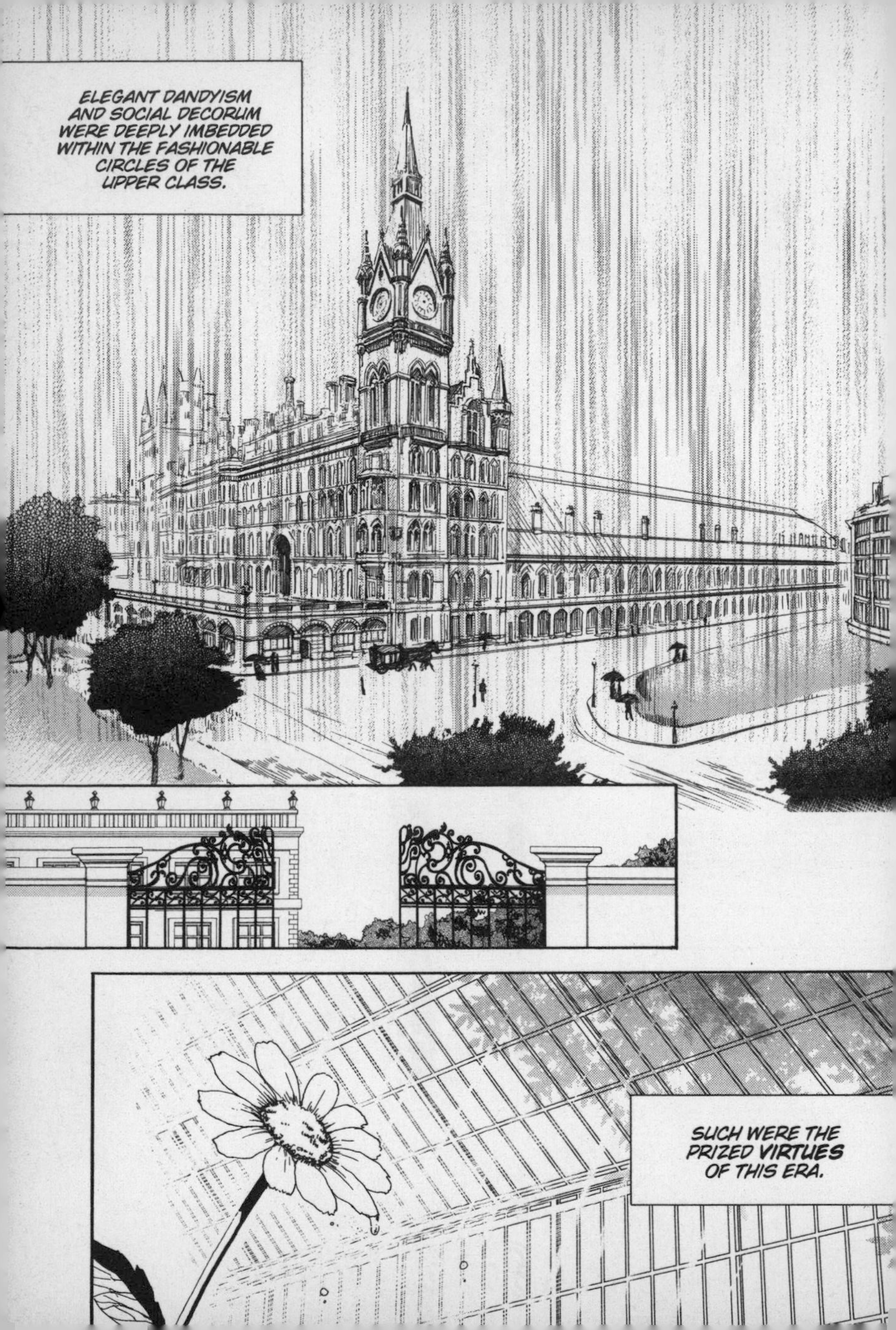
ELEGANT DANDYISM AND SOCIAL DECORUM WERE DEEPLY IMBEDDED WITHIN THE FASHIONABLE CIRCLES OF THE UPPER CLASS.
SUCH WERE THE PRIZED VIRTUES OF THIS ERA.

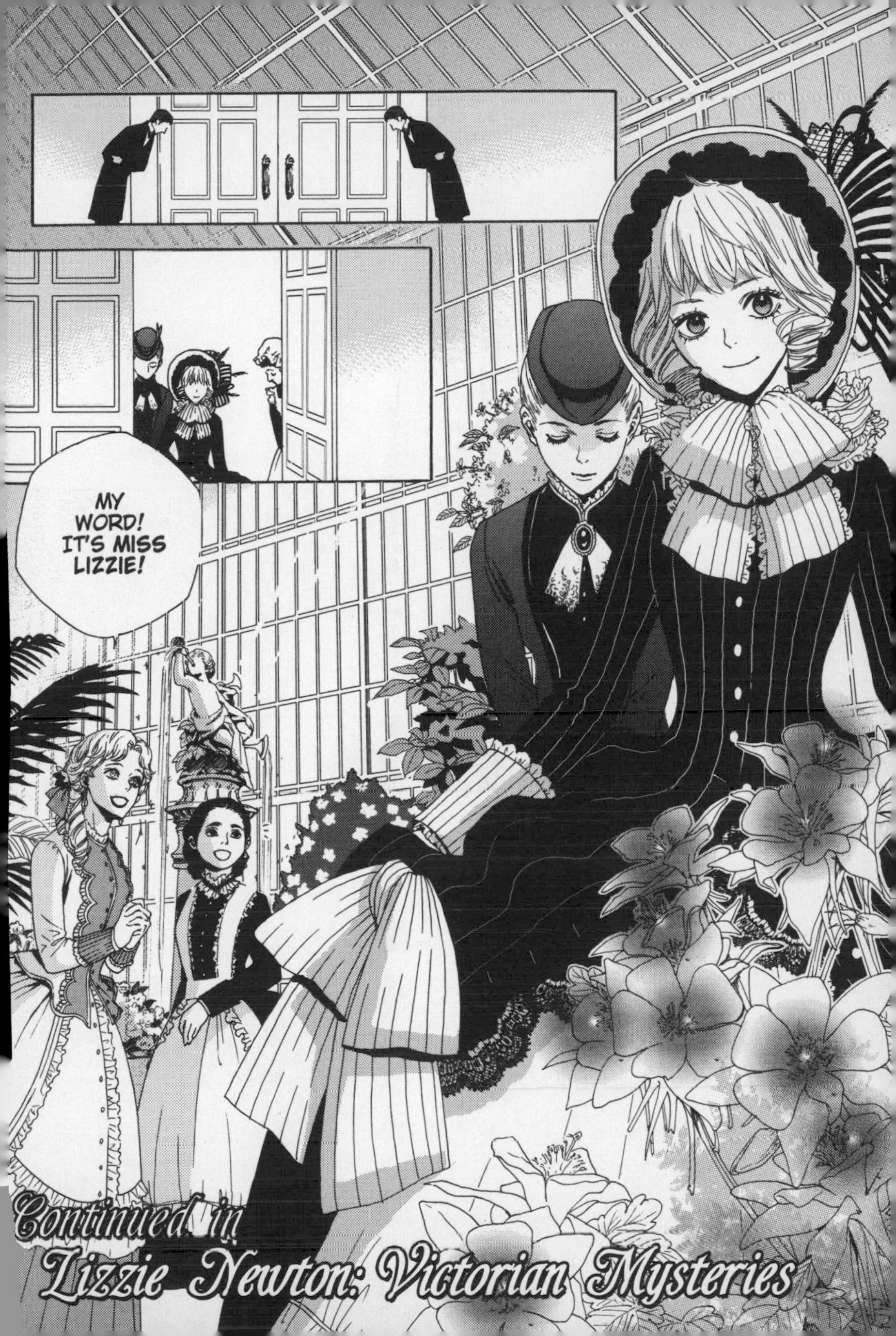
MY WORD! IT'S MISS LIZZIE!
Continued in
Lizzie Newton: Victorian Mysteries